ARTOIS

Namur

NAMUR

Cambrai

SOMME R.

MEUSE R.

RHINE R.

Amiens

St.-Quentin

PICARDY

Rouen

Noyon

SEINE R.

OISE R.

Château-
Thierry

Reims

ORMANDY

Evreux

Mantes

St.-Denis

Meaux

Dormans

LORRAINE

MOSELLE R.

ERCHE

Dreux

PARIS

Lagny

Epernay

Chartres

ILE DE FRANCE

Melun

RHINE R.

BEAUCE

MARNE R.

Nemours

CHAMPAGNE

SEINE R.

Orléans

URAINE

ORLÉANAIS

BURGUNDY

Blois

Tours

Amboise

FRANCHE-

Chenonceaux

NIVERNAIS

Dijon

COMTÉ

BERRY

LOIRE R.

MARCHE

BOURBONNAIS

SAÔNE R.

LIMOUSIN

Clermont-Ferrand

Lyons

SAVOY

Issoire

LYONNAIS

THE

ALPS

Usson

QUERCY

Carlat

AUVERGNE

LOT R.

DAUPHINY

RHÔNE R.

LANGUEDOC

Nîmes

Avignon

Béziers

PROVENCE

Carcassonne

Carlat

Narbonne

Marseille

MEDITERRANEAN SEA

ROYAL COUSIN

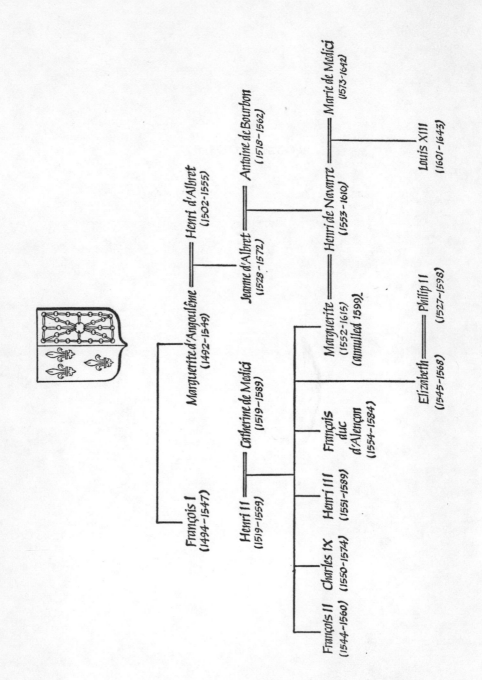

François I
(1494–1547)
    ═══ Marguerite d'Angoulême ═══ Henri d'Albret
    (1492–1549)   (1502–1555)

Henri II ═══ Catherine de Medici
(1519–1559)   (1519–1589)

Jeanne d'Albret ═══ Antoine de Bourbon
(1528–1572)   (1518–1562)

François II
(1544–1560)

Charles IX
(1550–1574)

Henri III
(1551–1589)

François
duc
d'Alençon
(1554–1584)

Marguerite ═══ Henri de Navarre
(1552–1615)   (1553–1610)
(annulled 1599)

Marie de Medici
(1573–1642)

Elizabeth ═══ Philip II
(1545–1568)   (1527–1598)

Louis XIII
(1601–1643)

ROYAL COUSIN

THE LIFE OF
HENRI IV OF FRANCE

❧❧❧❧❧

COPY 1

IRENE MAHONEY

1970

Doubleday & Company, Inc., Garden City, New York

Library of Congress Catalog Card Number 77-123700
Copyright © 1970 by Irene Mahoney
All Rights Reserved
Printed in the United States of America
First Edition

*To my father
who at every crossroad
chose Life*

CONTENTS

LIST OF ILLUSTRATIONS

INTRODUCTION

My first interest in Henri of Navarre began with a Christmas present when I was no more than nine. Both the author and the title have long been forgotten, and I recall only that the book had a dark blue cover and a frontispiece depicting a small boy in doublet and hose standing before a forbidding château, labeled "Pau"—and which in my ignorance of French vowels I mentally called "Pow." While my friends wandered through the cowboys and Indians of the American scene, my imagination strayed back to the small boy who one day became King of France. It was not, however, until many years later while doing some research on a French mystic and missionary, Marie Guyart, that I again came across Henri of Navarre—and found a resurgence of my childhood interest and curiosity.

Soon I was nosing out available material, and before long I was convinced of the need for a full-scale biography of this great French King. Certainly, as I soon discovered, there was no dearth of materials for such a study, which made it even more curious that no serious biography of Henri IV had appeared on the American scene since the turn of the century. Even though the body of materials is, as one would expect, considerably greater in France, yet even here the efforts at a full-scale study have been few. There are scholarly monographs in plenty dealing with specialized aspects of his life and work, but except for the work of Pierre de Vaissière (*Henri IV*, Paris, 1928) and Maurice Andrieux (*Henri IV*, Paris, 1955 and *Henri IV dans ses années pacifiques*, Paris, 1954) no effort has been made at a full-scale interpretive biography.

English readers have fared far more poorly, for authors writing in English have seemed content to deal with the more romantic and more lurid aspects of Henri IV's life—often fictionizing their accounts, or at best basing them upon questionable sources. While the history of "Le Vert Galant" is certainly not without its amorous interludes, it is unfortunate that such interludes should overshadow the real and serious contribution which Henri has made to French history. It is as a king and not simply as a lover that he has won the epithet "The Great."

Anyone who has pored through the materials dealing with the reign of this king must soon come to the conclusion that no fiction could surpass the colorful and exciting historical facts. One need neither embroider nor invent; the story is perfect in the simple truth of history. The biographer need only remain within the confines of historical truth to present a scene and a list of dramatis personae that are at once complex, absorbing, and utterly real. I have had, accordingly, no temptation to depart from historical fact into the paths of fictional conjecture. Indeed, there was no need. The facts themselves had a dramatic immediacy which fiction but rarely attains. I soon found that the people who emerge from the histories and diaries and memoirs were far more colorful than any that peopled my imagination. The task was not to embroider but to stay cleanly within the ambiance of historical fact. Such fidelity to fact was, I discovered, liberating rather than confining.

Since this biography has been written for the general reader rather than for the scholar, critical apparatus has been accordingly reduced to suit the interests of a general reading public. As the purpose of such a book is to recreate the life and personality of a man, it seemed consonant with this aim to keep the footnotes simple in both form and content, employing them to indicate the sources for direct quotations rather than to pursue the more abstruse problems of the professional historian. For the scholar this may be insufficient; for the casual reader it may be more than he requires. My decision rests on my own experience as general reader—an experience which has often been frustrating because of the lack of clear citations indicating where, precisely, I might find the material so tantalizingly quoted in the text. I can only hope that my own experience has not been unique and that other readers will also be happy to be given the opportunity of pursuing with a minimum of difficulty the material only briefly quoted here.

Since my footnotes indicate for the most part the material which I found most valuable, no effort is made to supply a complete bibliography. The materials for this period are overwhelming in their sheer bulk. Anyone pursuing research in the French sixteenth century

cannot help but be unfailingly grateful to those editors who have made
are invaluable. There are as well large numbers of individual memoirs
and letters kept by those colorful ladies and gentlemen of the Renaissance. The thirty-two volumes of J. J. F. Poujoulat et J. Michaud
(*Nouvelle collection des mémoires pour servir à l'histoire de France*)
and those edited by M. Petitot (*Collection complète des mémoires
relatifs à l'histoire de France*) containing memoirs of such contemporaries as Turenne, Palma Cayet, Villeroi, Cheverny, and others
are invaluable. There are as well large numbers of individual memoires
edited by such men as De Ruble, Rochambeau, Guessard—to mention
but a few. For my work, the two most important collections of letters
were those of Catherine de Medici, edited by H. de la Ferrière and B.
de Puchesse, and the *Lettres missives de Henri IV*, edited by B. de
Xivrey. The diplomatic correspondence of the time is also of super-
lative value: the correspondence of France and Tuscany edited by
Abel Desjardins and the Venetian correspondence edited by Eugenio
Alberi. There is also the vast Calendar of State Papers dealing with
English affairs in France, Spain, Venice, the Netherlands, etc. Notable
among the histories of the period are the works of Agrippa d'Aubigné,
J. A. de Thou, Enrico Davila, Claude Matthieu. There are also numerous collections which make available various contemporary accounts
and documents: *Mémoires de Condé, Mémoires de la Ligue, Archives
Curieuses*—again to cite only the most obvious. Among the diarists
special note must be given to Pierre de L'Estoile whose *Mémoires-
Journaux* provides one of the shrewdest and most meticulous comments
on the reigns of Henri III and Henri IV. Since, with the exception
of Nancy Lyman Roelker's edition of L'Estoile and the English edition of Sully, all this material exists only in French, all translations
are my own.

There are many to whom I owe much: the staffs of the Widener and
Houghton libraries of Harvard University, of the Library of Congress,
and of the Folger Shakespeare Library in Washington, D.C., as well as
to the librarians of the Bibliothèque Municipale at Pau. I wish also to
acknowledge my indebtedness to Dr. John Colaneri of the College of
New Rochelle for his help in interpreting difficult passages of Italian
and to Professor Raymond Ritter of the Sorbonne who shared with me
in long hours of conversation his own extensive research into the
life of Henri IV. To M. Edouard Morot-Cyr, formerly of the French
Embassy in New York, I am deeply indebted for his help in procuring a
grant which made possible months of travel in France. It is, however, to

Professor Nancy Lyman Roelker that I owe the most—and the best. Her own edition of the journals of Pierre de L'Estoile and her biography of Jeanne d'Albret were invaluable to me; but these are but small debts when compared to the generous and perceptive assistance which she has given me almost uninterruptedly since we first met in the spring of 1969. It is too facile to say that without her help this biography would not exist; it is true, however, that without her help something in the book itself would have been lost—and certainly something of the author's hope and courage during those difficult hours of composition which were made easier by sharing them with a friend whose enthusiasm never dulled her unrelenting critical judgment. For this, any public acknowledgment is but the merest gesture—made, however, in the belief that gestures are never empty but are freighted with all the loving desires which our mortal poverty can never fill.

ROYAL COUSIN

CHAPTER I

The World Awry: 1548–1572

I saw the mortal enmities, the passions, the caprices of men of power . . . the disobedience and turbulence of the people . . . I have seen everything turned upside down.

Venetian Ambassador

❧❧❧❧ The wedding which took place in the fall of 1548 in Moulins, the ancient capital of the dukes of Bourbon, was but a poor affair according to the standards of Renaissance France. That the fruit of this union would one day be numbered among the greatest and most beloved of French kings was a prediction too far-fetched even for the wizardry of the astrologers. To the members of the royal court who attended the ceremony, it was no more than a marriage of poor relations; if it had a distinguishing characteristic, it was that it was an affair of the heart. The groom, Antoine de Bourbon, was a handsome man whose love may have been alloyed with a native ambition which assessed his opportunity to marry the daughter of the King of Navarre as a chance of growing in royal favor. The bride, however, in this as in all things else, was single-minded. Although there was little of the flower of romance in the spare, angular figure of Jeanne d'Albret, she looked upon her marriage as a union of love.

Of all those present, however, the bride alone seemed to harbor such dreams. Henri II, ruling King of France since the death of his father François I little more than a year before, looked upon the whole affair with his usual brusqueness, hoping that the marriage of these poor cousins might bode well for the French state. Jeanne's father, Henri d'Albret, was annoyed that the young French King should have ended so peremptorily his own grand schemes for marrying his daughter

to the widowed Philip II of Spain. And Jeanne, who long years before
had come to realize that nothing she could do would ever bring joy
or approbation from her mother, was hardly surprised when Marguerite
d'Angoulême assisted at her daughter's nuptials still in mourning for
that single star in her sky, her brother, François I.

Jeanne's mother might well be forgiven her skepticism concerning
marital happiness, for no marriage had ever been less compatible than
that between Marguerite d'Angoulême and Henri d'Albret. Though
reared in sophisticated luxury, there was a coarse grain in Henri
d'Albret suggested in those portraits indicating the heavy nose, the
wide, mobile mouth and shrewd eyes. Finding his robust pleasures
distasteful, she retired to her lute and her classical meters and left him
to find other beds more to his taste. If the rumor reached her that the
city guards had discovered her kingly spouse, disguised as a chimney
sweep, running about after the farm women of Jurançon, her retaliation
was withdrawal to the court of her childhood where her brother reigned
in that Renaissance splendor which was to be forever linked with his
name.

The devotion which Marguerite could never give to her husband
had always been expended in full measure upon her brother. Her life,
her talents, her mind were his; and when she begot her first child,
this child, too, was placed at the service of the royal favor. Jeanne had
barely reached the age of reason when she realized that it was her
uncle rather than her father who directed her existence. Although her
mother's friend Clément Marot had called her the "mignonne of two
kings," she was anything but spoiled. In actual fact, she became little
more than a hostage for François who intended to use her in the
way most beneficial to his kingdom. Thus her early years were spent
far from her father's château in Pau and in the castle of Lonray, not
far from Alençon, where her education was presided over by Aymée de
Lafayette, a friend of her mother's. At the age of nine she was brought
to the sumptuous château at Blois where at every turn her eyes fell on
the symbols of her uncle's royal power. When it was learned, however,
that her father had assumed the initiative in negotiating a marriage
between his daughter and young Philip, son of the Emperor Charles V,
François found the thick ramparts of Blois insufficient to guard his
own interests, and in the summer of 1538 Jeanne was peremptorily
removed to the fortress at Plessis-les-Tours.

François soon countered with marriage plans of his own, and in
1540 Marguerite journeyed from court to inform her twelve-year-old

daughter that she was to marry Guillaume de la Marck, a slow-witted, ponderous youth, half-German, half-Dutch, whose major claim to fame now lies in his sister Anne who became the fourth in that endless marriage procession of Henry VIII of England. The reason behind the marriage had little to do with Jeanne. It was but another step in François' policy of weakening the Hapsburg power through strengthening his alliances with the German princes. Renaissance children were schooled to obedience, and Jeanne's schooling had been of a particularly rigorous type; yet with that uncompromising courage and inflexible will which were to stamp her life, she refused to obey her uncle's command. Not to obey François I was unthinkable, but it took persuasions and threats of a remarkable caliber before Jeanne d'Albret was brought to acknowledge this fact.

In the second week of June 1541, the bridal cortege moved slowly out of the shadows of Plessis-les-Tours through the green plains of Touraine until they could see the towers of Châtellerault above the quiet waters of the Vienne. Here on June 14, Jeanne, burdened to weariness with cloth of gold and silver and sparkling with precious stones, bent her head in stiff acquiescence to the words of the marriage ceremony. It was a ceremony of great pageantry, designed, as was everything François planned, for beauty if not for happiness. Shortly after the symbolic consummation, the main figures of the drama dispersed: the young bride back to Plessis, her mother to Poitou, her father to Pau, and the bridegroom to his disputed lands which he hoped to save, now with French help, from the encroachments of Charles V.

Yet the stubborn bride had her way after all, for Jeanne had prepared a document, officially signed and witnessed, avowing that this was a marriage of coercion to which she had never freely consented. Inconsequential at the time, such a document was sufficient evidence to invalidate the marriage, a fact which her uncle successfully utilized when, six years later, the bridegroom, now an admitted military failure, capitulated before the power of the Emperor Charles, marking himself an unacceptable figure to the King of France. Jeanne, liberated from the husband she had seen but once and bewildered by her own good fortune, soon did what any young girl might be expected to do: Jeanne d'Albret, heir to the throne of Navarre, fell in love.

Although Antoine de Bourbon, Duc de Vendôme and eldest son of the Bourbon line, had his heritage to recommend him, Jeanne's mother was less than enthusiastic about the union. Marguerite, although but fifty-six, was a woman already old, burdened with illness, and with the fire of her ambition quenched by the death of her brother. Perhaps only now did her maternal concerns, which had hitherto been subjugated to more ambitious projects, come to the fore. Her own marital experience had sharpened her sight and she may have discerned in Antoine some of that libertinism which had made her own marriage so unsatisfying. Henri and Antoine were both vain men, ambitious and greedy, yet without that penetration of mind and discernment of men which would have enabled them to perceive that guile and flattery with which they were so often surrounded. In an age when only great men succeeded, Henri d'Albret and Antoine de Bourbon had the unhappiness of being petty.

Jeanne d'Albret, although strongly marked by ambition, was in her marriage searching for something more complex than greatness; she was searching as well for admiration, affection, a reciprocal love which she found in this quick, affable man whose head was always bursting with schemes and who could express himself with such fluent charm. Had Antoine de Bourbon been gifted not simply with the ability to sway men but with constancy that would have made his influence lasting, he would have become one of the major leaders of his day, rather than that type of court-intriguer so easily won and so badly used.

Over this second marriage, the shadow of her uncle no longer fell, and Jeanne plighted her troth in freedom and in joy. "She does nothing but laugh," her cousin, the French King, wrote, describing the bride.[1] Moulins lacked the lavish display of Châtellerault, but Jeanne even then was impatient of show and pageantry and was proud to be married in this ancient Bourbon town, finding the simple gardens and fountains all to her taste. The occasion was not without splendor, however, for a young poet of Vendomôis, Pierre de Ronsard, had undertaken the epithalamion which predicted the joy of both heaven and earth if this young bride were to conceive a child whose face would mirror her own.

Those first months of their marriage were taken up with a festive visit to the Bourbon lands, followed by a journey through Béarn where her people welcomed the "Lady Jehanne" and her husband. It soon became obvious, however, that the small court of Navarre was not enough to satisfy the restless ambitions of her husband who used every opportunity to remind his Valois cousins of his position and his talents. No sooner had the bridal couple returned to Pau than Antoine rode northward to the solemn coronation of King Henri II's Florentine wife, Catherine de Medici.

Shortly afterward both Jeanne and her father left Pau—Henri summoned to court by the French King and Jeanne to join her husband—unaware that Marguerite's chronic ill-health had reached a critical stage. On December 21, 1549, she died alone in the "hermitage" she had built near the baths of Cauterets. It was a lonely death for a woman who had once charmed one of the richest and most sophisticated courts of Christendom. Her husband had grown more gross as her own health had become more precarious, and in her last illness it had been no surprise to find herself alone. Her body was carried northward to Morlaas, one-time capital of Béarn, and finally laid to rest in the cathedral of Lescar, resting place of the kings of Navarre. Even at the end she was forced to repose in alien soil, for surely she would have been more at home sharing the magnificent tomb at St. Denis which Philibert Delorme had designed for her brother.

With the death of his wife, Henri d'Albret found himself grown suddenly old. When, four years later, his daughter's first son died in infancy, he became obsessed with the need of an heir to whom he could entrust the kingdom of Navarre. Struck by gout and the diseases often attendant upon a dissolute life, he waited with impatience for his daughter, again pregnant, to bring forth her second child. That his wife had never given him a son had been a cause of enmity between them. A daughter had been of little use and, therefore, of little interest to him, until now when her womb could provide him with the grandson he so desperately desired, for no man in Europe had more dynastic dreams than the petty sovereign of Navarre. He had been only ten when Spain had seized "Haute Navarre," yet the enduring goal of his life was to reclaim this section south of the Pyrenees which he continued to feel was a rightful portion of his "kingdom." The tragedy of the "Navarre question" for Henri, and even more significantly for Antoine, was that neither man had the acumen to recognize that it was essentially a bait successfully employed by both France and Spain to draw the sovereign of Navarre to their respective (and mutually inimical) ends. But in the fall of 1553, Henri still had his illusory dreams, and, finding himself prey to age and sickness, he rejoiced in the hope that his daughter would soon give him a grandson to whom he could entrust his unwavering ambition to restore his kingdom to its original boundaries.

These were difficult months for Jeanne. The death of her first child, the little Duc de Beaumont, had filled her with grief, and now in her second pregnancy she found herself often sick and beset with periods of depression. Jeanne after five years of marriage was still extraordinarily dependent upon her husband. Even during her pregnancy and despite her persistent ill health, she continued to roam the countryside, never satisfied with the news she received of Antoine, constantly hoping that they would be able to be together again before her child was born. Antoine, caught up in those eternal wars between France and the Empire, tried to convince Jeanne that a soldier's camp would be unsuitable for her and begged her to find a quiet place where their child could be born in safety. Her father who had paid but scant attention to her for twenty years, now wrote urging her to be careful, to do nothing foolish, and suggesting that Béarn might be a proper place to give birth to her child. In September Antoine wrote that they were breaking camp and that he could join her for the trip south. It was October before they moved out of Picardy and began the long journey, southwest into Poitou, through the flat, marshy plains of Saintonge and into the rugged country of Guyenne and Gascony. They were met by her father at Mont-de-Marsan, who, seeing his daughter big with child, impatiently urged them into the last lap of their journey. When Jeanne reached Pau in early December, her pregnancy was almost at its term.

Ten days later, about one o'clock in the morning, she gave birth to a son. It is the inevitable fate of great men to have mythic elements entwined in the accounts of their births, and Henri de Navarre is no exception. One could tell from the very beginning, the legends ran, that he was to be a great king, a leader of men, but most of all a true Béarnais. He had the spirit of Béarn. Did not his mother, even as she gasped in the anguish of childbirth, sing the traditional song to the miraculous statue of the Virgin which ornamented the bridge between Pau and Jurançon. "Help me in this hour," she had sung, as all good Béarnais women of stout hearts should sing. "Beg God to deliver me quickly of this fruit of my womb, and may he give me the gift of a son." Soon she had, indeed, been delivered of a fine son, and hardly had the midwives finished their tasks for him than his grandfather had snatched him into his arms, rubbing his lips with garlic and pressing the strong good wine of Jurançon into his mouth. When the child made no demur, the old man was filled with joy, crying, "Thou wilt be a true Béarnais." And when young Jeanne reached out her arms to hold her child, her father put into them instead the long golden box which contained his will, saying, "This, my daughter, you may have; but this one here (tightening his arms about the child), this is mine."

Three months later, on the evening of March 6, 1554, the ceremony of baptism took place in the chapel of the château of Pau. The Cardinal d'Armagnac presided and the child's godparents were his grandfather, his uncle, the Cardinal de Bourbon, and his cousin, Claude de France. A silver font was cast for the occasion and, according to legend, the baby was carried to the sacramental waters in a giant tortoise shell. Here he received the name "Henri," and the hereditary title, Prince de Viane.

Henri's childhood has become as much of a legend as his birth. If one were to believe all the tales of his hardy rearing, his daring exploits among the foothills of the Pyrenees, his rude dress and ruder diet, one would conjure up an image of a stalwart, sure-footed peasant lad more apt for the soil than for the court. Yet the legends may not be so far from the truth, for in his first few years it was his grandfather who directed his life and his grandfather wanted his heir to be before all things else a Béarnais for whom the interests of Navarre would always come first. Even as his life ran out, he still dreamed of restoring the old Navarre, of wresting from Spanish power, by diplomacy if not by force of arms, that slice of land which had been conquered by Ferdinand of Aragon in 1512. Although Antoine often spoke glibly of his own plans for the restoration of Navarre, yet Henri had always been chary of this eager son-in-law who clung so readily to the stirrups of the great and thought it no degradation to fawn before his betters. The reckless independence of the Béarnais did not flow in his veins. As for Jeanne, she had taken quite literally the terms of her marriage vow and in the succeeding years she had followed her husband everywhere, spending far more time in the war camps of Picardy than in the court at Pau. No, it was not Antoine nor even Jeanne, but young Henri who alone could restore Navarre to its former glory, and for that task he was to be educated. If his first milk had been the wine of Jurançon, the milk which nourished him in those first few months flowed from the breasts of those sturdy peasant women of the region, carefully chosen by his grandfather. What, one of his adversaries was to ask many years later, could one expect from a man who had been nourished in his infancy on such milk? What, indeed, countered the proud countrymen of Navarre who saw in the reckless courage, the indomitable energy, shrewd mind and quick tongue only the result of that first sweet milk that had knit the bones of a Béarnais in his wiry frame and fashioned the heart of a Béarnais in his breast.

The old king, however, lived only to see the beginning of his dream, for less than two years after he had first held his grandson in his arms he died at Hagetmau. Once again Jeanne and Antoine were in Picardy and it was not until a month later that Jeanne arrived in Pau to bury her father beside his wife in the cathedral of Lescar. From this time on "Reyne Jehanne," as her people called her, was first and foremost Queen of Navarre. She went everywhere throughout her small kingdom, mingling with her people, giving feasts and balls, struggling against her natural reserve. This time Antoine returned to the war in Picardy alone.

By the winter of 1556, he was once again in the company of his family, for in December they traveled north to attend the court, then sitting in Amiens, to make a formal presentation of their young son who was just three years old. The Prince de Viane, even at this tender age, had recently been given fifty men at arms, and the ceremony which the people held for his parents at their official entrance into Limoges was one of the first fully ceremonious processions of his career. By February 4, the party had reached his father's ancestral lands at Vendôme and then traveled northward toward Paris. At court Henri II showed himself impressed by the small boy who seemed unabashed by his royal surroundings and already indicated that fearless independence which was to be such a marked characteristic of his life.

It was here that the event took place which has been chronicled by so many contemporaries and which Palma Cayet describes in its entirety:

> The king Antoine, his wife, and the prince de Navarre, their son, a spontaneous and handsome prince, came to court to visit the king, who, seeing the prince de Navarre so pleasing and cheerful, resolved from henceforth to bring him up with the dauphin, François. And so having embraced and kissed him several times, he asked him if he would not like to be his son. But the little prince, turning toward his father, answered, "There is my father . . ." The king, taken with his manner of expression, continued, "Then wouldn't you like to be my son-in-law?" to which he replied without second thought, "Oh, yes!"[2]

Antoine, always anxious to reaffirm his connection with the Valois family, immediately interpreted the incident as a sign of a forthcoming marriage between his son and Marguerite de Valois who was hardly older than the infant prince. Such an interpretation may have been built on ambiguous grounds; what was unequivocal was the character of the child who was to be neither cajoled nor intimidated by royal wishes. In the summer of that same year, Jeanne and her son returned to Béarn while Antoine remained to carry out his military duties.

The wars continued to go badly for France, and by the summer of 1557, French morale was dangerously low. When Henri II heard rumors that England might be coming in on the side of Spain he desperately urged the forces in Picardy to stand firm, for with Picardy broken, Paris would be an easy prey. But no royal exhortation could stem the power of the Imperial forces, and despite the efforts of the Constable Montmorency and his nephew, Gaspard de Coligny, St. Quentin was doomed and the north road to Paris clear. Paris shuddered, but the stroke it awaited never came; Philip II hesitated, despite the clamor of his captains who assured him that Paris was his for the taking. He had begun that habit of caution which saved him many defeats but cost him as well the crown of victory.

Meanwhile the only Frenchman who could be counted on to stem the series of Spanish victories was riding northward from his exploits in Italy to arrive at St. Germain on October 6. The name of Guise already had the aura of magic about it, and when the rumor ran that *El Gran Capitano* was riding home, the desolate French soldiers took new heart. François, Duc de Guise, was Philip's opposite in every way. While Philip waited to see the course of events, Guise propelled events upon their courses. What he attempted now was a typically Guisard venture: reckless, quick as lightning, and—most typical of all—successful. Even as Philip's troops withdrew before the new French commander, Guise continued to push north. Rumor was already abroad as to what he planned and as he followed his cavalry into Amiens, the English commanders at Calais became convinced that the rumors were true. The prize at which he aimed was the long-disputed town of Calais— Calais which had lain like an English taunt over the French countryside for over a hundred years. On New Year's Eve, Guise launched his attack against the demoralized English garrison, and on January 7, Calais and the disputed land of the Pale were in French hands again.

Throughout the war, Antoine de Bourbon had never lost sight of what advantages the conflict might have for his kingdom of Navarre. Even those who took him seriously as a man of war found his schemes somewhat bizarre as he enthusiastically described the possibility of capturing Philip of Spain in battle with immense consequences for both France and Navarre. In actual fact, his schemes were treacherous as well as bizarre, for even as he risked his life in war against the Spaniard, he welcomed the Emperor's envoy, Descurra, and listened favorably to a plan whereby he would place Navarre at the service of the Spanish King for the conquest of France, which would then be divided between Antoine and Philip. Following the French victory at Calais, Philip, assessing his depleted treasury, saw peace as the nearest way to victory, and with no immediate use for Antoine, informed him that their pact was no longer binding. In October a peace commission rode out from Spain, and Antoine, betrayed by war, now turned his mind to making peace serve his ends.

He wrote to Henri II, reminding him on his wife's part as well as on his own of their hope for "the recovery of our kingdom of Navarre or some recompense worthy of the loss we have suffered."[3] Perhaps, suggested Antoine, His Majesty would be gracious enough to mention this fact to the Cardinal de Guise, the Constable, and those who will be engaged in drawing up the terms of peace. In 1559, peace was formally established by the Treaty of Cateau-Cambrésis and the long series of conflicts between France and Spain were temporarily ended. The wars were over and after so many warlike dreams and flattering words, Antoine found that the little kingdom of Navarre had reaped no benefits from the treaty signed by the great powers. Calais was back in French hands and those three disputed bishoprics of Metz, Toul, and Verdun were to remain in French possession. But in the treaty he was now ordered to proclaim, the old territory of Navarre was never mentioned.

The period of tranquillity which France now anticipated was but shortlived, for on June 30, during the marriage festivities of his daughter Elizabeth to Philip of Spain, Henri II was mortally wounded during a joust with the young Comte de Montgomery. Montgomery had had no desire to break lances with his King, but Henri, always anxious to prove his strength, had insisted. Hardly had the contest begun when the Count's lance had slipped through the King's visor and entered his eye. From the beginning the doctors knew there was no hope of recovery. The lance had pierced the brain and for ten days the King lingered in torment. On July 10, 1559, at the Palais de Tournelles, Henri II died in the forty-ninth year of his age and the twelfth of his reign. He left four sons, the oldest of whom, François, just sixteen, was at once proclaimed king by the attendant noblemen and taken by carriage in the company of the Duc de Guise and his brother the Cardinal de Lorraine to the palace of the Louvre. The Guise influence, while always great, had been immeasurably increased when the preceding year their niece Mary Stuart—intelligent, beautiful, and ambitious—had married the Dauphin. As uncles and advisers, they were now in a masterly position to advance their own interests. Well aware that their influence would vitiate her own, the Queen Mother, Catherine de Medici did all in her power to keep them at a distance from her son the King. So desperate had she been to keep the center of control from this powerful clan that she had shocked half of Paris by refusing to observe the usual period of widowed seclusion, riding hither and yon, from the Louvre to St. Germain, so that she might never be far from the young king who, she hoped, would depend on her for advice and counsel.

As First Prince of the Blood, Antoine de Bourbon had every right to be a major influence at court during this period of jockeying for power. Even while Henri II lay dying, Antoine was looked upon by many as the most important man in France: Spain watched him nervously, fearful of the trouble he might cause; Elizabeth of England wrote flattering letters to him in an effort to gain his favor; and when the Guises heard that he was on his way north, they prepared as though for an invasion. But Antoine, although so often in the vanguard when he was not needed, now dallied indecisively on his way to St. Germain. He could hardly have played better into the Guises' hands. By mid-August the Guises were secure in the saddle, and when on August 18, Antoine rode into St. Germain, they could afford to treat him to a touch of that cold insolence which was to become such a marked element of *La tyrannie Guisienne*.

When François II was crowned on September 18 at the cathedral at Reims, the Princes of the Blood had obviously lost their position to the Guises. The coronation was an ill-omened ceremony in many ways. It was obvious to all that the crown was far too heavy for the frail boy-king who bore it. It was a tired child's face rather than the face of a monarch that acknowledged the smiles and applause of the people. The narrow shoulders, the weary eyes, bespoke those strange fevers and lassitude from which François had always suffered. Yet whatever his physical endowment, François reigned, undisputed King of France; and behind him, circling him about, reigned the powerful and astute minds of the House of Guise.

Although it was obvious that Antoine was no longer needed at court, still he tarried, despite the fact that he was poorly housed, often ignored, and sometimes treated with contempt. When Catherine de Medici suggested that he take charge of the embassy which would conduct Elizabeth de Valois to her husband Philip II, only Antoine failed to realize that this was less an honor than a convenient way of removing him from court. In October he began his journey, and was joined at La Flèche by his wife and their five-year-old son. In December they met Elizabeth in Angoulême, and after a sumptuous Christmas spent at Pau, the bride, conducted by Antoine, arrived at the monastery of Roncevaux on January 1. Here everything was on a grand scale: the heavily laden pack mules, the fifty pages clothed in white satin and cloth of gold, the lavish trousseau, the princess herself, her dark Valois beauty decked with precious stones.

As for Antoine, with his head still full of schemes for annexing Spanish Navarre, he now hoped to use this interview with the Spanish ambassadors toward that end. Thus with that vanity and arrogance which won him so much disdain, he insisted on receiving the Spanish delegates without rising and began at once a discourse on returning Navarre to its rightful owners. It was a dangerous breach of diplomacy which was palliated only by the enigmatic tact of the Spaniards.

By 1560 Antoine had worked himself into a wholly untenable position. Not only had he played a double game in the minor cause of Navarre, but also in a cause of far greater concern to the kingdom of France: the cause of religion. France had long felt the breath of the "new doctrine," that tempestuous movement for reform which would no longer be restrained by principles of obedience and conformity. François I with his breadth of vision had shown tolerance to those men who no longer found the spirit of God in the old forms and who sought to reform and revitalize the church of God; but his son, like most men of limited intellect, interpreted toleration only as a sign of weakness or an academic luxury he could ill afford. His father might well have encouraged with amused benignity the scholarly debates over new doctrines, but the new doctrines had now escaped from throne room and pulpit into the streets where they were caught more easily than the pestilence. The establishment of the *Chambre ardente*, the Edict of Compiègne, which imposed the death penalty on those not adhering to the Catholic faith, the rumors that France would soon have her Inquisition—all of these repressive measures which the heavy hand of Henri II had imposed upon his people were intolerable to the increasing number of Frenchmen who espoused the religious reform in one way or another.

From the beginning the kingdom of Navarre had offered asylum to many of the dissenters. Marguerite d'Angoulême with her sophisticated, inquisitive mind had listened with interest to the men from Geneva. Clément Marot had done his French translation of the psalms under her patronage, and when the controversial reformer Gérard Roussel was forced to flee from his diocese of Meaux, Marguerite had recalled him, first making him her confessor and then offering him the bishopric of Oloron. Her daughter, shortly after the death of Henri d'Albret, had written to the Vicomte de Gourdon, explaining that like her mother she was caught "in the matter of hesitation between the two religions," continuing, ". . . a reform seems so right and so necessary that, for my part, I consider that it would be disloyalty and cowardice to God, to my conscience and to my people to remain any longer in a state of suspense and indecision."[4] It would be five years before Jeanne would make a public profession of the new religion, yet in 1555 Theodore Beza, that "lively and subtle spirit" with his eloquent tongue and memorable face, could write: ". . . the King and Queen [of Navarre] begin to taste something of the truth."[5]

By 1558 it was well known, even in Rome, that the sovereigns of Navarre were encouraging preachers from Geneva. The Pope, alarmed at the increase of heresy, sent the Cardinal d'Armagnac into Navarre as his legate, and Henri II wrote a threatening letter to Antoine which at least partially intimidated that congenitally nervous sovereign. Ironically enough in the light of future events, it was in Antoine rather than in Jeanne that Beza and Calvin put their hopes, both writing to the King commending him for his stand, urging him to assume the leadership of the movement in France, and reminding him that for such a prize as the kingdom of God some earthly goods must be renounced.

This was the measure from which Antoine recoiled: he had but little talent for the difficult business of renunciation. He wished instead to set his course so that every movement, every event, every man might be subordinated to his own ambitions. But such a course is difficult to chart and even more difficult to steer. It demands courage, intelligence, patience, and high dedication. In its own way it also demands renunciation. It was a course for which the Guises were master pilots. Antoine wrecked his ship on the first shoal. As the Huguenots watched him falter at court in the fall of 1559 and saw how readily the weak mouth smiled, how easily insults were forgotten, and how avidly small honors were courted, they recognized that he was not the leader to champion the Huguenot cause. When François Hotman, one of the greatest of the Huguenot polemicists, wrote to a confrere that Antoine had betrayed all his hopes, he was voicing a common opinion.

The following spring the Huguenots, desperate under the continued policy of repressive legislation for which they held the Guises largely responsible, engaged in the "Conspiracy of Amboise"—an abortive measure to cast out the Guises, "free" the King, and win for themselves some measure of toleration. It was a plan ill-conceived and badly directed, resulting only in multiple executions, renewed favor for the Guises, and recriminations for the Princes of the Blood. Yet even the tragedy of Amboise did not end Antoine's ambivalent course. Even as he assured the King of his fidelity to the Roman faith, he was inviting Beza and Hotman to preach at Nérac. When in December 1560, François II died after a few days' illness, leaving the throne to his ten-year-old brother Charles, Catherine de Medici, who had had enough of uncles, made it clear at the first council meeting that she "as a loving mother should" would stay with her son and help govern the state. Antoine, as First Prince of the Blood, she named as first councilor and later that spring as lieutenant general of the kingdom. It was, however, not a call to power, for the Queen Mother's intention in these appointments was made abundantly clear in a letter to her daughter Elizabeth: "The King of Navarre is entirely in my hands and deprived of all power and authority except through my good pleasure. He is obedient to me and has no authority except what I permit him."[6]

Catherine had learned much during those anguished months when her first son reigned. She had learned the art of diplomatic fencing: to hold her sword arm steady, to feint and parry, to retreat and to attack. She had learned never to admit fear, to listen, to talk at length and to promise nothing. Gifted with a native shrewdness, she had tempered it into an almost perfect weapon, a weapon that with varied success would last her for thirty years. She had a woman's hatred of war, and she determined that for the remainder of her life she would pursue the cause of peace. The paths she chose to lead her to her goal were sometimes devious, often questionable, occasionally violent, but in the cause of conciliation no means seemed immoral to her. To keep France at peace and her sons upon the throne were from henceforward the twin goals of her life.

The course of conciliation as she saw it at the accession of her second son was to establish a delicate balance of power between the two main factions of the kingdom, Guise and Châtillon, so that her own power as "governess" of France would remain unimpaired. Having for almost eighteen months suffered under the ascendency of the House of Guise, she now sought to curtail that power by setting against it their traditional enemies. In effect, this meant a balance of Catholics against Huguenots, for by 1560 all three of the Châtillon brothers had espoused the New Religion. Condé, Antoine's younger brother, would also add weight to the Huguenot position and, as for Antoine, Catherine hoped by small plums and large promises to keep him where he would do her the most good. The Huguenots took heart as the Queen Mother favored them in unexpected ways, entrusting the education of the young king to Gaspard de Coligny (the second of the Châtillon brothers and perhaps the most talented), choosing as her chancellor, Michel de l'Hôpital, a man of liberal religious views, and announcing an assembly to meet in September at which both faiths would be free to discuss their respective positions.

Although the assembly that gathered in the refectory of the Benedictine monastery of Poissy on September 9 was impressive (thirty-five ministers, six cardinals, twenty-six archbishops, theologians from the Sorbonne, the royal family itself) little emerged in terms of concrete proposals. The colloquy did, however, by its attempt at open dialogue, prepare for an important measure which Catherine had already conceived. In the first weeks of 1562 there was promulgated that legislation which came to be called the Edict of January and which was to grant the greatest measure of religious liberty that the Huguenots would enjoy until the Edict of Nantes thirty-six years later. The response of conservative Catholics was immediate. The Paris Parlement at first refused to register the edict, and many years later Catholics still referred to it as the "fatal edict." For the Hugenots, however, it was a keystone of toleration, the most perfect legislation they would know for many years.

Shortly before the Colloquy of Poissy, Jeanne d'Albret had arrived quietly in Paris. "She comes to do all the harm she can," wrote the Spanish ambassador, enraged at such audacity, for Jeanne was now a professed Calvinist, having made her formal confession the preceding Christmas.[7] Her position made her religious profession of enormous importance to the Huguenots. During her trip north from Nérac she had been received everywhere by the heretics with great enthusiasm, as though she were a messiah, commented a disapproving historian.

Now in her apartments she daily received the members of the churches, invited preachers of renown, and did all she could to encourage the Huguenots to organize on a national scale. Beza himself was soon at court preaching in "open audience," even "communing" with the Cardinal de Lorraine who was heard to say that he was a "great personage and greatly to his liking." It was not long before even young King Charles seemed to have been affected by the new spirit, and the English agent, Throckmorton, reported that Jeanne d'Albret had told him secretly that one day when she spoke to her royal nephew, explaining why she did not attend Mass, he had said to her: "Surely, Aunt, to be plain with you (quoth he), if it were not for the Queen my mother's pleasure, I would not be there myself . . . and when I shall be at my own rule I mean to quit the matter."[8]

Such an atmosphere soon became intolerable to the Guises, and in November they left the court, followed shortly by their old enemy the Constable with whom they had now found a common cause. In order to strengthen their position, they tried to draw to it that vacillating Prince, whom they disdained even while they exploited him: Antoine de Bourbon, First Prince of the Blood. In actual fact, Antoine was once again besieged with lush promises from many sides, for every faction recognized that the adherence of the First Prince of the Blood would give sanction to its own enterprises. The Guises, knowing that no scheme was too bizarre for Antoine to espouse, suggested that as his wife was an admitted heretic, he might ask for an annulment from the Pope and marry their beautiful niece Mary Stuart. Thus the crown of Scotland would be his, and the crown of England not far off. Spain again entered the game with Philip exhorting his ambassador to keep up "Vendôme's" hopes for these could be put to good use in Spain. Shortly afterward Philip suggested through his agents that Antoine might accept Sardinia in compensation for Spanish Navarre. A little later Sardinia was replaced by Tunisia, a doubtful kingdom for Spain to give away since it was not yet in Spanish possession. Actually it mattered little what they promised; it mattered only that the bait be sufficiently tempting.

In this regard they need have had no worries, for Antoine, like a well-schooled ass, followed unwittingly whatever carrot was dangled before his nose. In March Throckmorton wrote in annoyance to his Queen: "The King of Navarre is all Spanish now," continuing, "the King of Spain has told the King of Navarre that he will travail for his satisfaction if he would live a Catholic and do his best to bring the Queen to do the like . . ."[9]

The first condition had already been met; the second Antoine found more difficult. In the first years of his marriage he would simply have had to beckon and Jeanne would have been at his side. But that was fourteen years earlier when the young bride was still responding to the ecstasies of first love. Jeanne was now thirty-four, a woman grave, mature—and disillusioned. The smile which had characterized her at their wedding was gone. Jeanne smiled but rarely now. She often sorrowed. The angular quality of her face had grown more pronounced, her bouts of ill health more frequent. One can only conjecture what she now felt for her husband whose petty vanity and vacillation must have gravely disappointed her. Perhaps it was pride as well as tact which kept her from expressing any derogatory opinion of the Prince in whom she had placed so many hopes. Only a single sentence from her *Mémoires*, written after Antoine's death, gives us a clue to what she must have suffered: "The withdrawal of the former king, my husband, from his first zeal for the Religion, was for me a very sharp thorn, not a thorn which pierced my foot but one which entered my heart. . . . it is more becoming for me to be silent rather than to speak of it further."[10] With this disappointment in her personal life, Jeanne turned with increasing determination to the political scene. More than ever she became the queen of her people and the savior of the Huguenots, busying herself with their causes, righting their wrongs, pleading for compassion and toleration on their behalf.

Although Jeanne's silence indicates that she wished, despite the cost to herself, to avoid a public scandal, such a scandal became inevitable when Antoine demanded that she return to the Roman faith. Such a step she could never take. Jeanne had too often been the pawn of kings not to recognize their designs. It was clear to her from the start that Antoine was concerned with neither her soul's salvation nor with the true religion; it was once again the visionary scheme of a kingdom which drew him on. When he commanded her to go to Mass, she refused. When he threatened, she ignored him. Antoine's tenacity could never match his wife's. Desperate lest Spain withdraw its promises if he could not meet its demands, he determined that since he could not convert his wife, he would repudiate her. Perhaps afraid to face her—Antoine's courage never reached much beyond the battlefield—he sent her a letter asking her to leave court. Jeanne had no love for the Valois court and to leave it would be a small hardship, but this time Antoine held the trump card, for he demanded that she leave her eight-year-old son behind.

It was more than a separation between mother and child; it was a separation between a woman and her dream, a queen and the future of her state. In the last two years she had done her best to ensure that her son be carefully instructed in the new faith, making certain that his tutor was a man solely devoted to the ideals of the new religion who would carefully school him in the responsibilities he would one day assume. One day he would be King of Navarre and upon him would devolve the happiness, the faith, even the salvation of his people. The future of Navarre was his. Upon her son rested all her hopes; now she stood to lose all. Legend has it that there was a long and painful scene of farewell between Jeanne and her son Henri. The Cardinal Legate, who could hardly be expected to show compassion for a heretic parent, wrote that she admonished him "never to go to Mass, in any guise whatever, even going so far as to say that if he disobeyed her in this, he could be sure that she would disinherit him and would not be known in the future as his mother."[11] Harsh words, perhaps, but the facts were harsh and upon this child's fidelity to what she had taught him were built Jeanne's dreams for the future of Navarre.

In early spring of 1562, Jeanne took the road southward toward Béarn. It was a bitter journey for she believed the gossip that her husband had promised the Cardinal de Lorraine that if she did not leave in eight days he would lock her up in one of his houses. "And when he made this promise," Jeanne wrote later, "the Cardinal with a solemn exclamation replied, 'This, Monsieur, is an act worthy of you! God grant you a good long life.' "[12] She was alone, without friends or support; no one could afford to help her, not even the Queen Mother, for with Antoine on the side of the Guises, Catherine herself was virtually a prisoner and the plight of the Huguenots more desperate than before.

Hardly had his mother left the court than the young Prince de Navarre entered upon his own period of lonely endurance, while all the forces of the adult world were concentrated on bending his stubborn will. His "heretic" tutor was replaced by the respectable and conservative

Jean de Losses. His father, his relatives, and "even the King of France himself" forbade him the practice of his religion, and by fear and coercion attempted to win him to their side. Their task was to be more formidable than they had anticipated. Once when they had led him as far as the door of the chapel he refused to enter; another time he fell ill. Whether the illness was real or feigned, no one seemed quite sure. That an eight-year-old child should be at once so determined and so ingenious caused the Spanish ambassador to write, "Although according to the opinion of some he is still very much a child, yet he is very alert, intelligent and good-looking and has shown himself very firm in his mother's persuasion." Even beatings did not move him, and on May 19 Chantonay, the Spanish Ambassador, wrote that Antoine had still made no headway with his son and that "Everything is still in the same state."[13] Of these events Jeanne d'Albret wrote proudly six years later: "I have always by the grace of God followed the right path . . . by this same grace, almost miraculously, my son has been preserved in the purity of his religion, despite the many assaults made against it. This is not through his own prudence, strength or constancy, for at the age of eight, which is what he then was, he could not have furnished all that. To God alone then be glory."[14]

Courage, ingenuity, shrewdness—none was enough, however, to counter the opposition permanently; and in the end, like his mother before him, he yielded to the pressure of the adults who governed his world. On June 1, Henri went to Mass with his father, "promising into his hands to cherish the orthodox faith and to die for it."[15] It was his first public capitulation which may have been dictated, even then, less by weakness than by a kind of realism which found tilting at windmills a hazardous and profitless occupation.

Jeanne's road home was not only lonely but perilous as well. She had but few retainers and in her arms she carried the additional burden of her infant daughter Catherine. She stopped briefly at Meaux where Condé was already massing a Huguenot army. Jeanne, however, resolved to remain neutral, fearing that if she should join any faction she risked losing the little she still retained. Somewhere along the way she met Theodore Beza, a meeting which provided her with one of those small comfortings that gave her courage to endure, for Beza with his quiet faith, his keen spiritual insight, his gentleness, was one of the few people in whom Jeanne's faith never wavered.

It was a comforting she sorely needed, for her plight was made more perilous by the open warfare which had broken out between Huguenots

and Catholics following the massacre of a Huguenot assembly gathered
for prayer at the town of Vassy. That the Duc de Guise later avowed
that the act had been contrary to his intention was not sufficient to
calm the storm, especially since it had taken place following the Edict
of January which had guaranteed the right of public worship to the
Huguenots. For Condé, who had assumed the leadership of the party
at the defection of his brother Antoine, it left the Huguenots no course
but that of arms. In his declaration announcing open war, Condé
wrote of "the horrible carnage at Vassy in the presence of the Duc de
Guise, which was committed on an assembly of unarmed men, women,
and children, who were worshiping in accordance with the pure religion and the Word of God." Already the Huguenots were envisioning
themselves not simply as the protectors of the new faith but as the
champions of France, the protectors of the crown against the encroachments of the House of Guise and its followers. Thus Condé explained their cause not simply as self-defense but as "the defense of
the royal authority, of the government of the Queen, and of the
tranquillity of the realm."[16]

This open warfare made Jeanne's trip from Vendôme to Béarn a
nightmare for during its course her dignified departure had changed to
open flight. Blaise de Montluc, lieutenant for the crown, was already
abroad in Guyenne, boasting that it was not hard to follow his course
because of the bodies of the heretics which he had left dangling from
the trees. His brutality had angered her but when she heard his lewd
joke that he would soon see "if it was as much fun to sleep with
queens as with other women," she was humiliated beyond endurance.[17]
Fearful lest she fall into his hands, she made her way into Béarn by
circuitous routes. Often too sick to travel, weakened by those sweats
and hemorrhages that had long plagued her, it was weeks before she
reached Pau and comparative safety.

At court, meanwhile, her son Henri listened in fear to the news from
the south: Guyenne smoking in the wake of Montluc's savage forays,
the mountains of Béarn no longer safe, men seeking to capture his
mother in order to imprison her, or perhaps bring her before the
Inquisition where she would be sentenced to that fearful death reserved to heretics. In late September he wrote to a friend of his
mother—the second of the letters preserved from the eight-year-old
prince: "Write to me to relieve my anxiety about my mother, for I
have a terrible fear that something has happened to her on her
journey. The greatest pleasure you could render me is to keep me in-

formed frequently."[18] Not long after his fears about his mother's safety were allayed, he suffered another loss. In November 1562 his father died of wounds received at the siege of Rouen. For Jeanne, Antoine's loss could not have been of tragic proportions for she had, in fact, lost her husband long before. In the letters of condolence that reached her, there was a note of congratulation. Now, the talk of divorce and annulment stilled—she would be free to steer her own course. With Antoine dead, Jeanne hoped that her son would be permitted to return to her; but although the Queen Mother acceded to her request that his former teacher, the Huguenot La Gaucherie, be reinstated as Henri's tutor, she made it clear that the young prince would remain at court with his royal cousins. Jeanne, increasingly fearful of the coercion exercised on her son, wrote sadly to the Vicomte de Gourdon: "They are keeping him at court, forcing him to sign and approve various requests false both to truth and his upbringing, reflecting hatred of the Reformed Religion and its adherents. . . . I am anxious and so distressed and sad at heart that I can find no joy or peace of mind."[19]

By the spring of 1563 feeling against the adherents of the Reformed Religion had reached a new peak, for in February of that year the Duc de Guise had been murdered by a Huguenot assassin Poltrot de Méré, who under torture named the Huguenot leader, Gaspard de Coligny as the instigator of the deed. Despite Poltrot's later retraction, the accusation was sufficient to stir up new hostility and set the Houses of Guise and Montmorency at each other's throats. If by killing the shepherd Poltrot had hoped to scatter the sheep, his work was successful, for on February 26, Sir Thomas Smith wrote to Queen Elizabeth: "The death of the Duke will make some great turn. The Papists have lost their greatest stay, hope and comfort. Many noblemen and gentlemen followed the camp and that faction rather for love of him than for any other cause. . . . He was so loved amongst the noblemen and soldiers of France, that now he is gone many will leave the camp; they begin to drop away already."[20] It was under this strain of Catholic disaffection that the Queen Mother was able to push ahead to the Peace of Amboise which ended the first civil war.

The peace which was signed in February 1563, was at best a temporary measure. In principle it granted liberty of conscience to the Huguenots, but they would never be satisfied until the full terms of the Edict of January were restored to them. Although the overt con-

flict had come to an end, France was still far from peace. Barbaro, the
Venetian ambassador, summed up his impressions in his official dispatch: "Such was the state in which I found the kingdom of France
upon my arrival: I saw from the very first that the administration
was without order, that justice was violated and besmirched; I saw
the mortal enmities, the passions, the caprices of men of power;
the conflicting interests of princes which change according to the
occasion, the religious disturbances, the disobedience and turbulence
of the people, the revolt and godlessness of the great. I have seen
everything turned upside down. . . ."[21]

For Jeanne, too, everything was upside down; not only was her son
still held at an alien court and her lands ravished by Montluc, but
in September of that year she was threatened with excommunication
unless she appear before the Inquisition within six months. Should she
refuse to recant, her property would be confiscated, her subjects freed
from their allegiance, and the kingdom of Navarre turned over to
another ruler. This was the weapon by which Pius V hoped to frighten
erring monarchs back into the bosom of the Roman Church; but
the weapon misfired, for the Queen Mother and her son, irritated
at this arbitrary action on the part of the Holy See, wrote a remonstrance to His Holiness on behalf of Jeanne. To confiscate kingdoms was not a prerogative of papal power and the letters that
went from France to Rome made it very clear that France would
not stand by and see an important vassal of the French crown subjected to the dictation of foreign powers. Although ultimately such
a letter did little to change Jeanne's position, she was grateful to
Catherine for the gesture, and feeling that perhaps there was no longer
any cause for fear, she accepted the Queen Mother's invitation to join
the court.

In the year following the Peace of Amboise, the Queen Mother was
at last in a position to carry out her long-cherished plan for a royal
progress through France to enable the people to see their sovereign—
a boy of fourteen now, tall, thin, with stooping shoulders, a narrow,
pointed face, and sharp, aquiline nose. Already he showed that passionate love of activity which frequently exceeded his limited physical
strength. Henri de Navarre was also part of that unwieldy caravan
that for two years was to wander like a nomad city throughout the
French countryside. Although his position was one of unimportance
compared to that of his king-cousin, yet he drew the limelight in a
number of ways before the progress was over. He had already established

a reputation for keen intelligence and the experienced English diplomat Sir Thomas Hoby did not hesitate to call him a "wise child."

Once his mother joined the entourage at Mâcon, Henri was again caught in the bitter religious feud which his mother's presence always stirred. Catherine had at first permitted him to leave the royal children and live in his mother's apartments, but when she learned that Jeanne had not only attended public Huguenot worship but brought her son with her to hear the preaching, she was outraged. "I will cut off the head of anyone who does not attend Mass," she swore as she commanded that Henri leave his mother and return to the royal apartments.[22] Command as she would, however, she could never do more than obtain an outward conformity from the young prince over whom she was never to establish any lasting influence. Nor could her threats succeed in cowing him, for when he overheard a rumor, while the cortege was at Bayonne near the Spanish border, that the Spanish intended to wipe out the Huguenot leaders, he unhesitatingly reported the news to his mother, thus diminishing even more the Huguenots' trust in the Queen Mother's good faith. Catherine must have been bewildered and frustrated at this child— not quite eleven—who could be neither cajoled nor frightened, and who clung with such courageous tenacity to the course his mother had charted. Even in those early days he differed markedly from his royal cousins. Catherine, shrewd observer that she was, must have noticed it.

It was when the caravan arrived at Salon, however, that the Prince de Navarre found himself the focus of attention. Here Nostradamus the famous seer of the age and a cherished friend of the superstitious Queen Mother, who had already cast the horoscopes of her children, came to visit the court. This time it was not Catherine's children whom he wished to see but the Prince de Navarre. He was, as the contemporary diarist L'Estoile later wrote, brought into the Prince's room during his levée and there for a long time he sat contemplating the child. This time his prophecy was anything but to the Queen's taste, for he predicted that this young prince would one day be King of France. "If God gives you the grace to live until that time," he promised the attending *gouverneur*, "you will have for your master a king of France and of Navarre."[23]

No one records the reaction to Nostradamus' prophecy. It must have seemed too far-fetched to be received seriously even by the Queen Mother's superstitious ears, for even should anything happen to King

Charles, she had two more sons waiting in the wings to be called to their destiny. No one in 1564 could easily believe that in a quarter of a century the Valois dynasty would have toppled and that the small boy who waited nervously, thinking that this was but an occasion for another whipping, would become the first Bourbon on the throne of France.

Even then, however, the seeds of Henri's future qualities as leader were beginning to show, and two years later a citizen of Bordeaux wrote of him:

> We have here the Prince de Béarn; it must be confessed that he is a charming youth. At thirteen years of age he has all the riper qualities of eighteen or nineteen; he is agreeable, polite, obliging and behaves to everyone with an air so easy and engaging, that wherever he is there is always a crowd. He mixes in conversation like a wise and prudent man, speaks always to the purpose, and when it happens that the court is the subject of the discourse, it is easy to see that he is perfectly well acquainted with it, and he never says more nor less than he ought in whatever place he is.[24]

For the next year and a half Henri continued in the royal entourage as it journeyed through France. His mother had, meanwhile, tried unsuccessfully to win from the Queen Mother permission to take her son back to Béarn with her; but Catherine, aware that there was no better bargaining point than a royal hostage, stood firm. It was not until two years later when the court had finished its progress that Jeanne managed once more to "escape"—this time taking Henri with her. By the end of January 1567, mother and son were at La Flèche; from here they traveled into Poitou and then with haste and secrecy completed their journey into their own domains. That fall, the tenuous religious peace gave way and the Huguenots provoked France into its second civil war—a conflict of six months' duration which terminated in March 1568 with the ineffectual Peace of Longjumeau.

By now Jeanne realized that her policy of neutrality was no longer practicable. Since her flight had been synonymous with the renewed outbreak of hostilities she found herself blamed as the instigator of the conflict. Despite her remonstrances, Blaise de Montluc had been appointed the King's lieutenant in Guyenne at the death of Antoine, and the Catholics, heartened by his support, had begun to rebel against the legislation forbidding the practice of the Catholic religion which

Jeanne had passed against them. With even her own lands in revolt, neutrality was impossible. It became even more so when on September 25, 1568, the crown formally revoked the Edict of January, thus reducing the Huguenots once again to the level of a seditious sect. Although the intention of such legislation was to repress, in fact it simply encouraged the Huguenots to subsume their differences into a stronger union.

These years were a period of apprenticeship for the Prince de Navarre—an apprenticeship both military and diplomatic. He had already shown a tendency to find his "delight" in "gambling, dancing, eating and drinking"—tendencies of which Jeanne not only disapproved but feared; to counter them she was firm in seeing that he continued the education which would train him for his future role. There was no doubt that he had the personality of a leader, but Jeanne was determined that he should be an intelligent leader with the knowledge and acumen which would elicit respect from his people and not a "donkey with a crown on his head."[25] She forbade him to gamble and when she caught him in a game of dice she ordered that he be punished. But not even Jeanne's severity could curb her son's lifelong weakness where money was concerned. If one avenue was cut off, then he would find other ways to get the funds he was always in need of. A contemporary noting his methods, observed: "He loves diversions and the pleasures of the table. When he wants money, he has the address to procure it in a manner quite new, and very agreeable to others as well as himself; to those, whether men or women, whom he thinks his friends, he sends a promissory note, written and signed by himself, and entreats them to send back the note or the sum mentioned in it. Judge, if there is a family that can refuse him: everyone looks upon it as an honour to have a note from this Prince."[26]

By the beginning of 1568 Henri had taken up his duties in earnest and in February of that year Jeanne sent her son into Basse-Navarre on his first task of "pacification." This was a question not of military but of diplomatic prowess, for the rebellion had already been put down and Henri's task was to bring the people back to their loyalty to their queen. In Bordenave's description of his address to the people, we find the beginnings of that rhetorical skill which was to serve him so well throughout his life:

> . . . since he could not capture them, he assembled the
> people . . . and demonstrated how wrong they had been to

follow the leaders of this sedition. . . . He said that his
mother, like all good mothers, wished her children to be strong
rather than weak, alive rather than dead, rich rather than
poor . . . and free rather than enslaved . . . and that they had
no reason to resort to arms . . . since they never appealed to
her without receiving a fair hearing and redress for their
grievances to the extent that the law and reason permitted. . . . He hoped that his coming would make them
wiser . . . so that in future . . . [they would] consider the
horrible consequences of their sedition before undertaking it.
[He pointed out] the ruin of their property and the misery
of their families . . . and he assured them that as their fa-
thers had benefited from the benevolence of their predecessors,
the Queen his mother and he himself . . . would never be sur-
passed in justice and good will toward their subjects. . . . If
they proved themselves worthy and obedient [his mother]
would never infringe upon their liberties . . . and privileges . . . nor force them in their religion. . . . He also offered
to act as their advocate to her and told them to address themselves to him without fear.[27]

Jeanne must have been pleased that her son, despite his penchant for
the lighter pleasures of life, was also manifesting that political acumen
by which a strong leader can cloak commands in language that wins
men rather than subjugates them.

Neither mother nor son, however, could calm the storm which swept
over them in those years, and Jeanne wrote in her *Mémoires*, "During
this turbulent time, I sent again and again to Their Majesties . . .
to cry 'Peace.' "[28] In answer there were only fresh outrages against her
people on the part of the King's lieutenant and rumors that the Queen
Mother planned to kidnap her son and bring him again to court. Jeanne,
abandoning at last her position of neutrality, traveled north with her
son, and on September 24 reached La Rochelle which Condé had
made his headquarters. It was at La Rochelle that Henri, not yet
fifteen, was given over to the care of his uncle who would instruct him
in the art of war. It was to be but a short apprenticeship, however,
for on March 13, 1569, Louis, Prince de Condé, was killed in the
Huguenot defeat at Jarnac.

No one felt Condé's death more keenly than his sister-in-law, for
she had found in him a friend, a leader, and a surrogate father for
her son. After his death, there was found in his pocket a blood-

stained letter from Jeanne, thanking him for his care of her son and expressing the now ironic wish that God would bless him with a long life. "I am so sad that I could hardly be sadder," she wrote to Henri at the end of March. "I know, my son," she continued, "that God has given you enough sense for you to feel the importance of this loss which for you is that of a second father who guided and protected you and held you very dear. . . . Your deceased uncle has left you the memory of his Christian life and his honorable death to be your patron saint, so that imitating the zeal he had for the glory of God you will make yourself the worthy nephew of such an uncle."[29]

Condé's death was in some sense retribution for the House of Guise, for like the death of the Duke six years before, it had been a treacherous murder wreaked on an unsuspecting man. Condé, already wounded, had surrendered to a group of Catholics who betrayed their own honor by killing their unarmed prisoner on the way to their camp. The deed but roused the enmity of the Huguenots to a higher pitch, and later that spring the English ambassador, Sir Henry Norris, wrote to Cecil, that there was but little hope for peace. It was an opinion that all who watched France shared, and the Venetian ambassador, Correro, commented darkly: "I have seen the kingdom of France in three different states, not so different, however, that one did not presage the next: at first there was a state of uncertainty and suspicion; then a bloody state of open war; finally after a short and counterfeit peace, a new state of war which I have given up without hope of ever recovering a lasting peace and union, at least for a long time to come, unless God come to their aid. . . ."[30]

For Jeanne the defeat at Jarnac and the death of Condé were blows from which she could barely rally. Not long after the King's forces had destroyed the Huguenot army, a Catholic force under Terride ravaged Navarre where Jeanne had left her ten-year-old daughter Catherine. Condé had been her hope and Condé was gone, leaving her son, still untried in battle, the nominal leader of the Huguenot forces. It was an age for young heroes: Henri d'Anjou, younger brother of Charles IX, had been the hero of Jarnac, and further north, Henri, son of the murdered Duc de Guise, was putting up a brilliant defense at Poitiers. Those young eagles, the three Henris, were already learning to swoop and soar, glide with the wind, or buffet it when necessary, and would soon be fighting claw and talon for the mastery of France. Henri de Guise might well have been the favorite to win, for to him had come the full inheritance of his father; intelligent,

diplomatic, brave, ambitious, there was not a Renaissance virtue which
he did not possess. But Henri d'Anjou had his share of courage and
of charm, and, in addition, the royal Valois blood ran in his veins.
Unlike his brothers, he had escaped the Valois curse, for those fevers
and periods of lassitude to which they were heir seemed to have
passed him by. At Jarnac his courage and skill had made him a hero
and there were already those who, assessing the pale, tired face and
dull eyes of Charles IX, were speculating that Anjou might some day
make a fine king.

Of the three, Henri de Navarre might seem to superficial observers
the least prepossessing. He had an unfortunate heritage: his father a
poor licentious pawn and his mother a heretic. Despite his years at
court he was still in some respects the mountain boy, the poor cousin
who must learn to be satisfied with the second place. But the Venetian
Correro, an astute observer of the court scene, did not write him off
so lightly when he noted that he was "a young man of wit, very carefully brought up in the new religion by his mother. The general opinion
is that he will become the scourge of our times unless God applies
some remedy."[31] Correro's report indicated that he felt that when
young Navarre came into his majority the Huguenot party would have
a redoubtable leader.

With the defeat at Jarnac, however, Jeanne d'Albret and many
with her began to wonder if they would not soon see the general ruin
of the Huguenots. The following November the meager hopes of the
party were again destroyed when at Moncontour their forces suffered a
bitter defeat. For a moment their confidence wavered, for the Providence in which they asserted an invincible trust had seemed to desert
them: their army had been routed and their treasury was empty. What
they did not know was that the Queen Mother and the King her son
were already talking of peace—not a peace in which the vanquished
would lose all, but a peace which would bring amity to France. The
Catholic party led by the Guises had proved its military superiority
and the Queen Mother feared that such undisputed power would
undermine the authority of the crown. In addition, the Catholic
victories had borne little fruit; the Huguenots were not perceptibly
weaker, the war was no nearer a conclusion. Money, too, was a matter
of prime concern, for the royal treasury was depleted, and without
money the mercenaries on whom they heavily counted would desert
them. Despite the disapproval of Catholic Spain and the admonitions

from the Holy See that peace could not be made with heretics, the Florentine Shopkeeper began her bargaining.

The peace would, doubtless, have been concluded sooner had it not been for the intransigence of the Huguenots—especially that of Jeanne who was determined that once the wedge had made an entrance she would push it deep. It took eight months of bickering before a peace was signed. "It was at last concluded at St. Germain-en-Laye," wrote Castelnau, who had played a large part in the negotiations, ". . . and in three days ratified and proclaimed by the Parlement of Paris. The articles were carried by Beauvais La Nocle to the Queen of Navarre at La Rochelle and by Teligny to the Princes' army, which then lay encamped on the frontiers of Burgundy, and received by them with the utmost joy and satisfaction."[32] They might well have received it with joy, for it gave, at least to the Huguenot nobles, more privileges than they had hoped for: full liberty of conscience, a general amnesty with the restitution of their confiscated estates, the right of public worship in the outskirts of two towns in each province, and four cities given them for security for a period of two years.

It was no surprise when Pius V, who had once said that there was nothing more cruel than compassion for the wicked, condemned with sorrow and regret this peace made with people "in open rebellion against God." He wrote to Charles sadly: "There can be no harmony between light and darkness."[33] The Catholics in France, taking their cue from the Vatican, inveighed against this "accursed peace," this "Devil's peace," this "limping peace"—and most contemptuous of all, the "Queen's peace." The last it most certainly was, the indefatigable work of that peacemaker who thought no haggling beneath her if it would deliver the kingdom of France from war.

There were those, however, who regarded it with neither enthusiasm or hostility; these were the realists who knew that the peace it aimed at would not last, but were grateful for the temporary surcease from war. Young Henri de Navarre, now almost seventeen, wrote later that month with the enthusiasm of youth to the Duke of Savoy, an optimistic letter describing the "joy and happiness" with which the peace was received, "the tranquillity" which has come to the kingdom at last, the "satisfaction" of the King at seeing his kingdom at peace again. What Henri de Navarre did not mention were the negotiations already on foot to ensure the enduring quality of the peace by marrying him to his Catholic cousin, the Lady Marguerite de Valois.

The proposed marriage between the Prince de Navarre and Madame

Marguerite was as "ticklish" as the peace itself. The most radical among the Huguenots, the pastors especially, warned of the evils of young Henri marrying a Catholic; the most radical of the Catholics— led by the Guise faction and urged forward by Spain—saw both church and state put at hazard if this young and influential Huguenot were brought into the royal family. The more moderate among both Protestants and Catholics saw it as a pledge of peace; and ten years of intestine war had taught them that peace could hardly be bought at too high a price. More than all his subjects, however, Charles IX favored this marriage, seeing in it an omen of peace and a means of strengthening his kingdom which had never known security since he had ascended the throne. With the "two religions married" there might be an end of war. Behind him was the Queen Mother who exulted at the opportunity to put the Guises in their place and push Spanish influence back to Madrid where it belonged.

What the young Prince and the intended bride thought, no one seemed to care. Rumor at a court rife with rumor whispered audibly that Margot was at best "disinclined." She was, they said, in love with the young Duc de Guise. Handsome, brave, intelligent the Duke undoubtedly was, but although Charles was not averse to employing his sword or his brain, the King assuredly did not think him worthy of marrying into royalty. That he should presume to raise himself so high quickened the royal blood with anger, and when Guise suddenly married Catherine de Clèves, tongues nimbly embroidered upon the gossip that the King had one night sent the Duke packing when he had come to attend Margot at a royal ball. Whatever the truth of the event, the talk did nothing to increase confidence between the Guises and the royal family, and indeed, little to placate Margot who had never taken kindly to being a tool in her brother's royal hand.

By the beginning of 1571 the Queen Mother had begun serious proposals to get Jeanne to court for discussions of the proposed marriage, assuring the Queen of Navarre that she had no cause to fear; but Jeanne still hesitated, using the uncertain state of her own affairs as excuse. On February 4 she wrote in reply to Catherine's urging: "I desire it more than you do, but our affairs are going so badly that they tie us here."[34] That spring Marshal Biron was sent into Guyenne to conduct personal negotiations for the marriage. Even that redoubtable warrior was somewhat intimidated by the "scowling face" of Navarre's Queen, understanding a little better what Montluc had meant when he had written: "It is not an unalloyed privilege to have to deal with the Queen of Navarre and her son . . . who is now grown, and being what he is, the greatest enemy of our religion. He lacks neither the courage nor the means to trouble us, both in Guyenne and in the royal council."[85]

During the first week of December 1571, Jeanne left Béarn for her journey to court, leaving her lands to the care of her son; and a few weeks later, Killigrew wrote to Burghley, "the Queen of Navarre makes all speed to court, whereof the King is very glad."[86] It was, however, mid-February before she approached Blois where the court was being held. After so many urgings, Catherine, in some embarrassment, now asked the Queen of Navarre to wait for a little while at Chenonceaux, for on February 7 Cardinal Alexandrini had arrived from Rome—sent specifically to speak against the marriage—and the Queen Mother could hardly house the two together. "I was constantly pressed to come, but nobody is in any hurry to see me now that I am here," Jeanne wrote bitterly to her son on February 21.[87] In a previous letter she had already reminded him of his duty "to attend the public sermons regularly and to say your prayers every day"; now, more distrustful than ever of Catherine's plots, she warned him not to leave Béarn until she should specifically send him word to do so. The letter she received in reply must have been some consolation to her in the lonely battle in which she was involved. "I am very sensible of the debt I owe you," her son wrote, "not only for bringing me into the world but for the pains you have taken for my welfare and advancement. . . . I pray to God every day for you."

They were prayers she needed desperately, for when on March 2 she arrived at Blois in the company of her royal nephew, she knew that she was to be treated as no more than a pawn in the Valois' dynastic schemes. Even here at Blois, in the château glorious with the splendor of the Renaissance, she was but poorly lodged. The wide corridors, the exquisitely carved furniture brought from Italy and Spain, the large rooms with their giant fireplaces, and the walls dazzling with gilt fleur-de-lys, none of this was for the gaunt, stern-faced woman from Béarn whose rooms were, she complained, poorly located and in bad condition. "I am in agony, in such extreme suffering that if I had not been prepared, it would overcome me," she wrote to her son. "I am not free to talk with either the King or Madame [Marguerite] but only with the Queen Mother, who goads me, as the bearer will tell you."[88] By the middle of March she was at the end of her rope, and she confided in a letter to Beauvoir, whom she had left to manage affairs in the south: "Everything is different from what I had been told, and all the hopes they held out to me have been cut off. . . . If I have to endure another month like the one just passed, I shall fall ill." Soon after, she became more explicit: "I am amazed at the way I bear the way they cross me: they scratch me, prick me, flatter me, defy me."[39] But it was not simply the contempt with which she was treated that was Jeanne's greatest concern; it was rather the spirit of the court. It was a hollow court, built on duplicity and guile and she was bewildered and disgusted by the trumpery, the licentiousness, the bright surfaces painted over dark scheming. Nothing was natural, nothing was true. She looked in vain for an unpainted face, an undevious word, and could not find one. When she looked into the eyes of her son's affianced bride, she was not comforted. Margot at nineteen was both beautiful and charming in the manner of the Valois. Ronsard in his poetry might compare her to Aurora, and the court, listening to her flawless Latin, liken her to Minerva, but Jeanne was inclined to agree with the recent hero of Lepanto, Don Juan of Austria, who, it was rumored, had once looked upon her while she danced and went sadly away, exclaiming, "She is made to damn and ruin rather than save." Even Jeanne's shy daughter Catherine, already self-conscious of that congenital lameness which marked the family of Navarre, fell under the charm of the Princess. She had already written to her brother, "I have met Madame who is very beautiful and I want very much for you to see her too . . . she has given me a little dog that I like very much."[40] The Valois had long known how to give presents where they would do most good, and the thirteen-year-old Catherine, flattered by Margot's attention, failed to understand her mother's sorrow and distrust.

In her letters to her son, Jeanne did her best to be dispassionate. Margot is indeed beautiful as all reports say. She has a lovely figure although she is "too tightly corseted." Unfortunately she paints so excessively that there is little left of her own face. "She spoils herself," wrote Jeanne, but added generously that it is really not her fault for everyone does so. "In this country painting is almost as common as it is in Spain," she explained. As to her religion—there are rumors that she may join the Reformed Church, but such talk is merely another will-o-the-wisp in which she can put but little store. Of one thing she is certain, however: after the marriage Henri must not remain at court, but return to the healthy atmosphere of Béarn as soon as possible. "Not for anything on earth would I have you come to live here.

Therefore I wish you to be married and to retire—with your wife—from this corruption. Although I knew it was bad, I find it even worse than I feared. Here women make advances to men rather than the other way around. If you were here you would never escape without a special intervention from God."[41] She was well aware that the Queen Mother and the court party had every intention of keeping Henri at their side, but Jeanne counted heavily on her maternal influence and on her son's devotion to the Huguenot cause which could not but be weakened if he failed to return to the south.

By the end of March, Jeanne, unaware that her son had fallen ill and presuming that he was on his way to court to assume his part in the negotiations, had written warningly: "Please note that the impression you make on your arrival will be the one that they will keep of you."[42] Many problems still remained: the place of the marriage (Jeanne was determined that it should not be in Paris, a city whose radical Catholicism she feared and distrusted); the question of dowry; the greater problem of papal dispensation because of both kinship and disparity of creed.

The Queen Mother, well aware that the devout Pius V strongly disapproved of such a union, sent carefully worded instructions to her able diplomat Ferals, saying that although she realized that it was a difficult case, she was sure that the Pope will agree when he thinks about it and the good it will do, concluding with her ace card: "Bring to his attention that England is now separated from the Holy See because of a refusal of such a dispensation . . . however there is nothing of this kind to fear in France, for my children are all very good Catholics."[43] Even in the face of this dangerous threat, Pius remained intransigent. When in May Gregory XIII succeeded to the Holy See, he reiterated the same position. Charles' response to this was one of uncontrolled rage. He was heard to call the Pope "that old hypocritical bigot," threatening to have his sister married in a Huguenot temple if the dispensation were not sent into France at once. Even though the dispensation was still withheld, on April 11 Charles IX, Catherine de Medici, and Jeanne d'Albret put their royal signatures to the contract of marriage between Henri de Navarre, First Prince of the Blood, and Marguerite de Valois, sister of His Most Christian Majesty. The wedding was to take place that summer in Paris despite Jeanne's remonstrances.

Jeanne was at last free to leave the court and journey to the ancestral Bourbon home in Vendôme there to await her son's arrival.

But Henri was still not well enough to travel, and when he had not arrived by mid-May, Jeanne left for Paris alone, arriving in the capital on May 16. Jeanne was never at her ease in Paris and now the high gray walls and narrow ill-smelling streets made her feel lonely and old.

She did not stay in the royal palace but took up residence at the palace of the Bishop of Chartres who was already known for his Calvinistic sympathies. Her daughter, who had been dangerously ill with pleurisy in April, was still convalescing, and Jeanne was alone in her visits to workshops and studios to arrange the necessary details of the wedding. She had not exaggerated when she had written in early spring that if she had to endure much more she would fall ill. She was already ill when she entered Paris and on June 4 she was stricken with a high fever and was forced to take to her bed. Rumors of poisoning ran rampant: her food had been poisoned, the Italian perfumer Bianchi had tampered with her scent, the Florentine leather given her by the Queen Mother had been treated with poison. It was instead an old pulmonary disorder that had asserted itself with sudden virulence and against which she had little stamina. On June 6 she was visited by the King and the Queen Mother and on the following day Sir Thomas Smith wrote to Burghley that there was no hope of her recovery. She had guessed from the first that her death was at hand and prepared for it in that calm, practical way that had marked most of her life. On June 8 she listened while her will was read to her, adding a codicil making it incumbent upon her son to uphold the Reformed Religion. In this, she stipulated, the Admiral de Coligny was to be his friend and guide. She reiterated the first article of her will that she was to be buried with her father in Béarn, according to the rite of the Reformed Religion. She made over her jewels and left instructions that Henri was to take his sister under his protection.

The following day Jeanne d'Albret was dead. She was laid out according to the formula for royalty: the room was draped in black and she herself clothed in white satin embroidered with gold and with a cloak of purple velvet about her. But no lighted candles burned near her and none of the familiar Catholic ritual was heard. Coligny was there to see that the orders for her funeral were carried out. The Cardinal de Bourbon who had hovered about her deathbed was given no chance to exercise his ministry. To many, the spare, stark ceremony seemed like a blight, and Margot, whose life was immeasurably changed by the death of her formidable mother-in-law, wrote wonderingly in her diary, ". . . no priests, no cross, nor any holy water."[44]

Yet Jeanne, who had fought so valiantly and lost so often, now in death lost her last encounter with the Valois, for the instructions concerning her burial were disregarded. Instead of the long journey down into Béarn, they satisfied themselves with a funeral cortege that went only as far as Vendôme, burying her in the church of St. Georges next to her faithless and ineffectual husband. To her enemies—and she had many—her death was not only a signal for joy but a sign that light would triumph over darkness. The dispatch that was sent to the Vatican read: "In a great proof of God's almighty power, on the day of Corpus Christi, the Queen of Navarre died in this city, this morning, on the fifth day of her illness."[45]

On June 12 the King's messengers arrived at Vertueil-sur-Charente bringing Henri word of his mother's serious illness. Had he himself not been detained at Pau by a lingering fever, he would have joined her, as she had planned, on the journey to Paris. But, as so often in her life, her plans had gone awry, and now both mother and son were denied the comfort of each other's company. On that same day he rode on to Chaunay, aware of how grave his mother's sickness was, for Biron had told him that "the only hope was from God alone—there was no human remedy." It was at Chaunay on June 13 that word of the Queen of Navarre's death reached him. It was Biron who received the messenger and who decided to wait until after dinner to tell the Prince. But as they attended a prayer service, the officiating minister was overcome with emotion as he tried to mention the name of the Queen; there was no need to tell Henri, for the faces about him betrayed the truth. When the prayers were over, he withdrew "with a set face" to another room where he could be alone. Here Biron and Beauvoir, who had been a close friend of Jeanne's and Henri's *gouverneur* since the age of nine, listened to the sounds of anguish, for, as Biron wrote to the King, it was a "keen blow" to the young prince who was too disturbed "at this terrible news" to write in his own hand.[46]

Even in those days of sudden death, the news had come as a great shock. Jeanne had been both queen and mother to him. She had been in every sense a valiant woman, a woman sorely bested and yet unvanquished, and her son had both loved and admired her. He wrote the same day to the Baron d'Arros, "I have just received the saddest news that has ever been brought to me, the death of the Queen my mother whom God called a few days ago." But the news which the messenger had brought had not only been the news of a

loss but of a new responsibility, a responsibility to which his mother
had groomed him during all his nineteen years and for which he now
found himself ready. He concluded his letter, "and now that my
mother is dead, I succeed her and must take as my duty all that was
in her charge."[47]

There was a new title to add to his signature now. He was Henri,
King of Navarre. It was in all practical ways an empty title, and he
a mock king without a kingdom; yet it was a signature full of pride
and of hope. What else it might betoken he did not know, but he
would sign it in memory of the days that were past, in pride of his
ancestry, and in hope of the good days that might sometime come
again.

CHAPTER II

The Darkest Day: July–August 1572

I see the coming storm all too clearly

Michel de L'Hôpital

❧❧❧ When in July of 1572 Mr. James Leche, a traveler from London, wrote to his friend Mr. Dannet that he might better spend his time in Paris than tarrying among the fisheries of Dieppe, for in Paris that summer there was much to see, he spoke more truly than he knew; for before that sultry summer was over, Paris would have seen sights from which her eyes would not easily recover. But in July, Mr. Leche could not have known such things, and even the Queen Mother, with all the paraphernalia of sorcery with which she tried to solace her fears, did not know all the summer was to bring.

One thing all of Paris knew: the days were hot and the nights no better, and the dark clouds which gathered for a storm would not yet break. They knew, too, that young Navarre was in the city and with him a retinue of Huguenot noblemen that set Catholic Paris agog. Despite the solemn mourning which he still wore for his mother, the Prince of Navarre showed himself to be an affable young man. His French was not quite that of Paris, nor was his hair quite in the manner of the court, but his eyes were bright and shrewd and his mouth quick to jest. Certainly he could not be called handsome, for his nose was far too long for his lean, beardless face—and would one day call forth the sally that the King of Navarre's nose was bigger than his kingdom! Yet he carried himself with an easy grace, riding with a little less punctilio than the young French nobles, but with a kind of leashed power that indicated that even at eighteen he knew something about holding the reins. He had, after all, already captained

armies in the field. Correro, with the well-trained eyes of the Venetian
diplomat (and the bias of the Catholic party), had already noted in
his dispatches that this "high-spirited young man . . . could easily
become . . . the scourge of our time."[1]

At the St. Jacques gate the Huguenot princes were met by the
King's brothers, Anjou and young Alençon, accompanied by the Duc
de Guise—now no longer in disfavor since he had settled into a
suitable marriage. The royal brothers were gay in their scarlet cloaks,
a marked contrast to Navarre who rode between them. Almost fifteen
hundred Huguenot lords followed in their train, and although they
carried no arms, they were a formidable array even so. That Coligny
rode with them did nothing to allay the suspicions of the Paris
populace. When the King's regular household was dislodged from the
Louvre to make ready for the gentlemen from the south, feeling simply
ran higher. Coligny had already hypnotized poor Charles, it was
reputed. He listened to all the Admiral said, deferentially asking his
advice, calling him "Father," and refusing to let him return to Châtillon, for he needed his counsel here in Paris. The Queen Mother
was half frantic with it all, for the King had turned his ear from her
and she could barely get a word to him in private. As for the Guises,
they were grim with outrage, for Coligny—whom they considered responsible for the murder of the old Duke—was their sworn enemy,
on whom some of them had promised a vengeance as bloody as the
one they accused him of taking on the head of their house. But
the King was a stubborn lad, and no one was sure how to turn his
head away from the grave speech of the Admiral which rang so
quaintly true in that court of flattery and duplicity.

Meanwhile Paris simmered—simmered through the weeks of an oppressive July and into August. The Seine was sluggish, and the narrow
street aswirl with dust. The Louvre bulged, and lackeys and maids
found beds where they could, while the kitchens almost stifled their
cooks as the royal ovens blazed to provide for hundreds of extra
mouths. Around the Cathedral of Notre Dame, sweaty workmen
hoisted huge wooden beams into place as they constructed the platform on which the royal wedding of Margot and Henri was to take
place; for this was to be a spectacle for all to see, not only those
lords and ladies of the royal household and those fortunate ones
who could have pressed through the great doors and into the shadowy
splendor of the nave. This wedding between a Catholic and a Huguenot
must take place outside the holy doors of the cathedral, for the bride-

groom himself was prohibited, because of his religion, from crossing beyond the flagstones of the *parvis*. No Huguenot—not even a royal one—might desecrate the church of the true God by his heretical presence. Henri might marry a daughter of the Valois, but the ceremony would not take place on holy ground.

By the third week of August, the enormous platform was completed and the King's artisans had arrived to hang the drapes and tapestries, to arrange for the placing of the royal standards, and to decorate the long porch along which the bridal pair would come. The choice of standards showed but little tact, for hung ostentatiously in the nave of the cathedral were the captured flags from the Huguenot defeats of Jarnac and Moncontour. This, the Huguenots soon learned, was but one in a series of humiliations to which they were to be subjected in the days to come.

On the evening of Sunday, August 17, the betrothal ceremony took place at the Louvre. The young groom signed the revised marriage contract and gave to his bride a ring with a diamond valued at 10,000 crowns. A supper and ball followed, and later that night Margot was escorted by her mother and her brothers, her sister Claude, and her sister-in-law Elizabeth to the residence of the Archbishop of Paris where, according to custom, she would spend the night before her marriage.

By early morning the square before Notre Dame was already filled with Parisians eager to see this brilliant spectacle. All available windows had been rented long before, but still the streets were thick with people jostling for place. By ten o'clock the aldermen and provosts of the guilds in their short, red robes, the sergeants and clerks of the court in more sober dress were in their places, and the archers and arquebusers stood ready armed. They were to wait for hours, however, before the marriage procession assembled. Finally, along the gallery which ran the length of the cathedral, stepped the hundred gentlemen chosen as a guard of honor, their battle-axes held high catching the sun; following them came the King's heralds, their short coats newly made and handsomely embroidered with fleurs-de-lys. Upon their heels came the royal musicians. Soon the clear pure notes of the trumpets arched over the crowd, piercing through the babble; while the sweet, melancholy music of the hautboys sent a hush over the waiting people.

A ripple ran through their ranks, reaching even those who could not see. Margot was coming—Margot as beautiful as a Greek goddess and as witty as a French one—Margot already a bit of a legend in Paris where grace and wit were no foreign commodities. At the same time from the other side of the cathedral, Henri de Navarre approached to claim his bride. He, like the other princes of the royal family, was dressed in pale yellow satin, heavily embroidered with pearls and other precious stones. Those who had never seen him except on horseback, as he traveled through the streets around the royal palace, were surprised and a little disappointed at how short he was. Accompanying them were the lords of the great French families—both Huguenot and Catholic: the Montmorency clan, faithful Catholics but a little too loyal to their Huguenot cousins, the Châtillons, to command the favor of the King or the Guises; the Dukes of Montpensier, of Nevers, of Guise; the Prince de Condé, and the Prince Dauphin. They walked together in apparent amity, almost it would seem without suspicion. Many hoped for great things from this "marriage of two religions" and the royal coin which had been minted for the occasion bore the emblem of a lamb and a cross with the significant inscription— soon to be fatally ironic—*Vobis annuntio pacem.*

As for the bride, she wrote later in her *Mémoires,* "I blazed in diamonds," and indeed her apparel was lavish beyond measure.[2] Her dress was of violet velvet richly embroidered with fleurs-de-lys and over it— despite the stifling heat—fell the royal mantle whose fifteen-foot train needed three princesses to carry it. At her side walked the King her brother, only two years her senior but already manifesting in the sloping shoulders and sallow skin that taint of the Valois which stalked the children of Catherine de Medici like some evil spell. Upon Margot's small dark head rested the full weight of the imperial crown, its heavy gold base set almost recklessly with enormous pearls, while diamonds, rubies, emeralds jostled for the light that would set them blazing. Behind her in maternal triumph came the short, rotund figure of the Queen Mother. Catherine had had her way, despite His Most Catholic Majesty of Spain, despite the Cardinal de Lorraine, despite the Pope himself.

When no dispensation had come from Rome by the preceding week, a French agent had been sent to Lyons to stop any communications from the Vatican and spare the King the embarrassment of having to act counter to a possible refusal. "You are to allow no courier to pass coming from Rome . . . until Monday be passed . . . taking care that they are not able to slip through secretly," Catherine had written.[3] Originally the ceremony was to have been performed by the almoners of the royal family, the Bishops of Auxerre, Châlons, and Angers, along with the Cardinal de Bourbon. But the Bishops hesitated nervously, and in the end it was the Cardinal de Bourbon alone, with a vacillation akin to that of his brother Antoine, who was coerced into the position of officiating cleric. Now he stood waiting, albeit nervously, to join in holy wedlock his nephew and Marguerite de Valois. He might have hesitated as he thought of the wrath that would soon fall upon him from the papal throne, but the King stood closer to him than the Pope, and the nearest evil seemed the first to be avoided.

If Charles feared hesitation, it was not from the pliable Cardinal, but rather from his obstinate sister. Margot, as he well knew, had a will of her own; and her will was not in this marriage. Did she, as eyewitnesses later whispered, fail to say "Yes" to the marriage question, and did Charles in repressed fury push the imperial crown so that her head nodded in what the poor Cardinal trusted was humble acquiescence? At any rate, all the actors performed their roles more or less creditably, and when the ceremony was completed, Henri, followed by his Huguenot retinue, descended from the scaffolding and led the way into the courtyard, while the Catholics entered the cathedral for Mass.

Unlike the bride, the groom left no record of how he felt on his wedding day. He was too much a political realist to be troubled by romantic dreams of marriage. This union, planned by those two strong queens, Catherine and Jeanne, was primarily an affair of state. That it might also be an affair of the heart was a secondary consideration; and from the outset, Henri was aware that Margot's romantic interests lay elsewhere. He could not have predicted the stormy course their marriage would take, but from the beginning he was faced with the fact that to most of the court he was, except for his blood, inferior to his beautiful and cultivated wife.

Following dinner at the Louvre, the company went to the Palais where the city officials and the members of Parlement were entertained. That evening the festivities were endless: supper and dancing followed by a masquerade, laudatory verses, musicians and an Italian troupe presenting a comedy. It was almost morning when the groom and his bride went to their chambers in the Louvre. Tuesday and Wednesday followed the same course—a round of dinner and entertainments in which, however, despite their variety, there was always one recurrent note: no matter what the drama, the Huguenot lords were always cast in the role of the foolish, the wicked, the vanquished.

When on the last day of the festivities a play was enacted in which
Navarre was placed in the role of a Turkish leader who was conquered
by a noble Christian warrior (the King), the Huguenots were wild with
humiliation and anger. In a city already in an inflammatory mood,
it would need but little to set off an explosion.

By Friday, August 22, the official ceremonies were concluded, and
that morning the royal council met after an interruption of almost
a week. The King himself was not present and Anjou presided, to the
annoyance of Coligny who knew that he had here no sympathetic
ear for the two matters which he wished to bring to the King's immediate attention: the violations of the Peace of St. Germain and the
Flanders War. Trouble in Flanders was no new thing, for the States
there were embroiled in efforts to achieve some kind of political
unity against the despotic rule of the Spanish king. Coligny hoped to
influence Charles to help the rebellious people of the Netherlands,
thus achieving his double goal of a break with Catholic Spain and
effective assistance for his coreligionists. Coligny was never a popular
man at court and this latest scheme only aroused his enemies further.
His influence over the King was, however, considerable—a fact which
simply exposed him the more to the enmity of the other court factions.
Eight months before, the English agent Henry Killigrew, in an effort
to sum up Coligny's precarious position, had written to Lord Burghley:
"The Admiral has secret intelligence from a councilor at court to look
to himself, for all is not gold that glisters."[4] But the Admiral listened
to none of the warnings, perhaps through a certain arrogance which
presumed that he who has the King's ear need fear no evil, perhaps because what he desired was of immeasurably more importance to him
than his personal safety.

The course he charted in the Flanders affair was espoused by few
even among the Protestant leaders. Coligny had at first counted on
English aid, but England had nothing to gain and much to lose from
French ascendency in the Low Countries. "Our sovereignty upon the
narrow seas will be abridged with danger and dishonor," wrote Burghley to Walsingham, then ambassador in France.[5] Yet without English
support Charles could hardly be counted on for an open rift with
Spain. The King's vacillation was his downfall, for early in July,
Charles, attempting to steer a middle course, had secretly given his
consent to the Huguenot Genlis to march to the relief of Mons with
4,000 foot and 600 horse. This decision was obviously the work of
Coligny of whom Walsingham wrote, "though he cannot obtain what

he would, yet doth he obtain somewhat from him."[6] The decision exacted a bitter price, for Genlis' expedition was routed and the King's role in it made known to the Spanish king. It was a difficult position, for Charles recognized that he was in no position to engage in open war against Spain. Still Coligny persisted, aware that among other advantages, war beyond France would leave his coreligionists more security at home.

Now fanatical in pursuing his course of action, the Admiral even dared to brave the Queen Mother with the threat: "Madame, the King refuses to enter on this war; God grant that another may not befall him from which he will not be able to withdraw."[7] In this, however, Coligny was vanquished, for on August 6 the King's council voted against an open war. Despite this victory, the factions opposed to Coligny—chief among them the Guises—still feared his influence over the King and rumors of various plots against the Admiral's life were abroad in Paris. Nonetheless, when his friends advised Coligny to leave the court before it was too late, he would have none of it, avowing that it was for the safety of France that he fought, adding: "It is better to die a hundred times than to live in perpetual distrust; I am weary of all these alarms at every event. I have lived long enough. I would rather have my body dragged through the streets of Paris than to engage in a new civil war."[8] The words were, although he could not have known it, a terrible prophecy of his own imminent death.

Although he had refused to follow the coward's path of flight, Coligny was too experienced a politician not to acknowledge that the threats against his life posed a very real danger. Even his present favor with the King might prove but a slender weapon against the full weight of so many implacable enemies. Even more than his enemies, he feared his "friends," wondering how far he might trust even his friend the King who was often so irrational and arbitrary in his behavior. A supper given in his honor, the use of the King's horses, a costly gift of fine silver plate—these were but trifles when weighed against that considered loyalty, that trueborn honor which Charles might never give because it was not his to possess.

Even amid his fears Coligny stayed on, with that austere devotion to duty which even the Papal Nuncio had noted with a certain admiration. Shortly after the marriage of Navarre and Marguerite, Coligny had written to his young wife: "The next three or four days will be taken up in games, banquets, masques and other pleasures.

The King assures me that he will then give me a few days to hear the complaints which are coming in from all parts of the kingdom concerning violations of the Edict of Pacification. I would far prefer to be with you than to stay here any longer . . . but one must put the public good ahead of one's private interests. . . . Do not worry, for I assure you that during all these feasts and pastimes I will do nothing that could cause a quarrel."[9] It was a blithe promise and naïve in an age when quarrels could be picked without reason and swords drawn without provocation. And, indeeed, no quarrel was picked with Coligny; instead, as he left the King's council on the morning of August 22 and walked with a few friends down the rue de Bethisy, two shots were fired in quick succession. Coligny, doubled in pain, nodded toward the house from whence the attack had come and from which the smoke of the arquebus could still be seen. Three of the Huguenot noblemen who accompanied him ran back to force the door and attempt to follow the course of the fleeing assassin, while the others helped the wounded Admiral to his residence. His left hand and right forearm were gravely injured by the shots which, by the merest accident, had missed their vital target; for Coligny, at the crucial moment, had stooped to fix his shoe and in that second the plot against him had, in a very literal sense, misfired.

Charles first heard the news while he played tennis shortly before noon with the Duc de Guise and Teligny, Coligny's son-in-law. His response was the petulant annoyance of a child interrupted at his games. "What, more trouble," he was heard to cry; "Shall I never have any peace!"[10] Those who later tried to implicate the King in the attempted assassination of the Admiral were forced to admit that Charles' reaction while not that of a grief-stricken friend was too frank and uncautious to be that of a conspirator. It was a far cry from the wary response of Catherine who heard the news as she lunched at the Louvre. She paled considerably, said nothing, and retired to her room. Catherine's opposition to the Admiral and her jealousy of his influence over her son were well known and it was but a short step to accusing her of a hand in the attack. The Spanish ambassador noted carefully that he did not think Catherine looked surprised when she heard the news, conjecturing, "I think she knew of this."[11] Yet if she knew of the deed she could not have known how it would misfire, and her pallor at that news needed no dissembling; for Catherine was far too astute not to realize the precarious position such a failure put them all in.

Despite his initial petulance, Charles' subsequent actions were those of a friend and son for a beloved father. He immediately sent his own surgeon, Ambrose Paré, to dress the wounds and satisfy him that for the moment at least Coligny was out of danger. That night, the King, accompanied by his mother, his brothers, and many of the Catholic lords, went to see the Admiral. To the King's wild ranting of discovering the perpetrator of the deed and seeing vengeance done, Coligny replied with a single, quiet sentence, "Ask Monsieur de Guise who has done me this service; he may tell you." In the hours since the attack on their leader, the Huguenots had been able to accumulate sufficient evidence to justify their suspicions that it was Henri de Guise who had arranged the deed. The murderer was Charles de Louviers, Sieur de Maurevert, a former page of the House of Lorraine and recently returned to Paris at the suggestion of the Duc de Guise's mother, the Duchesse de Nemours. The window from which the smoking arquebus was taken was in a house that belonged to Pierre de Piles de Villemur, one of Guise's former tutors. The horse on which Maurevert made his escape was unidentified, but had obviously been placed in readiness for a hasty departure. The name of Guise sounded too frequently throughout the narrative for there to be any doubt. There were those who said that while Charles had shaken his head negatively when the young Duke, still seeking vengeance on Coligny for his father's murder, proposed a duel to settle affairs, the Queen Mother had nodded when he had suggested murder.

At this moment it was hard for Coligny to estimate what Charles knew and for what he may have been responsible. Charles was an enigma, most of all, perhaps, to those for whom he professed friendship. He had been king since he was nine; he was but twenty-two now—a young lad to carry the burden of a troubled kingdom upon his shoulders. "The darkest day in that fair kingdom's history" had written one historian summing up the state of France: three civil wars with the possibility of another, war with Spain upon the horizon, strained relations with England, affairs miscarried in the Netherlands, Rome looking askance at the growing number of Huguenots and demanding a French Inquisition to put an end to them. No wonder the terror of it all endowed the boy-king with a kind of madness which sent him out upon the chase, finding in the lust of the hunt a surcease from his own failure, the weariness of his own blood, the Machiavellian advances of his court where the King might best be described as the crowned pawn. For if Coligny did not know where he could place his trust, neither did the King, as he watched the short, imperious figure of the Queen Mother deep in conversation with Anjou—Anjou only a year his junior but with a royal air, a boy already tested in battle while Charles was kept confined to his closet; Anjou with his smile, his counsel, his healthy body, who sometimes seemed to Charles to be assessing the royal strength, measuring the royal lifespan as he waited for the throne that might some day be his. There was little love lost between the King and his young brother—and less trust.

Now as Charles looked upon the tall man propped on his pillows, a man who looked more a saint than an admiral, a man who suffered like some Christian martyr as Paré's blunt scissors struggled to cut the burned flesh and probed to find the bullet, a man whom he had called "Father" and for whose safety he had made himself responsible, he saw clearly that this drama was written in the tall, masculine script of the House of Guise; whether behind it there was another script, more desperate, less confident, written in his mother's fine Italian hand, he did not know. The anguish of his uncertainty was as keen as the pain the Admiral suffered and he could avow with all sincerity as he bid his friend farewell, "The pain is yours but the grief is mine."

Navarre, feeling keenly his responsibility as head of the Huguenot party, had already been to see the King, in company with his cousin Condé, to demand satisfaction and justice. The King readily promised it and Navarre, placated, had returned to the house in the rue de Bethisy. The thought uppermost in the Huguenots' minds was that the shot that struck Coligny might be the first blow of a mass attack on them all. On Saturday morning they held a conference in the Admiral's rooms to discuss what course of action they would take. They were still "angry and menacing," "uttering imprudent threats," as the Venetian ambassador, Cavalli, later reported.[12]

At the same time, fearful of their own position, they appealed to the King for more protection. He immediately suggested that for his own safety Coligny be moved to the Louvre, but the Admiral, who had barely escaped with his life once, saw no point in placing it in jeopardy again, and no Huguenot could have looked at the Louvre as other than a death trap. Since they still demanded protection, Charles, at the suggestion of Anjou, sent them fifty men under the leadership of Jean de Cosseins, a colonel of his guards, and a Guise man body and soul. The presence of Cosseins standing guard outside his door could hardly have reassured the stricken Coligny, but he dared not resist lest he stir up more trouble. Navarre, unsure of his own position and uncertain of what could be done to ease Coligny's apprehension, made the futile gesture of leaving five of his own guard behind when he said farewell to the Admiral and walked home down the few streets that led to the Louvre.

It was less than a week since the ceremonious betrothal between Margot and Navarre, but the candles that burned this night cast a different glow. It was not a night for sleep, and Navarre spent a large part of it with the Huguenot lords surrounding his bed, discussing their best course of action. Margot stayed as long as she could in her mother's chamber with her eldest sister the Duchesse de Lorraine. The two sisters, frightened and depressed, sat together on a chest while Catherine prepared for bed. It was—in retrospect—a wonderful night for Margot who embroidered her diary with the bizarre and dramatic, losing none of the flavor as she wrote years later of her sister's imploring tears, her own nameless terror, and of the implacable Queen Mother who said that if Margot returned to her chambers and did as she was told no harm would come to her. Thus Margot kissed them good night and walked down the corridors to her own rooms. Navarre was already there and the room was heavy with that raw stench which sent Margot's elegant nose lifting in disgust and which later led her to write, "My husband smells like a corpse." She made her way to the high canopied bed, but not to sleep, for she wrote, "I found his bed surrounded by some thirty or forty Huguenots who were strangers to me as yet, as I had been married only a few days. All night long they talked of the accident to the Admiral, deciding to go to the King as soon as it was day to do justice on Monsieur de Guise, and if it were denied them, to take it into their own hands."[13]

What happened in the Queen Mother's chamber after she had peremptorily dismissed her youngest daughter no account can accurately report. Indeed, all the scheming, the plotting and counterplotting of which the royal family were variously accused slips far beyond the realms of historical fact into the giant shadows of conjecture and legend. It is a wonderful legend; however; sometimes contradictory, often misleading, but always flamboyant. It is a legend pieced together from that spate of contemporary accounts which poured from the presses after the terrible massacre was over. There is nothing objective about it, for the events which it describes could hardly have been interpreted objectively. Nor could there have been eyewitnesses to those events which rumor gave full rein. At best it was a question of hearsay, second- and third-hand accounts patched together to describe how the complex machinery of self-interest and duplicity slid into motion.

The evil genius fomenting the storm and shaping its course was, of course, the Florentine woman. When she had first come to France, Catherine de Medici had been no more than a subject of ridicule. Her Italian clothes and manner, her heavily accented French, her bourgeois background, most of all her inability to do what primarily she had been brought to France to do—beget children—these were the subjects of the scorn which was heaped upon her.

In the years that followed, when the Florentine shopkeeper had succeeded not only in providing heirs aplenty for the throne of France but even in managing that throne as *gouverneur* during her son's minority, ridicule had turned to something more deadly. Determined to strengthen her own position, she had surrounded herself with her "Italian creatures"—men like Albert de Gondi, Marshal of France; his brother Pierre, Bishop of Paris; and René de Birague, soon to be appointed to the office of chancellor. The Italian manner was never in greater disrepute, for as the fortunes of many French nobles declined, there arose a bitter anger against those Italians who had, it was said, exploited the French court to amass a fortune.

Ingenious though the Queen Mother undoubtedly was, she could hardly have been responsible for all she was accused of. The portrait that emerged was larger than life. "More cruel than Nero, more scheming that Tiberius," ran one rhymed attack, while a popular exposé had the descriptive if unwieldy title, "The wonderful account of the life, actions, and conduct of the Queen, Catherine de Medici, exposing all the means she has used to usurp the government of the kingdom of France and thus to ruin the state."[14]

Where the portrait errs most obviously is in suggesting that the massacre which was soon to sweep through Paris had been several years in the planning, that the visit of the Queen Mother with her daughter, the Queen of Spain, at Bayonne in 1565 had in reality been an occasion to plot this bloody deed, that Catherine had promised the Pope that she would provide another Sicilian Vespers for the members of the Reformed Religion. Catherine was at core an opportunist rather than a long-range planner and those who do her the honor of interpreting her schemes as projects of long duration miss the note of desperation, the quick, agitated movements of those delicate Florentine hands; for, ultimately, it was fear that marked her path. Coligny had been meant to die, but Coligny had bent his tall, spare figure at the second of destiny and had lost his finger not his life. A wounded Coligny was infinitely more dangerous than a wounded lion—for now it was the whole pride that would have justice, and to the Admiral's even reminder that he had but a wound in his arm, a hundred voices shouted that his arm was worth the arms of 30,000 men. France could not withstand such wrath as this, and it seemed to the Queen Mother that she had no choice but to catch the nearer way, bloody though that way might be. It was for her son's sake; that much was always clear to her. Had she known how deep the bloodshed would reach into the young King's soul, she might have hesitated; but Catherine was saved from overmuch imagining, and remorse was an emotion she never fully understood. Thus was concocted the plot which, in recognition of the day it occurred, became known as the Bartholomew Day Massacre.

The Huguenot lords were now conveniently massed in the Louvre or around the rue de Bethisy where a single, well-planned blow could annihilate them all. Cosseins and his capable guard were already in position; Le Charron and Marcel had been given their secret instructions to be passed on at the last minute to the armed men who had been summoned from each ward. Huguenot homes had been stealthily marked with a white cross. White armbands had been distributed to loyal burghers and soldiers to distinguish them from the perfidious heretics. In the minds of the underlings there was no doubt that this measure was but a counterblow to the perfidy which the Huguenots planned in retaliation for the attack on Coligny. His Most Christian Majesty was threatened and should he fall, France, eldest daughter of the Roman Church, would totter and be lost before these psalm-singing bravados with their black breeches and white capes who scattered the consecrated host of Christ in the streets and toppled statues of the Holy Virgin into the mud. The King himself had been heard to swear that by God's death he'd have no more of it. It was to be as holy a war as ever a crusader fought, and it was right that the great church bell on the steeple of St. Germain l'Auxerrois should be the designated signal.

What had taken place in the preceding hours that had brought such a plan to completion is at once the most conjectural and the most fascinating aspect of the flamboyant legend. As in all legends surrounding the Medici, there is the figure of a spy, one Bouchevannes, who pretending to be of the New Religion had sat quietly through the conferences of the Huguenot lords and then slid furtively back to the

Queen Mother's garden in the Tuileries to report on all that he had heard. There is also the classic element of the secret enclave, an *extremum consilium* in which those "creatures" of Catherine—Nevers, Gondi, Birague (and the Duc d'Anjou as well)—had agreed that no course lay open to them but a swift attack which would vanquish the Huguenots forever.

According to the legend, the King himself had had no part in these clandestine arrangements; his permission was the last piece of the plot to be fitted into place. It was, then, so the story goes, the evening of August 23 before the plan was presented to him. Eventually it was not Catherine who persuaded Charles but Gondi, that shrewd Florentine, who once as the King's tutor, had taught him, as the court gossip Brantôme later wrote, "every kind of perversion." But if Gondi had formerly led Charles toward evil, the perversion he now proposed was too monstrous for even Charles' blood lusts. Gondi was requesting that he sanction the order to kill his wounded friend as he lay in his bed, and then spit his supporters like so many huddled and bewildered sheep. The narrow face made longer by its pointed beard grew convulsed with rage, but Gondi's voice with its close Italian logic continued: Coligny's murder had not been entirely a Guise affair, others even closer to Charles had been implicated . . . for Charles' own good . . . no future in becoming involved in the Netherlands . . . the hopelessness of a war with Spain . . . the severe disapproval of the Holy See . . . And with the Admiral dead . . .

The Queen Mother and Anjou sanctioned all that Gondi said; they provided evidence that the Huguenots would take revenge unless they were stopped. Had not the Huguenot lords who attended him at supper made an ominously unfinished threat: "Unless justice is done . . ." The King, so often master of the hunt, was now at bay. The weak face was livid. The tired, veined eyes sought desperately for some means of escape. But as they each gave their counsel, voice after voice, they said but a single thing: one thrust of the sword tonight. Only that and France would be free. One thrust of the sword and the man to whom we had one day said, "Now we have you with us and you will not have to leave us again" would know to the contrary how wise the sacred psalmist had been when he had sung, "Put not your trust in princes."

From the outset the result had been inevitable. From childhood Charles had never been able to withstand his mother. Now as she stood before him, her body thickened with childbearing and overeating, her dark eyes opaque, her shrewd mouth determined, he bent his head passively. Then in a moment of rage he shouted those words which were later to be recorded in memoirs and printed in school books and mark forever this wicked King who was no more than a poor mad boy at bay crying in his anguish, "God's death! Kill them! Kill them all, so that none may come back to blame me! Go! Give the order quickly."[15]

The palace had grown quiet, but the candles burned on. The Louvre waited. The Seine lapped against its piles; the river smells drifted in the open windows, for Paris was still hot. There remained only the sound of the bell of St. Germain l'Auxerrois to send Paris leaping to her feet.

The sky was still dark when the *Marie* which had hitherto called the royal family to prayer now called Paris to murder. An unexpected incident between Huguenots and Catholics near the rue de Bethisy had set operations going long before dawn. Before the King had given the signal for the tocsin, he received word from Guise that the Admiral was already dead. This time the attempt at murder had been successful. Cosseins and his men arrayed themselves like a guard of honor before the executioners. Navarre's five guardsmen were hacked down in a moment, while the "baseborn Besme" (reputed by some to be the bastard son of the former Duc de Guise) led the way to the Admiral's room. It was not difficult of access for it had no bar; one of Coligny's servants had desperately tried to erect a barricade with a large chest, but to Besme and the dozen men who followed him this was no obstacle. What they found as they burst through the door, their swords jangling against each other in the small doorway, has been variously described: the Admiral struggling from his bed; the Admiral on his knees receiving a last blessing from Pastor Merlin; the Admiral severe and erect before his enemies. In any case, they found a defenseless man, his household fled as he had commanded them, his few friends gathered about him. He was still in his nightdress, his heavily bandaged hands useless at his sides. They killed him there and then threw his body down into the courtyard. It was not so easy a task as they had anticipated, for in his death agony one bandaged hand caught convulsively at the narrow window frame; but they pried him loose and he fell quite dead into the lower court where Henri de Guise, his uncle Aumale, and the Comte d'Angoulême waited. Yes, it was the Admiral. Guise could still easily recognize him, despite the blood that covered his face.

From here on, legend gives way to fact. There is no further need to conjecture or embellish, for the details of eyewitnesses are more lurid and more brutal than imagination could have conjured. With the Admiral's death and the sound of the great bell, the full strength of the machinery was set into motion. Paris blazed into light, the bridges and gates leading from the city were barred, and the guards, conveniently placed throughout Paris to "keep order," drew their weapons. The Holy Massacre had begun. Although the Huguenots had not been without suspicion, they had not dared to take precautionary measures. They had not dared to gather too closely together, had not dared to be seen publicly armed lest this be taken as a sign of their own plans for reprisals. Now the dozens of noblemen lodged around the rue de Bethisy were given no time to mourn or avenge the Admiral's death. They were killed as they stumbled bewildered from their houses or were dragged through the streets to be thrown half-dead into the Seine. No hunted stag was ever more doggedly pursued; everywhere in the dark, narrow streets, lurid with torchlight, gleamed the white armbands which marked the confraternity of the hunters. They waited in small bands on the corners of the streets; they prowled over rooftops, cutting off the escape of the pursued; they lurked in narrow doorways to catch a stray Huguenot as he tried to make his stealthy way to safety.

As dawn came, the streets became dangerously littered with bodies—many dead, some still living. Whole families lay together, for age or sex was no consideration. If one were to keep the tree from bearing evil fruit, then even the smallest buds must be sacrificed. Fortunately the Seine was not far away, and it made as good a sarcophagus as any other. To the Pont-aux-Meuniers in the area of the Châtelet and Pont-Notre-Dame which spanned the river directly in front of the cathedral, the living as well as the dead were dragged, summarily stabbed, and thrust into the waters below. As the sun rose, it glinted upon red patches which rose everywhere to the surface as body after body sank below the waters. Should the victims rise fighting to the surface, there were on shore that rabble, without arms, but who now found they could contribute their share by hurling rocks at the wretches who fought for their breath in the waters below.

By late morning even Marcel and Le Charron, the city provosts who had been placed in charge of operations, were frightened. Paris had become a mob—unreasoning, cruel, uncontrollable. The provosts' men could keep no order in such a scene. It was no holy war now, for out of the cellars of Paris had come crawling the thieves and cutthroats, the criminals of every sort to ply their trade where they would. The bodies that lay in the street were plucked naked before they were dead; homes were looted; shops were broken open and emptied of all their goods—and should the owner protest, the quick cry, "Huguenot, Huguenot," was enough to bring him to his death. Before noon, a terrified Le Charron arrived at the Louvre begging to see the King and demanding some action that would quell the rioting. Charles, driven beyond sanity by hatred and fear and perhaps already besieged by those ghosts who would haunt him till his death, agreed almost witlessly to whatever the provost could suggest.

The official report of the interview duly recorded by the city clerk rings with a bitter irony: "His Majesty was pleased to order the said provost and aldermen to take to horse and get themselves accompanied by all the forces of the said city, and have all murders, looting, plundering and rebellion stopped at once, and see to it day and night."[16] Charles was soon to discover, however, that the beast named Paris could not be so easily driven back to her cage. She had prowled abroad and tasted blood, and all the aldermen in France could not drive her back in until she had sated her lusts.

Charles himself was part of that great beast, for the halls of the Louvre ran as red as the Seine that Sunday morning. As soon as the tocsin had sounded, Navarre and Condé had been led under guard to the King's chambers. There they had been divested of dagger and sword and placed behind locked doors. Meanwhile their followers had been summoned individually from their rooms and led through the long corridors of the palace. At first they were simply surprised at the unexpected knock upon their doors, but when, under the leadership of the captain, Nançay, they were hustled with their retinues into a deserted wing of the Louvre, the meaning became desperately clear. Here they were disarmed and led into the courtyard. Their questions, their entreaties, their demands for justice were answered by silence or a laugh. As they were pushed into the cobblestoned court all their questions were answered at once, for there, drawn up two by two with weapons at the ready, stood the Swiss Guard. They killed with cold brutality, giving little thought to the choice of weapon—halberd, lance, club—anything would do, provided the man at their feet was dead and that when it was over they were paid for it. Among the first to be slaughtered were Pardaillan, Brichanteau, Beauvoir. Their confrères followed fast. Even La Rochefoucauld,

Charles' merry friend who only a few hours earlier had entertained the King at cards, met an ironical death at the hands of Chicot, the royal jester.

Soon the courtyard was silent but in the galleries of the Louvre a few desperate Protestants still sought escape. One of them, knowing little except that his life was in danger, ran to Navarre's room, battering desperately at the door until Margot's nurse opened it in terror. Margot, who had heard her husband leave sometime earlier but who knew nothing more, had fallen into a heavy, pre-dawn sleep when the wild-eyed Léran, already spurting blood from a wound in his arm, came leaping onto her bed. It is a scene which Margot makes the most of in her *Mémoires*, for it places her center stage in the role of a highly romantic heroine. She later wrote at length of the episode:

> He had been wounded in the arm and the elbow, and four archers were after him and rushed with him into the room. To escape, he threw himself on my bed. Feeling that man grabbing me, I slipped between the bed and the wall, and he slipped after me, still grasping me tightly. I did not know him and did not know whether he was there to insult me or whether the archers were after him or me. We were both screaming and equally frightened. Then, thank God, Monsieur de Nançay entered, and seeing me in such a state, he could not refrain from laughing, though he felt moved; and, getting angry, he sent the archers away, upbraiding them for their lack of courtesy; then he made me a gift of the life of the poor man who was still clinging to me.[17]

Thus, with Nançay to guard her, Margot made her way, still half-dressed, to her sister's room where she learned that her husband was at least safe from the fury of the mob.

If Navarre was safe from the fury of the mob outside, he was learning firsthand of those wild rages for which the King was noted. Navarre had not seen Charles since the evening before when he was vowing vengeance on all who had been implicated in Coligny's attempted murder. The change must have been stunning, for in those midnight hours Charles had passed beyond sanity into some dark world peopled with the phantasies of his imagining. It was terrible to watch him now, for with his long thin legs and jerky motions he must have seemed like some giant puppet engaged in some monstrous puppet show. His tongue, always quick with oaths, was doubly so now.

Translated into common speech, his terms were very simple: from now on there would be but one King and one faith. There was, then, for his cousins a choice of Roman Catholicism or death. For the others, the rebel Huguenot lords, there had been no choice; but because of the royal blood that ran in the veins of Condé and Navarre and out of pity for their youth he would grant them their lives if they complied with his demands. He awaited their answer.

Beside him Navarre could feel the reciprocal rage of Condé—Condé the fiery son of a fiery father, of whom the Papal Nuncio had written not so long before, "this Prince asks for danger and fight." No one ever came to doubt Condé's courage, but many came to doubt his wisdom. Now, at seventeen, he knew little of prudence—and in the fifteen years of life still remaining to him he would add little to his native store. Fortunately for the fate of France, it was given to Navarre, as First Prince of the Blood, to speak first; for Navarre was, even at the reckless age of eighteen, a temporizer. Threading his way through the maze of his gallantries, his derring-do, his follies, was the steady line of the diplomatist: to set one's eyes on the goal and chart a steady course toward it. Navarre was no coward, but to be run through with cold steel by the King's guard, leaving the Huguenot party (if, indeed, a party still remained) without a leader—this seemed to him like the sheerest folly.

His answer to the King was an adroit evasion of the issue: he reminded Charles of their kinship, of their friendship, of their mutual hopes for France; he reminded him that matters of conscience were grave questions needing serious consideration. In short, he committed himself to nothing and asked for time to make a decision. Condé was far less tractable. His speech was a staunch adherence to his Huguenot faith and a violent denunciation of all who so outraged it. To them both Charles gave three days to retract or to meet their deaths. They were then led into one of the King's chambers where Nançay was commanded to guard them with his life.

As the day wore on, Navarre and Condé received fresh news of other friends murdered by the mob: Caboche, private secretary to Navarre; Francourt, Jeanne d'Albret's former chancellor; Teligny, Coligny's son-in-law, who had tried to escape across the rooftops but who had been shot down by one of Anjou's men; Parenteau murdered with his pregnant wife. Some names, however, were conspicuously missing from the list of victims. No one had come swaggering in to boast of the death of Montgomery or the sympathetic Catholic Montmorency.

And in truth both these leaders had escaped, with almost a hundred Huguenots, for the plan to surround the St. Germain district on the Left Bank had miscarried, and despite Guise's efforts to pursue them, Montgomery, with his fine Spanish horse far in front, had led the group across the Vaugirard and out into the open country leading to Chartres.

By nightfall Paris was quiet. A little breeze began to ripple in from the Seine, but the courtyard of the Louvre was still piled with corpses which would soon begin to stink. Already estimates were being drawn up of how many victims had met their death: three thousand, perhaps, said a conservative estimate.

Still the massacre was not over, for on Monday it was discovered that God had wrought a miracle to manifest His approval of what was being done in His name: a hawthorn bush (a plant which flowered only in the spring) had suddenly burst into bloom in the cemetery of the Holy Innocents. The finger of God, the mob shouted; the white blossoms a symbol that the church has been purified according to God's holy will. Once again the crowds gathered, and once again they killed, armed now not simply with clubs and swords but with the invincible assurance that God himself was strengthening their hands. In their frenzy of self-righteousness, no one questioned the validity of the "miracle," and it was not until much later that the flowering hawthorne was discovered to be not a divine sign but a poor human ruse perpetrated by a few fanatical friars who wanted no questions or doubts to rise from the multitude.

Throughout that long day and the next, the now-terrified Charles sent his orders to the provosts: order must be restored; looting and burning must be stopped; the streets must be cleared. In turn the provosts gave their orders to the aldermen who arranged for groups of militia to patrol the streets and heralds were sent, mounted on horseback, to blow their trumpets and hoarsely repeat the King's commands. But it was to be a question of days not hours before Paris would be at rest again.

To such men as François de Montmorency, son of the old Constable, and Michel de l'Hôpital, who had long since recognized toleration as the only source of peace, it seemed that France had been driven to suicide. The latter had written to his daughter on the second day of the massacre: "I see the coming storm all too clearly. Use every means in your power to save your mother, your husband, yourself, for I do not think that there will be any great need to spend yourself in my behalf."[18]

Charles, well aware that his action would be variously interpreted abroad as well as at home, now set himself to the awkward business of explaining his position to the states of Europe. In most cases diplomatic dispatches had arrived long before Charles' official letter. The very night of Saint Bartholomew, the Spanish ambassador Cuniga, had written in exultation to Philip II: "As I write they are killing them all, they are stripping them naked, dragging them through the streets, plundering the houses, and sparing not even the children. May God be blessed who has converted the French princes to His cause."[19] Cuniga could hardly have sent a more favorable report to Philip, for if the Huguenots were annihilated he need have no more fear for the Netherlands or of a war with France. It was bruited about at the Spanish court that Philip the Solemn, with his long sallow face and compressed lips, broke into something akin to laughter when he read the news.

Rome received the news from many sources and the response of Gregory XIII was unequivocal. Salviati, the Papal Nuncio, a slight sickly looking little man, ill at ease amid the hostility of the French court, could hardly believe his good fortune at having such news to present to the Pope. In his long, undiscriminating report he explained: "When I wrote a few days ago in cipher that the Admiral was going too far and that he would soon get his knuckles rapped, I had already realized that they would not tolerate him very much longer, and I was strongly confirmed in my opinion when I wrote to you, in ordinary script, that I hoped soon to be able to give some good news to Your Holiness, although I could never have believed the tenth part of what I now see with my own eyes."[20] Salviati's report was underscored by the messengers sent from France to the Cardinal de Lorraine who was then at Rome.

Lorraine and Gregory were unequivocal in their responses from Rome: the messengers were richly rewarded, the cannon of Sant' Angelo were fired in ecstatic salvos, and September 8 was set apart as a day of solemn thanksgiving. Charles IX, so long considered by the Guises as fortune's fool, now became in Lorraine's heightened rhetoric, "the avenging angel divinely sent." Vasari was commissioned to prepare a series of frescoes portraying the event, and to ensure its lasting memory medals were coined by the Vatican representing the destruction of the Protestants by destroying angels and bearing the inscription *Huguenotorum strages* 1572. Whatever contempt Gregory XIII had hitherto shown for Charles was obliterated, and The Most Christian King found himself basking in the sunshine of the papal smile.

In England, however, no cannon sounded and no bells rang. England was in mourning. At the first news of the event, Fénelon as the French ambassador had tried to get audience with Elizabeth, but the Queen wished to give her disapproval as dramatic a form as she could. Fénelon was kept waiting eleven days for the favor of a royal audience. When it came, it was a far worse ordeal than even he had anticipated. He attended Her Majesty at Woodstock, and as he entered the audience room, he found the Queen assembled in full council. Everyone was in mourning, including Elizabeth herself. The heavy black robes made Elizabeth's thin face look unusually pale and reserved. As Fénelon advanced there was no sound but that of his own steps, and when he approached the royal throne there was no word of greeting. Into that silence the ambassador spoke, realizing even as he proffered explanations and circumstances that for English ears it was a thin story. He stumbled on, describing the danger of a Huguenot uprising, of the possible massacre of the royal family, of the young King's desperation. Elizabeth played out her role magnificently. For all her aggrieved silence and black mourning, she had no intention of severing her connections with France; let this poor fellow talk himself into imbecility and then she would condescend to accept his explanations, and even further, condescend to accept Charles' request that she be godmother to his newly born daughter. Friendship with France was too valuable a commodity for Elizabeth to forgo for a few thousand quarreling Frenchmen even though they shared her religion.[21]

Elizabeth, however, was not alone in her disapproval for even among Catholic sovereigns the deed was unpopular. Ferrière wrote from Venice that immeasurable harm had been done to the reputation of the French King by such a rash and ill-advised deed. In Austria, the Emperor Maximilian shook his head, saying, "Too bloody," refusing to believe that the massacre was not premeditated. "When all the birds were together in their cage, it was easy to take them all at once," he commented, adding, "When one has one's heart set on something, it is easy to find pretexts."[22]

All these reports were unnerving for both Charles and his mother, who now had to face the situation at home as well as abroad.

Their first scheme, to lay the blame for the massacre at the door
of the Guises, interpreting it as the bloody outcome of a long-standing
feud between Guise and Châtillon, met with failure; for the Duc
de Guise was far too astute to let himself be used so discreditably.
In any case, Charles found that his deed was not entirely unpopular.
Now that most of the Huguenots were dead, the atmosphere of
Paris was one of triumphant success. If this were true, then there
was no reason why Charles should not assume the full responsibility
for his acts. In this mood, dressed in full regalia, he rode to Parlement
on the morning of August 26 to hold that most ironic ceremony,
a Bed of Justice. How much of the irony he saw shall never be
determined. He was, during the ceremony, fully regal, fully in control
of himself. Sitting on his dais, his thin body, so long overwrought,
partially hidden by the robes of state, he made his speech to the
assembled Parlement. Charles could be eloquent when he chose—it
was part of his Valois heritage—and it behooved him now to use
his gift to the utmost. France had been threatened, he explained,
his royal person in grave danger, and in the midst of this danger
he had conceived the idea which he had later carried out, "an idea
which may have been put into my heart by His Divine Majesty."
What had been done was of his own decision and he alone would
assume the responsibility. The response was all that he had hoped
for. At that moment no loyal Parisian would dare to talk of royal
blame.

Secure now with the approbation of both church and state, Charles
drew up designs for a memorial of the event. Two medals were
coined. One showed Charles on his royal throne, under his feet
the bodies of the rebels; the other bore the figure of the King with
the inscription, "Charles IX, Conqueror of the Rebels," and ludicrously
enough, on the reverse side stood Hercules in his lion skin holding
a burning torch and an iron mace.

There remained only to assign a fitting punishment for the poor
scapegoat on whose head was heaped all the guilt for the monstrous
crime that had been committed. So, despite the fact that the most
careful search of his private papers provided none of the evidence
of treason that the Queen Mother sought so painstakingly, Gaspard
de Coligny, leader of the Huguenot party and Admiral of France, was
judged "guilty of high treason against the King's authority and of
being the principal deviser of the late conspiracy against his person."[23] His arms were ordered to be publicly broken by the common

executioner, his estates forfeited to the crown, his children to be declared ignoble and infamous, and his seignorial château at Châtillon to be razed to the ground.

On August 28, the church of Paris commemorated the event of the recent victory over its public enemies by a great procession. All Paris took part, including the King and the royal family. Through narrow streets still stained with blood, horses and men picked their way, passed looted houses where the doors swung open on their hinges, passed plundered book shops where the smell of burning leather and paper still hung heavy in the air, over the Pont-Notre-Dame so lately littered with the bodies of the dead, and finally into the great cathedral itself where God was fittingly thanked for his singular blessings to his faithful.

CHAPTER III

Years of Durance: 1572–1576

The sum and status of this kingdom seems to hang from a very thin thread.

Austrian ambassador

❧❧❧❧ From the beginning there had been no question in the court circle that sooner or later Navarre and Condé would be brought to heel, and by mid-September it was rumored abroad that the King of Navarre had begun to do his duty as a "son of the Holy See." Navarre had been deftly politic from the start, and in a letter that went to Tuscany shortly after the massacre, the Florentine agent had written that "the King of Navarre has always spoken very meekly, like a little lamb, declaring that he was willing to obey the King in all things and through all things, and even to die at his feet." It was, however, precisely his desire not to die at his cousin's feet that led Navarre to this unwonted act of meekness. With Condé, the case had been far otherwise, for, continued the anonymous agent, "Condé is not so sensible, and has spoken extravagantly, so that the King was constrained to reply violently."[1] When pressed to the conclusion of his position, however, Condé retreated and made his recantation on September 12. Shortly afterward, on September 26, Navarre read publicly his own long statement of abjuration, renouncing the errors of his heresy and begging to be readmitted to full communion with the Church of Rome.

Three days later, on the Feast of Saint Michael, he and Condé became the principal figures in an elaborate ceremonial held in the church of St. Germain l'Auxerrois. Once again the tower bell pealed— joyously this time—as the young princes were inducted in the highest chivalric order of the realm, the Order of Saint Michael. It was not the first time that Navarre had received this unique distinction; at the age of eight when, after months of valiant struggle, he finally accompanied his father to Mass, he had been "rewarded" by this same honor. It must have been, even to his child's sense of honor, a humiliating experience, an outward sign that he had capitulated to what his mother had taught him to hold in abhorrence. It was even more so now as he walked in solemn procession between the ornamented columns of the nave, clothed entirely in white, with his golden cape, richly trimmed in crimson velvet and embroidered with pearls. First Prince of the Blood though he was, he had been brought to heel; no one knew better than he what the courtiers who watched him thought. His mother's son in so many ways, he knew that what he did now might not have been her way; she would doubtless have faced the Valois challenge with the blunt determination to pay with her blood rather than temporize. But in this her son would never follow her. He had made his decision, and now his Béarnais pride demanded that he make the best of that decision. The lords and ladies who watched him follow the King in bringing his gift to the altar would not have the satisfaction of knowing that those steps cost him dear.

Beside him his cousin Condé bristled with anger beneath his finery, unable to forget that less than a month before he had vowed that he would face death rather than participate in a Roman Mass. Navarre, however, seemed less bound to his Protestant allegiance, and when the simply wrought collar with its medal of Saint Michael and its eight-pointed cross were placed over his shoulders, he indicated nothing but gracious acceptance. As he turned to walk to his place, he bowed gracefully to the royal ladies in the choir. To Navarre it was doubtless no more than a gallant gesture, but to Catherine de Medici with her eyes narrowed to catch the slightest nuance of manner, it was a public declaration of his defeat. In her exhilaration she laughed aloud.

It was a laugh that covered those long weeks in which she had haggled with Jeanne d'Albret. It was a laugh of victory as she remembered the stern, uncompromising position of that gaunt woman who knew nothing of compromise and little of duplicity—a woman whom she could neither impress nor intimidate. She had shown her the glories of the French court, paraded its opulence, its power, its sophistication before her; but the woman from Béarn had remained singularly unimpressed. She was indeed contemptuous, preferring the hard bread of the Pyrenees to whatever dainty fare Catherine de Medici could offer.

She had been proud beyond endurance, disdainful of that "fair show" which Blois had provided, and tenacious in her determination that following her son's wedding he should return to his own country lest he be besmirched by the Valois way of life. Had not the goal been so necessary, Catherine would have found the situation unendurable. But she had set her heart on this marriage and she had had her way. Not only was Margot safely married to the King of Navarre, but Navarre was neatly trapped in the one situation which his mother had been determined that he must avoid: Navarre was at court, bereft of his friends, bereft of his leadership of the Huguenot party, and now making public homage to the Church of Rome. Catherine's victory was complete.

Charles, desperate to procure Navarre's recantation, had done all he could to "induce him the sooner thereto"—even writing personally to Gregory XIII, begging him to absolve his cousin from all his past sins and suggesting, somewhat chauvinistically, that Spain might now look favorably upon a request to return the kingdom of Navarre to its former rulers.

Navarre has left no record of those days, and one is forced to deduce his responses from the later events of his life. He had not yet celebrated his nineteenth birthday, and although he had lived in an alien court a good part of his life, never before had that world shown its innate hostility in such violent form. He had been brought face to face with death—not death in battle, something which he had already faced, and in which he had found the exaltation of selling his life dearly in a cause to which he was wedded. This was another kind of death—the cold, pragmatic murder by which men of power annihilate those who stand in their way. To Navarre, there seemed neither glory nor honor nor value in such a death. Yet this did little to remove the bitter sting of humiliation as he publicly abdicated the position which his mother had given her life to, abdicated the party of which he was the rightful leader, the friends who counted upon him for loyalty and faith. If he masked the struggle, it was not because it did not cost him dear, but because he was learning that to dissemble was the nearest way to safety and to ultimate victory.

In the weeks that followed, Navarre set himself to the task of diplomatic correspondence, and in the first week of October a whole pouch of letters went out under his seal. To Venice, to the Swiss Cantons, to the German Princes, to Elizabeth of England—all carefully worded epistles explaining his present position, assuring them of his loyalty to the reigning King of France, begging their understanding of a difficult situation, and appending to each the tall awkward characters of his name with their life-long tendency to slant downward.

Of them all, it must have been the letter to His Holiness Gregory XIII that most greatly taxed his ingenuity. The promise to be a faithful son of that Church which had just chanted hymns of gratitude over the corpses of his dearest friends must have stuck in his throat and yet he recognized that his only hope for the future lay in precisely such a step. Even at the age of eighteen Henri was too politically sophisticated to believe that his personal sincerity would matter much to the Roman Pontiff provided that His Holiness was convinced that whatever Navarre's personal beliefs he would not act contrary to the Church of Rome. In such a tone Navarre began his letter: counting on "the hope of your paternal affection," having been strengthened by "the Most Christian King," having already asked pardon before the Nuncio Salviati, and now begging forgiveness from the Holy Father himself, urging him to remember that he was but a child when, under his mother's guidance, he had embraced the New Religion.

It was a simple letter of repentance from a humble young man who now wished only to walk in the way of salvation which had been pointed out to him so kindly by his relatives. As a token of his good will, he signed on October 16 an edict reestablishing the Catholic cult in Béarn and expelling the Protestant ministers, thus reversing the policy which his mother had maintained since her conversion in 1560. Gregory could hardly do other than reply with paternal benignity, assuring Henri of his own great happiness and encouraging him to use all his "riches, the gifts of his spirit, his greatness and power for the greatest praise of God!"[2]

As far as the French court could see, the "gifts of his spirit" were but few. Even the Queen Mother, who had, as Walsingham wrote to Burghley, "so many spies that they are afraid of one another," could find nothing to reproach and little to praise in young Navarre. The men of Béarn were noted for their hot tempers and long memories; but Navarre seemed of another race. He walked through the galleries of the Louvre apparently untroubled by the memory that they had so recently been awash with the blood of his dearest friends. He laughed and walked with Guise, gamed and hunted with him, as though all of Paris did not know the tale of how the Duc de Guise had prodded the dead body of Coligny with a contemptuous boot. Navarre, it was said with a smile, was but his father's son.

If Charles could then look at Navarre with a certain ease, it was but small solace in a sea of troubles. All those councilors who had promised that a "single stroke of the sword" would bring peace to France had been proven incalculably wrong. The blood that had turned the Seine red and stained the cobblestones of the Louvre had ended nothing. It had not driven the Huguenots into hiding or into the arms of what they were told was a merciful and maternal church; it had driven them instead into walled cities and battle phalanxes. For every lord who had been toppled dead or dying from the Pont-aux-Meuniers, there was a son or cousin or younger brother to take his place. Despite even the massacres in the provinces—for in the weeks following the Paris orgy, Bordeaux, Toulouse, Orléans, Bourges, Meaux, Troyes had all suffered their bloody fate—the Huguenot strength was terrifyingly strong. The blood of martyrs had bred not fear but courage, and something else even more unnerving for those who sat in the council chamber of the Louvre: a contempt for a government which could plot such perfidy.

In the weeks following the massacre, a change was apparent in the political stance of the Huguenots. So far, even throughout the period of civil war, they had never considered themselves as anything but the faithful servants of a government which in most things they adjudged to be rightful and just. They had represented themselves not as enemies of the crown, but as enemies to the House of Guise which they considered in its extreme intolerance and its dynastic ambitions to be dangerous to France and to the crown itself. Now, however, the ground had shifted, for the crown had betrayed them, allying itself with the Guisard faction. As they entered the period of the Fourth Civil War, they found themselves discussing the issues less in religious terms and more as a conflict *du bien public*. Exept for a small group of religious zealots, the division was no longer simply between Catholics and Protestants, but between opposed political ideologies. The Huguenots were now joined by a large body of *politiques*, a moderate Catholic faction headed by the influential house of Montmorency, which urged toleration and the healing of old wounds. Thus the movement was swelled by a considerable number of Catholics who despised the Queen Mother, distrusted the King, and feared the Guises. They were weary of arbitrary rule, insupportable taxes, refusal to call the Estates.

In such a spirit men began to question the Valois concept of monarchy, and soon the presses were full not only of those pasquinades whose attacks were often too scurrilous to be taken seriously, but also of judicious volumes that could easily set the throne rocking. Theodore Beza, that grave minister on whose advice and counsel Jeanne d'Albret had so much depended, pointed out that God alone had absolute power and that the power of the French monarchy was contingent upon the King's observance of his political duties. François Hotman, the noted French jurist, showed himself a little less violent than in his anti-Guisard pamphlet, *Le Tigre*, but nonetheless proposed in his *Franco-Gallia* that true sovereignty lay not in the King but in the people. Again and again the words "popular sanction," "election," "authority of the people" appeared, and in at least one tract, tyrannicide was defined not as a crime but as a legitimate right of the people when the sovereign has transgressed his authority. Charles' efforts to control the French presses were hopeless, and even had he succeeded he would still have had to cope with the inflammatory writings which were being smuggled into France from England and Germany and Switzerland: Had there been peace there might perhaps have been the possibility of discussing the concept of sovereignty, but Charles was never to know peace. He had believed for one short night that peace would be the fruit of death, but when the bloody swords had been wiped and put back in their scabbards, he found that he had been duped. In France there was no peace. La Rochelle was furiously at bay, Poitou and Limousin, with their fields bursting to harvest, were in arms, and the country of Languedoc seemed already lost.

At first Charles had hoped to settle the rebellion at La Rochelle quickly and peaceably. No dream indicates more clearly how little he knew of his people. From the beginning of the religious wars La Rochelle had been the headquarters of the Huguenots. Here the elder Condé had gathered his forces, here Jeanne d'Albret had joined him, encouraging her Protestant people, and writing that apologia which her later editor called her *Mémoires*. No city in France was less deferential to royal power and more open in stating its grievances. The news of the massacre at Paris had already propelled the Rochellais to arms and when they heard of the consequent massacres in other cities, they determined never to capitulate to the royal offers of peace. La Rochelle was a powerful city whose opposition to the royal power was made more dangerous because of its coastal position and its accessibility to England. When Charles' bastard brother wrote to the Pope that the capitulation of La Rochelle was of importance not only for France but for all of Christendom, he expressed the opinion of many.

Thus, he explained, "If it remains the way it is, it will become another Geneva, from whence will issue another kind of vermin, that is an infinitude of heresies. . . ."[3]

Charles, however, was determined to avoid an open conflict if at all possible. It was for just such crises as this that the King hoped to exploit his brother-in-law, and now Navarre was pressed into action to use his influence with his former coreligionists. It was a humiliating task, but one which he could not avoid. On September 10 he wrote to the mayor and councilors of La Rochelle declaring that he was sure of their "complete fidelity" to the "King, my Lord," that he wished their "good and conservation as much as you yourselves could wish it," and encouraging them to accept Armand de Gontaut, Baron de Biron, as their royal governor.[4] It was totally pragmatic advice, concerned with neither right nor justice but solely with political expedience, but the Rochellais would have none of it. That Navarre, their legitimate leader in the maintenance of their rights should now be advising them to accept the King's good pleasure when, less than three weeks before, he had watched the King's perfidy, seemed like a travesty to the Rochellais. They continued to repudiate Biron, and despite Navarre's advice, the gate of La Rochelle remained closed to the King's governor.

When Charles in a conciliating gesture appointed the Huguenot François de la Noue as governor of the rebel city, he met with no more success. When by December La Rochelle still continued intransigent, the King put Anjou at the head of the royal forces with orders to subjugate the rebel city by force. On January 12, Anjou left Paris for the west. Among his captains were Navarre and Condé, coerced into being part of that force set to vanquish the very people whom they were once destined to lead.

It was a hard winter for all of France, and by spring half the King's army was sick or dying from dysentery. For Navarre, however, there was a worse form of sickness—a fever of regret that he should find himself polishing his weapons before a city which had once given him so much happiness. When as a child he had ridden northward from Pau in company with his father and mother, La Rochelle had been a fairy city of delights. The great gates had swung open before them, and the heralds had announced the coming of Navarre. The small boy riding his horse with its bright saddle cloth must have loved it all—loved the tapestries hanging from the windows, loved the raucous, full-throated cheers of the Rochellais, loved the sight of the blue and

white harbor with its two massive towers and their enormous iron
chain which, its people boasted, could keep France safe from any in-
vader. When later, in company with his uncle Condé, he had visited
the city again, he had loved it still more, for by then he had learned
something of fighting men and courage and he understood what
his uncle meant when he said that no city in France was more loyal to
the Huguenot cause than La Rochelle. It was a noisy, turbulent city,
quick and gay and boisterous; but now in the winter rain it stood
ominously silent, cold and barred. He had foresworn his right to a place
within its walls; instead he must make his place among the muddy
ditches and wet tents. For although he was the sovereign of Navarre, he
was above all a King's man now and for that reason an enemy.

That June the full weight of his position as "King's man" came
home to him when he received a bewildered letter from the Baron
d'Arros who had been viceroy of Navarre under Jeanne d'Albret.
Some time before, D'Arros had imprisoned the Comte de Gramont, a
Catholic lord, who had recently been appointed Navarre's Lieutenant
General though he had fought vigorously against the Huguenots in the
South. From D'Arros' position, his action was commendable in every
way, since it spared the harassed Huguenots at least one thong of
the Catholic scourge. Henri, however, at the request of the King,
notified d'Arros of his extreme displeasure, commanding that Gramont
be given his liberty at once. The baron, hurt and angry at this unwarranted reprimand from his young lord, wrote that he had done
nothing except to try to keep the kingdom as it had been in Jeanne's
time, "thinking it my duty to remit this state into your hands, when
the time comes, without any innovation of that order and policy
established by the former queen your mother and authorized and
confirmed by you."[5] Once again Navarre felt the full anguish of what
he knew must seem his own betrayal. "Honor" had been one of the
dearest words in his mother's vocabulary and while he knew there was
no other course for him except the one he now followed, this conviction
did little to alleviate the pain of his own false position.

In March the last hope of a settlement with La Rochelle evaporated,
and its "governor" La Noue returned to the King's camp heavy with
failure. Four months of argument and persuasion had not been able
to balance the horror of a summer's night in Paris. To all of La
Noue's promises made in the King's name—and the terms he offered
were generous—came the single unanswerable question: Who can trust
the King? In reply the King's guns began to hammer at the citadel,

although most men agreed that La Rochelle was too well-placed ever to be conquered unless famine drove her to her knees. In April it seemed that succor was at hand, as the Rochellais saw the white sails of English ships making southward for La Rochelle; but long before they could reach the harbor they were forced to flee before the navy that Anjou had set in motion off the coast of Brittany.

Hardly had the first breath of spring brought a thaw of hope to the countryside, when out of the north came a winter frost withering the shoots of grain that had shown green and gold above the mud. All that winter the astronomers had called attention to an enormous star that had appeared in the heavens. It was they said the star of the Magi come again, threatening those who had plotted the massacre. But now it seemed to threaten all France alike—God's vengeance on the kingdom for the sins of the few. There were those who said that the end of the world was not far off, that God would soon come with his angels and their trumpets to judge the world in his justice. But to those who in these last years had seen death come in so many terrible and lingering guises, the final death of the world seemed not too terrible a thing.

At La Rochelle capitulation was inevitable and by mid-July the city which had stood as a symbol of integrity against perfidy, of liberty of conscience against unjust constraint, signed the peace terms drawn up by the King. By the peace, the Huguenots were granted freedom of conscience throughout France, but liberty of worship only in La Rochelle and Montauban. It was a peace unacceptable to both sides. While the Nuncio Salviati shook his head, murmuring, "This peace is neither good nor honorable for the Church," the Huguenots of Nîmes increased their preparations for war.

Long before the peace was signed, the royal army had lost its Lieutenant General, for some time earlier Anjou had received word that he had been offered the crown of Poland. Catherine de Medici, determined to people the thrones of Europe with her children, had left no stone unturned to win the vacant Polish throne for her son. Despite the fact that the Bartholomew Day Massacre had done nothing to enhance Valois popularity in Poland, Anjou had won the election. He had received news of his royal elevation with mingled emotions, however, for although Anjou shared his mother's lust for the pomp and glitter of a crown, he never shared her cosmopolitan attitudes. He was rooted close to the soil of France—and exile lay beyond her boundaries. The Queen Mother, however, was expansive with

joy, and Charles, who always found the court a more pleasant place
without his brother, shook himself free from his bad dreams long
enough to prepare a series of elaborate festivities in honor of Anjou.

Throughout the summer months and into the fall, the King-elect
tarried, letting the good French wine linger nostalgically upon his
palate, listening with a kind of horror to the guttural Latin spoken
with such ease by the Polish delegates.

It was the beginning of November, with the roads already bad
from the fall rains, before Anjou set out in company with his mother
and the Princes of the Blood. Charles had originally planned to go at
least part of the way, but he was stricken suddenly with small pox and
was forced to take to his bed at Vitry. The rest went on to Nancy,
and then to Blâmont where the final parting took place. Anjou's reluctance was apparent. Even Catherine, for all her fine talk, did not part
easily from this, her most beloved son. When the final farewells were
said, and the Queen Mother turned westward for the return trip to
Paris, some of the heart had gone out of her. So much to be
done—and her hands were growing a little stiff and old on the reins—
so many impossible promises to keep, so many enmities to counter and
friendships to juggle.

When she reached Paris she was further disquieted to see the
emaciated figure of the King trying so fiercely to cover that bodily
weakness which shamed him like some terrible vice that he could not
control. It was an anguish to watch him; for when he could barely stand,
he flung himself into the saddle and rode like a demon until, exhausted beyond speech, he was forced to take once more to his bed.
She would have done anything to save his life, but that was beyond
her power. By bribe or terror or intrigue she had often been able to
bring death, but the power of sustaining life was beyond even her.
She had watched her first son die. And now her second. The hemorrhages, the heavy sweats, the desperate gasping for breath—she knew
the signs too well to find comfort in the smiles and assurances of the
doctors.

As though her heart were not heavy enough, there was her youngest
son, Alençon, already looking with manifest envy at the posts which
Anjou's departure would leave open. Even while he had openly assisted Anjou at the siege of La Rochelle, it had been clear that he
was gathering secretly about him a body of malcontents. With his
brother gone he waited with greedy expectation to be made Lieutenant General of France in his stead. Alençon at the age of nine-

teen had little to recommend him unless it was his unflagging ambition. Like a chameleon, he would, throughout his short life, shift from cause to cause, from loyalty to loyalty in his frenzied efforts to be recognized as a man of parts.

Now, aggrieved that Charles had not appointed him Lieutenant General of the kingdom as he had hoped, he decided to play behind the colors of the *politiques*. From being a small group of theorizers with moderate ideas about sovereignty and religious toleration, the *politiques* had, since the massacre, emerged as a powerful party with a strong political organization. Guided by the political acumen of La Noue, the Huguenots had merged with the *politiques*, where in Languedoc and the Midi they had set up what appeared to the terrified court party as a rival government. Although both La Noue and Montmorency-Damville, governor of Languedoc and the second of the Montmorency brothers, were both willing to captain the movement, should a member of the royal family be induced to accept the leadership the cause would gain immeasurably. Thus was born the plot to wean Alençon from the Valois court to the court of the *politiques*. Should it be possible, the thinking went, to exclude Anjou from the line of French succession because of his position in Poland, then upon the death of Charles—surely not more than a matter of months—Alençon, neatly bound to the *politique* cause, could be placed on the throne and all civil strife be brought to a bloodless end. How much either the King or the Queen Mother knew of Alençon's secret aspirations it is difficult to say. That they had already recognized in him the possibility of treason is clear from the King's refusal to make him Lieutenant General of France and from the caveat Charles issued to Anjou at La Rochelle warning him not to place his young brother in charge of any major operation lest he betray it to the enemy.

This civil war within the bosom of her own family was intolerable to Catherine, the woman who had sworn herself to peace at any cost. Yet there was little she could do to keep her cubs from each other's throats. For some time she had lived in fear: fear of Charles' sudden death, of Anjou's ambivalent position, of Alençon's traitorous tendencies. Yet the man most dangerous to her designs she seemed to fear least. The Prince of Navarre, aimiable and aimless, had allayed all fears. He hunted with Guise, talked with the King, ignored his wife, and made love to Madame de Sauves. If he found his duress oppressive, he concealed it well. He smiled, he was amusing and amused; if he had had ambitions, the indolence of the Valois court seemed to have lulled them to sleep. He wrote the letters the King suggested, went faithfully to Mass, and acted with gallantry toward the Queen Mother. Catherine could ask no more. If she ever became uneasy over his spending so much time with Alençon, she consoled herself with the thought that they were merely recounting their secret amours.

The King, always susceptible to fear, now found himself a prey to suspicions of every sort. Convinced that his kingdom was seething with plots against the royal authority, he sent out in December 1573 a circular letter to his governors, warning them that he was "advised that in many places throughout the provinces of my kingdom there are persons who go from house to house stirring the lords and other people to rebellion and disobedience under pretext of public good."[6] That such "persons" were even within his own household became apparent in early March when the Queen Mother was advised of groups of men gathering in the neighborhood of St. Germain and of arms being carried secretly to Navarre's chambers. The Swiss Guard were immediately brought into position, the gates closed, and Alençon summoned into the presence of the King and the Queen Mother. Alençon was never a man to be counted on in times of crisis. According at least to the report of the Tuscan ambassador Cavalli, he now confessed all, attempting to shift the blame from himself, assuring his brother of his future fidelity, and begging only to be forgiven. "The Duke remains completely disheartened and half-silly," continued Cavalli, contrasting Alençon's attitude with that of Navarre who "has shown a very bold face without any fear of the consequences."[7]

Charles, however, convinced that his life was in danger, could not stop to judge innocence or guilt. He thought only to escape from the peril which threatened him. Boats, mules, carriages—every conceivable conveyance—were pressed into service, and royal chests and wardrobes were tumbled helter-skelter into the waiting vehicles. In a wild flurry, the royal family fled from the comparative fastness of St. Germain on to the open road for Paris. Charles, too sick and weak to travel, endured but badly the cold journey back to the capital. When his mother suggested, however, that they remain at the Louvre he would have none of it. If St. Germain had been surrounded by living enemies, the Louvre had worse terrors, for here walked the ghosts of the dead. Through the windows, even though they were shut against the drafts of March, he still could hear the Sainte Marie, the bell from the tower of St. Germain l'Auxerrois. At his own command, he took up residence south of Paris in the gray, impregnable fortress of the Vincennes.

Meanwhile policy had dictated that the royal family look lightly upon this aborted scheme as the folly of a small group of malcontents that had come to naught; to treat it otherwise would be to endow it with power, and this Catherine, perhaps wisely, perhaps blindly, refused to do. Dale wrote to Burghley in astonishment that the King continued to make merry with Navarre and Alençon, "using them with better countenance than ever he did."[8] It was, as always in the Valois household, amity by design, for Catherine knew her youngest son, knew that he thought himself wounded by negligence and contempt, knew that should the whip but flick those wounds again he would, beyond any consideration of family loyalty or royal pride, leap to the side of the enemy. This above all things she could not now endure. Thus when Alençon and Navarre made their official protestations of innocence, they were accepted by the King in good grace, and although the castle guard was noticeably increased, Catherine explained this easily as a measure taken "for the safety of us all."

Alençon, however, had passed beyond that boundary where clemency or kindness could keep him loyal, and less than a month later a further plot was discovered. This time the King's temper ran high and Alençon and Navarre were placed under strict guard. Again it is Cavalli who reports the details as he writes to the Signoria on April 10 of a "plot which has been discovered and which was to be carried into effect on Easter Day, against the persons of the Most Christian King, the Queen Mother, and the Grand Chancellor, and that the Duc d'Alençon was the head of this plot, being assisted by the King of Navarre and by Montmorency. Therefore all the guards in the castle have been removed, save those of His Majesty, and the Duke, the King of Navarre, and Montmorency are so far watched that they are not permitted to depart. During the whole of this day, all the gates of this city have been closed, because it is expected to effect the arrest of some accomplices, and I believe that they have already laid hands on fifteen."[9] Among the most important of the accomplices caught was Boniface de la Molle, a good friend of Alençon's and Margot's reputed lover, and Hannibal de Coconat, the captain of Alençon's bodyguard. "Strict justice must be done on these knaves," Catherine was reported to have said to the Spanish ambassador, who in turn praised her for "putting out the fire."

The Alleluias of Easter were muted for the two young Princes as they waited out the long hours of Easter Sunday behind their guarded doors. Little news reached them, for all who came and went were searched and only the Queen Mother's trusted servants were kept within the walls. It was rumored that the King, exhausted by his rage, was more ill than ever, that he had been heard to utter "dangerous and passionate words," that a trap had been set in the south to catch Montmorency-Damville which—if it succeeded—might undo not only the Montmorency clan but the whole *politique* party. The Queen Mother who had before urged clemency now wished the King to take stringent measures, and on April 14 she concurred with the Chancellor's argument: "Sire, matters have proceeded to such an extent, and the facts are so well known, that if you do not make an example and take severe measures, the means which hitherto Your Majesty had used out of pity and clemency will no longer be considered to have proceeded from the singular humanity and Christian charity which you have exercised toward your brother but rather from weakness and ir-resolution."[10]

Charles, taking this advice, had Coconat and La Molle executed, increased the rigors of the Princes' imprisonment, and sent for com-missioners from the Parlement of Paris to hear their case. In the sessions which followed, it was not Alençon's petulant protestations of innocence that drew the attention of the hearers but the long and deftly worded declaration of Navarre. As she listened, the Queen Mother must have found her judgment shaken. Perhaps it was not Condé or even Alençon whom she must fear, but the young Béarnais not yet come to his majority—this thin-legged prince with his wide mouth and long, bony nose, whose eyes were never without their glint of mockery. She thought she had bought him with trinkets and smiles and a few cheap promises; many an older knight had fallen asleep in that Bower of Bliss which Catherine tended so skillfully. It had been, she thought, an easy victory: a few good horses kept for him in the royal stables, and from her "court squadron" the sophisticated favors of Madame de Sauves.

Navarre, she was now discovering, was something more than a master of gallantry. What she heard from her dais was no frightened defense of a man begging for his life, but an apologia, strongly and cogently argued: he recalled his first trip to court when, at the age of seven, he had been brought by his parents so that he would learn to "love and serve" the royal family; he recalled how confidently he had come to Paris for his marriage, and the perfidy of the act that followed; how he had been "despoiled and abandonned" after the death of the followers who had trusted in his word. Yet even then such was his loyalty that he served at La Rochelle at the side of Anjou himself who could well testify in his behalf. By way of conclusion he explained his recent efforts to leave the court:

Seeing that my enemies have had such influence with Your Majesty that my efforts were powerless to dispel the distrust that you mistakenly had of me, I believed as true the rumors that had been circulated that there was an intention to harm me. Because of this fear, Monsieur le Duc, who heard them as well as I, told me of the plots that were formed against him and I told him of those against me. . . . Aware that Your Majesty's suspicions grew day by day and receiving fresh news of the harm that was intended to us, this was the reason why Monsieur le Duc determined to escape from this danger and to flee in order to safeguard his life. I promised to accompany him and from thence go into my own lands for my own safety as well as to re-establish order in Béarn and Navarre where, during my absence, I have never been obeyed. When we were on the point of departure, word reached us that Your Majesty was aware of our plans and thus you called us into your cabinet where we told you all we knew. There you assured us of our lives and told us that the King would take things in hand so that we would have no cause of complaint in the future.

Since then, while we were in the Faubourg St-Honoré, we heard the same alarms as before and were told that we were going to be taken prisoner to the Bois de Vincennes. Then the Vicomte de Turenne arrived . . . and confirmed the cause of our fears, alerting us to the danger to our lives. This was why Monsieur le Duc sent me a message . . . that he was determined to flee. Upon hearing this, I resolved to accompany him and to withdraw into my own lands for the same reasons that I have indicated before. This, Madame, is all that I know, and I beg you to judge whether I have not had just and manifest reasons for my departure.[11]

The ground of judgment had shifted; his judges had become the accused. It was no longer Navarre's treason that was on trial, but the perfidy of those who had treated him so badly and had now brought him to judgment. For all his deferential submission to the royal family,

Navarre emerged from the contretemps more master than servant. It is impossible to imagine how Catherine would have responded had she read Margot's later *Mémoires* in which her daughter avowed that the impressive declaration of Navarre was her work from beginning to end, written at the request of her husband who "being no counsellor, asked me to draw up his reply so that what he said would not cause any further difficulty to himself or to anyone else."[12]

The Princes' declarations of innocence did little, however, to change their position. Despite promises that they would soon be free, the guard in Vincennes did not diminish. Disheartened, they watched the castle being provisioned as though for a long siege. Charles' health was steadily declining, and Navarre sent word to the English agent that should the king die he feared death at the hands of the Queen Mother. By early May his fears were lightened by the news that the plot to trap Damville had been circumvented; with Damville still abroad, Catherine would hesitate to do anything that would bring the increased fury of the Huguenots upon her head.

On May 22 the fate of Alençon and Navarre was forgotten in the anxiety over the King who had been suddenly stricken afresh. All audiences were canceled and once again the physicians gathered in the royal chamber. "The king is reduced to skin and bone," the English agent wrote, "and his legs and thighs are so weak that he cannot hold himself up."[13] He had begun to hemorrhage from the mouth and soon subcutaneous hemorrhages broke out in all parts of his body. Although he said that he felt better upon hearing of the execution of Coconat and La Molle, it would need more than the destruction of his enemies to restore him to life. When the doctors shook their heads, Charles understood. He turned wearily, saying, "Pull the curtain that I may get some rest."[14]

For eight days he lingered, but despite the continuous hemorrhaging his mind remained clear. Later the Huguenots would people his death chamber with the ghosts of their numbers whom he had murdered but in truth Charles had already endured his nightmares and his last days were spent in the lassitude of approaching death. At the end he sent for Navarre, but the message he began to give him was lost in his weakness and he drifted off into an uneasy sleep. At the far end of the room, unneeded and unnoticed, sat his wife, Elizabeth of Austria. She had stayed praying throughout the night, saying nothing, crying silently. Two hours before noon on May 30 Charles died. His last words were said to be "Ma mère." Some who heard the phrase felt that it admitted many interpretations; Catherine knew of only one.

For the third time Catherine closed the eyes of a king in death, and once again she found that she had no time for grief. The day before his death Charles had written: "I have begged the Queen my mother because of my illness to assume greater care than ever for my affairs and those of my kingdom . . . until the King of Poland who is my legitimate successor should arrive. I have made my will known to my brother the Duc d'Alençon and the King of Navarre who have promised to follow and obey Madame, my mother, according to the love and devotion they bear her."[15]

Thus no sooner had Charles breathed his last than his mother assumed the task of regent, this time with the competent hands of experience. It was not a popular decision and Catherine's claim that her son had given her the regency won only "the great misliking of men of understanding" who felt that such power should reside in the Estates only. But the days when Catherine had thought to please the French people were long since over, along with other illusions of her youth. She had learned to take hatred in her stride provided only that hatred went unarmed. Fear she never learned to live with. She walked a hard course but fear made her stumble and lose her balance, and all too often it was fear that dictated her actions. Thus now, she gave orders for the court to move from Vincennes to the Louvre where she could watch Paris and hold it more effectively in check.

With her went those two thorny Princes, Alençon and Navarre, still under suspicion and consequently under guard. The death of Charles had only increased their fears for their own safety. It was, they knew, Catherine who had advised the King against excessive clemency, pointing out that kings could not afford mercy that might undermine their royal power. Navarre's earlier fear that the King's death might well herald his own was once again to the fore. He knew that he had already won the enmity and mistrust of the Queen Mother; this was part of his heritage, for she had hated his mother before him. His safety so far had lain in that casual veneer which had allayed her suspicions until she had come to think of him more as the son of the vacillating and ineffectual Antoine than of the proud and intransigent Jeanne. But given his involvement in two plots within weeks of each other, her mistrust was again stirred.

Fearful of what new plots might hatch in the weeks before she could expect Anjou on French soil again, she took further precautions against the "troublous princes," barring the windows of their apartments and increasing the guard at the exits of the Louvre. Yet even while she held them in further check she used them for her own purposes, and on June 1 a circular letter went out under Navarre's seal addressed to the governors of the provinces and reading in part:

> You know through the letter that the Queen has already written to you that it has pleased God to call to Himself the former king, my lord. This is a loss so great for this kingdom that I am sure that all his good servants will feel the sorrow and regret concomitant with such a disaster. Yet I console myself in my grief that His Majesty, foreseeing his end, indicated the desire he always had for the good of his subjects, and thus ordained by his last wish that the administration and regency for the affairs of the kingdom be vested in Madame while awaiting the arrival of the King of Poland. Being assured of her prudence and her long experience as well as her singular devotion to this crown, I am convinced that she will know how to order all things for the public good.[16]

It was not the first time that Henri had been forced to place his hand to a document which was far from his own beliefs. Two years at court, however, had increased his enmity and distrust. It could have been no easy act to affix his signature to a document affirming Catherine de Medici regent of France.

Now after two years of playing the role Catherine had cast for him, Navarre was seized with a passion for liberty. Even the massive fortress of Vincennes had not been enough to shatter his hopes. He encouraged Walsingham to bribe the guards and Margot to smuggle in women's clothes in which he and Alençon might make their escape. The old insouciance was gone and in its place was a reckless daring that would risk anything in the cause of liberty. When they were both moved to the Louvre, Navarre, in company with Alençon, tried unsuccessfully to escape into the city through an old postern gate which had been left unguarded; and even on the day of the King's funeral, there were rumors that the Princes intended to escape under cover of the crowd and excitement. Each failure simply increased their determination, and on July 31 the Venetian ambassador, Morosini, wrote at some length of the trouble the intransigent Navarre was causing: "The Queen arrived yesterday at the Abbey of St. Germain, accompanied by the King of Navarre, who, when in that place, attempted to escape so openly that it became necessary to give him warning which proceeding afforded him the opportunity of going to the Queen to make explanations. He then spoke many and violent words to Her Majesty asserting that the time had now arrived to set him at liberty, and that he could and would not endure to live after such a fashion and that he must have his remedy or otherwise he would find his way with his dagger; and he also used similar and more exaggerated language, indicating his intention to depart by force."[17] The Queen Mother's reply that he must be patient and endure his present position until the arrival of the Most Christian King, met with little understanding from Navarre who was overheard to say that if he could not make his way out with a dagger, he would burn the place down around them.

Open though this domestic warfare had now become, Catherine refused to acknowledge it, determined to keep family quarrels from public eyes. The facts, however, were all too obvious and when in an audience with the English ambassador, Catherine assured him that since the King's death she and the Princes lived "as one," Dale could not but be amused, adding in his report that Navarre in a secret message had begged him not to believe anything he said for it was all done under duress. As for Alençon, "he dares not speak to any man nor any man to him."[18]

Catherine, always ill at ease when she could not keep the peace and fearful of what new schemes Alençon might perpetrate for his advancement, received with relief the papers from Poland for which she had been waiting: an official statement from Anjou confirming her in her position as regent until his return. They were dated from Cracow June 15 and a few days later Anjou, now Henri III of France, clandestinely left the royal palace of Cracow for home. He left more like a guilty serving-man than like a king, for fearful that the Polish nobles would impede his departure, he made a stealthy and nocturnal exit, accompanied only by a few of the French gentlemen whom he had brought with him.

While Catherine anxiously counted the days it would take her son to make his way back to France, Henri was luxuriating in an Italian summer. His mother's desperate plea, "Do not in any way delay your departure . . . for we need you here" fell on heedless ears. It took him a month to get from Vienna to Ferrara and another month before

he left Turin for Lyons. Not only did he dally, he failed even to
write some assurance which would allay his mother's anxiety. In August
Dale wrote to Burghley, "From July 6 through August 6 there has
been no news from the King of France."[19]

After the dark Polish winter, Italy glowed before the new King
like some unfallen Eden. Even the glamor and sophistication of the
Valois court grew dim beside this paradise of pleasure. He visited the
studios of Italian painters, sat for a portrait by Tintoretto, and spent
the last remnants of his fortune (a fortune already borrowed) on
Italian gems and perfumes. In this gay and voluble atmosphere, his
own affability rose to the surface. The enthusiasm which greeted his
appearance was neither forced nor superficial. For once his Medici
blood was in his favor; he felt himself loved, and with this confidence,
his charm—which was also real—expanded. He left presents everywhere,
exquisite and costly presents, sometimes unblushingly borrowing the
money from his hosts to pay for them. One kingdom lay behind him,
impoverished, beset by enemies, torn by internal factions; and the one
toward which he journeyed could promise nothing better. His weeks
in Italy were not simply an interim vacation, but weeks snatched out
of time, the only truly carefree moments he would ever know. Perhaps
he guessed what awaited him; if he did no one could blame him for
tarrying.

When Henri reached Turin toward the end of August, his Italian
interlude was abruptly ended; for here Damville, leader of the *politiques*,
awaited him, anxious to treat for peace in behalf of the Huguenots.
Moderation had been the keynote sounded to the King by the diplomatic leaders in both Vienna and Venice, but the Queen Mother had,
conversely, counseled an implacable firmness in a document which
reached Henri through the hands of the Chancellor, "To enter his
kingdom like a prince" was Catherine's goal for her son. "You must
show yourself master and not let people think, 'He is young, we can
make him do whatever we please.' . . . When they see that you are
strong, they will come to their senses, or if they do not, you will
make them do so."[20] It was Catherine's advice that the young King
elected to follow, and Damville was turned away with the peremptory
reply that the King would treat with the rebels when he saw fit and
on his own terms. There was no hesitation in Damville's grim and
determined course as he turned west from Turin down into Languedoc
to cement the *politique* alliance with the Huguenots.

The first week of September, Henri at last arrived in Lyons

where Catherine and members of the court had been awaiting him. In her anxiety, the Queen Mother had left Paris early in August, sure that her son would journey with all speed back to the kingdom where he was so urgently needed. Catherine, who had written to Henri at the death of his brother, "If I were to lose you, I would bury myself alive," was beside herself with joy at his safe return. The state entrance which she prepared for him exhausted her ingenuity and, even more vital, her treasury. But no amount of pomp and pageantry could rouse the crowds to more than mediocre enthusiasm. Although the streets were lined with elaborate tapestries and the windows lush with flowers, the faces that lined the streets and peered from doorways were marked less with joy than with curiosity. The new monarch had a foreign air. They marked his Italian bonnet; they noticed a certain artfulness of manner, a subtle delicacy of dress more redolent of Venice than of France. His eyes, full-lidded and almond-shaped, seemed opaque and distant, placing limitless reserves between himself and the Lyonnais who watched the royal progress.

Catherine, too, found her son subtly changed. The warrior Prince who had won his spurs at Moncontour seemed to have sloughed off his soldier's coat for the affectations of a dandy. The aigrettes and earrings which he now affected, although they might have become him in Italy, would do little to win him the popularity of a people who sought the strong hand of a King, not the manners of a fop. Alençon and Navarre were among those who watched the King appraisingly, knowing that their future lay in his hands. Catherine, fearful of another *politique* scheme, had done nothing to alleviate their position, insisting that they remain under guard on the journey from Paris to Lyons. Thus Dale wrote in some amusement to Walsingham, "Her chickens go in coach under her wing and so she minds to bring them to the King."[21] Henri III, however, was willing to treat the "chickens" with greater liberality; and on November 1, the Feast of All Saints, they all heard Mass together, after which the Princes humbly avowed their loyalty to the King who on his part assured them that he would forget the past and count on their fidelity for the future.

This attestation of trust did little to change their position, however, and the Nuncio Salviati wrote realistically to Rome: "The King shows all sorts of affection to them; nevertheless they are always kept in sight and never go out without an escort."[22] From the beginning, Margot had placed but small store in her royal brother's avowals. She did not trust him; she did not trust his smile, his proffer of friendship, his protestations of good will. Later she wrote in her *Mémoires* of the Princes' first greetings with Henri: "As they embraced and welcomed each other, although the season was very hot and we so pressed together that we were stifling, there came upon me so great a chill that I shivered all over."[23] While Margot's comment is undoubtedly a result of hindsight rather than a "secret intimation of what was to come," as she later averred, it was an apposite comment, for in the months following the King's arrival the fraternal conflict reached new dimensions.

If Alençon's teeth had been set on edge with the new honors bestowed so prodigally upon his brother, Navarre seemed to have retreated into his former role. His passion for liberty was again in abeyance as he gave himself over to the pleasures the court provided. For his wife, if we may believe her *Mémoires*, he showed no more than an amused tolerance; he laughed at her tears and her tempers and left her free to love where she would. He himself took the same liberties, enjoying the charms of that accomplished intrigante Madame de Sauves, of whom Margot later wrote in indignation: "she used all her art to make the King my husband conceive an aversion for me; insomuch that he scarce ever spoke to me. He left her late at night; and, to prevent our meeting in the morning, she directed him to come to her at the Queen's levée, which she duly attended; after which he passed the rest of the day with her." Her husband's attitude bred in Margot a "coolness and indifference" which, she continued, "separated us altogether, so that we neither spoke to each other, nor slept in the same bed."[24]

So well did Navarre reassume his mask of indifference that his friends were heard to berate him for preferring to be a servant at court rather than a master with the Huguenots where he belonged. He was gay, witty, dynamic with little patience for the ponderous or melancholy. He knew how to amuse the young with his banter and charm the old by his respect for their wisdom and experience. He made friends easily and held no grudges. When the Duc de Guise was wounded at the battle of Dormans and taken half-dead to Château-Thierry, Navarre was soon at his bedside, offering his services and wishing him well. There were those among the Huguenots who could not stomach this easy affability with those who had murdered their leaders in cold blood. But just as Navarre had once capitulated to the Mass in order to preserve his life, he now capitulated again: for five months he had plotted and fought for his liberty and he had been worsted. This time he would try an easier course.

Meanwhile the King's position had been made incontrovertibly clear to all of France: he had no intention of granting freedom of worship, of changing his council, of reducing taxes, or calling the Estates. He had, on the other hand, a firm determination to clear the Rhône from Lyons to Avignon of enemy forces and then to subdue the recalcitrant provinces of Languedoc and Dauphiny. It was a wild and reckless threat made by a man who seemed to have taken but small stock of his own resources. While the Queen Mother had already brought Swiss mercenaries and German Reiters into France, they would not budge until they were paid, meanwhile ravaging the country until even the unarmed peasants turned upon them with scythes and staves in a desperate effort to recover their small possessions. When Philip of Spain offered troops to assist Henri in putting down the rebellion, it only entrenched the Huguenots in their position that they were saving the kingdom of France, while the King was willing to let it be ravaged by any foreigner who would join his side. Ogier de Busbecq, ambassador from the Emperor Maximilian, observing the King's brutal decisions, wrote of the suffering that would result from the King's order "that all the standing grain which could be reached in Languedoc or Narbonese Gaul be burned."[25]

At this moment there intruded a personal sorrow which made Henri de Valois less competent than ever to deal with the affairs of the realm: he learned of the sudden death of the Princesse de Condé, a young lady who had possessed the unique gift of eliciting a certain fidelity from the profligate King. When, after a week of hysterical grief, he emerged, it was in the bizarre dress of a mourner: his doublet and hose were black; the heavy rings and ornaments with which he usually bedecked himself were absent and in their place were death's-heads, elaborately carved. Henri's curious sensuality had taken another turn and his passion of lust was momentarily replaced by a passion for penance.

Although Catherine was shaken at the erratic conduct of the son on whom she had so long counted, she now took refuge in the golden dream that once Henri was anointed and crowned at Reims, all would be well. Thus, in the cold weeks of January, the royal cortege traveled northward out of Avignon, torn by the winds that swept the Massif central and caught in the snows that blew out of the barren crags of the Alpilles. Although it was rumored that the King's pages did not have cloaks to their backs, Catherine was determined to have a royal crowning; for, for the first time since 1547 when Henri II succeeded his father, François I, a man—not a child—was to be anointed King of France. Despite all the efforts of the Queen Mother, French nerves were too much on edge to enjoy the splendor of the ceremony. It was remarked somberly that twice the crown had slipped as the Cardinal placed it on Henri's head; and once the King was heard to murmur petulantly that it pained him. The tension was not eased when a few days later, "so sudden as to be almost clandestine," the King, again in the cathedral at Reims, married Louise de Vaudemont, a "handsome girl," but one who bore the ambiguous merit of being cousin to the Guises.

Shortly after the marriage festivities, the court set out for Paris where the King had agreed to meet the delegates of the party which had been formed under Damville's leadership. The six months which had passed since his return to France had proved to the King that his blithe hopes for frightening the rebels back under the shadow of the crown were folly. As he cajoled his unpaid mercenaries to keep in the field, patriotic Frenchmen flocked to Damville's standard, for Damville had declared the aim of his party to be "to save the kingdom for the King and against his evil councilors."[26] It was the statement of a patriot, not a rebel, and it drew men to him in droves. The King, aware that he had already lost many of the southern provinces, listened at first to the demands of the delegates with good grace. Their terms were hard, he commented, but he heard them to the end: freedom of worship, an increase in the towns held by the Huguenots, restoration of confiscated estates, the liberty of Montmorency, a declaration condemning the Massacre of Saint Bartholomew. When they began to argue the terms point by point, however, the King found himself pressed. While Henri de Valois might do much through a spirit of largesse, he would never be forced. He blundered again, and in a moment of rage dismissed the delegates. If he thought by his arrogance to strengthen the power of the crown, he was tragically mistaken. From the beginning he had alienated his people by his effeminate dress, his heavily embroidered shirts and Italian collars, his reserve which placed him beyond the sphere of even his nobles, his coterie of young dandies on whom he spent a fortune gleaned from an impoverished countryside. The grace of an occasional smile or the charm of a generous gesture was not enough to offset the general tenor of his actions. "The sum and status of this kingdom seems to hang from a thin thread," prophesied Busbecq to his master, the Emperor Maximilian.[27]

The strife which rocked France was at its bitterest within the royal family, for Alençon and Navarre still walked "fearful and distrusted." Although Margot, at the advice of her friends, tried to bring her husband and her brother into common cause, pointing out that they were equally in disgrace and that their only hope of success lay in uniting against their mutual enemies, even their common fate could not end their instinctive enmity. "One of these days they will cut the throats of one another," warned the English agent. The King, furious at Alençon's jealousy, reproached him sharply, warning him that unless he changed his ways he should be "chipped straighter." "It is a very hell among them," the agent continued, "not one content or in quiet with another, nor mother with son, nor brother with brother, nor mother with daughter."[28]

Into such a hell there took shape that nightmare against which the Queen Mother had desperately fought for more than eighteen months. "Yesterday," wrote Morosini to Venice on September 16, 1575, "the event took place, which has constantly been dreaded, and which may be considered to be the total ruin of this unfortunate and ill-starred kingdom, namely, that Monsieur the Duke of Alençon escaped from the court. . . ."[29] After several elaborate plots which had failed, the one which succeeded was markedly simple. Alençon let it be known that he was going to pay his respects to a "certain lady." Accompanied by a few retainers, he made his way to an address where he was already well known. It was the sort of errand on which a gentleman must be permitted his leisure, and by the time his trick was discovered, Alençon was far from Paris. Margot, although swearing to the King that she had no part in the plot, nevertheless provides a fairly detailed account: ". . . as soon as it was dusk and before the king's supper time, my brother changed his cloak and burying his face in it up to his nose, followed one of his servants who was not well known as far as the Port St. Honoré where Simier waited with a carriage borrowed from a certain lady. In this he traveled to some houses about a quarter of a league from Paris where there were horses ready for him. He mounted, and about a league farther on joined two or three hundred horsemen who were waiting at the rendezvous he had set."[30]

Alençon had headed due west for the town of Dreux hidden in the green valley of the Blaise. News of his escape scattered before him, and in town after town he was joined by men at arms. It was a victory for the *politiques*, and good men swarmed about him as though he were in truth a savior. By the time he reached Dreux, he had upwards of five hundred men at his side and promises of more with every mile. The King was beside himself, sending men out with orders to bring him back dead or alive. Nothing could have touched off so hot a spark as this. Was he to take arms against his royal brother? Bad enough that he should be forced to send mercenaries to cut down rebels in the field; bad enough that Frenchmen should take up arms in the dubious cause of saving the kingdom against its King. But if that King should take up arms against the royal blood of his own household—what then? He had but little feeling for Alençon, indeed from the beginning he had feared and mistrusted him; yet he had but to look at the sleepless eyes and pursed mouth of his mother to conjecture the fate that might befall the kingdom and the kingdom's sovereign, if Alençon were not brought peacefully to terms. Alençon, however, although but poorly graced with Valois gifts, had his own measure of shrewdness: he had got the bit from between his teeth at last and he would run a long mile before he would return to the stable. When Catherine, already old for journeyings about the countryside, followed in his track, begging him to admit her to his presence, she was denied. When she sent him word, begging him not to make one kingdom into two, her plea went unanswered.

The King, meanwhile, had sent the Duc de Nevers with his troops to try to keep the towns through which Alençon might pass from rising against the crown. He placed all ports under surveillance and deployed troops in strategic spots to keep his brother from crossing the Loire. Then, hoping that a gesture of kindness might do what troops would not, Henri, with a kind of largesse, sent to Alençon all his jewels, his wardrobe, his household furnishings, his silver plate. But Alençon had had enough of gestures; it was power he wanted— power and adulation. He had lusted for them long and he would not easily give them up now. A month after his escape, Busbecq wrote to Maximilian with his usual perspicacity: "They think that tomorrow Alençon will return to his mother in the town of Blois to obtain peace. But to me the whole thing is an object of suspicion and even if he should return, I think that nothing would be agreed upon."[31]

Throughout October the Queen Mother followed after him, from Mantes to Nogent to Courville to Blois, writing to the King on September 23, "He has told me that if I want to take the trouble to go to Blois he will speak to me"; and five days later, ". . . to lose a single

day is to lose all."[32] She grew yet more desperate when the news
reached her that Thoré, younger brother of Damville, had joined
Alençon with over a thousand horse.

There was now a force which called itself portentously "The Army
of Monsieur." Every messenger that returned to court brought the
same report: more and more men were flocking to Alençon. Henri
III, having exhausted his proffers of friendship, took refuge in rage.
But Alençon, who from his childhood had never had the power to
fight, had developed a sting like a nettle. He stayed near the Loire,
subtly suggesting that he might take Orléans, engaging in no battles,
never overtly refusing an overture to peace. He did very little in those
first few months of freedom, but he drove the royal family almost to
madness; and to Alençon that was as good as winning a battle.

From the sidelines Navarre watched it all with a kind of amused
detachment. The King was not sure what to do with him, and Navarre
played his part to increase the royal bafflement. Margot, appraising
Navarre's position following Alençon's escape, noted: "This flight did
not make the King show any better countenance to the King my
husband but continued to make little of him as he was accustomed to
do."[33] For almost three and a half years Navarre had lived under constraint at the Valois court. He had been not quite nineteen when he
had entered Paris in the July following his mother's death. He was
even then no novice to the intricacies of war or politics or religion. But
the years following his marriage had been a school of enormous value.
His natural perspicacity had been trained and refined; his political
acuity had been sharpened to a fine point. There was little he did not
observe and equally little that he was not able to interpret. In
January 1576 he wrote a letter to his cousin Jean d'Albret, which
provides a vivid picture of that court which he had now determined
to leave behind him:

> This court is the strangest you have ever seen. We are always
> ready to cut each other's throats. We carry daggers, wear
> coats of mail and very often a breast plate beneath our
> capes. Severac will tell you all about this. The king is as
> badly threatened as I am; he is more friendly with me than
> ever. Monsieur de Guise and Monsieur de Mayenne never
> move except with me. Lavardin, your brother, and Saint Co-
> lome are the heads of my council. You have never seen me so
> strong. In this court of friends, I defy everyone. Everyone
> in the League wishes me dead, out of love for Monsieur.

For the third time they have forbidden my mistress to
speak to me and they have reined her in so short that she
dare not even look at me. I am waiting for the moment when
I can give battle, for they say that they will kill me, and
I wish to strike the first blow.[34]

Less than a month later he had struck that first blow. On February
6, Navarre escaped from court. Navarre the affable, the lazy, the
debonair; Navarre, so easily satisfied, of whom the English agent had
written but a few weeks before, "they make but little of him"—Navarre
had fled. He had not even engaged in the melodrama of a "plot." He
had simply ridden off hunting and had failed to return.

It was a blow from the most unexpected quarter, for, as Dale wrote
to Walsingham the same day: "He was nothing mistrusted at this
time because he had been divers times a-hunting eight or nine days
together and used to return on the sudden and sometimes in the night
when he was least looked for."[35] When Navarre formed his hunting
party to go to Senlis, few were party to the motive that underlay it.
To allay any suspicion he had made a point of asking the Duc de
Guise to join him, fairly certain that he could expect a negative
response. Even among the few there was a traitor, however, and one
of Navarre's trusted company revealed the plan to the King the day
after Navarre's initial departure. The whole plot might have fallen
through with dire consequences for Navarre, had not D'Aubigné,
staunch Huguenot and friend of Navarre, aware of the treachery,
taken horse at once for Senlis. He arrived at Navarre's camp at the
dramatically appropriate moment, announcing, as he himself described,
"Sire, the king knows everything."[36] Navarre, sending the two unwitting members of the King's guard who had accompanied him off
on a wild goose chase to "find the King" and attended by only three
or four trusted friends, headed westward at once toward the town of
Alençon.

For close to four years Navarre had been kept in bonds. He had
learned to bow, to jig, to smile at insults; he had learned to dissemble
and to play the fool. Now he had his liberty again. He did not know
what the future held, but he vowed that they would never trap him
again. Catherine could sing herself out of breath before her son-in-law
would return to her court. When, at last, he crossed the Loire, he
turned to his companions saying, "God be praised who has delivered
me. . . . I'll never return unless I'm dragged."[37]

CHAPTER IV

Open Conflict: 1576–1578

In short, it is not possible to imagine a crab more twisted and
contradictory than the government of France.

L'Estoile

❧❧❧❧❧ The flight of Navarre left the court amazed. Catherine, for
all her astute vision, was taken completely off guard. She recalled
those shrewd eyes and knew that she had been fooled by them: all
of Navarre's camaraderie with Guise, his indifference to his wife, his
hostility toward Alençon, even his amorous attentions to Charlotte de
Sauves—all had been so much dissembling to turn her head in the
wrong direction. Catherine had been properly caught, but the Queen
Mother had a certain esteem for successful schemers and her anger
may have been tempered by admiration for this sly son-in-law who
could beat her at her own game. Catherine never came to like Navarre,
but he won from her that understanding and respect which she accorded few of her contemporaries.

The King, on the other hand, felt only impotent fury—a fury which
he tried to dissemble, for he recognized it as a sign of his own weakness. Yet he could not conceal his fear and bewilderment, and Dr.
Valentine Dale, in his report to Walsingham the day following Navarre's
departure, commented: ". . . the King is so discouraged with the
flight of Navarre that he will have peace come what may."[1] Henri,
always with a flare for the dramatic, now assumed the role of the injured and aggrieved monarch, writing on February 13 to Mauvissière,
his Keeper of the Seals: "I considered him so united to me that he
would never be able to separate himself . . . he told me that he intended to return to sleep here yesterday evening; but instead of return-

ing he sent me word by St. Martin that he had been told that I was going to have him arrested. As God is my witness, I have never had any thought or desire to do this. . . . I deeply regret this, for he leaves under such a false impression . . . that it will only hinder further the peace that I have done my very best to procure. It is all very discouraging."[2]

It became increasingly discouraging as reports of Navarre's activities poured in: 3,000 horse and 9,000 foot had come out of his own domains to "take their master home"; he had won approval everywhere by "reviling the Mass and all papistry," by assuring the Huguenots that what he had done at court was "not with the consent of his conscience," by attending the Reformed communion service and acting as godfather according to the Reformed ritual. Even worse were the reports that he was heading to join Condé, who, along with Duke Casimir of Bavaria and his German mercenaries, had penetrated into France, crossing in turn the Moselle and the Meuse and making record time southwest to Dijon.

Alençon and his men had already joined this army. Should Navarre join them in his turn, the King would be forced to sue for peace at any price. Hoping that minor concessions might lead to peace, he now wrote to Navarre assuring him of his continued friendship, sending him his horses and the men of his household along with his possessions. Dr. Dale watching the King's anguished maneuvers, wrote shrewdly to Walsingham: "The King of France would stroke him as a shrewd beast for fear of biting or striking."[3]

Had the King been aware of both sides of the coin, he might not have been quite so conciliatory, for Navarre himself was having difficulties. The first flight had been exhilarating, speeding westward through Dreux where Alençon had gone before him, then into the wooded hills of the Haut-Perche, past Senonches with its fortified château, past Mortagne and the great forbidding walls of the monastery of La Trappe, and down into Le Mesle, huddled along the gray spring waters of the Sarthe. It had been exhilarating to find fine horses waiting for him along the way and finer men whom he could call his own. Navarre was always a man of action and here in a single month he had found more action than the whole span of his twenty-three years had hitherto provided. He was, in that first month, all that his youthful dreams of bravado could have wished: he was a Prince escaped from duress, a Prince inventive and courageous, a Prince with a cause to whom men would flock and to whom victory seemed already assured. By the time he reached Alençon, however, during the first week of March, he was also a Prince who was suspect, a man who had saved his life by cheap promises on Saint Bartholomew's Day while his coreligionists were selling theirs at the costly price of blood. The Huguenots had seen him at the siege of La Rochelle standing behind the Valois standard, and they had heard rumors of his friendship with the House of Guise. Navarre needed all his charm to win back a people whom he had all but lost. In those first weeks of freedom, he found that before he could do battle with the King's forces, he would have to do battle with pen and ink, using every device of rhetoric at his command to convince his people that the last four years had meant nothing, that only now was he able to stand before them in his true colors. Letters went out in rapid course to the lords of the south assuring them of his desire for "the peace and tranquillity of this realm, and particularly for those of the Religion," begging them to muster as many of their friends as they can, to mount their horses as quickly as possible and come to join him for "the times are too urgent to remain at home." Aware of the grounds of their distrust, he pleaded with them to accept his word, "for it is very true."[4]

His charm, his energy, his determination were enough to win many, but when some weeks later he came to La Rochelle, he found that despite his recent public profession of the Religion, he was still regarded with mistrust. The Rochellais had never been known for their easy capitulation, and now even before this son of Jeanne d'Albret who had taken the title of "Protector of the Associated Reformed and Catholic Churches," they had little to show but suspicion. Although he wrote humbly to the mayor that he had no wish to make a formal entry but simply sought permission to come "as a friend with my own household," the citizens still remained adamant, recalling the Valois treachery of the past. When they finally agreed to his entrance, it was only with certain humiliating conditions partially disguised. Henri was asked to enter with a retinue of only fifty men—the citizens might become nervous, it was explained, should a large force be abroad in the narrow streets. At his side during his entrance rode his sister Catherine who had been sent to him from court. She was already a favorite with those of the Religion, for they detected in her something of the intransigent spirit of her mother. As they entered the city, they noted that the streets were lined with people; at first glance it looked like a very royal welcome, until it was noted that all were carefully armed and strategically placed to ensure their own safety should Navarre's promises prove false. Although it would soon be spring, there was a chill in the air at La Rochelle, a cold wind that kept Navarre from lingering.

Meanwhile the King watched Navarre's progress with a kind of despair. With Alençon, Navarre, and Condé leagued against him, he could see nothing but ruin for the crown. Thus during the month of March, the Queen Mother was given free reign to negotiate in the interests of peace and on March 13 the delegates of the Huguenots and *politiques* met with the King's council to discuss the articles which Navarre's party had submitted: that Navarre shall command the territory which his ancestors had governed before him; that all his men shall enjoy free right of passage; that his officers and servants shall enjoy the same privileges as those who serve the royal family of France; that he be obeyed as governor of the King in Guyenne; that the King assist him in recovering the old territory of Navarre from Spain. For a week they struggled through the thorny negotiations, but at the end the King's council, declaring that the petitions were exorbitant, walked from the council chamber.

Other diplomats might have despaired, but the "Florentine Shopkeeper," with her talent for bargaining, was indefatigable. Throughout April she traveled, she talked, she wrote letters, and toward the end of the month she met finally with the rebel leaders at Chastenay, an isolated house near Sens, set clear in an open field so that there could be no possibility of ambuscade or double dealing. In the talks that followed everything was on the side of the Huguenots and when the Peace of Beaulieu (or the "Peace of Monsieur" as it was often called in honor of Alençon) was signed, it conceded more than the Huguenots could have anticipated. They were assured universal freedom of conscience and worship except in certain restricted areas; special courts, called *chambres mi-parties*, were set up so that the people of both religions could be tried by an equal number of judges of both religions; eight fortified towns were given to those of the Religion for security. Condé received the government of Picardy and Alençon a magnificent appanage including Anjou, Touraine, and Berry. Navarre was confirmed in the government of Guyenne. In addition, the family of Coligny was reestablished and a public apology was made for the events of Saint Bartholomew's Day. On May 8 the Queen Mother could write at last, "after having been for so long a time engaged in the business of peace, yesterday it was concluded according to the power I hold from my son."[5]

As usual she received but little thanks for her efforts. The Huguenots remained unsatisfied, the Guises were infuriated, and the clergy in general outraged at so many concessions to the heretics. It was rumored that the King had wept when he signed the Peace of Beaulieu and tears would not indeed have been amiss, for the peace threatened his prestige on every side. From his childhood the Queen Mother had quoted to him the prophecy of Nostradamus who had written, "At the head of the whole world will be the great Chyren." "Chyren," she had explained, was but an anagram for "Henri"—for he was to be the greatest of kings. The glories of Chyren seemed far from him in the summer of 1576. Chyren would have been a man of energy, of wealth, of daring. Henri had had those gifts once, but he had lost them. Although he was but twenty-five, he felt himself growing old. Once he might have fought through those obstacles which piled before him in nightmare confusion but now with that neurotic insouciance which was the despair of his counselors, he turned from affairs of state to spend his nights in the brothels and convents of Paris and his days with those fair young men whom he called his *mignons* and on whom he squandered the money that should have gone to buy him an army.

When in late July he returned from a vacation in Normandy with his carriage filled with multicolored parakeets, baskets of lap dogs, and chattering monkeys, there were open jibes at the King of sport who took no advice but from his *mignons* with their long, curled hair and little velvet bonnets "like those of girls in brothels." Paris saw in him no "Chyren" who would lead the world; they had their own titles for him. In the first days of September placards went up all over the city proclaiming, "Henri by the grace of his mother, uncertain King of France, imaginary King of Poland, Janitor of the Louvre, Warden of St. Germain l'Auxerrois."[8]

The wave of insolence could not have been more adroitly timed, for on August 16 the King had issued the edict to convoke the Estates General at Blois in the fall of the year. By this measure, he hoped— he was not sure how—to reverse the terms of that peace which he now so bitterly regretted, and to re-establish something of his royal prestige. Yet long before the Estates had met, this last weapon turned in his hand, for the Huguenots who had been among the loudest to demand the Estates the preceding spring now repudiated them, accusing the King of suborning this body to strengthen his own position against those of the Religion. It was no surprise to them that the assembly which met in the château at Blois on December 6 was composed almost exclusively of Catholics.

For the King's purposes, the château at Blois was psychologically perfect, for everything at Blois bespoke the brilliance and glory of France. Henri, with a strong feeling for atmosphere, had planned it well. Following the opening Mass, he made his solemn entrance into the Estates. The macebearers who preceded him were dressed in new finery, their short coats heavily embroidered with fleur-de-lys. Then came the canopy under which the King himself walked, handsome and royal in his white satin doublet and cloak of purple velvet. As the royal procession reached the entrance, the members of the Estates rose to their feet. The great wave of episcopal purple flanking the King was balanced by the flamboyant robes of the peers of the realm and the more sober dress of the Third Estate. Behind the King walked his mother, his wife, and his brother Alençon. The King ascended the dais, accompanied by the members of the royal family. For a moment the illusion of royal splendor was about him like a nimbus and the great hall bowed in instinctive homage before the fleur-de-lys of France. The jeweled hand, graceful and commanding, gestured and the delegates took their places. The Estates had opened.

On the right of the royal throne sat Catherine, a portly woman of fifty-seven, who was beginning to show the effects of her years. At the King's left sat Queen Louise, her pallor and hesitant manner made more noticeable by her robes of state. Beyond the Queen Mother in a great armchair which his puny frame could not fill sat Alençon, that "wandering son," brought like some royal trophy to dazzle the public gaze. When Henri rose to speak, his audience was still captive to the spectacle of royal power. For this solemn function the affectations of dress had been put aside: the earrings and bracelets were for the time gone. The *mignons* were gone, too. The man on the dais was gifted with great charm. His face was too narrow, his mouth too weak to be called handsome, but he had about him a presence, a grace of manner, and a quality of voice which had won him the reputation for being one of the most eloquent princes of Europe.

His opening speech was a moving plea for peace, for loyalty to France above every other claim; it was eloquent, tempered, yet almost passionate in its personal appeal. For a moment the royal presence had made itself felt, and Catherine seeing her son at his regal best must have felt one of those surges of optimism which alone could have carried her through her stormy life. No hour of eloquence, however, could ob-

literate the months of misrule: the offices bought and sold with little
regard for merit or integrity; the taxation which ground the people
into despair that vast fortunes might be spent on spectacles to amuse
the court and please the King's favorites; the licentiousness and folly
of the King's own life which undermined his authority. Even as he
publicly promised to observe inviolably "all the regulations and ordinances that may be made by me . . ." Navarre was writing in indignation of the continued violations of the peace and demanding
that royal justice be exercised toward his people.

Later that month, further incensed by the turbulent citizens of
Bordeaux who continued to stir up trouble, Navarre addressed a letter
to his people of Guyenne. It is one of the first of Navarre's letters
in which are revealed those qualities which were one day to make him a
powerful and beloved king. There is little of the Valois charm about
it, but there is a vigor, a cogency, a toughness of mind that knows
how to measure the real against the ideal, a perception that strips
away illusions and forces men to face things as they are. It was a plea
to observe the terms of the Edict of Beaulieu and to remain loyal
and obedient to their lawful King. It was also a pledge to uphold his
people against those who wished to exterminate them. Thus, he concluded:

"Let us, then, take a firm and needful resolution, Messieurs, to work
for our own general conservation against the schemes and artifices of
the enemies of our peace; and I swear before God, who is our judge
and who sees the depths of our hearts, that under the authority of my
lord the King, I will uphold all those who are under my protection. I
will, with the help of your counsel and of the chief lords, as well as of
all lovers of peace and tranquillity, oppose all violence, mobs and
oppressors . . . and in so doing I shall spare neither my life nor the
means which God has given me."[7]

Despite the King's initial stance, the Estates had not been long in
session before it became clear that the King had a master. The Duc de
Guise, subtle, adroit, constant, pursued a policy carefully charted in
every detail: France must remain Catholic. This was the essential;
all other policies were at best subordinate. Building on the local
associations of Catholics that had banded together against the Huguenots, the Guises had set out to construct a war machine superior to
anything the King had at his command. For several years, especially
throughout the north of France, the citizens had banded together into
so-called "Catholic leagues," which had as their purpose the protection

of the Roman faith. The religious nature and motive of these associations was sufficient coercion for most Catholics and membership in the leagues was high. The religious terminology of the oath ("In the name of the Most Holy Trinity and in the communion of the Precious Body of Jesus Christ . . .") was sufficient to ensure continued loyalty. It was the genius of the Guises which gathered these local unions together under a unified leadership, thus placing at their command thousands of ardent Frenchmen who had publicly sworn "to use all our power to maintain the exercise of our Catholic, Apostolic, and Roman religion in which our ancestors were nourished and in which we wish to live and die."[8]

The King had, unhappily, persisted in minimizing the importance of these leagues and the importance of Guise influence until, in November 1576, the Huguenots published a pamphlet, which they alleged had been found among the possessions of a Guise agent, in which was a carefully formulated plan for placing the family of Guise on the throne of France. The Guises, the report affirmed, were the true successors of Charlemagne, "the green and flourishing shoots" of the great French leader. The Capets, from whom the Valois were descended, were but reprobates, no more than dissolute failures unequal to the task of governing a great country. The Duc de Guise, then, was to be put at the head of an army which would free France of the Huguenots, imprison Condé and Navarre, send the King and Queen to a monastery, and ascend the throne himself, thus restoring the glory of Charlemagne.[9]

Although many argued that the "David Memorial" (taking its name from the man among whose effects it had been found) was simply a Huguenot ruse to divide the Catholic faction, the King could not take the risk of ignoring it. Knowing himself too weak to oppose the Guises, he came more and more to veer to their position. Throughout December the discussion of religious liberty continued, but by the end of that month the inevitable decision had been taken: the Estates resolved that henceforth but one religion was to be tolerated within the kingdom. *Un roi, une foi, une loi* had again become the law of the realm.

Once the step had been taken, a delegation was immediately sent southward to Navarre and Condé to inform them of the decision of the Estates and to beg them to comply with its terms. Such an embassy was hardly more than a piece of protocol from which little was expected. Part of the delegation under the Bishop of Autun branched westward to seek Condé around the marshes of Saintonge. He met them toward the end of January in the fortified town of St. Jean d'Angeli. It was less a confrontation than a volcanic eruption: Condé refused to accept the credentials of the delegates, refused to listen to their position, refused even to break the seal on the documents they presented. He lashed out against the "suborned and corrupted Estates of Blois" which had acted contrary to the public faith, and had perjured itself by acting contrary to the solemn oath of pacification taken less than a year before. Condé's only answer was a declaration that he would resume arms "to restore the kingdom in its full splendor."[10]

Condé's vitriolic response was no more nor less than had been expected; if there was any hope of peace it was to be found with Navarre. In late December, Navarre, angry and disturbed by the constant violence erupting around him, had written to the people of Guyenne begging them to follow the terms of the peace despite provocations to the contrary. "If we reenter these ways [those of war]" he had written warningly, "we will soon see an inextinguishable fire which will lead to inevitable ruin." "Each of you," he continued, "both nobility and clergy . . . must unanimously agree to obey His Majesty. . . . Let us not use the veil of religion to cover our falsities. . . . I wish to render equal justice to everyone—of whichever religion he is. . . . Those who follow a right conscience are of my religion."[11] It was the tone of such a letter as this with its underlying conviction that loyalty to the throne and the establishment of peace were the most essential elements of French policy which gave whatever faint hope they had to the delegates who were welcomed by Navarre in his city of Agen.

The Archbishop of Vienne, an able diplomat, headed the delegation. He reminded Navarre that the King by his very coronation oath was bound to uphold the Catholic faith, that the preservation of this faith, whole and undisturbed, was a fundamental law of the kingdom, assuring Navarre that if he were to accept this basic principle he, in turn, could promise him that "those of the new opinion would not be harmed." The Archbishop, encouraged by Navarre's respectful attention, reminded him that he could hardly hold the King to the Peace of Monsieur when such a peace was manifestly prejudicial to the kingdom at large. As Vienne launched into a recital of the horrors that would come upon them all should France be plunged into war once more, he felt a slight hope, for Navarre was visibly moved. But Vienne had misread the emotion he had seen on Navarre's face; it was a sign of sorrow, not of acquiescence, for what was being asked of him was beyond his power. Nothing he could surrender would bring peace now; he knew that if the King did not. Guise knew it, too, and would play it for his own ends. There had been a day—perhaps no further away than that of the King's father—when a monarch could decree "one King, one faith, one law," but that day had gone. No decree could stem a wind —and it was a wind that rushed through the south of France, leaped rivers, bent grain before its weight, and already battered at the royal portals. Should Navarre acquiesce to the King's demand, abdicate his position, and disband his army, nothing essential would change. Another leader would take his place: Condé, Damville, Thoré. There was no lack of leaders who would take arms against bonds which had become intolerable. Their fight as they saw it was not against France but for France, not against the King but for his interests—and the tragedy was that he was too blind to see it. "After the King and his brother, I have a greater interest in the restoration of the kingdom than anyone else in the world," Navarre wrote later in explanation of his position. To Vienne and the other delegates, he replied "modestly enough," even mildly. He did not see, he answered the Archbishop, that the proposed scheme would make things any better. He could not but question the good judgment of those who asked the King for one religion in his kingdom. Faith could not be regulated by the sword. He, too, wanted truth, and should he some day see that his own ways were in error, he would reconcile himself to the Church of Rome. But that time was not yet. He had no further message for the King except to repeat his profession of loyalty.

As the delegates turned in disappointment from Agen, the interminable debates continued at Blois. The decision to reestablish a single faith had in actual fact settled nothing. The outlawing of the Calvinist religion was tantamount to declaring war and it was obvious to most that France could ill sustain further internal conflict. While from Spain came the deliberated approval of Philip II, and from Rome the paternal blessing of Gregory XIII, no equal enthusiasm swept through the Estates. Only the Guise faction favored war, for war was the instrument they had fashioned to wrest France from the King and win it for themselves.

All of this was in the Queen Mother's mind when she rose in the assembly begging for whatever course would keep the country at peace. It had been to the Guises that she had chiefly looked as she proclaimed in her accented French: "I am a Catholic and I have as good a conscience as any. . . . I am now fifty-eight years old and I am ready to die and go to heaven. But I will not authorize the Catholics to destroy this kingdom. If there are those who do not care about the loss of the state in order that they will be able to say that they have maintained the Catholic religion, or if there are those who hope to profit by its ruin, then I have nothing further to say, but I will not be one of them." If she hoped to win public commendation from her son she was disappointed; instead he reproached her for what he considered her persistent opposition. "Madame" he was overheard to say, "this is the third time you have spoken to me about peace; I tell you quite plainly, do not speak to me about it again, for I do not wish to hear it."[12] This arrogant disapproval coming from the very quarter for which she was willing to risk all wounded her deeply, but it did not defeat her. She simply turned to find other ways in which she could serve her son and his kingdom.

If she could not establish peace, she might at least try to diminish the power of the enemy. Should she be able to procure the defection of the leader of the *politiques*, Montmorency-Damville, the Huguenot cause would be irreparably weakened. To this end the Queen Mother bent her efforts. In January, she wrote to her son: "As for Marshal Damville, it is he whom I fear most, for he has the ability, the experience, and the largest following. I urge you, therefore, to spare nothing to gain him. To my mind, success or failure rests upon his action. . . . Offer him anything and everything he wishes in order to overcome his mistrust and calm his suspicions."[13] Catherine's scheming was perfectly timed, for Damville, bitterly disillusioned by those of the Religion, now found himself a solitary leader. The Huguenots, mistrustful of his allegiance to Roman Catholicism and annoyed by his autocratic rule, had repudiated him as governor of Montpellier and elected their own governor in his place. Humiliated and lonely, Damville was in a perfect state to succumb before the King's assurance of pardon and friendship. By March of that year, Catherine de Medici watched in triumph as the former leader of the *politiques* took up his position at court.

When that same month the Estates were formally closed, France was once again plunged into civil war. The brilliance in which the Estates had opened sadly waned, and in the scuffle of argument and compromise the King had lost the aureole of kingship. Something

had died at Blois: something of France and something of Frenchmen's hopes. Diverse expectations had been brought to the Estates
when they had opened three months before, but none of them had
been fulfilled. Some had hoped for an increase in the power of
the Estates; some had hoped for a peaceful return to a single faith;
some few had hoped to discover in the person of their King that
valor and determination which had made him a favorite before he
ascended the throne. However disparate their goals, they were united
in their desire to avoid war, yet war was the single, palpable fact
which emerged from the Estates. Even Guise had been betrayed,
for the King had won a tactical victory when he announced himself the chief of the Catholic League. Thus Guise instead of finding
himself the leader of a strong force against which the King would be
powerless, found himself instead a subordinate member of that League
which was now captained by the King himself.

Lady Fortune, whose wheel is never still, had played him false.
After years of careful plotting, of adroit diplomacy, he had maneuvered
himself so close to the throne that a single vaulting leap would
have placed him where his vanity already sat; now he rode down
the steep, uneven cobblestones through the gate of the château and
into the March wind that blew bitterly from the gray, opaque waters
of the Loire. Two armies had been formed; the King had placed
them under the command of Guise's brother Mayenne and young
Alençon. Guise himself was left empty-handed, and he did not love
the King any better for this overt insult.

France was at war and France was impoverished, yet still the
King continued to squander his people's money on elaborate balls
and spectacles and presents to his favorites. When that summer, a
terrible storm swept across the countryside, ruining crops, killing cattle
where they stood in the fields, setting barns and mills afire, it became
clear to many that the powerful hand of God had fallen in chastise-
ment on a wicked and dissolute land. Rumors grew of a strange
beast that appeared not far from Paris, a beast who changed his
shape, who talked in human tongues, and who successfully eluded
all pursuit. The devil, perhaps, was abroad in France, and no man
could catch him. The devil would have them all, God help them,
unless the Florentine and her bedizened son should somehow save
them from the beast of war that raped and ravaged and would not
be placated.

No one was more profoundly in favor of peace than the Florentine herself, and toward the end of May the Duc de Montpensier had been sent to Navarre to probe the possibility of an immediate end of the war. A few weeks later the King was able to confide to the English ambassador that Navarre had expressed a wish to see him which he construed as equivalent to seeking peace. The King's determination for peace was further augmented by a message from Mauvissière, the French ambassador at Whitehall, who reported preparations underway for sending English forces to help the Huguenots at Brouage and La Rochelle. Wearily the English ambassador, Sir Amias Paulet, wrote in his report to Burghley: "All things rest here after the accustomed fashion, unconstant and uncertain."[14]

The beast still roamed and the King could not stem the violence that had been unleashed by the resolution taken by the Estates at Blois. The hope that the King's opening speech had inspired had long been forgotten for the King now seemed unable to play any role but that of King of Trifles. He still sponsored with childish delight the Italian comedians who had first played at Blois and who were known for their skill in "lewd song and play." He publicly insulted his nobles and could make no reasonable explanation when the Pope reproached him for using Church funds for matters far other than the prosecution of "this holy war." It was, of course, upon the *mignons* that the King lavished his fortune—now largely borrowed—and his scandalous affection. "Florid and frizzled," described L'Estoile with his diarist's eye and keen wit. "With their ostentatious manner, their hair ornamented, their crests raised high" they arrived at Olinville to visit the King, "leaving a sickening trail of perfume behind them, in the streets, in the houses, in every place they visited."[15] It did not help the King's prestige when in August presents reached him from Poland—child's presents to delight a child's heart: a wild ass and a little dwarf "no bigger than a child of three" who claimed more of his attention than the affairs of his kingdom. It was solid advice that his councilors gave him when they suggested that he increase his guard because of the violent hostility which swept in waves through the impoverished districts of Paris.

In the south, Navarre was as desperate as the King to terminate the war. With the defection of Damville, the distrust between Huguenots and *politiques* had increased. The Catholic captains—Laverdin, Duras, Gramont—in whose personal devotion Navarre knew he could trust were outraged by the contempt shown them by such ultrareformers as Turenne and Favas. Even more dangerous to his leadership was the disapproval leveled against his own person. Mornay, that tight-lipped leader who might well have passed for Calvin's next of kin, was not slow to indicate his disapproval of Navarre's impetuosity, of his amorous follies, of his racy tongue. None of this, Mornay made quite clear, was what the Huguenots expected from their leader. Navarre's position was not strengthened when Casimir, to whom he had appealed for help, indicated quite openly that he did not trust Navarre because of the "evil counselors" who surrounded him, because of his own partiality for the Valois court, and his tendency to make arbitrary decisions without the consent of the Churches. When the rumor began to circulate that Navarre had threatened to make his own peace with the King of France unless Casimir came through with immediate aid, his reputation was further clouded.

If the Huguenots were seeking a republican leader who would give the Churches deliberative votes in the affairs of the country, they would not find him in Navarre. He had not been brought up in a Calvinist assembly, but at a court—a court where kings ruled supreme. He was too wise not to seek advice, but he would never feel himself governed by it. He was an autocrat—but he was many other things as well: he was frank and free in his relationships; he was just; he was, in an age of brutality, remarkably humane. His letters were filled with a kind of blunt honesty that was, in truth, the highest diplomacy. Yet now no amount of personal loyalty could balance the news of defeats and ill fortune that poured in from east and west: by sea the royal forces under the command of Lanssac had descended upon the island of Oléron, captured Brouage, and greatly inconvienced La Rochelle. The momentary victory at Mont-St. Michel was reversed twenty-four hours later when the Catholics recaptured the citadel and sent the three seditious monks who had opened the gates to the Huguenots hurtling from the pinnacle into the sea below. Issoire was reduced to rubble, the whole countryside of Guyenne was ravaged by brigands, the fields lay fallow while the peasants took up arms to play their part in the chaos of war. It was with good reason that 1577 came to be called "The Year of Bad News."

It was inevitable that by the end of August, Nevers and Montpensier should meet once more to negotiate for peace. On September 17, 1577, despite the opposition of the Guises, of Spain, and of the Holy See peace was concluded. The Peace of Bergerac—or the "King's

Peace" as it was called to distinguish it from the shameful "Peace of Monsieur"—was no more than a *modus vivendi* which admitted the existence of another form of Christianity while continuing to restrain it. Although many of the liberal concessions of the Edict of Beaulieu were revoked, the Peace of Bergerac at least granted to the Huguenots the right to dwell unmolested in any part of the kingdom, even while curtailing the public exercise of the Religion to certain designated places. Only a small number of mixed tribunals were provided for, and even in these two-thirds of the membership was to be Catholic. The eight towns which were given as places of security were to be handed back to the King at the end of a period of six years.

There was little enthusiasm for the peace in any quarter; it granted at once both too little and too much. When on October 5 it was publicly proclaimed in the squares of Paris, the people paid but small notice. Peace they wanted with all their hearts but they had grown a little cynical over the years, for who, they asked, ever kept the treaties that were so easily signed? Sir Amias Paulet, who had seen the King play fickle to his sworn word before, represented much of France when he wrote dubiously in his report to Elizabeth: "God grant that it may be made with that sincerity that becomes the oath of an anointed king."[16]

For one man, however, peace held no charms. Alençon's few small victories over the Huguenots had whetted his appetite for glory, and war was the arena in which glory would be found. Here, he thought, he could prove himself and perhaps win a kingdom as well—for Alençon's dreams of power had now become imperious. If France no longer needed his military leadership, there were other countries that did; and in the spring of 1578 he turned his covetous eyes to the Netherlands. Trouble in the Netherlands was of long duration. As far back as the reign of Henri II, the advocates of liberty had solicited help from France against what they claimed to be Spanish tyranny. The Netherlands question had always been a ticklish business, for while France was more than willing to undermine Spanish power, she was never in a position to openly oppose Spanish policy. Tenuous advances had already come out of the Lowlands suggesting that the French might come to their assistance, but the King could ill afford a public commitment. He feared Spain, and he feared England as well for Elizabeth had made it more than clear that she would consider French meddling in the Netherlands a threat to

English influence. To Alençon none of these considerations mattered when weighed against his personal glory. If he was slow to accept the tentative and secret proposals that were made to him, it was simply that he wished to be sure of his footing before he made the leap.

It was precisely here that Margot with her shrewd intelligence, her beauty, and her daring might be of use to him. Thus the scheme was concocted that Margot, for reasons of health, would request the privilege of journeying into Flanders to visit the spa at Liège. To this the King had no objection and on July 6 an elaborate cortege began its way up the Picardy road. Margot, a good traveler and keen observer, missed little of the scene around her—the variations in architecture, the different patterns of the gardens, the public lighting which made the streets of the cities as "bright as day" even after sundown. She noted with special delight the curious clocks at Valenciennes, intrigued with the moving figures and the melodies which accompanied the striking of the hours. She never forgot her principal task, however, for it was the people far more than the clocks and gardens which required her scrutiny. She had inherited a certain adroitness in pointing the conversation where she wished it to go and even in the midst of a ball or a dinner she tested the reactions of the people to Spanish rule, to their new governor, Don Juan of Austria, to their hopes for independence. Even before she reached Liège, she had formed the opinion that many of the people opposed Philip and considered it treachery on Don Juan's part to bring back Spanish troops upon their soil. Quite tentatively she was able to suggest that perhaps her brother Alençon might be willing to help them gain their freedom.

Liège, Margot found, was a lovely city with sufficient wit and gallantry to keep her amused through six indolent weeks. She might easily have prolonged her stay had it not been for a letter from Alençon telling her that at court "all is changed"—that the King is angry with him, jealous of his victories, and suspicious of Margot's prolonged absence. Further, Henri in exasperation had suggested to the Spaniards that Margot's visit might well have a motive injurious to the Spanish state and the Spaniards in response were already laying plots to capture her. It was obvious to Margot that she must leave Liège at once, though how she was not sure for she had no passport and was hardly in a position to obtain one. It was mid-

October when, after weeks of hazardous travel, she rode into La Fère where Alençon awaited her.

The peace which France was now enjoying was at best nominal. Spain had already manifested its displeasure over Alençon's possible interference in the Netherlands; the Holy See had clearly indicated that it found the Peace of Bergerac far too favorable to the Huguenots. Meanwhile the Huguenots themselves, using the freedom given them by the Peace of Bergerac, had convoked a national synod at Ste-Foy-la-Grande. Although it was essentially a religious and not a political meeting, the temper of the discussions indicated that the Huguenots had lost none of their militancy. The goals of the synod coupled with the increasing complaints of Navarre that the rights of his people were being constantly infringed upon, that the Peace of Bergerac was being broken by the very people whose duty it was to conserve it, should have made it palpably clear to the King that peace in France was more tenuous than ever. His hopes of limiting the power of the Huguenots by keeping Damville close to court had long been shattered. Damville, ambiguous though his position was with those of the Religion, was a man of far too much pride and integrity to let himself be duped by a puppet sovereign. No sooner had he been confirmed in his office than he began to work toward peace and friendship with Navarre. It was a coalition of two powerful men; between them they controlled the south. This was an incontrovertible fact which the King was forced to admit.

Into such an atmosphere of distrust and apprehension had ridden Margot with her exotic schemes for finding a kingdom for her misshapen brother. If the King did not at once condemn the scheme, it was only that he knew that Alençon would brook no outright refusal. Instead, he dallied; and the *mignons*, catching their signals from the King, toyed with Alençon in their own way. He was again the butt of their jokes and their daily skirmishes; they mocked him for his looks, his size, his failures in both love and war; and Alençon, knowing he was no match for them, hated them the more. Unable to endure their ridicule, he confided to Margot his secret plan for escaping from court to pursue that glorious destiny which he saw waiting for him in the Netherlands. He would escape, he told her, by night, through her windows, with one or two of his trusted men. "And thus," wrote a contemporary, "the First Prince of the Blood, heir presumptive to the throne, escapes through a window at the risk of breaking his neck."[17] First had gone Alençon, dangling like a monkey at the end of the rope, then Simier, his secretary "pale with fear," and last of all Cangé—a poor soul unfortunate enough to be Alençon's valet. There was little of gallantry about the huddled figures that clung to the rope and less of royalty—and the drama turned to pure farce when as Margot tried to burn the incriminating rope in her fireplace, the chimney caught on fire. For Margot detection was inevitable, and as Alençon threaded his way through the Latin Quarter to gain the road for Angers, the Queen of Navarre stood before her royal brother who threatened that she would pay with her life for this brother whose loyalty she had so much protested. Margot, however, was a bold-faced liar. She denied any part of the escapade, indeed any knowledge of it; before her blanket refusals, the King was helpless and more to save his face than her neck he pretended to believe her. Actually it made little difference who had contrived the escape; the fact remained: Alençon was gone again, gone into the countryside to do what mischief he could. Recalling the hornet's nest he had stirred the last time, the King acceded to his mother's suggestion that once again she pursue her elusive son.

Thus as Alençon galloped northward to Angers, his mother—now almost in her sixties—followed little more than a day behind him. She did not expect a filial welcome, and she received none. Instead, she was kept waiting in what lodgings she could find, while her son occupied the battlemented château at Angers. Some time later Alençon agreed to meet his mother at Bourgueil, a little town near Saumur; without protest he agreed to all she said, and this frightened her beyond any argument he might have proposed. She reminded him that if the rumors were true—and there was little reason to doubt them—that Guise and Spain had formed a coalition, then it was more essential than ever that the King and Alençon be reconciled. She begged him to have nothing to do with Flanders, and offered him in exchange a magnificent southern appanage as well as new marriage negotiations with England. He smiled, he agreed, he reassured her—and every word he uttered rang false to Catherine's trained ear. She returned to court in mid-March utterly disconsolate with her failure to reach her son. By the end of April Monsieur was levying troops for his Flanders' expedition as she knew he would.

CHAPTER V

The Quest for Peace: 1578–1581

If God does me the grace of doing what I wish, I hope that this
realm will benefit from my work and that it may remain peaceful.

Catherine de Medici

❦❦❦❦ As Alençon continued his journey toward war, his mother
prepared herself for one of those "journeys of pacification" in which
she spent much of her life. She proposed to travel south into Guyenne
to bring back to the King of Navarre his lawful wife Margot, and at
the same time to strengthen the peace which was being so ill kept.
On August 2, 1578, Catherine, with Margot at her side, began the
long trip from the King's residence at Olinville to the territory of
Navarre.

What she hoped to gain from this journey was simply stated in
a single imperative. "We must have peace." Everything must be
risked for this goal: comfort, wealth, pleasure—even honor, for Catherine realized, as her royal son did not, that France was on the brink
of disaster. The fertile land that had formerly produced crops of
wheat and grapes in such abundance lay parched and cracked. France
lay sterile, waiting for rain. Processions were formed, prayers of petition were chanted that God might remove his curse from the country
and its people. But the only answer was increasing waves of heat,
thunder, and lightning without the blessing of rain. The cost of food
soared, and the countryside was ravaged by brigands who took what
they wanted, killing or maiming the desperate farmers who attempted to interfere. Springs and streams dried up entirely; the Marne
moved sluggishly along its banks, and the Seine was lower than
anyone had ever seen it. The windmills stood quiet, as did the

hopeless people who knew not where to turn. They had cried to God and he had not heard them; perhaps they should cry again to their King. The King, however, had passed beyond the point where he could hear the cries of the poor. When his ministers remonstrated with him, he agreed to be less the gamester and more the king; he proposed some helpful legislation and concurred in the plans to keep down expenses. Yet no sooner had he agreed, then he lost himself in some new frivolity, forgetting the cause he had promised to espouse. When in their desperation, the poor rose up in Normandy, Brittany, Burgundy to protest the impossible burden of taxation which Henri continued to impose, the King still failed to realize his responsibility, blaming the insurrections on the Machiavellian policies of the Guises and their League. Generally so vacillating, Henri now became resolute, refusing to decrease taxes and murmuring, it was rumored, "I'll show them I'm a greater master still." Blind to the real causes of unrest, he failed to realize that he had far less to fear from the people, and even from the Guises, than from those close to him who turned his head with their flattery and ruined his kingdom with their advice.

No one recognized more clearly the danger into which the state had fallen than Navarre. Early in July he had written to Henri that despite the King's commands the peace was not being kept, that the very men who wielded the King's power wielded it for his own destruction. Knowing that a weak king was often a greater danger than a wicked one, he wrote as tactfully as he could, "Your authority must be strengthened, for if it is not, I will be governor in name and title only." Twelve days later, in a letter to Damville, he wrote of the absolute necessity to work in harmony for the cause of peace, warning the impetuous Damville that such a goal would take both time and patience. Thus he encouraged him "to do everything possible for the execution of the Edict and particularly to put an end to every raid, pillaging, or other hostility and to take as one's duty to return things to a state of peace. I beg you to consider that the establishment of a general peace within this kingdom after so many occasions of distrust, of violations of that peace, of massacres, is not the work of a single day and will not be achieved except by time and patience." Some time later he wrote, "I will spare nothing, not even my own person" and proved his pledge by selling his forests of Champrond, Chateauneuf, and Castelmoron, hoping that the money from the timber would keep his army going for a few months longer. He anticipated Catherine's journey with high hope, writing again to Damville that he was looking forward to this as a means of "ensuring peace." As for the return of Margot, this, too, he seemed to look forward to, writing of "the happiness it will give me to see my wife and have her here with me."[1]

To those who watched the French court from the sidelines, Navarre's hopes seemed far too sanguine, for they were inclined to see Catherine's journey as another clever ruse to draw Navarre away from the Huguenots and back to his Valois cousins. Paulet, who missed few of the nuances, wrote to England: "I think no man can tell what will come of this second marriage between the King of Navarre and his wife, in which nothing is omitted that may hinder the journey. . . . If she goes she will make sure of returning shortly, and her husband with her." They go, wrote another English agent, not for reconciliation but that "they may have the wolf by the ears."[2]

It was with distinct misgivings that the Huguenots learned the size of Catherine de Medici's entourage. A household of more than three hundred persons had set out for Guyenne: grooms and coachmen and ostlers of every degree, lackeys to ride beside the Queen of Navarre and to take care of the minor nobles, muleteers responsible for the litters, wagon men to lead the unwieldy wagons loaded with tableware and kitchen utensils, head cooks and second cooks, fruiterers, fishmongers, salad chefs and bakery chefs, carpenters and goldsmiths and haberdashers for both men and women, leather workers and spur makers, tailors and barbers. It was a movable city that made its slow descent into Guyenne. It was, however, more than a city of comfort and style; it was, as well, a city of the most astute politicians and the most sophisticated court beauties. Among her advisers the Queen Mother had chosen the finest to accompany her on this mission: La Mothe-Fénelon and Saint-Sulpice, former ambassadors to England and Spain; Paul de Foix, councilor of state, who had already carried out important diplomatic missions in London, Venice, Rome; Cardinal de Bourbon, uncle of Navarre; Guy du Faur de Pibrac, polished orator and diplomat; and Lanssac, her own confidential secretary who was responsible for the dozens of lengthy letters which went northward to her son during the twenty-two months which Catherine was to spend in the south. They were all men of impressive stature, and yet for courage and fortitude they had more than met their match in the Queen Mother. Now in her sixtieth year, stout almost to obesity, ridden with rheumatism, still she journeyed cheerfully over the rough roads, in her litter or on muleback with no

personal complaint so long as what she was doing would make
for the good of the King her son. Shortly after she had begun
her journey, she wrote to her trusted adviser, Pomponne de Bellièvre,
whom she had left at court to help the King: "I would infinitely
regret the trouble I have taken to come here if I were obliged
to return like a disabled ship, and if God does me the grace of
doing what I wish, I hope that this realm will benefit by my work
and that it may remain peaceful."[3]

On September 18 her party arrived at Bordeaux where a house
had been prepared for them overlooking the water and where the
city officials came to pay them homage. Only one thing went wrong
during her ten days at Bordeaux: Navarre had made no move in
her direction. Although he had written every encouragement to her,
once she found herself close to the seat of his power his interest
waned. She waited as long as she could and then finally wrote to
him: "It is not possible to come to any good decision unless I
have a chance to speak with you . . . come to dine or to stay the
night, whichever you please, just so long as I have an hour to talk
with you . . . and put an end to so many comings and goings."[4]
Still Navarre made no move even when Pibrac was sent to assure
him of safe conduct; he had once been badly treated at Bordeaux,
and "the wolf" for all his daring was not without a sense of danger.
His hesitation was part of his wile, and by it he eventually won
the trump card; for Catherine, anxious and impatient, willingly conceded to whatever rendezvous Navarre stipulated. At his suggestion,
they met at La Réole, not far from the town of St. Macaire. Here
on an unseasonably hot October day, the two queens dismounted
and were greeted by Navarre who was accompanied by an impressive
escort. At last, after more than two years of separation, Margot
again met her husband. Now in his twenty-sixth year, he was no longer
the light gallant; he had become a soldier, a king, and what he had
always been destined to be: a leader of men. The easy charm was
still there, but now it was but a small part of the man. His ability
to attract, to be gracious and amusing was his as before, and Catherine
could write in all honesty to her son of the "gracious welcome"
accorded her by the King of Navarre.

The Queen Mother was, in general, pleased with this first meeting,
and she wrote that night to the King that she had every reason
to hope that "my journey will be of help to you." The most immediate
obstacle to peace was the enmity between Navarre and Biron who

had been named by the King governor of Guyenne. Biron was essentially a military man; admired by his soldiers for his courage and skill, he was never a popular man outside the camp. He was arrogant and sometimes brutal, with an intelligence too blunt to perceive the line of diplomatic distinctions. It was, however, for these very qualities that he had been made governor of Guyenne which he held with stubborn force against the claims of Navarre. Navarre openly accused him of holding his title unlawfully and of stirring up unrest throughout the province; but nothing budged Biron. Although Charles IX had called him his "dear and well beloved lord," Catherine had little love for him; yet she preferred his friendship to his enmity and saw that he had his usefulness in keeping Navarre in check.

On one issue Biron and the Queen Mother agreed: Navarre must be won to their side. Catherine's determination was reinforced when Biron told her that he had reason to believe that Navarre had already been approached by Philip II with overtures of great promise if he would join Spain against the interests of France. Catherine winced at the thought, and enlisted Margot's charm to beguile Navarre into accepting Biron as an ally rather than an opponent; yet when some days later Biron appeared, all hope of friendship was swallowed up by the implacable enmity between the two opposing leaders. Italian rhetoric and French charm proved powerless against the unleashed anger of the two men. Catherine was, as she later confessed to her son, exhausted by the violence of the scene and by her terror of what the end might be for in their fury the two men were soon facing each other with drawn swords. For a moment she feared that the swords would find their mark and that she would soon have either a dead Navarre or a dead Biron at her feet. Either would have made her own position intolerable and would have ended any hope of peace. But the swords had been sheathed and the two leaders had parted at least in peace if not in friendship. It was with a sense of deep relief at this narrow escape that she wrote her son describing the scene: "Biron found the King of Navarre in my room, who spoke to him more roughly than your sister and I had expected because of what had taken place between them. The Marshal was very angry. I assure you I did not know what to do to straighten matters out; but the good offices of your sister and the Cardinal de Bourbon and the great pains I myself took with both of them succeeded in restoring their relations after a fashion."[5]

Margot, whose relationship with her mother had often been a stormy one, now found herself in good favor as she took her "good offices" seriously and did all she could to mend the rift between Navarre and the court party. It was apparently a sincere effort on Margot's part, for sometime during those months she wrote a lengthy letter to her confidante, the Duchesse d'Uzès, expressing her desire to serve her brother in the cause of peace: "I am determined to do everything in my power for him," she avowed, "in whatever will not be prejudicial to the greatness and maintenance of my husband . . . in order to persuade him [Navarre] always toward peace and to bring him to conform himself to the will of the King . . . in whatever will be for the peace and tranquillity of the state. You must believe that I will do this and that there is nothing dearer to me than this; for I would prefer death to war."[6]

Although little of a practical nature was accomplished in the first meeting between Navarre and his mother-in-law, it ended with a promise for a longer conference to be held at the end of October on L'Isle-Jourdain where the Articles of Peace would be studied by councilors appointed from both sides. Meanwhile the Queen Mother intended to continue her journeys, bringing, she hoped, the King's blessing of peace to the cities of the south. As she traveled down the east bank of the Garonne, the cities of Marmande, Agen, Toulouse all received her with elaborate ceremonies. Although it was largely through the heavy hand of the Catholic Biron that the ceremonies were initiated, Catherine, so set upon the unity of her son's kingdom, preferred to believe that France was already reaping the blessing of unity and peace. When on October 12 Margot made her solemn entrance into Agen, riding in regal splendor under a canopy of white satin down streets hung with tapestries, and with the last fall flowers strewn at her feet, the Queen Mother tasted for a moment the cup of joy. And when later in the month she gathered together in the episcopal palace the Catholic aristocracy of Guyenne for one of those extravagant receptions by which she thought to uphold the glory of the Valois, she hoped the cup might be hers forever.

It was, however, but a fleeting hope, for even as the people paid homage to the wife of the Béarnais, the Béarnais himself again remained at a distance. The conference planned for L'Isle-Jourdain was indefinitely delayed as Navarre, always skillful with excuses, protested that it was the Huguenot delegates and not he himself who postponed the meeting, that even as he wrote he was setting out, that were it not for the many small items of business which demanded his presence he would already be at Catherine's side. But Catherine who knew something of the machinery of diplomacy had little difficulty in discerning the core of truth: Navarre remained distrustful. Despite her promises, her affectionate phrases ("my dear son," "my good son," her letters called him) Navarre feared a trap. He had learned the lesson of skepticism well during those four years he had spent at the Valois court. He had learned to doubt Valois promises and Valois endearments. No man knew better the full implications of Catherine's phrase, "I use every man as he can serve me." Life and honor were expendables in Catherine's code, provided only that her own son's life and honor remained protected. This was a truth in which Navarre had been painfully tutored; he understood it and in his way he respected it. Had his cousin who sat so restlessly upon the throne of France understood it half so well, he might have entrusted his own weakness to his mother's strength; but the day for such hope was past.

Thus throughout October Navarre hedged and procrastinated, while Catherine, restive, remained in the safety of Catholic Toulouse. The English agent, impressed by the dexterity with which the young Prince managed to gain the whip hand wrote, "The Queen Mother and all her old and grave counselors are at the end of their Latin . . . finding him to be furthest out of their danger when they think he is already in their snare."[7] Saint Michael's Summer was long past, the last of the crops had been harvested, and the vines drooped with the first frost. Still Catherine waited for Navarre to fulfill his promise. With the Feast of All Saints the autumn sun grew cold and the dampness of winter settled into the stone walls of the palace. L'Isle-Jourdain, a fairyland of gardens and green meadows in summer, had little to recommend it when, finally, believing Navarre's latest fervent avowal, Catherine journeyed to meet him there in the second week of November. For twelve days she waited while messengers rode to and fro; but Navarre still hesitated. It was hard to believe that this was the land which Navarre had called an "earthly paradise," for now the great shade trees were bare, the waters of the Vienne cold and sullen, and jagged rocks rose menacingly above the tide. Catherine with her tendency to be more impressed by the works of man than those of God, longed for the well-ordered domesticities of the Louvre. What good could come to her in this place, she must have wondered as she waited on, and indeed no good did come, for "the Wolf" waited cautiously beyond the circle of what he feared might be a trap.

After the first three impatient days of waiting, she had written to the King: "I am furious and annoyed as well at having been here for three days without hearing any news from my son, the King of Navarre, nor from Fénelon whom I sent to hurry him up. I have just sent another messenger. . . . I hear he is sleeping at Mauveisin in order to be here for dinner tomorrow. If that is so, I hope that in a few days we shall know their real intentions." But on November 11, Fénelon returned alone with the exasperating message that Navarre was "coming." By November 13 he had still not arrived, and in her letter to her son the Queen Mother made one of those rare references to her own physical inconvenience, writing of "the suffering I have endured in taking such a long journey in such a bad season," adding, "if he had any consideration for my person, he would act very differently." When the following day not Navarre but his messenger Guitry appeared with the suggestion that they put off entirely their proposed meeting at L'Isle-Jourdain and arrange instead for an interview at Pamiers, Catherine reached the end of her patience. "I was angry," she wrote to her son, explaining that she considered Navarre's conduct tantamount to insolence. What does he take me for, she continued, "showing no respect for me," but suggesting that she go "to a city in the mountains with a climate so bad that there is still snow there in June; and bad as all that is, the roads between here and there are worse." Her interview with this latest messenger was a stormy one: when she suggested Condom as a meeting place, he hesitated; when she suggested Nérac, he pointed out the difficulties of crossing the Garonne in winter. In short, he placed an obstacle before each of her suggestions, and it took all her self-control not to lash out in anger. Schooled so long in patience, she now put her virtue to good use, writing with some satisfaction to her son, "Through it all I have tried to act gently and kindly . . . knowing that this would be what you would want."[8] When finally on November 19 she left the fortified town of L'Isle-Jourdain, it was with another promise wrung from Navarre for a meeting to take place during December at the Huguenot town of Nérac.

Catherine had been gone from home for over four months and she had little to show for it—promises and shadows of promises, little more. Fearful lest her son think she dozed in his service, she wrote placatingly, "Hour by hour I try to hasten things," "we do not lose any time," "I have missed no opportunity." But Catherine's sense of urgency found no match in her son. He had his prayers, his vigils, his *mignons*, and his pleasures and for long stretches of time this was enough. The world beyond, which he could never cope with, he had learned to obliterate. In reply to the long and sometimes daily letters of his mother, he contented himself with silence or a dilatory note. Above and beyond the personal grief this brought Catherine was the larger grief that by such conduct he impaired his own authority. "Please let me hear from you more often," she pleaded; "I suffer very much when I do not hear from you for fifteen days. This is very prejudicial to your own interests."[9]

As her son's indolence increased, Catherine's activity increased accordingly. Since her projected meeting with Navarre and his Huguenot delegates would not take place until December, she decided to spend the interim visiting additional cities in the south. Thus her "wandering city" moved eastward to Auch in the heart of the Gascon countryside. On November 20 she made a splendid entrance in a great carriage drawn slowly through the streets to the door of the church of Sainte-Marie where she alighted to enter the church for a solemn *Te Deum*. The days following, Margot arrived, gracious and smiling in her royal litter of black velvet; and on Saturday Navarre himself appeared, ostensibly to see his wife whose health had been a matter of concern and to plan the entertainment with which he would fill the days which the royal party would spend at Auch.

On December 15 the major event of the month took place: Margot made her formal entrance into Nérac. Seated on a white palfrey between her husband and his sister Catherine, she was her most captivating self. Feeling herself admired, she was in her turn lavish with praise for the spectacle that had been arranged. The native poet Du Bartas had been asked for an appropriate tribute and he had composed trilingual verses in Latin, French, and Gascon for the occasion. If Margot was taken aback by the unfamiliar sounds of the Gascon dialect, she did not show it but listened with eager joy as young Mademoiselle Sauvage recited her praises:

O Blackbird, Nightingale, . . .
Greet with a sweet song the most beautiful creature
in the world.[10]

Margot was never averse to being called "the most beautiful creature in the world," even when such praise was couched in the rude patois of Gascony. With a spontaneous gesture she removed her richly embroidered scarf and put it in the hands of the young speaker. It was a gesture typical of Margot—impulsive, gracious, generous; it was not far from the gestures of her royal brother which won him friends even as it lost him France.

The feast which followed was as sumptuous as Navarre's resources could make it. For days wagons had rumbled across the western drawbridge bringing dozens of casks of choice white wines and claret and a tun or more of the native wine for the servants. Brace after brace of quail and pheasant were plucked and hung in the huge kitchen. Fish were brought in great loads from the mountain streams, and thrushes were forced to sacrifice their song to please the delicacy of royal palates. Even Margot was satisfied, and Saracini wrote to the Grand Duke at Florence of the "true and reciprocal love" which she was showing at last to her royal husband. From the sidelines it seemed that the Queen Mother's plans were tending to a happy conclusion and Saracini continued to express his satisfaction for the "great reverence" which the Huguenots were showing in their full observance of the ceremonial prescribed for royal persons. Yet some among them did not hesitate to show their contempt for the ungodly rounds of merriment in which the days were spent; and at least one of them wrote that the time was spent doing nothing but laughing, dancing, and tilting at the ring. If Navarre would not go to Paris then he was determined to bring Paris to Navarre, and for a while the staid streets of Nérac were noisy with gaiety. Candles burned far into the night in the ball room of the château and a music far different from that of the Protestant psalms rose and fell in the winter air. Margot, always happiest when she glittered most, found Nérac not a bad second to the Louvre. As for Catherine, who had learned that a ball can sometimes do as well as a conference, she watched contentedly while she made her final plans for the convocation now set for mid-December.

If, however, Navarre had found a way of pleasing Margot at last, it was not without sacrificing something of the honor he had been at such pains to reestablish among the Reformers. A leader of men, not a leader of dances, was the role for which they had cast him, and his present conduct was not entirely appropriate. When during a ball at Agen, the candles were suddenly snuffed out by the young gallants and "deeds of dishonor" took place in the darkened room, Huguenot sensibilities were shocked. That the sun rose upon fewer maids might be a quip among the gallants, but to the grave ministers of Nérac it was a scandal that stained the honor of their King. The lavish display, the madcap bear hunts and boar hunts in which the Béarnais risked life and limb, were all sources of reproach. Suspicion of the Queen Mother and her purposes increased, and men who believed that Navarre could never be worsted in a battle feared that he might be vanquished at a ball. They feared the skillful meshes of the Florentine without realizing that their King, for all his bonhomie, had himself a certain skill in laying traps.

Once again the conferences were postponed, and Catherine spent the time between Christmas and Candlemas Day in the old abbey of Paravis. On February 2 she returned, journeying the three leagues along the windy banks of the Garonne into Nérac for the opening of the conferences on February 3. Many of Catherine's household had warned her of the dangers of holding the talks in a Huguenot stronghold, but the Queen Mother unwilling to delay longer, only reiterated her resolution. She had suffered much during the last six months. Her health had been poor during the winter and shortly before her return to Nérac she had written to a friend, apologizing that the letter could not be in her own hand, but explaining that her arm was so badly swollen and inflamed that she could not use it. There was a deeper suffering, however, than that of physical discomfort and that was the recognition that there were many on both sides, as she herself wrote, who wished to do nothing but stir up trouble; but, she concluded with her remarkable resiliency, "as always I try to rise above all that."[11]

The day following Catherine's arrival, the formal sessions of the conferences began. Writing to her son she commented: Yesterday I saw the deputies . . . they all look like Huguenot ministers."[12] They presented a formidable array, these grave men with their "cast-iron countenances" armed with cahiers containing their "rights" and "a long list of their grievances." But if Catherine was intimidated, she did not show it. Her speech to the assembly was "relevant and lively," and Damville's secretary, who took full notes of the meetings, noted that her French was better than many had expected.

The tone of the conferences was somewhat different from any that had preceded them. Now the questions were not being argued on grounds of dogma but on the practical problem of political rights. Catherine was determined as far as possible to hold to the articles of the Peace of Bergerac, while the Huguenots a return to the more favorable Treaty of Monsieur. They were particularly concerned that they have sufficient towns of surety and that the mixed tribunals composed of Catholics and Protestants be maintained. Always, of course, they continued their demands for full liberty of worship. For three weeks the debates continued in full heat with Catherine's vitality pushing the delegates to the boundaries of endurance. Mass was said each morning by the Cardinal de Bourbon; when the poor man overslept, it was the Queen Mother who routed him no matter how late the conferences had continued the night before. From Mass, she led her party to the conference table, often keeping them without their dinner until almost noon. It was often midnight when she called a halt to the discussions. Although some of the delegates fell ill with fatigue, Catherine's energies seemed only to increase.

Finally on February 28, after twenty-five days of discussion, the Articles of Nérac were signed by Catherine de Medici and Henri de Navarre and were sent on to the King for his ratification. The Queen Mother had held the line as best she could. She had reduced the towns of surety to fourteen and insisted that the Reformed Religion could be practiced only in certain places. Yet she conceded enough to satisfy at least for a time "those grave ministers" whose vision was so different from her own.

Two months later Catherine bade farewell to Margot and Navarre, and the leavetaking gave her great satisfaction, for Margot assured her that she would never again leave her husband. She was happy, too, that Margot seemed disconsolate at her mother's departure, for nothing gave Catherine greater joy than the thought that her children needed her. She wrote to Henri of her departure, telling him that Margot "wept with sadness"—although Margot herself in describing the scene says nothing of such an emotion. The following day Navarre joined her at the monastery of La Prouille to thank her, to recommend himself to the King, to wish her God speed. There in front of the crowd that had assembled he bid her goodbye, saw her safely into her carriage, and then remounting, rode gallantly at her side for "three French leagues." Although he had refused to journey with her to Paris, they had nevertheless come to terms on many issues, and her estimate of Navarre had changed despite his annoying tendency to "let time cool." Even if he continued to mistrust her, she was willing to trust to his good will; thus she wrote to her son shortly after Navarre had left her, "He spoke with complete sincerity or else I am the most mistaken woman in the world."[18] She had come for peace and friendship and she was satisfied that she had not come in vain.

As the Queen Mother journeyed eastward toward Carcassonne, Navarre and his wife turned toward Pau, capital of Béarn and birthplace of Navarre. They stopped first at Coarraze, the little town not far from Pau where the Béarnais had spent part of his childhood. After dinner they went on to Pau where they made their solemn entrance in mid-afternoon of May 24. The inhabitants felt a special bond with Navarre for this was not only his birthplace but it had been the city of Jeanne d'Albret whom they held in veneration. Although Pau was not a gay or expansive town, no care or expense was spared to make this solemn entrance a magnificent ceremony. The guildsmen of the city, elaborately dressed, came in a body to meet their King and a company of soldiers in full ceremonials acted as their escort. They entered the east gate, beneath the great city bell, then traveled down the main avenue which was hung on every side with rich taffeta tapestries worked predominantly in green. Here before the dark walls of the château, the soldiers honored the King and Queen with a ceremonial salute, their white plumes catching the breeze which swept down from the mountains. Behind the château rose the Pyrenees, so dearly beloved by the Béarnais, with their purple shadows, still capped with snow even in late May.

Nothing was omitted to make Margot feel at home, but from the beginning she felt alien at Pau. She who loved laughter and wit found little of it here. Jeanne d'Albret was still alive here, casting her shadow over the frivolities of the Valois Princess of whom she had never approved. No number of carefully wrought tapestries, no amount of decoration, no number of elaborately furnished rooms could ever make Margot feel at home within the grim walls of the royal château. Jeanne d'Albret was still here—in her own austere room, in the great room with its enormous fireplaces in which she had given birth to Navarre in the cold of a December night. Wherever Margot walked, the forbidding presence of her mother-in-law was before her. She was too much her mother's child to experience her husband's exhilaration at seeing the Pyrenees rising in the distance. She had been able to make a little Louvre out of the château at Nérac but here she never could. Here there was nothing of the light, graceful galleries of the Renaissance; another spirit ruled at Pau: the spirit of reform, of austerity, of control. It was less a palace than a citadel with its narrow windows and high, battlemented towers. As for the people, they had a spirit which could never be hers.

Ever since the days of Jeanne d'Albret, Catholicism had been outlawed in Pau, and even Navarre's wife was forced to practice her religion clandestinely. She was permitted to hear Mass only in a small chapel, which she explained in her *Mémoires,* was but "three or four feet in length and so narrow that it could scarcely hold seven or eight persons."[14] During the time of the service, the draw-bridge was raised so that those from the town might not attend. When on Pentecost Margot invited some Catholics to participate in the Whitsunday service, Navarre's secretary, the overzealous Le Pin, came with his guard and arrested them all. The quarrel that followed was violent, and although Navarre assured his wife that he was on her side, yet Margot knew that the spirit of Pau had worsted her; and when some weeks later she left to accompany Navarre to Montauban, she vowed that she would never return to "that little Geneva," as she styled it.

While attendance at a Huguenot synod was not quite what Margot would have chosen for a holiday, it was at least no worse than being confined at Pau. If she was fearful that she might have lost some of her husband's affection during their stay at Pau, she was now able to recapture it in full measure, for Henri fell ill on the way to Montauban and for seventeen days Margot was his nurse, assuaging the violent headaches and high fever that racked him. Margot, with her family talent for role-playing, now became an unparalleled nurse, sitting at her husband's bedside during the long night hours and, as her *Mémoires* carefully note, snatching only a few hours sleep whenever she could. By the end of July the synod was over and by early September Margot and her ladies were again established in Nérac where of all the cities of the south she felt most at home.

By its very location the château at Nérac had a graceful charm, a charm augmented by the careful architecture of several generations. Built on the left bank of the Baïse, it formed a quadrangle flanked by six battlemented towers which were later razed to make way for the more pacific style of the Renaissance. Of the wings, it was the northern one, built less than a hundred years before by Alain d'Albret, which most charmed Margot. It had about it much of the air of the Italian Renaissance; it was light and graceful with a charming Italian loggia whose columns with their striped shafts and ornamented chapters spoke more of the Valois than of the Béarnais. Beyond the château itself stretched the royal gardens with their fountains and orangeries and groves of laurel. A wooden bridge joined the garden to the right bank of the river whose gray-green water moved imperceptibly between its fertile banks. There was an aura of romance about the château with its shaded groves, its rustic park and quiet water. It was easy to forget the vestiges of war—the towers and drawbridges—and to imagine all the world at peace, lulled by the tranquil beauty of river and woods. There were, as Margot pointed out, many games played at Nérac—hunts, tilting at the ring, tennis, skittles—but chief of all was the game of love. In such a game Margot was always a willing participant and, she soon discovered, so was her husband. It was, however, a bit of a surprise to find the thin, angular sister of the King, with her shy manner and congenital limp, playing along with the others with the Huguenot Turenne as her chief partner.

Once Navarre realized how much Margot enjoyed Nérac, he did all he could to embellish it. Tapestries were brought from Pau to ornament the walls, Venetian glass ware was ordered, ornately decorated with mother-of-pearl and gold, peerless mirrors with frames of ebony were hung in strategic places, new chests, intricately carved, were ordered from Spain and Italy. Even the cost of a silver urinal is found among the household expenses. New utensils were bought for the kitchen, huge vessels for boiling and baking, roasting pans and turnspits to cook the enormous quantities of food Navarre ordered for his court. The expense account for a single Friday suggests that even on days of penance no one went hungry at Nérac: 150 gudgeons, 100 frogs, 300 oysters, 500 flounders, 19 codfish, 12 mackerel, a dozen shad—and for those who might not favor fish, 700 eggs were on hand. Navarre who had been proverbially careless about his clothes, suddenly spent money lavishly on his own wardrobe. His personal expense account for 1579 lists doublets of silk and satin, yellow satin breeches, shirts of Holland linen, scarlet riding cloaks, and elegant Spanish hats. Even gold for fixing the King's teeth was carefully noted. He was no longer the careless and sometimes ill-washed leader of men, but the elegantly dressed lover of women, as he rode out in his doublet of tan velvet, his embroidered green breeches, his collar trimmed with imported Moroccan leather and his wide felt hat.

If Henri dressed well, he was but a shadow of his queen, for he bestowed on her presents far beyond his means: an emerald ring, a collar of twelve hundred seed pearls, four gold rings embellished with diamonds, expensive orange velvet for her caps, plumes from a bird of paradise, and soft leather gloves, delicately perfumed and trimmed with amber. For a little while Margot cherished the illusion that perhaps she had not been married to a mountain boy bred on goats' milk and garlic, but to a true European prince. She was twenty-five, confident, beautiful, and experienced in both love and diplomacy—two games she dearly loved. Since she could not be at the Louvre, she determined to make a little Louvre out of the court of Nérac. She hired musicians: two lute players, six violinists, and a music master to train her chapel singers. For Henri who "liked to laugh" she engaged one Nicolas Léon, who was good at playing the broad farces which Henri so much enjoyed. Du Bartas was called upon to contribute verses in honor of the royal couple and responded by titling Margot "the ornament of France," comparing her in his poetic extravagance to the biblical Judith who had merited the appellations "the glory of Jerusalem, the joy of Israel, the honor of our people."[15] When native talent grew thin, troops of Italian players were brought in to add a cosmopolitan note to the court of the Béarnais.

Meanwhile Margot continued to dazzle the court by both her manner and her dress. Realizing that her lovely white neck was one of her chief attractions, she managed to show as much of it as she dared; proud, too, of her luminous black eyes, she rarely made use of the custom of the mask. She was also proud of her abundant black hair which she curled and fanned until it sat high upon her head, sparkling as it caught the light of the candles. It was, no doubt, with Marguerite in mind that the next Huguenot synod held in La Rochelle the following year fulminated not only against moral laxity in general but against the paints, the tassles and hoops and open bosoms which did nothing but sap the virtue of both sexes. D'Aubigné, that staunch Huguenot soldier, wrote in retrospect of this court at Nérac: "Such luxury draws vice as heat draws serpents. Both spirits and arms have grown rusty while the Queen of Navarre has been there. She taught our King her husband that a cavalier lacks spirit unless he is in love."[16] D'Aubigné's statement was, unfortunately, a condemnation of Navarre as well as of his wife.

The condemnation meant little to Margot, however, who wrote later, "Our court was so brilliant that we had no cause to regret our absence from the court of France. Here there was the King's sister and I who between us had a good number of ladies-in-waiting, while the King my husband was surrounded by a fine troop of lords as handsome as the most gallant I have ever seen at court; I could have nothing against them except that they were Huguenots."[17] If Margot felt she could be indifferent about the complaints of the Huguenots, Navarre realized that he could not afford to offend them. Despite the Articles of Nérac, peace had not come to France. He had no sooner taken his leave of the Queen Mother than he was forced to write a series of letters to Henri III, all with the same message: the terms of the treaty have not been kept; even those towns promised as security had had their walls razed, their houses destroyed, their citizens killed. When will justice be done and those responsible for setting France afire be given their merited reward? Most painful of all is the fact that he knows that the King's ears have been filled with "noise and false reports."[18]

In the midst of the darkness, however, one element of light emerged: Damville, who, following the Estates of Blois in 1576, had been maneuvered into throwing in his fortunes with the royal party, was beginning to recognize the folly of his move. It was apparent to him almost from the start that the King was using him for his own purposes, that even while he coerced him with gifts and promises of gifts he never actually trusted him. When in April of the preceding year, his eldest brother died of apoplexy while visiting the Louvre, Damville became the head of the large and powerful Montmorency family. Now more than before, the weight of his influence would be enough to tip the scale. As he watched the Huguenots' hopes betrayed again and again by the King's cupidity or his passive acquiescence to the advice of his self-interested councilors, he began to reexamine his own position. There was much about the Huguenot cause which was alien to him and many of their leaders whom he could never trust, yet he recognized that his sympathies were with them rather than with the conservative Catholics of the court. For a time he had been lulled by royal favor, but the warrior in him was beginning to reawaken at the sight of the brutality and injustice which he saw on every side. "Robbery and brigandage are the order of the day, all under the cloak of religion," he had written to Navarre not long after the Queen Mother's departure. Once again the conviction that all Frenchmen must be permitted liberty of conscience and of worship took hold of Damville and in December 1579 he agreed to meet with Navarre in the hilly town of Mazères, not far from Tarbes. By the end of the conference, the "docile servant," as Catherine had called him the year before, had begun to think seriously of allying himself with Henri de Navarre.

Navarre could well use the influence and power that Damville would bring to his cause, for by the beginning of 1580 it had become increasingly apparent that the Articles of Nérac were but paper promises and that in actual fact France was already at war. The issue which was forcing them into open conflict was that the time had expired for turning over the towns of security which had been conceded to them at Nérac. Although the King was within his legal rights in demanding that these places be surrendered, yet in actuality such surrender was tantamount to extinction for the Huguenots unless some provision of freedom of worship was made. Henri himself might have agreed to some adjustment since he realized that neither side was in a position to engage in another war, but the forces of the Guise were too strong for him and Navarre's pleas went unheeded. Added to Navarre's solicitude for the Huguenot party was his increasing concern over his own life, for twice during these months attempts were made to assassinate him, once by an ambuscade as he rode to Nérac and again by poison in the house of a lord he had promised to visit. In both cases he had been advised in time, but now his anger was unleashed. If this continues, he warned, he might be driven to "extreme remedies," not against the person of the King but against "those who under the cloak of the King's authority do all they can to destroy us."[19]

By mid-April he had sent a summary of grievances to the King, begging some redress and yet careful not to blame Henri but only those who by their deeds proved themselves enemies of them both.

When that same month he issued a "Declaration and Proclamation," indicating that no one could expect the Huguenots to be bound by a "peace which is scorned and broken by the other side," it was Catherine and not the King who replied. "I cannot believe that you want to ruin this kingdom as well as your own, yet this is what it will mean if war breaks out again," cautioned the Queen Mother, and continued, "What occasion has the King given you to do this. . . . He asks only that you observe what you have already sworn to." She concluded with a touch of the maternalism which was one of her favorite weapons: "I beg you to believe me and you will see what a difference there is between the counsels of a mother who loves you and those who do not. . . ."[20] To Navarre, however, such counsel was but empty words, and the time for words had passed.

Thus was begun the conflict which later historians graced with the amorous if meaningless title, "The Lovers' War." Again Navarre wrote bitterly to the King reviewing the circumstances under which he had been forced to take up arms, describing "the misery to which we have been reduced through the fault of your ministers and officers," and listing the towns taken, the inhabitants massacred, and the women raped, concluding that throughout he had attempted to keep the peace, for "I have cherished your good grace more than my own life."[21]

Uncertain of Damville's position, anxious about the help that Condé was attempting to get through Casimir of Bavaria, Navarre wrote a final plea to the Earl of Sussex, hoping to win Elizabeth's ear through his intercession. "Were I to tell you of the murders, massacres, assassinations, taking of towns, etc. . . . the list would be too long," he wrote in a letter which was to prepare England for word of renewed war. "For two months the papists have been in arms in Languedoc, especially Marshal Biron, so that were it not for our extraordinary patience we would be in arms long before this."[22]

Navarre, always opposed to war, deeply regretted that the idyllic life at Nérac should be invaded by conflict. In a letter addressed to Margot in early April he apologized that war and not peace should be his gift to her, adding, "It is a profound regret to me that in place of the happiness I wish to give you, things turn out just the opposite."[23] But although Margot loved the leisure and luxury of her life at Nérac, she was sufficiently an intrigante to be pleasantly stirred by the excitement of war—especially when Nérac was declared to be neutral territory. She liked to think that she had married a brave soldier, a man with a quick sword arm, one of those impetuous lords of the south who liked danger as much as they liked their strong wine. To be the wife of a hero was, to Margot, more exhilarating than to be the wife of a peaceful monarch. Thus, when the people of the south cheered for Navarre when he captured the all but impregnable town of Cahors, Margot, too, was quick to rejoice at his exploits, commenting, "In the capture of Cahors my husband showed himself . . . not only a prince of renown but a resourceful and daring captain."[24]

It was not because Cahors was a great city that its capture became a legend, but because the deed was surrounded with a kind of derring-do. Foot by foot the Béarnais scaled the rocky walls which protected the city and gained entry with part of his force only to find the citizens armed to the teeth and prepared to fight him step for step. For four days the struggle continued, for, as he wrote to his colleague Scorbiac, "we had to conquer the rest foot by foot, barricade by barricade." When on May 31 he had won the city, he was tired unto death, but with a consideration which was later to be one of his most lauded traits, he took time to write to the wife of one of his captains: "Although I am still covered with blood and powder, I will not undress until I tell you of our good news and send you word of your husband who is safe and sound."[25]

The taking of Cahors was a victory, and Henri de Navarre was sorely in need of victory. Since the rich equipage bearing Catherine and Margot had traveled into the south, since the days when the zealous Huguenots leaders had watched their prince trotting on horseback beside the royal litter, their old suspicions had revived. They recalled that although this Navarre was son of good Queen Jehanne, yet he was as well the son of that vacillating Bourbon, Antoine de Vendôme, who had slipped from faith to faith with the ease of a salamander, courting favor wherever it was to be found. Perhaps too much of his father's blood ran in the veins of this young Prince who smiled so easily and talked so well, who won men by the simple charm of his camaraderie. Was he to be trusted? They scarcely knew, as they watched the wagons making their way to Nérac piled high with silks and imported linens, watched the servants unload casks of wine, dozens of pheasants and trout, peaches and plums. Was he their man or a Valois man, they asked, as their eyes followed the graceful movements of the Queen, her blond wig—for blond wigs were in fashion—which covered her own black hair, and noted with moral indignation her bared throat, her painted face. Jezebel, murmured some; daughter of Jezebel, murmured others who had heard rumors of how Catherine de Medici managed her court. Even the kindest among the Huguenots looked at Navarre with a kind of pity mingled with fear. When would he awaken, this prince of pleasure, whose ears, so long attuned to the music of the viol, might not hear the drum of war should it beat? With Cahors all that changed. Seeing him bloody and torn, fighting on horseback and on foot, placing himself always in the vanguard so that his men would have a leader to follow, they knew that this was in truth the son of Jehanne the good, in whose veins ran the blood of Navarre and on whose heart was stamped the symbol of the New Religion.

In Paris, however, the taking of Cahors sounded a very different melody. It was one more cause for alarm in a court where the Florentine agent, Renieri, wrote that all was in *gran discordia*. By mid-summer it had become obvious to both sides that the war could not continue and Navarre, losing town after town to the superior forces of the King, knew that the sooner peace was made the better bargain he would be able to drive. Finally on November 28, 1580, a treaty was signed at La Fleix which ended the short but turbulent Lovers' War. Yet if the Treaty of La Fleix brought peace to Navarre and his enemies, it succeeded in stirring up enmity among the men whom he had counted as his friends. Condé, who from the beginning had shown his displeasure at the war—largely perhaps because Navarre's decision had been taken without consulting him—now showed himself equally opposed to the peace. During the talks at La Fleix, Condé remained in the Huguenot stronghold of Nîmes trying to arouse the Protestants of Languedoc, Provence, Dauphiny against accepting another paper peace, promising that if they continued their fight that he would bring German troops to assist them.

There had always existed a basic enmity between Navarre and Condé and the latter's arrogant refusal to accept the peace came as a disappointment rather than a surprise. There was, however, disapproval from other quarters which Navarre found more serious. La Rochelle and Geneva, always more inclined to the bellicose policies of Condé rather than to the conciliations of Navarre, showed themselves but ill-pleased by the Articles of La Fleix. Soon after the peace was signed, a letter came out of Geneva which questioned Navarre on the advisability of a peace which gave more to the

Catholics than to the Huguenots. Its author was his mother's devoted
friend and spirtual counselor, Theodore Beza, whose Calvinistic position Navarre never wholly espoused. Navarre's answer, written at the
end of November, was a long letter of explanation and justification.
He attempted to explain the conditions under which the war had
been undertaken and to explain that the peace, while not ideal,
was far better than a state of continued war. "This peace," he
wrote, "is not to our disadvantage. It ought to be read and welcomed
by all for the reestablishment of our religion. . . . I beg you to
prepare people to receive it and to write about it to those who are
essential to its acceptance, especially my cousin Condé and Duc
Casimir, so that our union among ourselves may be strengthened—
for this is the most essential element for our conservation—and that
we may thus be led to serve God and to rebuild on our old
ruins."[26]

When a few months later he received a further letter from Beza,
this time questioning his personal life, his apologia was more difficult
to handle. The morality of John Calvin would never be his; he
could not deny his follies, his gambling, his flagrant love affairs. He
was well aware that in the eyes of Beza, as in those of many of
the reformers, he seemed a less zealous Huguenot than his cousin
Condé. It might have been possible for him to endure such judgment
if it involved no more than a personal slight; but he recognized that
such judgment would inevitably weaken his leadership of the Huguenot
party and consequently weaken the party itself. Of all the responses
possible to him, he astutely chose the one which would most quickly
reinstate him in Beza's good graces; he wrote as a penitent son,
willingly chastised by the hand of a wise father. "Please continue
your warnings to me just as though you were my father," he wrote.
"I beg you to tell me every time, speaking to me freely and can-
didly. If I do not profit as I should from your holy admonitions,
at least you must believe that I do not mean to reject them."[27]

Alençon, who had acted as mediator in the Peace of La Fleix,
continued to be a further subject of dissension, for the Huguenots
were suspicious of Navarre's continued friendship with him. Following
the peace, Alençon had stayed on in the south, happy to be in
the company of his sister who, for one reason or another, continued
her enthusiasm for his dreams and schemes. He enjoyed, too, the
sense of success that came with seeing himself the pivot between
Navarre and the King—a position he interpreted, as always, as more

important than it actually was. In January Navarre waited to bring Monsieur to Nérac where he rejoiced at the chance to "feast him in his own house." Throughout the winter months their amity continued and it was not until March that Alençon began his preparations for returning to court. Rumors had long been abroad that Navarre would return to Paris in company with Monsieur; it was a rumor that Navarre found to his advantage to keep alive, since nothing flattered the Queen Mother more than the thought that she had somehow allayed her wary son-in-law's suspicions of the court. But, as in the past, when the moment for departure approached, Navarre bid his guest Godspeed while he "regretfully" stayed behind to tend to his lands.

Navarre was at this time hardly in a position to leave the south, for despite the peace things were still in turmoil. Although the Articles of La Fleix had been far from a Huguenot victory, they had brought two decided assets in their wake: Biron, so long a thorn in the side of the Huguenots, had been removed from his office of governor of Guyenne and been replaced by Navarre's friend Matignon; Damville had openly broken with the King and declared himself on the side of Navarre. On the debit side of the ledger was Condé who continued to decry the peace and to influence the provinces of Languedoc and Dauphiny to refuse to accept it. Throughout the winter Navarre continued to send emissaries to explain the peace terms and to urge the provinces to accept them, but it was not until April that he could write to the King that there was quiet at last in the turbulent provinces of the southeast. Even so, the peace was at best tenuously kept and the remainder of the year was spent in remonstrating with the King and the Queen Mother over the barbarous injustices still wreaked upon the Huguenots. In March he wrote to Catherine begging her not to believe the lies and calumnies that "run fast" about him but to trust that he acts only to have "a good and workable peace."[28]

Despite the King's assurance that he would do everything in his power to assuage these harsh conditions, little changed. In truth, little was left in the King's power. Forced into a situation which he could not control, he had long since ceased to try; and in the spring of 1581 Claude Haton noted in his *Mémoires*, "The King has left the care of public affairs to his mother, and while Catherine de Medici remains at Blois, he has withdrawn to St. Germain-en-Laye, according to some for the cure of the shameful disease which afflicts him, to others to wait for the execution of the pact recently concluded between the Catholics and Protestants of the Midi."[29] Again and again Navarre wrote in increasing anger—that his right to his ancestral château of Vendôme was being questioned, that the Seigneur de Fressinet was laying claim to power in Guyenne, that the Duc de Mayenne, brother to Guise, was doing all he could to encourage war, that the towns of Tarascon and Périgueux—among others—had been taken by the Catholics without cause. In return, the news from Paris was simply that the King busied himself in choosing clothes for the Duc de Joyeuse's wedding and that the Cardinal de Bourbon had given an elaborate party to amuse the King.

At such a moment, with his loyalty to the King sorely tempted, Navarre received overtures from another quarter which might have proven an invincible temptation to a less wary prince: Philip II sent emissaries from Spain to renew his request—this time "with insistence" —for the hand of Navarre's sister Catherine. The marriage alliance was but one part of what Phillip offered. He assured Navarre that if he agreed to such a marriage he would give him sufficient help to establish an independent kingdom in the south consisting of Navarre, Foix, Béarn, and Bigorre. The old glory to which the D'Albrets had clung so chauvinistically would be theirs again. In addition, Philip reminded him that Spain's influence with the Holy See was such that he could easily procure an annulment of Navarre's present marriage, after which he would give him his own daughter, Clara-Eugenie, granddaughter (through her mother Elizabeth) of Catherine de Medici and Henri II. Not only would this reaffirm the Spanish alliance, but as the wily Philip pointed out, strengthen Navarre's claim to the throne of France should the present king die without issue.

The plan was flawless—if one could trust the King of Spain, but that Navarre would never do. Throwing in his lot with Catholic Spain was a tricky business and one which would not only make him traitor to France but win for him the enmity of Protestant England and of his own Huguenot people. Navarre refused the proposal on the grounds that his conscience would not permit him to espouse his sister to a Catholic prince.

While Navarre could juggle adroitly the external forces ranged against him, he was less successful in managing the domestic affairs of his court. Theodore Beza had chastised him more than once for the license in his personal life, and his Huguenot minister, Du Plessis-Mornay, that rigid "Pope of the Huguenots," as he was called, was reputed to have admitted sadly during an audience with Elizabeth that his master was sometimes snatched away from his duty by "the hot blood of his youth." "The hot blood of his youth" was something which Navarre would never completely outgrow and whatever the uncertainties of war he found time to take his pleasures.

Even while Margot freely pursued her own pleasures, she noted carefully the maids of her court who fell before her husband's charm. There had been Dayelle, the beautiful, dark-eyed Italian who had traveled in the Queen Mother's suite; then Rebours, "that artful young person who never liked me," as Margot noted; and the more trivial affairs with Mademoiselle de Tignonville, "the woman Caichicot," and the "trollop of a man named Goliath." These had all ended in time, and Margot, as casual as her spouse, took but small notice. It was not until Navarre fell enamored before a fifteen-year-old child, one Fosseuse, that their domestic tranquillity was seriously threatened. "She was much more beautiful than the others," wrote Margot, "and was at that time young and really a very lovable person."[80] Throughout the winter of 1580 and into 1581, Navarre continued to shower presents on Fosseuse whom he called "my little girl." Always prodigal in his gifts, Navarre won the affection of many of the women at the court by his little presents of apricots and yellow pears brought from Tours and boxes of sweetmeats from Italy; but to Fosseuse alone went the imported boxes of marzipan in which she took a child's delight.

Margot might well have forgiven the gifts, since at the same time she was receiving precious gloves embroidered in gold and silver, but when it was reported that Fosseuse had been heard to say openly that if she had a son Navarre would marry her and she would be Queen, Margot could not brook her insolence. Since her pregnancy was common talk, Margot sent for her to suggest that she withdraw from court in order to avoid a scandal. But Fosseuse, perhaps in arrogance, perhaps in fear, refused to acknowledge that she was pregnant, screamed in anger at the Queen, and ran for protection to Navarre. The tale as Margot tells it leans heavily to one side: "Now she shunned my presence as much as she had been accustomed to seek it," she later wrote. "She endeavored to make all the mischief she was able between us. For his part, he avoided me; he grew cold and indifferent." It is the tale of the virtuous woman, wrongfully treated, as one reads it in Margot's *Mémoires*; and like the tales of most virtuous women, virtue had its revenge.

One morning at dawn the royal physician gained entrance into the King's bedchamber "and greatly embarrassed my husband" with news that Fosseuse was in labor. Margot never had the opportunity for a better story, for, as she tells it, her husband, desperate to keep secret what was already public, begged his wife to go to Fosseuse's apartment and help in the delivery. More virtuous than ever, Margot arose to do her husband's bidding, "for," she continued, "I had too great respect for him to be offended at anything that he should do." Calm and efficient, Margot suggested to her distraught husband that he go out hunting for the day while she removed the frightened Fosseuse "to a solitary part of the palace" and "saw that she wanted for nothing that was proper to her situation."

Margot's care while sufficient to save Fosseuse was not enough for the child, and after some hours of labor, the girl who had hoped to please the King by bearing him a son, gave birth to a stillborn female child. Before the end of the day Fosseuse was carried back to the quarters occupied by the Queen's maids. Henri, who had followed his wife's advice and spent the day hunting, returned toward evening to learn the conclusion of Fosseuse's pregnancy. Margot had little compassion for the girl who had so flaunted her position as the royal favorite, and when Henri, often indiscreet in his affections, begged his wife to go to Fosseuse again and console her in those difficult hours, Margot refused. When he pointed out that it was her custom to attend personally to her maids when they were ill, Margot pointed out that he had already routed her from her bed at dawn, that she had done far more than her duty or position demanded, and that there was little that she could do for Fosseuse now. The King, Margot carefully recorded, instead of being grateful for all she had done, grew angry at her refusal.

It was the beginning of a serious domestic rift, for even when the event was over and Navarre's ardor for Fosseuse had somewhat diminished, the coolness between Margot and her husband persisted. Margot, bored and petulant, began dreaming of the Louvre, of the dances and masques of which her mother wrote, and perhaps also of a young nobleman, Champvallon, whom she had met in Alençon's suite when her brother had visited the south. When some months later her mother wrote asking her to come to court for a visit, sending her 1,500 crowns to cover her expenses, Margot accepted and began to plan her journey to Paris.

CHAPTER VI

The Ways of Love: 1582–1584

I do not offer you anything of my own both because it is already yours and because there is nothing worthy of you.

Montaigne to Corisande

꧁꧁꧁ Margot's return to Paris was not an impulsive step, either on her part or on that of the Queen Mother by whom it was largely planned. Like most of Catherine's moves, it was instigated by many motives, chief among them her unswerving desire to get Navarre back to court. Margot's motivation was less political: Nérac no longer amused her. She was weary of its country style, irked at being so far from the French court, jealous of the child who had replaced her in her husband's interest. Almost a year earlier she had written to her mother, "On my part, Madame, you can imagine what boredom I am enduring, being so far away and subject to all sorts of false rumors. . . ."[1] What had been at first merely irksome, became unendurable when Fosseuse overshadowed her on all points. Margot never adverted to being childless until with Fosseuse's pregnancy she made plans to take the waters at Bagnères. On June 1, 1581, Bellièvre wrote to the Queen Mother, "The Queen your daughter is going to the baths near Pau; she says she does this because of the extreme desire she has to satisfy the King her husband's desire to have children." Bellièvre's letter was followed shortly by one from Margot herself who concluded, ". . . I will let you know what results I have from this."[2]

For the next few months she continued to hope, and for a while all the rumors were that the Queen of Navarre was soon to bear a child. Renieri wrote to Florence conjecturing that the Queen Mother's plans to bring her daughter to court might now have to be cancelled because of the latter's pregnancy. Renieri, however, underestimated Catherine's ability to make all events converge to her own purposes. To the Queen Mother, her daughter's pregnancy was but another strong motive for her journey north and she wrote to her advising that she defer her trip until her seventh month in order that she might be delivered at court. Nothing would give the Queen Mother greater power over her son-in-law than the possession of his child; if Navarre could not be coerced into coming to court through his wife, Catherine had no doubt that he would come for his child—especially if this child were a boy.

This time, however, all the subtle scheming went for naught, for by January it was clear that Margot's rumored pregnancy had been a false hope; by the beginning of 1582 Navarre's letters indicate that plans for his wife's immediate journey were already in full swing. Although Navarre was firm in his decision not to go to Paris, he did agree to accompany his wife on the initial stages of her journey. When, on March 13, they arrived at St. Maixent, they learned that the Queen Mother, despite her recent illness, had set out to meet them. Since Navarre would not make the journey to Chenonceaux which she had urged, then, sick or well, in her litter or on mule back, over the muddy spring roads she would make her way to him. It was, she knew, important for the King's welfare that she confer with Navarre, and where the King's welfare was concerned she was indomitable. Past experience had taught her that she would be but ill thanked for her services; this hurt her, but it never stopped her. Thus Navarre and the Queen Mother met at the château belonging to Lanssac at La Mothe-Sainte-Héraye, a few miles southeast of St. Maixent. Here they dined, and afterwards discussed the problems of the Huguenots and the cause of peace.

Navarre placed as much importance on this conference as did Catherine herself, for shortly before he had written to Beza: "I hope that we shall see the Queen in about ten days; I feel that this is necessary for the good of the peace and the welfare of our Churches." Although their talks resulted in no definite steps, Navarre, at least, was pleased at the atmosphere they created, and wrote later to his friends Bourlie and Scorbiac that he had been given "great assurances of future tranquillity."[3]

On March 31 the two queens took the road for Chenonceaux alone, arriving on April 28 to find the King awaiting them. Although the Queen Mother was satisfied and happy with her encounter with

Navarre, nothing she said cheered the King who, it was reported by the English agent, continued in a "heavy and sad countenance." He had put too many hopes in the rumors that Navarre might become a Catholic to be contented with the news brought by his mother. Nor was he happy to have Margot back at court. Despite Catherine's assurances that Margot had worked zealously for the King's interest during the months preceding the conferences at Nérac, her brother could feel nothing but mistrust for this sister who in so many ways was his superior. Although she was but two years his junior, she was still beautiful with a vitality and decisiveness which he had lost before his time. Not yet thirty-two, he was irreparably marked by failure and infirmity. From their childhood Margot had been his enemy, and now her continued friendship with Alençon and her apparent reconciliation with her husband goaded his fears and suspicions.

Margot, however, refused to be put out of countenance by her brother's manner, and as they journeyed to Paris her delight in the familiar countryside grew; not all was familiar for she had been gone almost four years and there were new faces at court, while some of the old faces wore a different look. The Duc de Guise, once her reputed lover, looked thin and old, she noted, aged, perhaps, with too much plotting and mistrust. The Duc de Mayenne, his brother, had changed in a contrary direction, for, as Margot wrote to Navarre, he had become so fat that he looked almost deformed as he tried to keep pace with his gallant brother. So much had her opinion of the Guises shrunken that she wrote to Navarre who, she thought, hesitated to make his way to court for fear of them: "As for fearing those of the Guise faction, please believe me when I say that they have neither the credit nor the means to do you any harm." There were, as she continued to point out, other and more positive reasons for coming to court: "You would be a person on whom others depend," she wrote, for she would be willing to stake her life on the King's friendship with him. She continued, "You would have gifts from the King himself; you could take care of all your affairs and could do far more for those of your party—being here at court and near the King—than all those in your service would ever know how to do by their solicitations."[4] It was a well-worded plea, enthusiastic and directed to what she knew were Navarre's interests.

About those things which gave her most pleasure—clothes and manners and entertainments—she was silent, for she knew that they would mean little to her husband. Banquets were still as lengthy and balls as extravagant as she had remembered them. Margot who had always loved the dance found it here to her heart's content, and exulting in her freedom from Huguenot restraint, she whirled through the measures of the gaillard as she had done in those days when she had first dazzled the French court with her grace.

Besides the general pleasures of the court, there was as well the renewed pleasure of continuing her romantic attraction for Jacques de Harlay, Sieur de Champvallon, whom she had first met in Alençon's entourage when they had visited the château of Foix-Candale near Cadillac in 1577. Champvallon, who held the position of Master of Horse for Alençon, had all the qualities which Margot valued: he was popular, a duelist of repute, and one of the most handsome men of his time. She had met him again in 1581 when Alençon visited Nérac. When, in the summer of 1582, he married Charlotte Catherine de la Marck, Margot was inconsolable; but on her return to Paris, Champvallon was easily able to convince her that his love had not changed, that he dreamed of no one but her, and his marriage was a misery to him.

Margot, for whom the proverb, "Absence makes the heart grow fonder," never rang true, soon found that in this atmosphere her recollection of her husband was growing dim, and that when she did remember him he seemed brusque and unpolished compared to the courtly grace of Champvallon. Her relations with her husband were further impaired by renewed difficulties over Fosseuse whom she had, for diverse motives, brought to Paris in her suite, but whom, on her mother's advice, she had later dismissed. Although Navarre's love for Fosseuse had waned, he took as an affront to his authority the fact that Margot would so peremptorily dismiss her without his consent. The letters between Navarre and his wife grew increasingly bitter, and by mid-June Renieri wrote in his dispatch to Florence: "The Queen of Navarre has declared that she no longer wishes to live with her husband who is a liar and a Huguenot."[5]

Navarre had lived too long among the Valois to be seriously disturbed over the bruit he had stirred. What Margot did and said had long been her own business; and as to Fosseuse, he had lost interest in the ambitious child who thought he might some day make her his wife. To her sorrow she had been too naïve to realize that Navarre bestowed his smiles and his favor as easily as his gifts of marzipan. Sometime in 1582, however, Navarre discovered that his affairs, always embarked upon so casually, were taking on a new dimension.

He was seriously in love, not with a child who had the gift of her virginity to offer him, but with a widowed countess who called herself by the romantic name of "Corisande" and whom he had first met fifteen years before. He had been present as a boy of fourteen when on August 6, 1567, Diane d'Andoins had been espoused to Philibert de Gramont in the garden of the château at Pau. With his mother, he had witnessed the marriage contract and wished well to the bridal couple. He had seen little of the bride after that, but later when he returned to his own lands in 1576 he found himself at war with the Catholic Gramont who had removed his wife and two children from their château high on a hill in Bidache to the colorful coastal city of Bayonne.

The Comtesse de Gramont (and de Guiche) was among the faithful Catholics who had welcomed the Queen Mother and Marguerite on their entrance to Toulouse on their way to meet Navarre in 1578. Not long after, the enmity directed at Catholics in Béarn had led the count to move his family to the safer city of Bordeaux. This step did nothing to protect his own life, for he was killed at the siege of La Fère in the summer of 1580. At the death of her husband, the Comtesse de Gramont moved south again and so had the opportunity to renew her friendship with Catherine de Bourbon, Navarre's sister.

Navarre had doubtless seen her earlier, but he seems not to have seriously noticed her until he returned to Pau on a spring day in May 1582. Six weeks before he had watched his wife and the Queen Mother ride off on the Poitou road toward Chenonceaux while he had ridden west to La Rochelle in an effort to improve his relations with Condé who, it was rumored, would just as soon people came to him as their "Chief Protector." There he had been taken seriously ill, and it was some weeks before he was well enough to make the journey back to Pau where he arrived on May 5. With his arrival the streets rang with the Gascon cry *Bibe lou Rey,* and soon the courtyard was filled with the bustle of horses and mules, with lackeys and ostlers, although it took but few servants to carry the yellow and orange valises which formed Navarre's meager baggage.

His convalescence was slow, and it was some time before he joined his sister and her women in the great hall. It was here, legend has it, that he first noticed Diane de Gramont, her fair head bent as she sewed seed pearls on a crimson gown. She had neither the ebullience of Margot nor the winsomeness of Fosseuse. She was a year or two his senior. She had borne two children and her figure had begun to thicken; nor was her face perfectly proportioned: her nose was a trifle short and her forehead too high for perfect beauty. Yet there was about her an air of high intelligence which had moved Montaigne to send her a book of verses with the note, "I do not offer you anything of my own both because it is already yours and because there is nothing worthy of you."[6] What Montaigne expressed so gracefully, Navarre, though he thought of himself as a warrior not a poet, also felt. A part of his heart, sensitive, alive to nuances, a part that had hitherto gone untouched, began to take shape in the presence of this fair woman with her quiet hands and gentle voice. It was with a passion tempered with reverence that Navarre approached Corisande d'Andions.

Corisande stands unique in Navarre's life, not perhaps because she loved him more than the others—for some indeed loved him so well that they preferred death to the emptiness he left behind him—but unique for loving him for what he gave her in each moment, rather than for the things he might give in some future moment. Romantic, idealistic, she was also a realist. She loved the moment she could grasp, knowing that dreams were often illusions and that Hope, cruel sovereign, often played her vassals false. She knew enough of time and change to know that no moment is eternal, that the shape of permanence is in itself a shifting thing. When in the night at Hagetmau Navarre swore that he would love her forever, the moment of her ecstasy never slipped beyond the moment of experience. Forever was another thing; kings, being close to the gods, might speak of it; but kings' mistresses never. Yet this was no limitation on her love, but rather its fulfillment. Lost in the present, she never asked of him more than he had to give. She had no need to seek the comfort of permanence, for each moment of their love was for her rounded, timeless, in some sense infinite, so that there was no need to search for what might lay beyond.

When letters continued to arrive from Paris begging Navarre to join the court at the Louvre, they were opened by hands that barely noted the royal seal. It was no longer the wary soldier and the astute politician that kept Navarre in the south, for he now found himself a captive of another kind. To leave the reality of the love that he had found in Corisande was unthinkable; beside this, Margot's protestations of loneliness, her assurances of joy in having him with her once again were but tinkling bells lost in a deeper resonance. When protestations of her brother's loyalty achieved nothing, when her comments that it was those who were jealous that he might come too close to the King who led him astray by their counsel, fell on deaf ears, Margot resorted to her husband's innate love of pleasure. She wrote of the balls held at the Louvre, balls that lasted until morning with music so beautiful that all the surrounding houses opened their windows that they might miss no note of the royal entertainment; and she concluded, "If you were a decent man, you would leave your fields and the moods of Timon and come here to live among true men."[7] Margot's jibe could not have been more ironic, for Navarre was further from the cynical misanthropy of Timon than he would ever be in his life. He was a man in love and like all lovers he found the world limitlessly beautiful. What need had he of the music of the Louvre; Corisande was his music, for, as he told her again and again during those first months, she was his life, his everything, to whom in return he gave all that he was. That platitude of correspondence, "I kiss your hands a thousand times," was no longer a conventional phrase; it expressed his heart and it seemed no extravagance to him to want in truth to kiss unendingly those graceful hands which he had first noticed as Corisande had sat embroidering in the hall of Pau.

Corisande, however, was no coquette; she was almost thirty, with an experience of danger and conflict behind her. There was little of vanity in her love for Navarre. Their embraces were her ecstasy and yet her hands freed him for the work she knew was his. She had seen France too long at war; she longed for peace, and she believed that if any man could bring the violence and discord to an end it was Navarre. If peace lay on the road to Paris, she would have helped him mount his horse. She was no stranger to loneliness, and she would willingly have endured a little more if it were in accord with the cause of peace. They both knew, however, that nothing would be gained by a visit to court.

News from Paris grew daily more disturbing. Lorenzo Priuli, the Venetian ambassador, wrote in his report to the Signoria: "The condition of this kingdom, as I hear from persons who are well-informed and who are faithful servants of the King is very bad. . . . I lament that the King should take so little care for the dignity and the interests of the crown and should think more of his pleasures than is becoming."[8] The King, always capricious, now seemed almost childish in his manners. The Queen Mother he addressed even publicly as "Maman." His memos to Villeroy, his secretary of state, often closed with "Adieu" written four or five times in large childish letters, followed by a row of "X's."

Navarre had rightly determined that his cause could never be fostered by his presence at court and when in August news reached him of the terrible scandal which pivoted about Marguerite, he thanked his stars for the provinces that separated them. Like all scandals, particularly those concerning royalty, each recital embroidered the facts until all Paris was reaching tiptoe to catch the latest word of the lurid actions of the royal family. Whatever had touched off the incident, the fact remained that Margot was in disgrace, a disgrace particularly humiliating even in a family and at a time when reputations rarely went unsullied. Some maintained that the episode had taken place at a ball where, in the absence of Queen Louise and the Queen Mother, Margot was presiding, attending her brother on the royal dais. For reasons which no one overheard, the King was seen to fly into one of his fits of fury and there before the gaily dressed dancers to charge Margot with every kind of profligacy, enumerating her lovers and even accusing her of bearing a child to Champvallon. When he demanded that she dismiss at once the "evil companions" with which she had surrounded herself, Margot realized that this storm would not blow over easily.

The Queen Mother for whom family strife was more painful than war between nations was beside herself. Following her daughter's "public disgrace," she sent for her in the garden of the Tuileries with its long green lawns and shaded walks which always represented for Catherine the seat of her feminine power to cajole and conquer in her Florentine atmosphere of fountains and flowers. She assured her daughter that the King would be willing to see her to discuss the matter and reach some amicable solution, provided only that Margot, on her part, did not speak "sharply or sourly" to him. Margot, however, who never inherited her mother's ability to temporize, would make no promises. She saw no reason why the accused should respond with humility while all the terms for peace remained in the hands of the unjust accuser. Catherine, for whom justice and injustice had long been among the most hypothetical of terms and who lived in a world where only actualities were real, could reach no terms with her intransigent daughter.

If the Queen Mother had hoped by this interview either to frighten her daughter or move her to compunction, she had failed; and the English agent who, like everyone else near the court, watched every detail with nervous anticipation, wrote in his report: "Thus the daughter departed from the Queen Mother without weeping or changing of countenance, passing forth into the next chamber where with a cheerful countenance she took her leave of the princesses and all the other ladies."[9] Margot would leave the court, for there was nothing else she could do; but she would leave like the princess she imagined herself to be: controlled, beautiful, with her charm unblemished no matter what might have happened to her honor.

With Margot's departure, however, the King found himself in more troubled waters that he had anticipated. It was not only his own sister whom he had treated thus, but the wife of the King of Navarre; and the King of Navarre must now be reckoned with. Navarre had received the first inkling of the affair in a letter which reached him while he was hunting at Ste-Foi-sur-Dordogne. It was a letter worded so carefully that he was hard-pressed to reach the core of it. What it said ostensibly was that the King wished to inform him that his wife would soon be on her way back to Navarre, and that he, the King, had taken the liberty of removing two women from her company because of their bad influence. The inference, that the virtuous Queen of Navarre was being corrupted by her serving maids, must have amused her husband who answered the letter promptly in terms as veiled as those he had received. He thanked the King for his "great good will" in advising him of these circumstances, assured him that some word of scandal concerning the women involved had even reached the south, and that he was delighted that the King had taken steps to do what seemed best.[10] It was not until later that the true aspect of the matter reached Navarre, and when it did his anger was unfeigned. He refused absolutely to receive his wife who, it seemed, had been such a blemish on the Valois court that she had to be sent packing like some common courtesan. The Queen Mother, astute enough from the beginning to see where all of this might lead, took to her bed, sick in body and mind that her daughter, exiled by her brother, was now repudiated by her husband. As usual the King had gone too far and his regrets would avail him little.

No common letters would heal the breach, and from both sides the most astute politicians were called in to attempt a solution to the imbroglio. At the Queen Mother's advice, it was Bellièvre, so often called upon to untangle royal snarls, who was sent south to present the case in person to Navarre. The king in an effort to palliate Navarre's anger had only augmented it when he had written, according to L'Estoile, that "even the most virtuous princesses were not always exempt from calumny and would remind him that false accusations had even been made against the late Queen his mother." It was hardly a tactful comment, and Navarre, wryly amused at the unwitting insult, "took to laughing" and replied to Bellièvre, "The King does me too much honor in these letters. In the first he called me a cuckold, and by this one, the son of a whore."[11] If the affair were to be ended, it would not be through the diplomacy of Henri de Valois. On August 29 Bellièvre, who knew Navarre and had assisted skillfully in the conferences at Nérac three years before, wrote to the Queen Mother: "I do not think, that it will be easy to persuade the King of Navarre to take back his wife without some suitable satisfaction that will be performed publicly."[12]

Meanwhile Navarre had sent his Huguenot minister Duplessis-Mornay, from Nérac on August 17 to present his case to the court at Paris. The King, however, had already left the Louvre and the Huguenot leader was forced to make the hot, dusty journey southward to Lyons where the King had taken refuge from his own mistakes. Duplessis-Mornay was too much the enemy of license to argue his case diplomatically. He had long blamed Margot for her husband's frivolities and sighed audibly for the days long past when Jeanne d'Albret would permit no traffic with Catholic immorality. Yet Navarre had chosen his emissary with deliberate care, for Navarre had chosen to play to the the hilt his role of aggrieved husband and insulted monarch. While Duplessis-Mornay, with his forbidding black doublet and stiff white ruff, argued with moral indignation—which was with him no pose—that his sovereign could hardly be expected to receive to his court and his bed a wife who was "publicly besmirched," Navarre made overt plans for war. The King in terror withdrew to his prayers and left the management of the diplomatic mission to his mother.

Navarre, despite his overt moves, had no intention of plunging into fresh conflict, but neither was he to be satisfied with verbal apologies. He had discovered that the whole affair might be used to his own advantage and with his gambler's instinct he planned his strategy. The Huguenots needed towns of security and Navarre intended to use Margot's disgrace as a bargaining point to this end. Thus he sent Pibrac, Margot's chancellor, to the court to deliver a strenuous ultimatum demanding reparation for the ill-treatment accorded Margot who was manifestly innocent of the accusations brought against her. Inserted into Pibrac's remonstrance was the hint that if the King should remove his troops from several towns in the south the negotiations concerning Margot might move forward with greater expedition.

As in her marriage she had been used as a pawn by her brother Charles, now she found herself used by her husband, although to what political end she was not to know specifically for several months. Margot, however, was too much her mother's daughter to give in without a battle and soon she journeyed on to the fortress at Plessis-les-Tours where her mother-in-law, Jeanne d'Albret, had also learned the lesson of fortitude during the lonely years of her childhood. From there she wrote to court that she would not budge until she was promised some kind of security. In a letter to her mother she commented bitterly, "If, as they say, kings are like gods who love afflicted hearts, then mine should be very pleasing to him."[13] No state was worse than inaction for the energetic Margot, and after six weeks of waiting, she wrote to Bellièvre: "I cannot rest until I am liberated from this purgatory, for I can find no better name for it, since I do not know whether I am to be consigned to Heaven or Hell."[14] Yet months would pass before her destiny would be decided, for Navarre was determined to strike a hard bargain. By the end of January even the patience of the Queen Mother was somewhat frayed, and she wrote in annoyance to Bellièvre: "I am most displeased at the answer the King of Navarre my son has given you about my daughter—that he should prejudice her reputation after such a long period of waiting and all her manifestations to do whatever he wants."[15] Navarre, however, could well afford to bide his time and he knew it, for despite the Queen Mother's words, it was very obvious to all of France that it was not he but her own family who had "prejudiced her reputation."

The King was loth to give Navarre what he asked for, and his instructions to Bellièvre were to get his cousin to receive Margot first and then to talk about removing the royal garrisons which, the King argued, are "not at all as dangerous" as Navarre was indicating. But Navarre was too shrewd for this measure and he wrote with implacable determination to Matignon, his governor in Guyenne, "Just as soon as I learn that the garrisons are withdrawn I will leave for Nérac to receive my wife."[16] By March the King could hesitate no longer, and Stafford wrote to Whitehall that the King's troops had been removed from the towns specified by Navarre and that the latter had agreed to receive Margot; but, added Stafford, "men think that it shall be as late as he may and whenever it is, it shall be full against his stomach."[17]

When Bellièvre had spoken to Navarre on Margot's behalf toward the end of 1583, he had received but small comfort and had written sadly to Margot, "I beg of you, Madame, not to impute to me any lack of good will."[18] The following January Navarre himself wrote to his wife, but it was a letter which did little to further the negotiations, saying only: "It is very necessary for both of us that when they see us reunited it will be with our full consent. . . . I want it to appear to everyone that I do nothing by coercion and that I believe none of all these calumnies. This, my love, is all that I can say to you for the present."[19] It was not until early April that Navarre advised Bellièvre that he would come to Nérac where he hoped to find his wife waiting for him. He could not come during Holy Week, he explained, because "it is the time of devotions," but he would like to be reunited with Margot immediately after Easter. What he had not seen fit to explain to either Bellièvre or his wife was that he spent the intervening weeks at Pau where Corisande was the guest of his sister. The months of Margot's absence had been far from lonely for her husband, for he had found all he needed of love with Corisande. Now as he bid her goodbye, it was with promises that he would return as soon as diplomacy permitted, for neither he nor Corisande considered Margot any more than a diplomatic affair. To the King Navarre wrote with cold formality, "Following the command it has pleased Your Majesty to give me . . . I have come here to receive my wife. . . ."[20]

The reunion of the King and Queen of Navarre took place on Easter Friday, April 13, at Port-Ste-Marie. From here they made the journey to Nérac, riding together up the long avenue of trees tipped with their first green. In the chill shadows of late afternoon they crossed the bridge over the Baïse, high with the spring rains. It was not very different from their entrance on that spring day in 1579 when Navarre had brought his queen with high celebration to Nérac for the first time; that had been in May when the promises of spring had already burst into flower. The orange grove which Margot grew to love so dearly had been in blossom and the waters of the Baïse had run green and cool. This time it was early April and the King and Queen slogged their way over roads deep in mud. The bridge over the river seemed less picturesque and beneath it the waters ran brown and turgid from the spring thaw. Five years ago the whole town was out to meet them with excited anticipation at the fabled elegance of the Valois princess. Now their train was smaller and less elaborate, the welcomes were muted, and the conversation strained. Margot was not unaware that Navarre's first minister, Duplessis-Mornay, had called her "a woman publicly besmirched." Her brother's insults still rang in her ears and the lonely days spent looking over the bluffs of Chateaudun as she fought against the new emotion of angry despair were still with her. Worst of all, she knew that Navarre himself had used her as a pawn to bargain for greater security for his Huguenots. The letter she wrote in her pride to Catherine de Medici does not quite ring true when she assures her mother of her "great happiness" and of the "honor and great kindness I have received from my husband and friend."[21]

That night they dined in the banquet hall at Nérac—a hall which Margot had always admired for its grace and sophistication. The dinner was of elaborate proportions, but there seems to have been little of the gaiety of a homecoming about it. Although the Venetian ambassador wrote that the King of Navarre had received his wife "lovingly," only a single witness committed to paper a description of those first hours that the pair spent together and that was La Huguerye, "the most Huguenot of Huguenots," a man little known for his objectivity. He noted that they walked together in the gallery of the château until evening and then went to dine in candlelight. Margot's eyes, he observed, were red with crying and her cheeks wet with tears. He continued, "Her husband was entertaining himself with the men who were around them without bothering to speak to her which made me think that what Du Pin had told me was true, that he had taken her back under duress."[22]

Although with the reconciliation completed, the Queen Mother had breathed a sigh of relief, still she could not trust her daughter's discretion and wrote a long, last letter to Bellièvre without whose soothing presence she feared the reconciliation might not last. "I pray God," she wrote . . . "that she may live like a woman of good character and honor and like a princess of her position ought." She should, the Queen Mother continued, be surrounded only by good and virtuous people. "Should she say that I am not, tell her . . . being what I am, known by everybody, having lived as I have up to my present age, she can do the same without offense to God nor scandal to the world. . . . But now . . . I think she should reject everyone who is not worthy to be near a wise and virtuous princess, who is still young and who perhaps thinks herself to be prettier than she is. I don't know who will say this kind of thing after you have left, for, of course, now that she is with her husband I won't write to her any more for he'll see the letters." Then came Catherine's concluding shot to maintain peace between this erring couple: "Tell her," she concluded, "not to let him make love to the women of her household."[23] It was her last word; she could do no more.

Margot's exile was at an end, painful though that end might be, and with it went a little of the apprehension in which France had lived. The Queen was with her husband and the kingdom remained at peace; yet what Henri de Valois had sacrificed by his public reproach of his sister, he would never win back. He had been known for his vacillation, his evasion, his weakness, for most of his reign; but somehow the royal dignity had been at least partially preserved, in his own eyes at least. He was a king; he clung doggedly to this belief, playing role after role in his effort to fulfill the divine destiny he was sure was his. After the folly of his affair with Margot, something of hope went out of him. When that same summer he planned an assembly of the principal men of his kingdom to be held in the early fall at St. Germain-en-Laye, it seemed doomed from the beginning. It was not until mid-November that the assembly opened and after some weeks of useless debate the deputies returned to their own lands having accomplished little except to remain loyal to the policies of the people who had sent them. No one seemed either angry or surprised at the failure of the assembly; failure now had come to be the expected conclusion of all the King turned his hand to.

Unable to make the decisions which his government demanded, the King turned to religion with an abandon that drove his ministers to distraction and his mother to tears. Earlier that summer the Tuscan ambassador Busini had written home, "He wears the habit of a penitent, goes frequently to Holy Communion. About his neck he wears a collar of ebony with death's-heads carved in ivory. Above all, he frequents the church of the Capuchins, taking his place with them in the choir, listening to the Divine Office, kissing the ground, and singing with them for three or four hours to everyone's amazement."[24]

Even these practices of piety were not enough to satisfy his bizarre devotion, and in December of 1583 he had formed a new confraternity, the most elaborate of them all. This was his brotherhood of "Jeronomites," who were to live in a hermitage constructed for that purpose in the Bois de Vincennes. There, in the murky atmosphere of the château where his brother Charles had died, Henri took refuge. The atmosphere was ideal for his purposes: the somber walls, the high, impregnable tower, spoke more of death than life. To this dubious honor were brought twelve of his friends, numbering five cardinals, three bishops, four dukes, and the King himself. Their habits, made by the royal tailor, were of gray cloth with a white cross on the left arm. Their cells, too, were to be hung with gray, and their food platters, their two carafes, and their candlesticks were to be of muted silver. To those for whom it was not tragic, it seemed ludicrous. The English ambassador wrote wryly: "Their order is to go apparelled in the color as before, to go barefoot, to have stones in their hands to knock their breasts when they be at their prayers, and to live of alms."[25] No one, not even the most pious, could take these caprices of the King seriously, and the Tuscan dispatches no longer called him "King" but patronizingly, *Il Vescovo*, "the Bishop."

Meanwhile he had washed his hands of the Margot affair as though he had had no part in it; and once again Bellièvre and the Queen Mother were left to bring order out of the chaos her son had wreaked. As for Navarre's letters from the south, angry letters not only concerning his personal affairs but dealing with the multiplied injustices against the Huguenots on the part of the King's ministers, they went unanswered or received responses too wide of the mark to be of any help. Even the storm that Alençon had stirred in the Netherlands seemed unable to rouse the King's full interest.

Alençon had never heeded his brother's threats or his mother's pleas to give up his plans for involvement in the Netherlands. He was flattered by the offers that came to him from the Lowlands and too enamored with his image as a liberating hero to recognize the truth of his situation. For a time, he continued victorious and to some extent popular; yet what Alençon never faced was the fact that the people who had called upon him to help them wished to use his power but never to be subjugated by it. They had no desire for a sovereign who would "nibble at their liberties"; and when they invited Alençon it was with the understanding that they would keep "a good muzzle" on him. Alençon, however, too much a Valois to be satisfied with anything less than absolute power, conjured a scheme to reduce by trickery the people he had come to champion. In January 1583, despite the well-founded objections of his generals Biron and Montpensier, he engaged upon that piece of treachery which has come to be called "the French Fury." It might better be called the Folly of Alençon, for by it he condemned himself to irredeemable disgrace. On pretense of reviewing the troops, he had the gates of the city opened and his own French troops in uncontrolled bands poured in. The people of Antwerp, no strangers to treachery, acted with an alacrity he had not anticipated, and the French troops found themselves trapped behind the gates and drawbridges of the city. Twelve thousand Frenchmen were hacked to death by outraged peasants and burghers. "Since France was France," wrote Roger Williams to Walsingham, "France never received so great a disgrace."[26]

Alençon, "Duke of Brabant" and "Liberator of the Netherlands"— empty titles which he himself had vilified—withdrew to French soil. Another man would have given up, but the desire for success ran like fever in Alençon's blood and he could not cool it. The following July the thin, dwarfed figure, already wracked with bouts of what his physicians called "tertiary ague," again planned to muster an army. It was a hopeless plan, the last stand of a desperately disappointed man; for Alençon, with little talent for making friends or winning subjects now stood clearly alone. In September, Stafford, recently arrived at Boulogne, wrote to Walsingham, "If Monsieur has no better reputation all the rest of France over than he hath here, it is very small, for truly poor and rich cry out of his dealing in the Low Country."[27] When in Middelburg in Flanders his arms were pulled down and those of the hated and feared King of Spain were put up in their place, the case was clear.

For Alençon there was another, equally humiliating, ramification of his action at Antwerp. For eleven years marriage negotiations had been in progress between Alençon and Elizabeth of England. Elizabeth had never been enthusiastic, but she had found it to her interests to play for time. Twice the French duke had come to England and on his second visit, during the winter of 1581, Elizabeth had publicly avowed her intention to marry him and had given him a ring in token of her fidelity. Consequent events in the Netherlands had changed all that, however, and when Alençon, now bereft of glory or hope of success, wrote seeking her aid, he received not the letter of an affianced bride but that of a calculating sovereign, contemptuous of the misshapen "Frog" who had failed in all his enterprises. It was, although Alençon was unwilling to admit it, the end of his proposed marriage to England. Already mortally ill with a fever that never left him, he retired to Château-Thierry to brood upon the glory which he had so nearly grasped.

In March the Queen Mother, despite her own ill-health, journeyed to Château-Thierry where, as L'Estoile noted, "Monsieur lies very ill, bleeding at both nose and mouth."[28] He was too weak to rise, too weak even to talk, and the hours were spent in a lassitude that ominously reminded the Venetian ambassador of "King Charles of happy memory." When the crisis passed, Catherine returned, always hopeful, to Paris where the doctors had already advised the King that his brother could not recover. It was obvious to all save to his mother that the Prince "shall never escape the fall of the leaf." By mid-April word reached court that Alençon "was given over of the physicians as no man of this world." A few days later the English agent wrote from Château-Thierry that "everyone was in Monsieur's chamber ready to pull the sheet over his face" but to their astonishment he rallied and attempted to continue his correspondence.[29]

It was a moment of false hope, and by the end of May the Queen Mother was again at Alençon's bedside from whence she wrote a short business letter to Bellièvre, explaining that her grief kept her from writing more, for she is overwhelmed with unhappiness at "seeing all die before me."[30] When, however, Alençon died in mid-afternoon of June 10, he died alone with no member of the royal family in attendance. News had reached the Louvre in the middle of the night, but the King waited until morning before going to the Queen Mother's bed chamber to tell her of the death of her youngest child. Her sorrow impressed those in attendance with its sincerity, and Busini noted that twice he saw her delicate hands raised to wipe the tears from her cheeks. Inconsolable in her grief, Catherine waited at the Louvre for the body of her youngest child to make its journey to Paris. For three days the funeral cortege passed through the towns which had so largely feared and hated the spindly prince whose allegiance none could trust.

Whatever there had been of dishonor in his brother's life, the King was determined that the final obsequies would be royal in every way. The body, brought by Biron at the head of 400 horsemen, rested first in the monastery of St. Magloire in the suburb of St. Jacques. On Sunday at evensong the King and Queen with the Queen Mother came in procession to pay their homage. Before them came the Swiss Guard with muffled drums, then the King riding slowly upon a Spanish horse covered with violet cloth. The King, too, was dressed in violet mourning, his head covered with a square cap and attended by the Princes of the Blood. The cardinals also wore violet robes, while the other members of the court were garbed in black, seated upon white horses. The Queen Mother, slow and ponderous in her funeral robes of tawny with a veil of cyprus crepe covering her whole body, rode in a litter. Next to her rode the ladies of the court, clothed in black and seated in black coaches drawn by white horses.

The following day the Prince's body was brought to Notre Dame des Champs, then to the Cathedral of Notre Dame, and on Wednesday to St. Denis where the burial took place. There the heir apparent, the last possible Valois successor to Henri III, was laid beside the kings his brothers. At least in death he had found his place beside kings, as he had wished for all his life. From childhood he had lacked the stamp of royalty; the Valois charm had passed him by while its vices had bred in him like maggots. He belonged to a dying family; conceivably he knew this better than the others and was driven on by a desperate hope to make his mark upon his world before it was too late. He had never felt that he belonged—and yet perhaps no member of his family symbolized the Valois destiny so well as the Duc d'Alençon, heir apparent to the throne of France, betrayed by his own blood at the age of twenty-nine.

CHAPTER VII

Heir Apparent: 1584–1585

On one hand the crown of France; on the other a pair of psalms.

Roquelaure

✤✤✤ Alençon was dead, and the news outran the riders who brought it. Talk ran high through towns and roads that if ever a thing could pitch France back into war this was it. The heir apparent dead and the Huguenot Henri de Navarre the next of kin. What would the King do now, or the Queen Mother, or yet more to the point, the Guises, those powerful brothers who wore their Catholicism as sharp and ready as their swords? But to the surprise of all the Queen Mother did nothing. Still draped in mourning, she sat heavily in her apartments, "in great domps" as Stafford wrote, unable to rally from the death of her youngest son. She had buried three kings, all of them dead before their time. She no longer needed to study the vast ceremonial for a king's burial; she knew it by heart. Yet always before the duties of regent had fallen to her charge and her grief had been swallowed up in business. Now, for the first time, she was not needed, and the helplessness of age and of her position swept over her. *Regina Madre* had always had a lovely sound in her ears. Queen, and mother too. Queen because she was the mother, that was what pleased her. For it was true, as a contemporary wrote, that her favorite image of herself was that of the great *Genitrix*, that dynamic force which kept infusing new life into the veins of France.

The image of life-giver had, however, slipped and become distorted as one by one she had watched her children die. She must have recalled those early days of her marriage when her husband and her dominating father-in-law François I had watched with impatience for her waist to thicken that they might be assured of an heir to the French throne. For years she had failed them and felt the cold wind of repudiation blow close to her. She recalled the humiliation of public prayers to remove her sterility, of the indignities the doctors had heaped upon her with their mysterious and futile rituals for making her womb fertile. It was in those days too, that she had learned of magic, for no means of making her conceive a child were left untried. Then finally in a burst of triumph, life stirred within her and she brought forth a child with an exaltation that was not far short of the Madonna's. She had given birth to a son; France had its heir. In rapid succession had come other sons and daughters until her fertility became proverbial. The "Great *Genitrix*" in her pride could not be stopped. There were children aplenty, children not only for the French throne but children for all the great thrones of the Continent. She would people the thrones of Europe with her seed.

This had been her great dream, and she had held to it steadily despite the death of her two eldest sons. She had held to it even while the marks of death became visible in Alençon, still doing what she could to keep warm the marriage plans with England and, lest this should fail, engaging Philip II for a possible Spanish marriage. With Alençon's death the dream faded beyond her grasp, and she told one of her intimates that "time might wear this grief away to the show of the world, but out of her heart never."[1] She herself wrote to Elizabeth in the hope that the woman who was to have married her son would best understand her own grief. Elizabeth's reply was what her mother's heart had sought: "But for myself," Elizabeth wrote, "I find no consolation if it be not death, which I hope will make us soon to meet. Madame, if you could see the image of my heart you would there see the picture of a body without a soul; but I will not trouble you more with my plaints, having too many of your own. It remains at this present that I vow and swear to you that I will turn a great part of my love for him to the King, my good brother, and you, assuring you that you will find me the faithfullest daughter and sister that ever Princes had."[2] At another time Catherine would have sought for "some tail" in such fulsome words, but now she was content to take them for what they seemed. She did not know, but neither would she have cared overmuch, that Stafford had specifically recommended to Elizabeth that she be very nice to her "and use her while she may serve her turn, for I think she will not live long to do it."[3]

It was not her personal love for Alençon that wounded the Queen Mother so sorely; he had been far from her favorite child, and he had too grievously afflicted the state to win her affection. It was, rather, the loss of a dream. For her, France was inextricably bound up with the Valois dynasty. It was inconceivable that the fleur-de-lys should pass to another family. Yet the fact was manifest: the last of the Valois now sat upon the throne of France. This thin sallow man with his prematurely gray hair, with his propensity for boils and earaches, for orgies of love and religion, this man whom Busini noted as "pale and thin" with a doctor in attendance for fear of his health—with him the Valois line would end. All France knew it as well as Catherine, and fond of anagrams as the French were, they had coined another one for the reigning king: *Rien*. A king of nothing; nothing accomplished, nothing to hope for. *Rien:* the last of the Valois.

With Alençon's death, the problem of succession was brought into dramatic relief. The legitimate successor was, of course, the First Prince of the Blood, Henri de Navarre, but to most of France he had forfeited that right by his stubborn adherence to a heretic sect. It was unthinkable that France have any but a Catholic king; this was a fundamental law of the realm which neither king nor parlement had the right to change, a law which was reaffirmed by the King's coronation oath which demanded not only that he be the chief protector of the Roman faith but that he solemnly promise to extirpate heresy from his kingdom. Whatever Navarre's blood claim—and of this there was no question— he was as a Huguenot a totally unacceptable candidate for the throne of France.

There was, however, one possibility: should Navarre agree to abjure his heresy and return to the bosom of the Roman faith, there would be no reason why he could not assume the role of heir apparent. When, therefore, during the last days of Alençon's mortal illness, it was learned that the King was sending Epernon into Guyenne, the mission became a matter of high conjecture. Those less politically astute accepted the ostensible reason that he journeyed to visit his sick mother; others conjectured a marriage with Catherine de Bourbon or a negotiation with Damville. It was L'Estoile, however, who came closest to the truth when he conjectured that the royal letters which Epernon carried contained a plea for Navarre to come to court and there hear Mass, thus proving his right of succession to the throne.

Although Navarre could foresee little but additional contrariety in Epernon's visit, he was in no position to refuse to receive him, especially when, while visiting the little river town of Pamiers, he received word of Alençon's death. He returned at once to Pau where he, his sister Catherine, and the whole court "disappeared under their veils," while the royal apartments were draped in black. The letter of condolence which he wrote to the King was a masterpiece of ambiguity: "The news . . . has brought me great sadness for I recognize my inestimable loss; but of course how much greater is this for Your Majesty, and yet I am sure that since you have so often overcome so many adversities you will be able to surmount this one, seeing in it the will of God." But, wrote the English agent, "their thoughts were of another color."[4]

However Epernon's journey was interpreted in Paris, the zealous Huguenots of the south saw but one motive: to win Navarre back to court. Despite the eight years he had spent among them, years of poverty, hardship, danger, still they did not entirely trust their Prince. Once again they feared that he might be misled by green promises into abjuring the Reformed Religion. The realist Roquelaure, who recognized the temptations involved, was said to have turned on one of the "proud ministers," as he hammered away at his prince, saying that it was no easy choice for a man faced with "the crown of France on one hand and a pair of psalms on the other."[5] For Navarre, however, the issues were more complex. He knew too much of Valois' ways to put much stock in Valois' promises. The agent who wrote to Walsingham from Paris at the end of June showed himself a novice in the ways of the French court when he promised, "We look daily here at the court for the King of Navarre, the Prince of Condé, and Monsieur d'Epernon."[6] Navarre had but little intention of going to court, least of all on the tether of the King's *mignon*. The King's hopes were as groundless as Huguenot fears, for from the beginning Navarre knew what the conclusion of Epernon's visit would be. He would gladly have avoided it if he could, for he feared the bitterness that might result from his refusal of the King's proposition. He had no doubts about his course of action, and yet he knew the turmoil which would overtake France should the line of royal succession remain unestablished.

When he and Epernon finally met, however, it was, as Busini wrote, with a show of "cordiality and friendship" that greatly contented His Majesty. Actually there had been little doubt that Navarre would—if he met with Epernon at all—acquit himself as a gracious host; it was Margot who made the Queen Mother nervous, for Margot had an avowed enmity for the Duke. At first she peremptorily refused to meet him, but Catherine, implacable in her resolve that her capricious daughter should do nothing to impair this last chance to settle the perilous question of royal succession, sent Bellièvre with letters to Margot, begging her, for the sake of them all, to receive Epernon. Overcome by this concerted pressure, Margot at last surrendered to her mother's wishes, writing later to Matignon, "I saw the Queen so grieved by the loss we have sustained, that the fear I had of irritating her and of losing her has made me do violence to myself in a way that I thought was beyond my power."[7]

On August 4, Epernon, accompanied by Biron (whom Margot equally despised) arrived at Nérac where they were treated in sumptuous fashion. Although his reception at Nérac was impressive, its success was all in its outward show, for in the matter he had come to treat of there was only failure. He had already talked with Navarre at Pamiers and again at Pau and had found the Prince, despite his reputation for hedging, uncompromisingly direct: he would neither come to court nor become a Catholic, even though the throne of France depended on it.

Those who knew him best were not surprised, as the Huguenot Villiers testified in a letter written that July: "I noticed in his youth always a constancy in resolutions. There has never been any fickleness or change of purpose or opinion."[8] What the Huguenots called resolution, the Catholics called stubborn adherence to heresy; and the Nuncio wrote in annoyance to Rome: "This Prince does not seem eager to receive the light of faith. Weighing things with only the balance of human prudence, he said openly that he did not wish in changing his religion to lose friends of whom he was sure, to acquire others about whom he was doubtful."[9] The bishop of the ancient see of Lombez, not far from Pau, wrote a long letter begging Navarre to accept Catholicism not only for his own interests but for the peace of the kingdom, assuring him that he had special power from the Holy See by which he could absolve Navarre. But Navarre had his mind firmly established, and he wrote in reply: "Having been nourished and raised in the religion I now profess, it does not have roots so weak that they can be easily moved; and as this matter is the only one that we are accountable for before God, it is from Him that I await clear and certain inspiration." He continued that such a rapid change on his part would argue "hypocrisy, inconstancy, infidelity," qualities which would make him unworthy of being king.[10] It was a show of constancy that cheered the Huguenots and increased their loyalty to their leader.

It was perhaps the Catholics rather than his fellow religionists who were closer to reading the mind of Navarre. For Navarre it was largely a question of "human prudence," as the Nuncio had called it, for had the end been clearly in his favor, he might have taken the step proposed to him. But that the throne would be his remained doubtful, that the Catholics would accept this second baptism into their faith more doubtful still, and that Henri III, "greedy, disdainful, vacillating," could ever be trusted was the most doubtful of all. The safest course was to stay where he was and read the meaning of events only as they occurred.

Navarre's answer, although he may have foreseen it, must have staggered Henri de Valois, for this had been his only hope to establish the succession peacefully. A Huguenot was unthinkable as The Most Christian King and yet in what other quarter was he to seek for a successor? There were renewed rumors that he would seek an annulment of his marriage with Queen Louise and seek to provide an heir to the throne through another marriage; but those who knew him best knew that he would never risk a second marriage that might prove his own sterility and not the Queen's. Under this additional stress, the paradox of his personality grew to full measure and he became daily more secret, more willful, more violent—and more religious. "He is so strange a man of disposition and so unknown in his proceedings that no man can settle any judgment upon his actions," wrote Walsingham; "he is become since Monsieur's death (whom he stood in fear of) to care for nobody and so keepeth everyone about him in awe, that mother, counsellors, minions, and all quail when he speaketh."[11] Warned of the possible plots of the Guises, Henri belittled them; cautioned about the secret machinations of Spain, he shrugged his shoulders and predicted the early death of Philip himself. Neither his counselors nor his mother could pierce through the piety or luxury with which he armored himself against the knife edge of despair. One day when she begged him to see her for his own good, "he neither came to her nor suffered her to come to him, so that she went back again weeping and marvelously discontented. . . . if he had a foolish toy in his hand or a monk's weed to make or an *Ave Maria* to say, he would let his state go to wrack," Stafford ominously predicted.[12] "The Capuchin King," Cavriana had come contemptuously to call him in the dispatches he sent secretly to the House of Medici.

If the King's conduct was a source of great anxiety for most of

France, there was one family at least to whom it gave great pleasure. The House of Guise watched Henri de Valois squander his kingdom with infinite satisfaction. It was eight years since the Estates of Blois had closed and Henri, Duc de Guise, had taken his cold way down the cobbled path that led to the Loire. He had been a bitterly disappointed man, a man of enormous capabilities passed over by lesser men, a man who watched the instrument of his power—the Catholic League which he had shaped—plucked by Henri de Valois who could no more control it than he could control his own vices. On that day Guise had vowed himself to patience; and now he intended to harvest the fruit of his vow. He had watched with speculation from his window in the Louvre while Alençon's funeral procession passed in the street below. He had watched with anxiety while Epernon made his way on his ambiguous mission into Gascony and listened in relief when the news reached Paris that Navarre had announced that he would remain in the Reformed Religion.

Although most of France was in agreement that it would be impossible to have a Huguenot on the throne of France, the Duc de Guise knew that impossibilities sometimes come to pass unless one took the proper measures to defeat them. Some members of the court might describe Navarre as a pauper prince cooped up in a corner of Guyenne, but Guise was too shrewd a man to underestimate the greatness of others. Himself a leader of men, he sensed the quality of leadership in Navarre, sensed not only his military daring—obvious in such fabled attacks as those on Cahors and Mont-de-Marsan—but his political acumen as well. A prince with no pretensions except to be the champion of a group of religious zealots fighting for their rights? Perhaps; but Guise did not think so. He was aware of Navarre's close and cordial relations with England and aware, too, of the means Navarre had recently taken to establish firm friendships with other Protestant nations.

The summer before, Navarre had written to the Duke of Saxony and other German princes, to Charles, Duke of Sweden, to Frederick of Denmark, to Rudolf, Emperor of the Holy Roman Empire, fulsome letters of praise for their accomplishments, with the suggestion that once trouble came to an end at home he might indulge the pleasure of visiting them in person. The point of these letters was to suggest the possibility of a stronger union among all the kingdoms espousing the Reformed Religion, and the answers he received were, for the most part, approving and sometimes enthusiastic. It was Navarre's first excursion into a role that would look beyond France into the realm of continental politics.

Guise came closer to assessing Navarre for what he was than anyone else in France—even his coreligionists. He assessed him as a danger of significant proportion, against which the full battery of his own power must be directed. He had watched not only Navarre's tentative approach to princes outside of France, but had watched as well his increasing union with Damville. When Henri de Valois had asked Damville to relinquish his governorship of Languedoc in favor of his *mignon* Joyeuse, he had made a mistake that won him an eternal enemy. Damville, as any man who knew him would have predicted, had refused the King's request; and the rift between Languedoc's governor and Joyeuse, the Lieutenant General, became daily more violent. Despite Damville's tendency to moderation, he was inevitably thrust closer to Navarre who used all his influence to establish a lasting union. Hopeful of what such a union could mean for the Huguenots of the south, Navarre had written to Damville earlier suggesting a meeting "to confirm and strengthen our friendship more and more by an indissoluble bond, making it, as I have promised you, perpetual and unbreakable, so that it cannot possibly on any occasion suffer any alteration on my part, for I have no other desire than to remain forever your most affectionate cousin and perfect friend."[13] The King's response to such a possibility was violent and illtimed: he threatened that he would deal with Damville as a traitor, ruining his lands, imprisoning his family, and confiscating his personal property to the crown. Damville's anger was more than justified and he vowed that if the King would make him desperate, then he would do desperate things that would make the King regret his action. In such an atmosphere the meeting between Damville and Navarre took place, and the amity which followed was all that Guise had feared.

Guise longed for Navarre to make some move that would discredit him at court; instead, the Prince outwitted him on every score. When Spain made overtures to him, he not only repudiated them, but at the first opportunity saw that they were reported to the King. Not only did he turn Spain's advances to his own ends, but gained valuable information that he could well use to blackmail Guise. The House of Guise had long been in secret communication with Spain, but it was not, however, until June 1583, that there appeared in the reports of Juan Batista de Tassis, one of Spain's key diplomats, Philip's conclusive sentence: "I am accepting the offer of Hercules."[14] "Hercules" was the code name of Henri de Guise and "Jacobo" that of his brother Mayenne. From then on the code names appeared regularly in the Spanish correspondence and a series of payments began in earnest. "The offer of Hercules" was to work toward the abolition of Protestantism in France and the Netherlands, to ensure that the decrees of the Council of Trent be accepted throughout France, and to hinder successfully the Huguenot Prince from the French throne.

The first two clauses might be worked out with care and diplomacy, but the third was a thorny problem. If Navarre was not to inherit, then a line of succession must be designed in another direction. Thus there was pushed to the center of the stage, a man already old by Renaissance standards, Charles, Cardinal de Bourbon, younger brother of Navarre's father. Never a man of great intellectual acumen, in his old age he was no more than a pawn for the House of Guise. Péréfixe, one of Navarre's earliest biographers, described him with both disdain and compassion as "that good man doting with age, permitting himself to be flattered with these vain hopes, [making] himself the bauble of the Duke's ambition who by this means drew to his party a great number of Catholics who considered the House of Bourbon."[15] Lest his cardinal's robes blend poorly with the fleur-de-lys, it was rumored that he might "put off his hat and purple" and strengthen his alliance with the Guises by marrying the sister of the Duke, now widow of the late Duc de Montpensier. There would be, then, no need for Guise to seize the throne by violence, since he could direct the course of the state by sitting at the right hand of his brother-in-law the King. "The House of Guise is closely leagued with the Cardinal de Bourbon," wrote the Nuncio. "He is their ass to bear their whole burden," commented Stafford, weary of both the intrigues and indolence of the French court.[16] Although the King lived in terror and suspicion of the House of Guise, he took no practical steps to hinder their plots, and the Queen Mother, sick with gout and out of favor with her son, could do nothing. "Poor woman," commented the English ambassador, "she dare say no other than the King will have her say for the world is not with her as it hath been, though in show there is as much honor to her as ever was."[17]

Meanwhile Guise, away from court and free in his own territories of Lorraine, set in motion the machinery planned so long ago for a Holy League: a union of militant Catholics for whom the conservation of the Catholic faith was their primary goal. Its clearly defined objective was to prevent the crown of France from falling into the hands of a heretic. The central thesis of its political philosophy was that religious unity was the social foundation of any state. Thus, the head of the government must be a Catholic and the rallying cry was the old one, "*Un roi, une foi, une loi.*" It is undoubtedly true that the idea of a Huguenot king was so generally intolerable that some instrument would have been fashioned for stopping Navarre even had Guise not been at hand; yet the credit or blame for the form and drive of the Catholic League must remain his. All the old arguments presented at the Estates of Blois were again to the fore, this time with more urgency since the prospect of a heretic king was now that much closer. The terrors of what happened to Catholics across the Channel were graphically presented and English exiles were called upon for lurid eyewitness accounts: Catholics burned at the stake, Catholics drawn and quartered, Catholics imprisoned without redress and exiled without funds or friends. This was the royal patrimony Navarre would bring with him to the throne of France. Fanning out from Paris, always a seat of conservatism, the carefully organized movement spread to the provinces. Government officers, university students, merchants, peasants—all were rocked with the thought of the terrors that awaited them and all joined with a desperate desire the League that alone could save them.

The King, aroused at last from his lethargy and frightened by the continued rumors of secret pacts with Spain, issued on November 11, 1584, a declaration against the League: ". . . against all persons, making leagues, associations, intrigues and practices against the estate of this realm."[18] But the declaration was as impotent as the King who signed it. Far more important was the secret pact signed on December 31 between Spain and Guise in the old feudal castle of the Guises at Joinville. The chief emissaries of Spain were Juan Batista de Tassis and Juan Moreo; Mayenne and Guise signed in their own right. The defined ends of the treaty were to defend the Roman faith, extirpate heresy, and affirm the right of the Cardinal de Bourbon to the throne of France. In addition, certain private bargains were struck with Philip: Guise promised to fight the Flemish rebels, to return to Spain the disputed territory of Cambrai in return for Spanish money and Spanish troops. All, however, was to remain cloaked in the utmost secrecy until March—the time assigned for an open movement.

The King, despite his suspicions of what was going on in Lorraine, did nothing but indulge in further luxuries and more erotic devotions. Those who loved France wept at what seemed her inevitable ruin.

Those closest to the King pitied his impotence. The populace of Paris was less kind. The pulpits—all with their Guisard ministers—fulminated against this puppet king, expostulating that a king who rules badly no longer has the right to the throne, for only well-ordered power can be from God. Soon a spate of literature poured from the presses in a tide no man could control. Busini commenting on the nature of these pamphlets and lampoons described them accurately as *pasquini sceleratissimi*, scurrilous pasquinades which reduced the King to a caricature of royal power. Every move that the King now made played into the hands of the patient and astute Henri de Guise. Within a month, 6,000 people, it was estimated, had turned their backs on the King to join the League. By mid-March Guise was ready for open action. He had levied a sizable army at home, was helped by Spanish funds, and even had promises of aid from the Vatican for his holy enterprise. Thus on March 31 was issued the formal declaration of the League, a manifestation of open hostility against those "who are seeking to subvert the Catholic religion and the entire state."

The Declaration of Péronne, as it was called, was an impressive document, written, as a contemporary noted, in a "strong and noble style." The goals it set for itself were equally "noble" and most of France responded to it. It struck hard at the monarchy, although never overtly referring to the King himself. It pointed out that if the faith of France was in danger, this was because of the bad government to which France was subject. It complained of those who had "insinuated" themselves into the King's friendship and weakened his authority in order to aggrandize their own. It deplored a nobility "enslaved and set aside," a clergy "crushed by tithes and subsidies," a people "squeezed by taxes of every kind." The task of the League was to restore these people to their rightful positions; the League, in Guise's rhetoric, was to be an instrument for the common weal. Although the declaration implicitly insulted her son, it did not hesitate to flatter the Queen Mother, stating fulsomely, "together we very humbly beg the Queen, Mother of the King, our honored lady, without whose wisdom and providence the state would have been lost, for the faithful testimony she can give to our faithful service . . ."[19]

All this was but peripheral, however, to the main point of the declaration: a statement by the Cardinal de Bourbon declaring himself heir apparent to the throne. Since, as Navarre later pointed out, the King was but thirty-three and the Cardinal already sixty-two, such a declaration seemed more like a joke than a serious political move. The

Cardinal himself took it in great earnest, even petitioning the Holy See that he might be released from his priestly vows to follow this other holy vocation opening up before him. Bourbon was a soft man who loved his ease; he had small intelligence and no great motivations; thus he was a perfect tool for Guise who showed him great deference to his face but was heard to call him *Le petit homme* behind his back. It was not a flattering nickname, but it was infinitely kinder than that coined by the Huguenots who with the robust humor of the south dubbed him "the Red Ass."

From March 31, the warfare was in the open. The King issued a counter declaration against the League but in both tone and matter it failed to meet the crisis. Knowing he had failed, he wrote to Navarre: "I have not been able to prevent the wicked schemes of the Duc de Guise; he is in arms; keep on your guard."[20] Guise was indeed in arms and successfully so. He had already taken Châlons-sur-Marne, while his brother took the precious and beautiful city of Dijon. By April word came to the King that not only Spain but Savoy as well was helping the League, and that the Pope himself was an accomplice, promising indulgences to those who assisted it. Sadly the King replied to the Nuncio, "A prince such as I am . . . should not be blamed and accused of lack of piety and zeal for religion, and yet, to my sorrow, I am."[21] "We are here marvelously troubled," wrote Stafford; "the Queen Mother weepeth and taketh on and cryeth out upon the King who having listened to none of the warnings now cannot put three men together. . . . The poor old woman is in her bed, sick for very melancholy." "If he were my king," concluded Stafford, "I would pray God to help him."[22] As the news poured in of increased membership in the League, the towns taken, the violent fulminations against the King from every quarter, it seemed that God alone could help the poor sallow figure who bore the ultimate responsibility for the ruin of France upon his shoulders.

When an offer of help did come, however, the King was loath to accept it: his cousin Navarre, whose position had stirred up the broil, offered himself and his army for the support of the King. He promised that he could have 24,000 foot and 3,000 horse at the King's service by the end of May. He would also bring with him three powerful Huguenot leaders, Damville, Turenne, and Condé. The offer served but to increase the King's anxiety. It was true that such a force might stem the Guisard tide, but what would it do to his reputation as The Most Christian King were he to league with heretics against the manifestly Catholic faction in his kingdom? He could hardly afford to alienate the Papacy and although the Guise influence in Rome had been mitigated with the accession to the throne of Peter of the cautious and moderate Sixtus V, the King knew that he must still step warily. Sixtus had, at first, been suspicious of the League; but the King knew that Olivares, the Spanish ambassador to the Vatican, was a persuasive man and that he had spoken long and cogently into the Papal ear. He was not surprised, then, when he received a message from the Pope, saying, "Tell the King I want to help His Majesty with all my power, but only on the condition that he does not mix himself up with the Huguenots, rather that he must drive them out of his kingdom. I am now given assurances that the League has only this end in view."[23] The persuasive Olivares had won his point. In the light of such a message Henri could do nothing but refuse Navarre's offer, even though he recognized that by such a refusal he was but levying another army against himself.

On April 25 Busbecq summed up the situation in a letter to the Emperor Rudolph: "All here are in the terror of a sudden war which had not been anticipated; it was all the time before the King's eyes but he could not see it. It is more than two months ago since the Duc de Bouillon had written to inform him. . . . It is said that the King is in a terrible state for having paid no attention to this information. The Cardinal de Bourbon is the supposed author of all these troubles, but actually, if I am not mistaken, it is the Duc de Guise, Mayenne, and the Cardinal de Lorraine along with their uncles the Duc d'Aumale and the Marquis d'Elbeuf, as well as the Duc de Mercoeur, brother of the Queen and governor of Brittany. . . . The Queen Mother still with the Duc de Guise is forced to listen to the ugliest complaints about the conduct of the King her son."[24]

If Henri de Valois had failed to interpret the signs that surrounded him, his cousin Navarre had been more alert. Even before the publication of the Declaration of Péronne, Navarre had met with Damville to decide upon a common plan of action. For a week they met in the town of Castres, just north of Carcassonne, and from their meetings emerged a declaration of their own, signed by Navarre, Damville, and Condé. They condemned the policy of the House of Guise, accusing them of trying to substitute the House of Guise for that of Valois, of misleading the King, of having fomented civil war for a quarter of a century. They agreed that if the Guises would put down their arms and give back to the Huguenots their rightful positions, they too would relinquish their arms, warning, however, that if a single violation took place, France could expect total war. At the same time that Navarre offered his services to the King, Damville also wrote to him, repeating that he had the honor of walking in his father's footsteps—a man of great devotion to the Church but one who had always stood first for the cause of peace. Any other course, Damville reminded the King, already stood condemned by the test of experience. Countering the King's charge that his alliance with Navarre was contrary to the loyalty he owed to his King and his country, Damville declared himself to be a loyal servant of the King and not of the Spaniards. There was no need to spell out the implications.

Navarre, too, wrote to the King reiterating his loyalty. "You have only to command me," he assured the King, pointing out, however, that he "waited from hour to hour" while "others less close to you are given commissions." "Surely I cannot be forgotten," he continued, reminding the King that almost two years earlier he had informed him that the Guises had begun to plot with Spain. Yet even these protestations of loyalty went unheeded and some weeks later when Navarre sent Chassincourt to court, he advised him, "Tell the King that I grow impatient while I watch things grow worse which could in a moment be amended." Concerning the Declaration of Péronne, Navarre warned, "They have addressed it to me in particular and to those of the Religion; but it is obvious that I am only a pretext and that their principal ends tend directly against your person and against the state." Still the King hesitated and by the end of April, Navarre, watching the gains of the League, wrote to his lieutenant Matignon, ". . . they advance foot by foot while we do nothing to oppose them." As the League seized Castets, Montignac, Ste. Bazile, he wrote in an agony of haste to Ségur, "Hurry, hurry, hurry; hurdle every obstacle, delay will ruin us."[25]

Even as Navarre recognized the immediacy of the peril, the King urged him not to move, to keep the peace as long as possible, assuring him foolishly that nothing would be done prejudicial to his interests. Navarre answered with a blunt realism: "I have forbidden anyone of the Religion to move, as you commanded, assuring them that Your Majesty knows how to overcome the enemy and maintain his servants"; yet, added Navarre, "it is difficult to sustain this argument when there is so much evidence to the contrary." Still the King would not authorize him to move, and in the beginning of May Navarre wrote to one of his captains, "Never have I put my trust in God as I do at this moment."[26]

Navarre's trust in God, however, never diminished his human activity, and the first weeks of May were taken up with efforts to secure help from the Protestant nations. As often in the past, Elizabeth of England was his first recourse. As early as March 12, even before the Guises had made an open declaration of their position, Navarre had written to Elizabeth, asking for no specific help, but wishing to assure himself of her support for the troubles he foresaw. It was a letter that made its point obliquely in favor of Elizabeth's own interests, since Navarre was well aware that mere philanthropy would never move England's Queen. He is grateful, he told her, that God has put her in a position where she can help the oppressed, for, as she is undoubtedly aware, this same oppression may very well touch her own kingdom unless her wise prudence intervenes to keep it from spreading. By April 5 the Guises were in the field, and Navarre wrote again to Elizabeth of the ruin that would face them all unless prompt action were taken. It was Elizabeth's passionate hatred for and fear of Spain that he played on, commenting that the Guises were but tools in the hands of that wily and ambitious monarch who hoped by ruining France to lift Spain to further power. It was the strongest point he could make, for Elizabeth's fear of Spain might move her when nothing else could.

An even more pointed letter had gone to Robert Sidney, Earl of Leicester, warning him of the danger to England as well as France, for, as he wrote, "It must be obvious to you that the ruin of one means the ruin of the other." Again the fearsome name of Spain was used as a wedge, as he pointed out that "the ambition of Spain, which has overcome so many lands and so many oceans, thinks nothing in the world inaccessible to her."[27] It was far from an empty threat, for Philip, egged on by the Guises' ambition to seize Scotland, had begun his plans for the Armada. Letters had already gone out from Navarre to the King of Denmark, to Duke Casimir, to James of Scotland, all of whom waited to see what steps England would take. "All Christianity is waiting upon your prudence and authority," Navarre wrote to Elizabeth by his emissary, Ségur, whom he had sent into England to give the Queen a full report of the "tragedy" that played itself out in France. Even faced with the possibility of Spanish aggression, Elizabeth hesitated, fearful of winning the enmity of France should she overtly assist Navarre. Toward the end of June, Navarre wrote wearily to Ségur, "We live in uncertainty, waiting for the decision of war or peace and always sure that either way will lead to evil."[28]

There was little hope in France that spring as the people watched their King take sanctuary in his hermitage, casting off his robes of state for the gray weeds of a monk at a moment when France most needed a king. "Rouse yourself from this long sleep," wrote Navarre to his cousin; but it was too late. Elizabeth, looking across the Channel at the impotence of her brother monarch, commented in contempt, "Jesus, was there ever a prince so smitten by the snares of traitors without the courage or counsel to reply to it."[29] Only the Queen Mother continued to hope with her active courage which still believed that events might yet be turned to their favor. Her son, who had so often passed her over in these last years, now implored her help. In mid-March, despite gout and catarrh and toothache, she set out for a meeting with the House of Guise.

She arrived at Epernay, a pretty town on the Marne, and took up residence in the celebrated abbey. Here she awaited the conferences which the Guises had promised her. When the conferences finally opened in May, League successes in the field had placed them in a position to bargain as they would, and the Queen Mother knew herself worsted. The Duc de Guise made his demands very clear: the Cardinal de Bourbon was to be recognized as heir apparent to the throne, the Roman religion alone was to be permitted in France, Guise himself was to be given command of the royal troops.

For once the Florentine Shopkeeper had nothing with which to bargain. If she did not accede to their wishes, the Guise were in a position to force them on the kingdom by violence. Perhaps more than their arrogance, she hated their pretexts—that all of this was done as loyal sons of Rome, as humble members of the one, true Church. Even the Roman Pontiff seemed dubious about the place of religion in the French troubles, and to the Cardinal de Bourbon who had expected a bull of approbation he wrote: "We can only praise your zeal for religion; but even an end so legitimate as this should not be attained except by legitimate means; and before all else, you owe homage and obedience to the majesty and authority of the King."[30]

By the first week of July Catherine knew that the long weeks of bargaining were to no avail. Heavy with the rheumatic pains that made travel a torture and heavier still with a sense of failure, she made the journey south to Nemours where the treaty between the Guises and the crown was to be concluded. In all the journeys she had made before, she had always won something—not always all that she had hoped, but never before had her travels left her with empty hands. This time she had failed; despite her brave words to the King, her assurances that things were going well but slowly, she had seen from the first that Guise held the rein hand. She, who had known so long what it was to be accounted a power in the state, found herself now bereft of everything save her maternity; she was the King's mother and no more. She had failed her son, failed her own dreams of glory, failed France. Everything lay heavy on her, most of all that weight of loneliness that set her apart from the others as they sat at the council table at Nemours. Here on July 9 she appended her signature to the Edict of Nemours, knowing as she did so that she had not only strengthened the sword arm of the House of Guise, but that she had added a jewel to the crown of that most hated enemy, the King of Spain. Her signature condemned her son to servitude, and with words that weighed heavier than stones she wrote to him to interpret as he would the simple fact: "I have this morning sent the articles of peace to you."[31]

It was a peace which gave the Guises all they asked for, preserving the King in name only. To L'Estoile, as to many intelligent Frenchmen, the Edict of Nemours seemed the end of an era, since it placed the King in servitude to the League. It was with a doomsday finality that L'Estoile noted in his journal: "after so many difficulties and debates, comings and goings, the treaty was concluded at Epernay between the King and the House of Lorraine. By this it was decided that there should be but one religion in France, and the other exterminated. . . . This was the only subject dealt with, because on the matter of the reformation of the kingdom, of which there has been some talk before and since, they were afraid that it might have to begin with them. . . . The worst part of this is that the King is on foot and the League on horseback, as is proved by his penitent's sack and their cuirasses."[32]

It was, of course, upon the Huguenots that the blow fell hardest; while they had feared such a measure, they had hoped that Navarre's influence with the King would keep him from betraying them. For Navarre it was the end; he sat without moving, his head buried in his hands for several hours. Nothing could comfort him; nothing give him hope. When, finally, he raised his head, it was reputed that half of his mustache had turned white with the intensity of his sorrow. On July 10 he wrote a letter, powerful in its restraint, to Henri de Valois: "I understand, my Lord, that peace has been made both without me and against me. You have joined your enemies to ruin your servants, your most faithful subjects, and those who have the honor of being your nearest relatives. Even more, you have divided your forces, your authority, your resources to make them strongest who are armed against you. . . . I find this very difficult and almost unendurable. . . . Even so, my Lord, I cannot abandon the hope I have always had in the goodness, justice, and love of Your Majesty for your servants, your subjects, and your state."[33]

Even as Navarre wrote, the King, at the monastery of St.-Maur, outside of Paris, was receiving the Duc de Guise and Cardinal de Lorraine "with a smiling and joyful countenance," kissing them twice as a sign of trust and affection. Yet no one was fooled, and Cavriana expressed the fears of all when he wrote: "Friendship between them is not possible; rather there is a distrust which grows from day to day which will perhaps erupt into some disastrous event."[34]

Although the Edict of Nemours was the greatest blow that Navarre had so far to sustain, it at least made the path before him clear. As early as June he had already made a public declaration of his position in reply to the Declaration of Péronne. It was a document of some length prepared by that careful statesman, Duplessis-Mornay. It indicated the falsity of the accusations made by the League, reiterated his belief in the Christian religion, and his willingness to "change for the better as soon as the better should be taught him." It deplored the folly of declaring the aged Cardinal de Bourbon as successor to the King, and concluded by challenging Guise to single combat or to combat between small forces in order to avoid universal bloodshed. To this, Guise, arrogantly sure of his sword, replied that he must refuse lest in killing a Prince of the Blood he be guilty of parricide. In the cover letter which accompanied the document, Navarre wrote: "I am sure Your Majesty will not find it strange that being what I am, a man filled with a spirit of courage, I cannot pass over in silence these monstrous insults." Wishing to clarify his position not only to the King but to all Frenchmen, he begged that his statement be printed "in order that through it I may make my intentions clear to everyone."[35] The King, however, hesitated at such a request, fearful that such a step on his part might increase the animosity of the Guises.

Receiving no answer to his earlier letters, Navarre wrote again to both the King and the Queen Mother, describing the state of France as it appeared to him, and predicting the inevitable horrors ahead. "He is arming these rebels against himself," he wrote in warning to the Queen Mother, adding, "I console myself with my innocence, my integrity, and my devotion to both Your Majesty and the state." With the League in open war against the Huguenots, he no longer felt bound by the constraining measures laid upon him by the King and actively solicited help from England and Germany and massed what forces he could in the south. That energy which was to mark his reign so clearly from that of the Valois was now to the fore, as he wrote to Ségur a letter couched entirely in imperatives: Raise as large a group of Reiters as possible; do everything to get a good number of Swiss; raise a second army by means of the King of Denmark and other princes; pick the best army leaders available; employ for key posts the young ardent members of the nobility—and lastly and most typically—"Make haste!"[36]

For his part he was in haste to strengthen the parties within his kingdom, and in August he met with Condé and Damville at St. Paul-Cap-de-Joux near Toulouse. The document which emerged from this meeting bore the ponderous title, "Concerning the peace made with the House of Lorraine, the chief instigators of the League, to the prejudice of the House of France." It was a careful exposition, drawn up once more by Duplessis-Mornay, of all the machinations of the House of Guise from the time of François II to the present. The chiefs of the League were labeled "enemies of the King, of the House of France, and of the good of the state." All their interest in religion, the document stated, was no more than a pretext to hide their well-known designs: "to destroy the House of France and lodge themselves in its place." The conclusion was—as befit its authors—dynamic and unambiguous: "We shall wage war with them to the utmost and shall exterminate them by every means in our power."[37]

Frightened by the vise in which he found himself and impelled by the Queen Mother, the King responded by sending an embassy to meet with Navarre at Nérac at the end of August: its purpose was to regain him to the Catholic faith. In addition to the King's carefully chosen counselors, there were in the party two theologians from the Sorbonne who urged Navarre for the peace of his own conscience as well as for the good of the crown to become a Catholic. His answer was unswerving: since he was not aware of any error in the religion in which he was raised, he considered that it would be unbecoming to abjure it through either fear or hope. The King's last hope had failed.

Following this meeting, Navarre once again framed a declaration of his position, this time addressed to various princes in an effort to convince them of his primary loyalty to France. Referring to the conference that had just been so unsuccessfully concluded, he wrote: "I do not think that anything ought to be required of me, so that merely because of their desires I should be forced to violate my conscience." His statement, however, was more than an apologia or a condemnation of his enemies—it was a blueprint for action as well, cogent in its argumentation and moving in its rhetoric. What was done at Nemours must be condemned, he declared, for it was "a peace made with strangers at the expense of the Princes of the Blood; with the House of Lorraine at the expense of the House of France; with rebels at the expense of obedient subjects; with agitators at the expense of those who have bought peace by every means in their power. . . . I intend to oppose it with all my heart; and to this end to rally around me, according to my position in the kingdom, all true Frenchmen without regard to religion, since at this time it is a question of the defense of the state against the usurpation of foreigners."[38]

It was a manifesto of leadership such as France had not heard for many a year. The rhetoric rang true with no alloy to diminish its power. Mornay, that scrupulous keeper of Navarre's conscience, had advised him not long before to put aside those love affairs in which he wasted so much time and instead "make love" to France. It was in some ways an unnecessary admonition, for Navarre had always loved France. He had not loved the Valois ways. He had hated passionately what had happened on Saint Bartholomew's Day, had hated the false bonhomie with which he had had to live during his years of detention at the Valois court. France he had always loved and wept to see her torn and wounded; yet if he must fight to keep her from falling into the hands of Guise and Spain, then he would fight. Not all Catholics were Guisards and many were won by the open sincerity of Navarre's position. Stafford observed that many good Catholics flocked to his standard, and it was already in the minds of many that of the three Henris, it might be Henri de Navarre who would emerge victorious.

The possibility of victory receded, however, when word reached France in September, 1585, that the Roman Pontiff, despite his mistrust of the League, had capitulated to their demands—powerfully backed by Spanish coercion—and had issued a formal sentence of excommunication against Henri the "so-called King of Navarre."

CHAPTER VIII

The League Triumphant: 1585–1588

The most important thing here today is that Guise has made the leap; he is pledged.

The Spanish ambassador

❧❧❧❧ The language of the document which excommunicated Henri de Navarre was impressive:

The authority vested in Saint Peter and his successors by the infinite power of the Eternal King surpasses all the power of earthly kings and princes. Founded on a firm rock, unmoved by winds or storms—either favorable or unfavorable—its decisions and judgments are irrevocable and thus it zealously guards its duty to see that its laws are kept. When it finds anyone transgressing the laws of God, it punishes them severely, depriving them of their offices, however powerful they may be, and crushing them as ministers of Satan.

Thus, following the duty and responsibility which has been given to us by all churches and nations . . . and so that we may not be accused before God of neglecting our duty, we are forced to take up arms—arms which are not simply our own human weapons but those of the all-powerful God himself—for the destruction of those powerful enemies, those two children of wrath, Henri de Bourbon, formerly king of Navarre, and Henri de Bourbon, formerly Prince de Condé. Should anyone presume to encroach on this act, let him know that he will thereby incur the wrath of the all-powerful God and of the Apostles Peter and Paul.[1]

Such a statement left little doubt about the status of Navarre or his cousin Condé—or the responsibility of all good French Catholics to repudiate them.

The Guisards were triumphant and those who had been led to believe that Brother Felice Peretti would make a moderate pope realized they had been duped. Yet the bull had scarcely been signed when it became obvious that the apostolic aim had missed its target. Except for the most fanatical group, Frenchmen were enraged at what they considered papal interference in national affairs. What new papal privilege was this, they asked, to depose princes by the power of Peter? No one saw the ramifications of the bull more quickly than the King who, reported the Tuscan ambassador, was furious with the Apostolic Delegate's demand that he should have the bull promulgated at once. "It seems that the Pope would like me to act as his provost marshal in France," rasped Henri de Valois, more ticklish than ever over his royal power.[2]

It was the Queen Mother, however, who saw even more clearly than her son the dangers behind such a papal act, and she wrote with a sense of inevitability to Villeroy: "In all this I see only harm for the King, for if I saw that he had the means to be strong as I wish he were, I would not give a button for all those practices and dealings. . . . I would be sweet to all of them, popes and kings, to win such forces as would enable me to command and not to obey them."[3] Once again Catherine was right; it was neither the accusers nor the condemned who suffered most, but the hapless King caught between enemy fire. Although the bull drove some moderate Catholics from the League, it was not the King's cause they espoused but Navarre's. Despite his military weakness, the King could no longer risk accepting his cousin's offer of help, for in the light of the bull any communication with the heretic Navarre would be construed as a betrayal of the Catholic cause. The trap was proving even more effective than the League had anticipated.

If it paralyzed the King, it stirred Navarre to further action. He was not slow to respond to Rome, and in a matter of days denunciations appeared on the chief streets of Rome in which Navarre addressed himself in mimic style to "Monsieur Sixtus, the self-styled Pope." The occasion was ideal for the rhetoric of the Huguenot jurist, Hotman, whose pamphlets rang with fiery denunciations against this "stinking excommunication." Navarre, however, never adopted Hotman's tempestuous rhetoric and the letters which the Prince addressed to the

French King, to the Sorbonne, to the Paris Parlement, as well as to various European princes, were marked by an eloquent logic which won him in some circles the compliment of being "the most reasonable man in France." To the Paris Parlement which had already indicated its reluctance to register the bull, Navarre wrote cogently of his own position, concluding in a tone to win further sympathy: "However, it has happened (and I am certain that you see all the wrong that has been done to me) that the enemies of the King and of the kingdom are authorized and armed against me. Thus my patience and obedience must bear the pain of their rebellion, so that the foreigner may be satisfied at the expense of the householder, and the servant at the expense of the child of the house. This is something, my lords, which in truth is very hard for me. But I have God for my protector, France for my judge, all of you as my witnesses, and the King my Lord (for I cannot doubt him) as the vindicator of my sincerity."

To the Third Estate he assumed a different tone, a tone of a leader who understands the suffering of his people and would do everything possible to assuage it. Navarre's great gift was to win men by his humane understanding of their position, and now after years of indifference on the part of their rightful sovereign, the people of the Third Estate were moved by this Prince who assumed his own suffering so lightly and indicated a compassionate regard for the burdens which they bore. "It is not myself I pity, but you," he wrote. "I pity myself only because I do not have the power to defend myself without causing innocent people to suffer. . . . I was born a Frenchman. I sympathize with all your evils. I have tried every means of saving you from civil war, and in order to shorten it I will not spare even my life. . . ."[4] Had not the propaganda of the League been so telling, the response to Navarre's letter might have been far more favorable. But all that he said was immediately countered by such pamphlets as "A Warning from an English Catholic to French Catholics" which promised untold horrors to the simple Catholic citizens forced to live under the rule of a Protestant sovereign.

It was, however, to the King himself that Navarre made his most powerful appeal, pointing out what the Paris Parlement had already indicated: that such a bull, implying the Pope's right to free people from their allegiance to their king, might be more dangerous for the King of France than for the King of Navarre. This is, he affirmed, simply a veil for the aggrandizement of papal power. Is it the policy of the church for the shepherd to close the door to the sheep that have wandered, instead of searching to bring them back? "If this were truly in the cause of religion," Navarre commented caustically, "then they would wish to convert me rather than to subvert me." The letter which he wrote to the Queen Mother on the same day concluded with a warning, the truth of which she knew but too well: "I can foresee the day, Madame, when both you and the King will see, perhaps too late, whose hands you have armed."

Navarre's charges that the papacy and the League had acted in bad faith, that their zeal for the cause of religion was but a screen to conceal their ambitions, were bolstered by the fact that when he asked for a national council to discuss his conversion, he was refused. On October 11 in a formal letter to the Sorbonne he had written: "Judge then, Messieurs, which of these two parties has right on its side, which of the two should be given respect for this right; which of the two proposes a course of action salutary for this state and favorable to the church. . . . There is no doubt that you must choose between a civil war or a council; between the annihilation of one part of this state by the other or the reunion of two parts of the kingdom into one. . . . To conclude: I tell you, Messieurs, that I ask and agree to a general council, and to facilitate matters I will not refuse a national council. . . . If despite my request and against all the orders of the church, these proscriptions, murders, and other barbarities continue . . . I resolve to oppose them by a just defense; and may the curse fall upon those who have troubled this state under the false pretext of the church."

It was a powerful plea, but the Sorbonne, composed of the most reactionary theologians in France, could not stomach it. No move was made to accept Navarre's offer; instead the Paris pulpits inveighed against him as a relapsed and stubborn heretic whose intransigence now plunged France anew into civil war. Where, asked Navarre sardonically, was that Good Shepherd who, according to the Gospel, would leave his fold to seek the lost sheep? Where were those zealous missionaries who did not hesitate to journey to distant lands to preach to the infidels? What desire was here to instruct in the faith when they would condemn a man before listening to him! "Judge by this, my Lord," he wrote to the King, "the intention and plans of those who have solicited this wretched bull."[5]

With the refusal to consider his plea for a national council, war became inevitable and Navarre turned from rhetoric to arms. War had actually broken out in his own household six months before the bull of excommunication was issued. It was once again Margot who had stirred up trouble; this time not simply by a domestic squabble but by an armed revolt. If Margot had a dominant motive it is difficult to discover, for all the "indignities" which she had suffered had merged in her mind into a general spirit of revenge: revenge against the Huguenots who had never accepted her, against her brother who had publicly belittled her, against her husband who had humiliated her by months of repudiation.

Perhaps her response was caused by the discovery in her husband of a power she thought he lacked: the power to love. His affair with the Comtesse de Guiche bore little resemblance to the passing adventures he had shared with Rebours or Fosseuse. This was more than either gallantry or passion. There was a quality of tenderness and mutual response that placed it beyond the amorous intrigues that Margot had accepted as a conventional element of court life. What Navarre had felt for the others had amused Margot, for she had understood it, understood the ground from which it sprang, and its inevitable denouement. She had understood it because it had been her own experience. She, too, had known the exhilaration of power, of playing goddess to lesser noblemen, of leading her lovers along perilous paths in their search for her. Like any game of chance this game had its dangers as well as its rewards—but both Margot and her husband were inveterate gamblers. Yet now Navarre's gambling instincts seemed dead; he was not playing for a prize, was not even playing to win. He had given himself to Corisande without caution and without vanity. The game no longer had rules, for it had ceased to be a game. Corisande on her part did not guard her trophies, did not reign from her victor's throne. All that he gave her she returned to him with the gift of herself. Margot, thrust into a drama she did not understand, hated and mistrusted what she could not fathom.

Loneliness increased her anger, for Nérac which had once been a pleasure palace now had little to divert her. Navarre, occupied with the demands of love and war, spent most of the winter months in the saddle and on January 6, the Day of the Three Kings, always a feast of great revelry, the Queen found herself alone with her servants. Angry and aggrieved, she wrote to her husband: "If I thought that news from Nérac would be important enough for you to bother reading, Monsieur, I would tell you about our Feast of the Kings which we have solemnized in the usual way. . . . The feast would have been very lovely if it had been graced by your presence; for without that nothing seems very pleasant to me."[6]

Despite these recriminations Navarre stayed on at Pau, where, doubtless, Corisande remained the guest of his sister. If when he returned to Nérac late in February he feared to be faced with the tears and accusations of a jealous wife, he was mistaken. It was a Margot quiet and reserved who asked his permission to spend the weeks of Lenten devotion in the Catholic community of Agen. Conversely, if she expected either apologies or complaints against her proposed absence, she, too, was disappointed, for her husband was reputed to have said with apparent relief, "That's fine, my love; and pray for me, too."[7] On March 19, accompanied by a few of her ladies-in-waiting and a small number of cavaliers, Margot left Nérac for the short journey to Agen.

It is difficult to assess how complete Margot's plans for rebellion were when she left Nérac. Later, Matignon was to attest that the Queen had confided to his wife that she was already in close contact with Spain through the agency of the Duc de Guise. In the first months that Margot spent among the people of Agen, however, there was no suspicion that she was any more than a devout Catholic seeking to be among her own religionists during the days of solemn devotion preceding Easter. They found nothing strange in the fact that this good Catholic queen should wish to spend these days of penance and prayer apart from her heretic husband.

The townsfolk found their guest charming, pious, and generous. They were soon to discover that she was also that most romantic of ladies—a beautiful princess in distress—for about a month after her arrival she met with the principal men of the city and confided to them that she was in great danger from her husband, urging them to fortify Agen for their sakes as well as hers. At first even the perceptive Bellièvre had no suspicion of what she intended and wrote to the Queen Mother of the tragedy of the wife who had been forced to flee from her husband because of the "evil designs" of the Comtesse de Guiche.

When on March 31 the League issued the Declaration of Péronne, proclaiming the Cardinal de Bourbon the heir to the throne, Margot, recognizing this as the first step of the League to open power, began to manifest herself less as a guest and more as a mistress. Little by little, on the plea that she must protect herself from the double threat of her husband and the King's lieutenant Matignon, she brought more and more troops into the town until soon she had twelve hundred men in Agen. By the middle of May, the city was hers. With the keys of the city in her hands she could make her own plans as she would. She fortified the city, stationed soldiers under the leadership of her friend Duras, and kept Guise informed of her movements.

Margot's action was soon common knowledge and on May 5 Stafford wrote to Walsingham: "The King of Navarre's wife is plainly discovered to be of this League by letters of hers to the Duc de Guise . . . wherein she calls him her Hercules, her Alexander, and such other terms, and assureth him that she . . . desireth him not to spare the King of Navarre and the French King."[8] For the Queen Mother this latest news, which came to her as she was fighting her losing battle with the Guises, was too heavy to bear and she wrote: "I am so upset that I am ready to die. . . . There is not a single day that does not bring some new trouble. . . . I have never suffered so much. . . . I realize that God has given me this creature for the punishment of my sins."[9]

By September it was apparent that Margot was receiving Spanish subsidies, and Navarre, furious at her treachery not only to him but to France, gave Matignon full rein to besiege Agen. But by then no outside force was needed to vanquish Margot for she had completed her own ruin. In August she had sent Duras to Spain to treat with Philip over increased subsidies, but Duras had returned empty-handed. As a result, Margot was forced to increase taxation—never a popular solution. She had already lost the favor of the citizens by billeting her soldiers in private households where they demanded as their own the small quantities of food available, as well as the wives and daughters of the householders. Their liege-lady, Margot, who had spoken so movingly at her arrival, and whom they had welcomed so joyfully, was proving a tyrannous mistress.

Margot's imperious behavior and her indifference to the welfare of the citizens made her role increasingly unpopular. When in late summer, with the plague already raging in Agen, she refused permission for the citizens to leave the city, her rule became intolerable. A tumult arose and Margot, frightened by this sudden violence and warned that the townspeople would not hesitate to throw her from the ramparts, fled, her dignity and possessions left behind her. In an effort to recapture for Walsingham something of the French atmosphere, Stafford wrote, "Tumultus Gallicus."

At the fortress of Carlat, not far from Aurillac, Margot finally found refuge. Here high on a forbidding rock of black basalt, impregnable to men but the target for high winds blowing from the Auvergne, Margot took her stand. Here, constantly ill from the cold that penetrated through the broken windows and ill-fitting doors, Margot spent the winter of 1586. Soon, however, fearful of capture, she left Carlat for her mother's château at Ibois. She dared not take the easier roads, but fled over precipitous mountain paths, forded streams, slid down the slippery shale of the hills. She arrived at Ibois at night, groping her way through the unfamiliar courtyard and finding but a questionable sanctuary, for, the accounts record, there was "neither protector nor provisions—nothing but some walnuts, bean pods, and some lard."[10] She had barely closed the gates behind her, when she was assailed by a group of horsemen under the Marquis de Canaillac, come, on her brother's order, to take her into custody. Scandal upon scandal had frayed the royal patience and there were some who said that the brother would have had his sister killed, were it not for the restraining hand of his mother. Carted from place to place, Margot was brought finally to the high château of Usson where Louis XI had kept his prisoners, boasting that they were safer at Usson than at any other prison in France. So impregnable was the château that a contemporary noted, "Only the sun can force an entrance here."

It was at Usson, first heavily guarded by the King's men, then set at liberty through the devices of the Duc de Guise, that Margot was to spend the next eighteen years of her life. There is no need to think that the Tuscan ambassador exaggerated when he wrote that during those first terrible months, Margot fell prey to a despair so black that she lost the desire to live. Ultimately she chose life rather than death—even life under duress. Here at Usson she outlived both her mother and her brother, growing ridiculously fat, dressing out of fashion, painting grotesquely, and forgotten by that court which had once proclaimed her "a goddess from heaven rather than a creature of earth."

In the summer of 1585, however, neither her royal brother nor her royal husband could have predicted that Margot's scheming would come to such a wasted end. The King, fearful of everything, exaggerated the harm she might do; but once Navarre's initial rage was cooled, Margot's treachery affected him but little. He doubted her constancy to any cause, even that of the League, and doubted even more her ability to hold Agen against Matignon or the Huguenots.

She was of little danger as a military enemy, and as his wife her position had long been negligible.

His love for Corisande continued unabated, despite the opposition of the Huguenots who feared that the Catholic countess was but drawing their leader into a dangerous snare. D'Aubigné later acknowledged in his *Mémoires* that he had openly accused Corisande of being a sorceress "who had bewitched my master, and I had even gone to consult a doctor, Hotteman, to find out if he did not know some philters which could disenchant my master."[11] D'Aubigné's attitude was, as always, extreme, but Turenne expressed the opinion of many when he wrote: "I fear that the pleasures of the Comtesse de Guiche will retain the King of Navarre longer than the welfare of the general good requires."[12] In actual fact, it was Corisande who inspired Navarre to the activity of the next few months. It was to Corisande that he explained the advances of the League, the encroachments of the Duc de Mayenne, his own plans for increasing his forces and for besieging key cities held by the Catholics. He could explain it all to her because Corisande with her intelligent imagination knew how to listen. She loved too well the man of arms ever to dissuade him from personal danger; she loved too well the Prince who might some day be King of France to do other than encourage him to succeed. When, lonely and worried about his welfare, she wrote begging him to come to Pau, she was immediately ashamed of her request and countered it with another, entreating him, if he loved her, to put off his journey. Although sending messages through the occupied territory was always hazardous, Corisande did not hesitate to entrust notes to her inventive couriers who hid them in the linings of their caps, the heels of their shoes, the scabbards of their swords. The messages she received in return were hardly love letters: a friend is dead, a town is taken, a comrade is wounded, his army is suffering from plague; then almost as an afterthought came the affectionate conclusion, "Live assured of my fidelity; if possible, it is stronger than ever."

From time to time, however, he found time for a longer letter, the kind of letter he might have written often had war not become for him a way of life. On June 17 he wrote from Marans, not far from La Rochelle, an idyllic spot which war had not yet ravaged:

> I have never seen a place so suitable for you. With this in
> mind I intend to make some exchange for it. It is an island

enclosed by woodland marshes, where every hundred steps
there are canals so that you can explore the woods by boat.
The water is clear and rather fast-running. The canals are
wide and the boats all very splendid. In this woodland there
are a thousand gardens which can be visited only by boat. . . .
The land is full of wheat and is very beautiful. One can
be tranquil here in time of peace and secure in time of war.
One can rejoice in the presence of someone you love or
lament in his absence. . . . My soul, keep me in your grace
and believe that my fidelity is pure and spotless; there has
never been its equal. . . . Your slave who adores you madly.[13]

But Corisande, although sometimes a romantic, sought no tokens
from the man she loved. It was not so much his protestation of
love which shook her heart as the news that he had successfully
confronted the foe. His cause had become her own, and she sent
her son to his service, cut down her forests and sold the timber,
listened to the insults both Catholics and Protestants hurled against
her name and never wavered. She had too active a mind to find
satisfying the long weeks at Pau spent in the company of the sickly
Catherine de Bourbon but she was willing to wait in expectation
of those brief visits when Navarre with a few soldiers, successfully
evading enemy troops, would knock upon the gates of the château
to spend the night with her.

These nights became increasingly few as the power of the League
waxed and Navarre gave himself wholesale to the business of protecting his lands. At the end of 1585 he had written to one of
his lieutenants, "The news that I have received from court is that
Mayenne is on the march with the largest possible force. The King
has agreed with everything they wanted, so we shall soon have them
on our hands. That is all I can say for the present." Once again
he wrote to the French clergy and to the nobility trying to open
their eyes to see their "true enemy." "I fear and bewail the fate of
the poor and the innocent who will bear the horrors of war," he wrote,
but all to no avail.[14] Again he stated his willingness to appear before
a national council to discuss his religious position, but the League,
for whom such a council would be disastrous, successfully fought
such a possibility. Underscoring the policy of the right-wing Catholics,
Olivares, the Spanish ambassador to the Vatican, wrote to the Pope
warning him to distrust anything he might hear concerning Navarre's
conversion. "I hear from France that steps are being taken with

His Holiness to obtain permission for the Béarnais to recant," Olivares wrote; "thus it is hoped to ensure for him the possession of the kingdom. This would be simply setting fire to France. . . . Let His Holiness be undeceived with regard to the supposed sincerity of the Béarnais. We might believe in it if he only asked to retire into a monastery and do penance; but as it is the means for him to succeed to the throne, it is clear it is only a pretence."[15] Retiring to a monastery was a Spanish solution, not a French one, however, and Navarre no matter what the obstacles arrayed against him never gave up the hope of victory.

There was little that spoke of hope in the spring of 1586. The help he had requested from the German princes was slow in coming, and Elizabeth, as always, hedged before the expenditures necessary to help her fellow prince. Meanwhile Mayenne was abroad in Guyenne and while Navarre was reputed to have said tauntingly, "The Duc de Mayenne is not so terrible a person as to stop one from walking about Guyenne," yet he knew he was not ready for a major combat with the League. Navarre, knowing Mayenne to be a cautious man, ponderous and slow both in his own movements and military commands, realized that his own strength lay in his speed. "Put wings on your best horse," he wrote urgently to his old comrade Batz, who had fought at his side at the victory of Cahors. "I have told Montespan to run his to death. Why? I will tell you at Nérac. Make haste, run, come, fly. This is the order of your master and the prayer of your friend."[16] By June his haste had reaped some small rewards: the port of Brouage was fortified, and the towns of St. Jean-d'Angéli, Royan, Taillebourg had been taken by the Huguenots. The obese Mayenne, who, Navarre claimed, spent more time at dinner than he did in bed, was having a harder time than he had bargained for.

Meanwhile Navarre had recognized that he could hope for nothing from the King. In May he had sent La Mersilière to court to attempt once more to present his position and to assure Henri de Valois of his desire to help him in any way possible. But La Mersilière could hardly get a royal audience, for as L'Estoile recorded, ". . . one can hardly get the King out of a monk's cell and the more he thinks about the situation, the weaker is his side and the stronger is the League."[17] As the first summer heat hit the capital, bitter epithets and mocking verses were scrawled on the streets. "The sluggard king," was the Parisians' contemptuous title for him as he sought

sanctuary from their pleas and accusations in the Bois de Vincennes.
Elizabeth who had long entertained nothing but disdain for Henri
de Valois but who feared Spanish power in France should he concede
totally to the demands of the League, wrote to him in June 1586:
"Pardon me, but it is my affection which dares me to speak so
freely. Before God I have no other motive but my love for you.
I am amazed to see you betrayed by your own council, by those
closest to you in the world and for you not to have wind of it.
. . . For the love of God do not sleep too long a sleep. I understand that there is a truce of some days; use this to strengthen
your own position and be careful not to agree to their conditions
which will only lead to your own disgrace and the loss of your
state."[18]

Her letter came too late. Henri de Valois could not rouse himself
from his lethargy—a lethargy which his fears only increased. That
summer famine struck Paris and the starving population took to the
fields where they cut the half-ripe grain where it stood, threatening
to use their knives on anyone that tried to stay them.

War and famine—the scourges of which the Evangelist John had
spoken in his Book of Revelations. The red horse and the black
horse with their fearful riders were abroad in the countryside while
the King scourged himself and mumbled his prayers to no avail.
War and famine were enough to ruin France, but there was more:
in September the Loire overflowed and from Roanne to Nantes the
country lay beneath the flood waters. League after league lay covered,
while houses and bridges were swept away in the current. When the
waters subsided, the crops were ruined, silt lay heavy upon the fields,
and the carcasses of cattle rotted in the fields.

The King, more helpless than ever, empowered his mother to set out
on another "journey of pacification." Thus, once more, in the interests
of peace, Catherine left Chenonceaux to travel first to Tours and the
white splendor of the château at Azay-le-Rideau and finally southward in
an effort to arrange a conference with Navarre. The "eternal negotia-
tor," now in her sixty-seventh year, still had not lost hope in her
ability to manage men—even such men as her evasive son-in-law;
but Navarre, seeing no point in an open clash between himself
and the Queen Mother, spent the autumn months evading the retinue
which pursued him relentlessly.

Catherine, as truculent in the cause of peace as most men are in
the cause of war, had vowed to follow her son-in-law wherever he

went, and thus she journeyed south into Poitiers and then westward into St. Maixent, the town where in 1582 she had said farewell to Navarre as she and her daughter had made their way to court. The four years that had passed since that meeting had brought the burden of age to Catherine; her resilience was gone. Her stomach was often queasy and her legs swollen from the long hours of travel. For two weeks she waited at St. Maixent but Navarre as always pleaded urgent business elsewhere. In the penetrating cold of December she still waited with no consolation but a short letter from her son which she cherished for his kindess to her.

It was not until December 13, after days of wrangling over security measures, that Navarre met with the Queen Mother at St. Brice, a little river town between Jarnac and Cognac. Navarre had arrived with a sizable body of troops, but these he left beyond the city walls while fifty Catholics and fifty Huguenots were chosen to stand guard at the gates. There in the hall of an isolated house, with the cold, winter light sifting through the high arched windows, the Queen Mother met her son-in-law at last. Both were flanked by their diplomats: Nevers and Lanssac on Catherine's side; Turenne and Duplessis-Mornay with Navarre. But essentially it was a combat between the keen-witted prince and his persistent mother-in-law. Legend has obscured much of what actually took place at St. Brice, but it is colorful legend well suited to the actors who played the drama. The Queen Mother upon greeting Navarre was noticed to "cover him with infinite caresses" embracing him, running her hands over his sides, until finally with a laugh he undid the buttons of his doublet and baring his chest announced, "You see, Madame, I keep nothing covered."[19]

The talks, begun with mutual distrust and divergent aims, were inevitably doomed. None of the wiles on which Catherine had counted was successful in winning Navarre. Still inclined to think of him as a light young prince whom she had kept trotting at her stirrup during his years at court, she had brought with her her "flying squadron," hoping that a beautiful face would soften his obduracy. But when with a typical double meaning, she assured him that he could have "anything he wanted," she was met with the plain answer that he saw nothing that he wished. Evasion, ambiguity, procrastination were all weapons she used with master skill, but Navarre countered them all. Uanable to weaken her son-in-law's tenacity, Catherine grew petulant. Why, she asked, do you insist on bringing ruin to the kingdom;

why will you not obey the King? adding peevishly, "Have I not always been a good mother? . . . You used to be so friendly and tractable; now you have changed so." Navarre, annoyed by these accusations which placed France's ruin upon his shoulders, lost a little of his equanimity as he replied, "I have not obeyed the King for eighteen months. I am not afraid of him; I know what he can do. Yes, you were a good mother in my youth but not for the last six years. . . . It is not I who keep you from sleeping in your bed, but you who keep me from sleeping in mine. Madame, you grow strong on this trouble; if you had peace you would not know how to live."[20]

Navarre's show of self-confidence at St. Brice had been sheer bravado. He was desperately in need of men and of money to retain the soldiers he already had. Now at Fontenay-le-Comte he wrote once more to the King of Denmark thanking him for his good will but obviously hoping that it would be replaced by something more substantial. Early that spring, Guitry, unsuccessful in his efforts to win assistance from the German princes, wrote urgently to Walsingham: "Knowing as we do your good judgment in a matter of such great importance not only to us but for your state as well and fearing that if this prince sees himself abandoned by Her Majesty as he has been by the rest of Germany, great harm will come to the Christian Republic; while, on the contrary, if Her Majesty gives courage to this prince who is full of zeal and piety, we will predict the speedy delivery of France."[21] Her Majesty remained silent, however, and when Navarre's ambassador to England reported that he had been unsuccessful in soliciting from Elizabeth the 100,000 crowns which the King needed, he sent a further emissary, Buzenval, with the single instruction: "Rouse her up to help us."[22] Buzenval openly averted to what Guitry had but hinted at: if the League assisted by Spain were to be victorious in France, then Elizabeth might well have to look to her own safety. No better way to render ineffective Philip's covetous glances toward England than by assisting Navarre in his struggle against the League.

Elizabeth's consistent policy of hesitation was now reinforced by further Anglo-French difficulties, for on February 18, 1587, Mary Stuart, sister-in-law of the King of France, had been beheaded at Fotheringay Castle. The death sentence had been passed the preceding October and in the intervening months European feeling had been stirred in favor of the ambiguous figure of the Queen of

Scotland. Henri III had sent his most able diplomat, Bellièvre, to plead for clemency; Philip had reactivated his plans for an English invasion; Mary's young son vowed that the deed would not go unpunished; while the Papacy inveighed against this latest barbarity of the heretic Queen. "If to offend all the world be a good course of government, then can we not do amiss," wrote Walsingham bitterly to Leicester.[23]

Catherine de Medici also spoke in denunciation of her daughter-in-law's execution. Although the Queen Mother had bitterly resented Mary of Scotland's influence over her young husband, François II, during the few tumultuous months she ruled as Queen of France, now she showed herself full of maternal sympathy for "one of the most beautiful women in the world." She saw her death as a "threat to Catholic monarchies," leaving the way open to regicide. It was not only Catherine but all of France that bitterly resented Elizabeth's action, and Stafford wrote in consternation to Walsingham, "I must needs write that I never saw a thing more hated by little, great, old, and young, and of all religions than the Queen of Scots' death and especially the manner of it."[24] This ill-timed execution served the Guises well for they played to the hilt the tragedy of their Catholic cousin put to death on trumped-up charges by a heretic queen. The implications were obvious: in a country where a heretic wore the crown, no man's head was safe. Let Frenchmen think well before advancing the cause of the Béarnais! Stafford fearful lest the interests of the King and the League meet in this common cause warned Elizabeth that France might well turn against England unless the King "have some good offices" at the hands of the Queen of England.[25] Should the King of France ally himself with the League and Spain, England would be in serious danger.

Philip, however, had no intention of an alliance with the Valois; his plans were more circuitous. He was at last after so many years, so much reflection, so many abortive plots to embark upon "The Enterprise of England." The schemes for conquering England which his bastard brother, Don Juan, had spun so wildly many years before, were now to be worked out with a care and prudence that would make them invincible. Philip's cause had been strengthened in many ways by Mary of Scotland's death: she had named him as her successor; the Catholic cause in the British Isles had lost its champion; Elizabeth of England must be punished for her machinations against the Church of God—of which Philip saw himself increasingly as the only true and strong defender. Thus the plans for the Armada were hastened, and Philip, usually so cautious, now prodded his generals and goaded his shipbuilders, for he would brook no delay.

So shrouded in secrecy were Philip's schemes that even Elizabeth's Spanish agents could not inform her of what was being planned in the Escorial, but she knew enough of Philip to know that he could not be named to a kingship without trying to win the prize. Her own political situation had never been more difficult. When continued pleas for help came from Henri de Navarre, she hardly knew what to do. In the light of events in Spain and France she could ill afford to succor Navarre, whatever her private sympathies, yet neither could she afford to have him vanquished for she saw in him a bulwark against Spanish power in France. It was this latter view which Walsingham sought to encourage when he wrote to Lord Burghley in the fall of that year: "There is no way so apt to stop the Spanish expeditions against this realm, as the upholding of the King of Navarre and the keeping under of the House of Guise, whom Spain seeketh to advance. If Her Majesty shall lose this opportunity, either by long delay in resolving or by not sending such a portion of treasure as may do good, she shall have cause to say, 'Farewell my days of peace.'"[26] With this in mind, Elizabeth consented to secret subsidies, deviously paid, to keep mercenaries in the field against the League.

Thus by the end of the summer the Huguenots were supported by Germans and Swiss who traversed Lorraine and Champagne, passed over the Seine and marched on to the Loire. Navarre heading eastward from La Rochelle intended to join them in Bourgogne. Joyeuse, watching Navarre's progress, saw this as his opportunity to regain his lost favor with the King and with an army noted more for its elegance than its experience, he set out to intercept the Béarnais at Coutras. Navarre, aware that he was ill-equipped to fight so large a force, counted on the Huguenots' ability to move with speed and thus avoid the trap that Joyeuse was attempting to set. But this time Navarre's calculations were too optimistic, and Joyeuse's ponderous forces "all of gold, with feathers, embroidered scarfs and velvet cloaks" reached the Dronne before him, effectively checking his plan to cross the river and travel north to join the German army. Unable to avoid a battle, the Béarnais deployed his troops in the most advantageous positions. Although he could not match Joyeuse's force in size, his leaders were his most skilled and experienced soldiers. At his side were the old veterans of Jarnac and Moncontour and leading his cavalry were the fiery Condé and his brother Soissons, who though he might lisp at court spoke clear and true in battle. It was daybreak as the armies maneuvered into place and the sun was high above the Dronne when the first charge took place. However religion may have been used as a cloak for ambition on both sides, the Huguenot preacher Gabriel d'Amours who accompanied the troops wished to make it manifest that this contest was no mere struggle for mortal gain. He insisted that they kneel in prayer and that their war cry be the French translation of David's psalm of victory: "This is the day the Lord has made; let us rejoice and be glad in it." Joyeuse, close enough to see the Huguenot troops on their knees, first took this as a sign of weakness, but as the first shock struck the royal forces he knew he had underestimated the enemy. "They seem meek and humble," his lieutenant Lavardin had warned him, "but when it comes to the charge, you will find them devils and lions."[27] It was not D'Amours alone, however, who had put fire into the veins of the Huguenots for Henri had that day, so legend goes, placed on his helmet a plume of white feathers that he might be distinguished in the midst of battle —a plume that soon became not only a personal symbol but a symbol of the whole Huguenot cause. Neither long prayers nor long speeches pleased Navarre and his address to the leaders was that of a man of war: "I shall say nothing else to you but that you are of the House of Bourbon; and if God live, I will now show you that I am worthy to be the first-born of the family." "They are ours," he concluded, looking at the enemy; "glory be to God, service to the King, our sovereign Lord; may honor be ours and salvation to the state."[28]

By mid-afternoon the Catholic forces were routed and Joyeuse himself for all his "fine plumage" lay dead on the field, surrounded by hundreds of his fellow soldiers. It was a victory unparalleled in the history of the religious wars and they listened for the signal to pursue the retreating remnant north into the Leaguers' own territory. Poitou lay open before them, but the order they awaited did not come. Instead Navarre announced that he was traveling south, and taking a small troop of men with the twenty-two conquered flags as trophies of his victory, he made his way through Guyenne to Nérac to lay his trophies at the feet of Corisande. It was a move which came close to costing him the loyalty of his captains for whom victory was too costly to be thrown away so easily for love. He listened to their arguments but he did not swerve from his decision. "He threw their words to the wind and his victory to love," wrote D'Aubigné bitterly. And even six years later, the zealous and truculent D'Amours, trying to curb the license of his king's life, recalled to him that bitter day: "Did we not tell you that if we did otherwise, the victory which God had given you would prove to be of no account in the future! You broke up your army; you went into Béarn; you understand me well."[29] Only Duplessis-Mornay, determined to be loyal to his leader at any cost, found excuse for Navarre in saying that caution was most needful, that it would have been folly to pursue the royal army into their own territory, especially since this would have prohibited them from joining with the mercenaries who were waiting for them at the Loire.

Navarre's journey to Nérac was made at a great price; it was his first great victory in the five years that Corisande had been his mistress and the standards which he placed at her feet were not simply a symbol of a battle won, but of a kingdom which might yet be his. The three days they spent together should have been the fulfillment of five years of dreams; yet something had gone: a spark of passion on Navarre's part, and on Corisande's the free gift that love can attain only when it knows itself secure. As he presented to her the flags, blood-stained and cannon-torn, she knew that he gave her the truest share he could in his greatest victory. It was much to give, a symbol that the victor often gave to God alone, yet it was not all. In the year and a half since she had seen him, a bit of Navarre had wandered astray and she could not bring it back. Corisande was too sophisticated a woman to have believed that Navarre could remain physically faithful to her. She had heard that in the preceding March Esther Ymbert had borne the Béarnais a son. She must have heard also of his affair with the pretty Suzanne des Moulin, married to a pompous grammarian too absorbed in his Chaldean texts to notice where his wife found her bed. These were those *passades* which Navarre took so lightly that he never thought of them as encroachments upon his love. Perhaps Corisande had thought that she, too, could take them as lightly as her lover.

"Live assured of my fidelity," he had so often written to her, and she had been amused at his vehement protests; now she found his protests empty, and she began to do what once would have been inconceivable to her: cling to him as he rode beyond her reach. She was thirty-five, an age when the moments of present happiness were no longer enough to keep her mind from assessing the future. She had grown heavy in the five years they had been lovers, and her skin had a blemish which paint could not conceal. She had come to her peak and passed beyond it; his still lay before him. Throughout November and into December, he stayed with her intermittently at Bidache and then at Hagetmau, writing to her between times: "I will be your faithful slave until death." On December 4 he arrived at Hagetmau for the last time. Although neither of them knew it, it was to be their final week together. On the morning of December 11, with news that all ways were blocked by the enemy, Navarre took to the saddle with the joy he always found in reckless exploits. He promised as always that he would return; there was no reason to doubt his word, but Corisande, whose intuition outweighed her logic, may have sensed that it would not be so.

In fear and uncertainty dawned the new year of which Péréfixe wrote ominously: "Now began the year 1588 which all judicial astrologers had called the wonderful year, because they foresaw so great a number of strange accidents, and such confusion in natural causes that they were assured that if the end of the world came not, there would happen at least a Universal Change."[80] The ominous prophecies were brought close to mens' minds when on the last Sunday of January Paris was darkened with so thick a fog that, as L'Estoile reported, the people in the streets groped like blind men while torches were lighted to pierce the inexplicable darkness. It would take more than candles to bring light to this darkened city where the King sat rattling his death's heads to avert the evils that no man's hand could stay. Earlier the Spanish agent had written to Philip: "The King has done nothing but dance and masquerade during this carnival without cessation. The last night he danced until broad daylight and after he had heard Mass, went to bed until night. He then went to his Capuchin monastery where he now is, refusing to speak or to see anyone. His carnival madness was, it would seem the greater, in order that he might be able to accentuate his asceticism afterwards."[31] The King was a driven man, a man without hope, who sought refuge not only from events but, as the Papal Nuncio observed, even from his own thoughts and wishes.

Every false move of the King underscored the power of the League.

The Guisard alliance with Spain was now fast; Mendoza had written
to Philip the preceding June, "The most important thing here today
is that Guise has made the leap; he is pledged."[82] The League had
agreed not only to Spanish money but to Spanish forces as well,
hoping, however, to bring them in under the banner of Lorraine
which would, they felt, somehow mitigate the affront of having Spanish
troops on the Ile-de-France. The ruse fooled but few and De Thou
wrote sadly: "Spain has been transplanted into France to walk proudly
with its head raised through the streets of Paris."[83] More and more
Navarre realized the truth of the declaration he had made over two
years before: his task was not simply to achieve religious liberty for
a small group of dissidents, nor even to put an end to civil war,
but to save France from a foreign force bent upon her subjugation.

Despite the victory of Coutras, fortune had not dealt kindly with
the Huguenots. Stafford, usually favorably inclined to Navarre, now
cooled in his praise, fearful, as he wrote, that the Béarnais might
throw away his cause in the interests of love as he had already done
after Coutras. Corisande's charms, he pointed out, might be a dangerous net set by the Catholics to catch the Prince. "The Countess
of Bishe [Guiche] . . . governeth the King of Navarre as she listeth
and is a very dangerous woman; and who marreth the King of
Navarre's reputation throughout the world; for he is altogether as-
sotted, as they say, upon her."[34]

Stafford's denunciation of Corisande was ironically timed, for it
came when the rift between Navarre and his mistress was becoming
daily more evident to them both. Her love had conquered her reason
and she could no longer hide her disquietude. She began to do
what she had vowed never to do: to complain to her lover of his
lack of fidelity, of affection, of constancy. Even as she wrote, she
knew that she only harmed whatever chance she might have to win
him back, but she had passed beyond reason into an anguish of
loneliness that she could not control. In mid-March, in answer to
her accusations, she received a letter from Navarre, a letter which
brought her no comfort, for instead of asking her pardon for the
faults of which she had accused him, he simply turned the accusations
upon Corisande herself: "I have received your letter, my mistress,
in which you tell me that you wish me no harm but that you
cannot feel any assurance in anyone so changeable as I. It was a
great pleasure to learn the first; and as for the other, you are very
much mistaken to remain in such doubt. You begin to interpret your

suspicions and they fall upon me. I am faithful in my love and my service is beyond all quarrels."[35]

Throughout the spring his letters continued with their avowals of his fidelity, but where in the past he had risked ambushes and bands of marauding soldiers to make his way south to the château on the hill of Bidache, now he made little effort to see her. The letters which protested that he lived to kiss her hands, that he was her slave, that he would be faithful forever were no longer her comfort for they seemed to protest too much, to lack the spontaneity which had been one of her greatest joys. As the winter snows cleared and travel became less difficult, she held to the hope that he would come to her at least for a day, but by May the hope had waned and in a melancholy which once she would have disdained she wrote to Navarre: "After tomorrow your arbor will be finished and every day your walks grow more beautiful. I can easily relate to you all the news here for that is all I have to do. For a long time now I have come to loathe this house and the whole place. It no longer speaks of nightingales. As a matter of fact, I have forgotten what their song was like, although I shall be very happy to hear the first one for its sad music will bring to birth some lovely thoughts in my heart; as for that, everything has that power, even the kestrels which fly before my window. Goodbye. It is so late that I do not know what I am doing."[36]

It was not a letter which would draw Navarre to her and she must have known it even as she wrote. Corisande had so long been his strength that he could not brook this sudden change at a time when he was most in need of support. The winter months had been hard ones for his troops, for Coutras had been followed by failure at Vimory, a failure which Guise made the most of and which he followed by a further victory at Auneau. "Saul killed his thousands but David his ten thousands," sang the Paris preachers in exultation of the League's triumph. Navarre had never more bitterly regretted his use of German mercenaries, for each encounter showed them more undisciplined. Their leaders were inconsequential men who were willing to risk no more than their pay demanded. Heavy with unwieldy baggage, they plowed through the country around the Loire, alienating the farmers by destroying their crops and sometimes their homes. Unable to cope with the muddy roads, they were forced to leave behind everything but their most essential arms, losing sometimes even their shoes in the sucking mud through which they marched.

Ravaged by dysentery, they were often too weak to march at all, but lay huddled along the river, cursing the French soil on which they were dying. Even Guise, long used to the horrors of war, was shocked by the state of the Reiters and wrote to the King: "I would never have believed their terrible death rate, if I had not seen it, having been on their trail for a day. . . . I swear to you on my honor that I have seen more than eight hundred fallen bodies . . . Your Majesty would be horrified to see the course of their army where there are not less than three or four hundred persons left dead or abandoned."[37]

The failure of the Reiters shook Navarre's confidence, but unlike his Valois cousin he responded to failure by a renewed burst of activity. These were exhausting months for Navarre as he wrote letter after letter to Elizabeth begging her not to fail him now, rode ceaselessly from La Rochelle to St. Jean-d'Angéli, down to Nérac and north again to exhort the unpaid, ill-fed Huguenot troops and decide on the best course for dealing with the hapless Reiters. Sully who accompanied him on most of his journeys observed that sometimes he was so tired that he could barely sit his horse, and Navarre admitted in a letter to the Duc de Montpensier, "I haven't slept in a bed for fifteen days."

Into the midst of this fatigue came a blow that left Navarre reeling: the Prince de Condé, after a three-day illness, was dead at St. Jean-d'Angéli. Condé, the fiery leader, the man who would temporize with no one, whom many considered a more able leader for the Churches than Navarre himself—Condé, dead at thirty-five. As in all such cases of sudden and mysterious death, rumors of poisoning soon solidified into accepted fact, and the Huguenots directed their anger against the Catholics who, they were sure, were implicated in the death of their leader. Although in many ways Navarre and Condé had been rivals, the Béarnais, sick with what his loss would do to Huguenot morale, wrote to Corisande on March 10: "one of the greatest tragedies I could ever fear has just happened to me: this is the sudden death of the Prince. I mourn for him as he ought to have been for me, not as he was . . . they have poisoned him, the traitors . . . the Romish preachers canonize this wonderful deed and the hand that is responsible; they admonish all good Catholics to take example from such a Christian act—and you belong to this religion."[38]

When the results of the autopsy performed upon Condé could not be explained by the physicians in terms of natural causes, death by poisoning became the verdict, with suspicion falling upon his wife, Catherine Charlotte de la Trémouille. The page who was accused of administering the fatal drink was interrogated, as was the Countess herself, but the evidence was insufficient; and since Condé's wife was four months pregnant, her trial was postponed until after the birth of her child. Rigorously guarded by the angry Huguenots and repudiated by her own brother she was imprisoned—and forgotten—at St. Jean-d'Angéli.

Meanwhile both Huguenots and Leaguers kept their eyes on Navarre to assess his reactions, the former fearful that now that the intransigent Condé was off the scene Navarre might temporize with the League. Stafford, in analyzing the results of Condé's death for the Huguenots, feared lest it might cause more dissension, since, as he noted, "they are all at inward jars, mistrust, envy and piques one with another."[39] No matter how the issue went, it was a triumph for the League: a military leader of experience and daring was gone and they, like Stafford, wondered if Navarre would not modify his position now that his "right hand" had been cut off.

There was, however, no longer the possibility of a middle course, even if Navarre had been the man to take it. Since the League triumphs of Vimory and Auneau, Guise's popularity knew no bounds. With Spanish gold solidly behind him and his own ambition to prick him on, he had the sweeping confidence of a master. As he assessed his position, there seemed no limits to what he might hope for. Navarre he knew for a talented soldier and a shrewd man, but Navarre alone with his weary, ragged troops could not carry the war. The King, poor pawn, he could move as he pleased; and the people—the people were his. After an early spring spent in Châlons, in April Guise moved west to Soissons. Meanwhile the King's agents brought in tales of "designs against the King" being formulated by the League; and in Paris the crowds grew restless to welcome their protector, who had saved them from the Huguenots and brought the spoils of the German mercenaries to attest to the completeness of his victory. Even Henri de Valois, blind to so much that he could not bear to witness, was forced to recognize the revolutionary temper of the Paris crowds.

Accepting counsel only when it was too late, he began to fortify his position by increasing his guard and doubling the protection at the Louvre. At the same time he sent Bellièvre to Soissons with a message which was an open declaration of his impotency. The message forbade the Duc de Guise to come to Paris, warning him that if he did, he would be held accountable for any excitement that might ensue. Guise understood the message far better than the terrified man who sent it, and elated by this avowal of weakness he gathered a small group of horsemen and set out for Paris. With his seven companions he rode all night, breakfasted near St. Denis and at noon of May 9 entered Paris. When he reached the city he made his way through the Porte-Saint-Martin to the Queen Mother's residence at Les Filles Repenties, where the astrological tower which she had built to read the stars rose useless above the convent buildings. She needed her astrologers no longer for the stars were easy to read these days. She read the signs in her son's sallow face and in the quick step of the man who now sought entrance into her apartments. And if she missed these signs, there were the cries in the street which she could not miss, the full swell of voices shouting, "Long live Henri, long live Guise, the pillar of the church." When she was told of Guise's arrival, her composure deserted her. She thought she was ready for anything: for battle, for an uprising in the streets, for some strange bizarre gesture on the part of her son; but this open disobedience on the part of Guise startled her. She would have thought him more politic.

When he entered her room, however, she had regained her composure and could greet him with the dry welcome: "I am very happy to see you but I would have preferred you to come at another time." What happened in that confidential interview can only be conjectured, but if the Queen Mother had hoped to protect her son from confrontation with his mortal enemy, she failed, for Guise insisted on seeing the King. She sent a servant to notify her son and then in her litter, for she was too ill to go on foot, with Guise walking at her side in white damask doublet and black cloak, his handsome head bare, they went through the gathering crowds to the Louvre.

The King had already known of Guise's arrival, for Bellièvre had come to him at once on returning from his futile mission. Fear and anger, those two emotions which when combined make desperate men, had seized the King. To Alphonse d'Ornano, his Corsican captain, he explained briefly: "Monsieur de Guise has just arrived in Paris, contrary to my express command. What would you do in my place?" It was in a sense a rhetorical question for no one had any doubt what d'Ornano would do, and the captain with a single gesture made himself very clear. But the King's other advisers warned against Guise's death, fearing that they would not be able to hold out against the Paris mob. The argument was hardly settled when Guise himself, followed by the Queen Mother appeared in the chamber.

As Henri watched the Duke walk the long length of the room, he wondered why even then he did not give the signal to the compliant d'Ornano. "Strike the shepherd and the sheep will be scattered," someone had reminded him. Perhaps it was true; but even as he reflected, his moment passed. It was to be his destiny to the end, this ruinous inability to keep to his course, this fatal weakness to think too much until he had let the moment slip away in some idle speculation. Had he been able to analyze Guise's position, he would have realized that even this powerful duke would not wish to risk a display of military power against the reigning monarch. The King's first anger, however, was lost among his fears. He was doomed, doomed in this terrible year of which the astrologers had predicted: "If, in this year, total catastrophe does not befall, if land and sea do not collapse in total ruin, yet will the whole world suffer upheavals, empires will dwindle, and from everywhere will be great lamentation."[40] He was the ill-starred king caught in this web of prophecy. Fate had pursued him, doomed him, trapped him. For three hours the discussion between Duke and King continued assisted by the conciliating efforts of Bellièvre and the Queen Mother. At the end, with nothing concluded, Guise left to spend the night at his residence. "God save us all," wrote Stafford as he finished his notes for the day.

It was a weary and anxious Paris that went about its duties on May 10. The tide of excitement was sweeping toward its climax and the citizens watched with mingled emotions of fear and hope those two opposed citadels: the Louvre and the Hôtel de Guise. The Louvre had never gone to bed; the windows were bright with candlelight until dawn and within the corridors was the shuffle of the changing guard and the subdued voices of the King and his officials attempting to arrive at a course of action. Guise was more subtle, and the Sixteen, that secret committee of revolutionists who for years would hold Paris in the palm of its hand, put the final touch on their arrangements with quiet efficiency. Arms were already amply stocked in the Hôtel de Guise, in obliging convents and monasteries, in the homes of those "good Catholics" who saw in this movement the salvation of the Roman Church.

The following morning Guise again made his way to the Louvre, this time with four hundred gentlemen secretly armed, for Guise had had sufficient experience to know that in the hunt the most desperate

animal is the first to spring; but his visit was uneventful. The Queen
Mother listened to what he had to say, but the King barely favored
him with a glance. Each appearance of Guise in the Paris streets was
like some triumphal procession. "Now that you are here, we shall all
be saved," came a voice from the crowd, and this messianic cry swept
over the people until they were reaching out to touch his cloak, praying
for his blessing, trying to touch his person with rosaries and medals. He
could well afford to shout back to them, "My friends, you will be my
ruination. Cry 'Long live the King' instead!"

By the following day the King had regained a little confidence, for
assisted by Biron and Grillon, his military tacticians, a plan had been
worked out by which the King might hold Paris. That night 3,000
Swiss troops were quartered in the suburbs with orders to march into
Paris at dawn. While it was still dark on the morning of May 12, the
citizens of Paris were awakened by the roll of drums, the jingle of
tambourines, the shrill notes of the fife. The King's Swiss and French
guards had moved into the city. It was a movement brilliantly planned
and efficiently executed: The strategy neatly separated the strongholds
of the League from each other and should, according to its engineers,
place the King in power over all of Paris without the shedding of
blood.

In those first hours the plan worked without a hitch. It was, however, but a short-lived victory, for the leaders of the League also had
their strategy: the barricades—obstacles that any citizen might construct, that depended on no trained military skill, no regular arms or
ammunition. Soon the citizens were in the streets again, pushing
heavy boards across the narrow streets, heaping up piles of rocks and
cobblestones, rolling barrels heavy with earth and stones into strategic
positions. There can be no doubt that the strategy of the barricades
was no spontaneous act on the part of the people; it had been a long
time preparing in the minds of the Sixteen, ever since the Spanish
ambassador had suggested the efficacy of this simple, inexpensive measure. Soon the builders of barricades had turned into soldiers and their
full wrath fell on the bewildered Swiss who knew only that the King's
command was that they should not draw their arms. Trapped beneath
a reign of stones and blows some of them fell mortally injured while
their companions, in whatever phrases of French they could recall,
attempted to explain that they were "Bons Catholiques," friends not
enemies, men sent to save Paris not to destroy it. They felt desperately
in their pockets and around their necks for medals or rosaries which

would indicate their alliance with the citizens; they dropped their arms, called for mercy, knelt with their hands joined in supplication.

The King who had often read doom in events less harsh, now read it correctly here. Seeing no other course possible, he threw away the scraps of royal power left to him and sent a plea, like some abject vassal to his lord, begging Guise to bring Paris to order. The Duke received the message in his residence where he had spent the day, careful to distance himself from the rebellion in the streets. Now at the King's request he went into the streets, still dressed in white, neither booted nor armed, his leather riding crop his only weapon. A messiah needs no weapons, and Guise played his role to the last detail. He was calm, at ease, almost paternal as he admonished these wayward children to put down their weapons and return to their homes. The master had spoken and the sea grew calm. The people were his disciples and the King his debtor. That night he wrote to a friend: "I have defeated the Swiss and a part of the royal guard, and am holding the Louvre so closely besieged that I expect to give a good account of all within it. This victory is so great that it will be remembered forever."[41]

Late that afternoon the Queen Mother again had her sedan chair brought and despite the danger made the journey to the Marais for another interview with the Duke. No doubt she knew that her journey was futile, for why should the victor give quarter to the vanquished? Guise's demands were exorbitant; she shook her head reproachfully, accusing him of trying to "put shackles on the King and pluck the crown from his head."[42] Yet hoping to gain a little time, for Catherine still believed in her powers of persuasion, she begged him to come to the Louvre, promising that the King would give him as much he could; but the Duke replied coldly that he did not trust the Louvre. He would concede nothing—for everything was already his. Yet even Guise could not want a bloody revolution and that at least might be stemmed if she played her cards adroitly. It was evening when they concluded their talk, and the way had been left open for further conferences. Her perilous journey—it had taken her two hours to get from the Louvre to the rue St. Antoine—had not been altogether wasted, and once again she set out for the Louvre in her indefatigable efforts to keep her son upon the throne of France.

Paris did not sleep that night, for although Guise had put a halt to the brutality of the Paris mob and enabled the Swiss to make their way back to the Louvre without being torn to pieces on the way, yet he had only excited their desire to rid themselves of the Valois monster and put the crown of France upon the man who was already the King of Paris. The indefatigable preachers goaded the people on, students from the Sorbonne pitched their inflammatory speeches higher, everywhere bonfires blazed in the streets and citizens prowled armed and restless around the environs of the Louvre. The King, defeated, brooded in silence; he could not be moved to action for he was bereft of hope. His mother had told him of Guise's demands: a meeting of the Estates, complete military power placed in the hands of the Duke, the *mignons* and the King's other trusted friends dismissed, and the Duke's mortal enemy, Epernon, deprived of all honor and power. What was left to the King under such conditions except to wear the fleur-de-lys, smile upon his betrayers, and say Amen whenever a royal amen was needed. Yet if the crowd that gathered about the palace broke through his guard, he would not be left with even so much. Although he could not believe that anything would come of it, he gave his permission for his mother to visit Guise once more the following afternoon.

Catherine de Medici had never been a popular figure in Paris and she must have known that she was taking her life in her hands as she climbed into her chair and gave the order to be taken to the Marais. By now barricades were thrown up close to the Louvre and at every few steps the Queen Mother was stopped and questioned. They insulted her, they threatened her, and predicted her son's ruin; but they let her go on unharmed. Perhaps they admired the courage of this old lady with her cumbersome body and watery eyes who with her house in ruins continued to fight until the end. Perhaps they feared her reputation for magic, not daring to touch her lest she catch them up in some dire spell. At any rate, she reached the Hôtel de Guise and began again the interminable—and useless—negotiations. As they quibbled, a messenger brought Guise news which made him rise from his chair crying, "Madame, you gull me! While you have kept me talking, the King has left Paris and gone where he can stir up more trouble for me. I am a ruined man!" The Queen also arose, avowing that she knew nothing of this, refusing to believe that her son was not still in the Louvre awaiting her return.

The return to the Louvre seemed endless. Bewildered and frightened, she waited before each barricade caught between hope and dread. When, finally, she reached the Louvre she found what all her life she had tried to avoid. The throne was empty; the King her son had fled.

1. Henri IV (Photo Giraudon—Paris)

2. Marguerite de Valois
   (The New York Public Library
   Astor, Lenox and Tilden Foundations)

3. Marie de Medici
   (Photo Giraudon—Paris)

4. Catherine de Medici (Photo Giraudon—Paris)

5. Henri III (Photo Giraudon—Paris)

6. Charles IX (Photo Giraudon—Paris)

CHAPTER IX

Thrust and Counterthrust: 1588–1589

Time often brings many things which one cannot foresee and we
admire those who know how to yield to time in order to preserve
themselves.

Catherine de Medici

❧❧❧❧❧ In the silence of her son's apartments she was forced to
acknowledge the truth. The first dread fear that had plagued her during the first sterile years of her marriage and that made her submit to
anything in the hope of bearing children, the dread fear that had
followed her relentlessly in the thirty years since her husband's death
and that she had worked herself to death to vanquish, had at last
vanquished her: the throne was empty. The sacred places where royalty
had reigned were bare and she who had gloried in her role as *"genitrix"*
was bereft of the last of her sons. The only bargaining point she had
had during the long humiliating hours with the Duc de Guise had
been taken from her hands; for against all his ambition, his avowed
championship of the Roman Church, the manifest devotion of the
populace, she had placed the royal presence of her son: Henri de
Valois sat upon the throne by Divine Right and no man dare topple
the sovereign whom God's holy oil had sealed. The King is in Paris and
there cannot be two kings, she had argued desperately in an attempt to
get Guise to leave the city. But the King was not in Paris; the King had
fled.

Meanwhile Henri III rode southward, accompanied by only a few
followers, some of whom were not even booted and spurred, so
precipitous had been the King's order for their departure. That night
they spent in a little town not far from Paris where the gates were

securely barred lest Guise should pursue the escaping party. There
was little left of royal presence about the man who sought refuge from
anyone who would give it. He had spent the afternoon, "pale and
exhausted," in an anxiety of waiting while he listened to the mobs in
the street below and counted the dead among his Swiss Guard. As the
May day waned and the chill fog of the Seine filled his room, he
could stand it no longer, and like some palace knave fearful of being
caught by his master, he slid through the back gates of the Louvre and
with eight companions took to the southern road. They headed for
Chartres where the King felt certain that the bishop, Nicholas de Thou,
a royalist in his sympathies, would give him refuge. Even though there
was no pursuit, they rode hard and on the following day the gates of
Chartres opened to the weary party.

For the moment he was out of the fray and back among people
who would not question his authority or his deeds, but were proud to
have their King housed among them. It was once again left to the
Queen Mother to untangle the knots that the royal hands had tied.
He had sent word to her of his whereabouts, warning her not to follow
him until she received fresh orders. The court, too stricken to act,
waited while Catherine took up once again the thread of her conferences with Guise. "I would prefer to die today rather than tomorrow
if this game is going to continue," wrote Villeroy, the secretary of
state.[1]

Although Stafford wrote to Walsingham, "the Duke of Guise is not
remained full master," yet he was certainly close to it, as the more
fanatical Catholics, not content with their cry, "Long live Guise," had
added the more triumphant note, "On to Reims." Guise, however,
was far too clever a politician to follow the will of the rabble, what
he sought was a far more substantial victory. His terms were his own
to dictate now and he presented them without compromise to the
Queen Mother: he was to be made Lieutenant General of the kingdom; Navarre was to be excluded from succession to the throne; the
Duc d'Epernon and other enemies of the League were to be deprived
of office; the King's personal guard was to be disbanded; the principal
government posts were to be given to faithful Catholics.

Meanwhile in order to quell any rumors that he had coerced the
King by his show of arms, he wrote to all the principal cities of the
realm explaining that the trouble in Paris was the result of the King's
evil counselors and the presence of foreign troops which had frightened
the people into an armed response. His own entry into Paris was simply

his last faithful effort to prove to the King that all the calumniating rumors about him were false. He had been able to quiet the mob, save the Swiss Guard from being massacred and protect the Louvre itself from encroachment. The letter was adroitly worded and even more adroitly timed; those who read it had little choice except to conclude that their King was either a knave or a fool.

When, a week later, a letter went out from Chartres under the royal seal explaining "what had happened at Paris," it came too late. As for the King's benevolent gesture of absolving the citizens of Paris from all blame, the hand raised in absolution no longer had the power to touch them. It was the King of Shadows who spoke when he avowed to the delegation that came to him at Chartres: "I love the Parisians, in spite of themselves. . . . What I did on the Day of Barricades was with no thought but of their good and conservation as I hope to prove at a convenient time and place. Go back, continue your office as usual . . . and show yourselves as good subjects as I have shown myself a good King."[2]

To the Frenchmen who watched the struggle for power, it seemed obvious that Guise was, on all fronts, the victor. What many of them did not yet realize was that he had made himself master of France only at the price of becoming the valet of Spain. The Day of Barricades had undoubtedly been to his advantage, yet the initiative had not been his. Guise's actions had been part of a larger plot to keep the eyes of Frenchmen focused on their own troubles, while a Spanish fleet, long in secret preparation, waited for the signal that would set it on its unobstructed way to England. The plot was adroitly timed, and earlier that winter Mendoza had written, "the King's hands will be so completely tied that it will be impossible for him even by his words and much more by his actions to come to the aid of the Queen of England."[3] What happened to Henri de Valois meant little to Spain; whether he fled or held his ground was all one. What mattered was that France, in the grip of her own revolution, would be powerless to give assistance to England. If it was true that Guise ruled the King, it was equally true that Guise had his own master.

Only Navarre remained clear of this web of intrigue. Already excommunicate, already in open war with the League, the events in Paris made no immediate change in his position. L'Estoile recorded that Navarre had been lying on the grass when the news of the Paris troubles reached him, and that after a few minutes' silence, he had responded: "They still haven't caught the Béarnais!"[4] His first impulsive words soon gave way to a more careful analysis of what these events would mean for France. Early in June he wrote to a colleague: "I suppose you have already heard the worst news, with the most dangerous consequences, that has occurred in centuries—the things that have been happening in Paris: that Guise has seized the city and the keys to the citadel, forcing the King to flee to Chartres, from where he is in touch with the Catholic princes and his nobility, writing to his towns to persevere in the obedience and fidelity they owe him. . . . You can imagine my feelings of sadness and displeasure to see these things happen which could have been foreseen and which there was sufficient time to avert; even yet there may be a remedy provided the King is faithfully served by his subjects and that they do their duty. Now is the season when we shall recognize true Frenchmen. For my part, I have no desire other than to use everything in my power, and my person as well . . ."[5]

His own position was to pursue relentlessly the goals he had set forth in the manifesto issued following the Declaration of Péronne: to reassert the unity and integrity of the French kingdom, loyalty to the reigning monarch, and peace—the only means by which France could be saved. He had little confidence in conciliation with the League, for as events in Paris had made incontrovertibly clear, the League had small interest in fair compromise. The Day of Barricades had made it more obvious than ever that for the League religion was not the cause but simply a pretext to be used skillfully for their own ends. If he had ever doubted his own wisdom in refusing to return to the Church of Rome, his doubts were allayed now. Had he acquiesced to the pleas of the royal family, he would now be as neatly caught as the King himself. As it was, he was free, he had his army, and—even more—he had an inflexible resolve. When he received a letter begging him to take a more conciliatory stance, he replied, "I know that the advice you give me is the result of your friendship, but you know my resolution; I do not think I should change it, nor should you counsel me to do so. . . . I have always told you that this is not a matter of religion but of the state, and this you can clearly see in what has recently happened in Paris, with the attempt that the League has made on the King who is more Catholic than anyone."

In the weeks following the King's flight, Navarre, like most of France, could do little but wait. "We still do not know what will come of the enterprise of Paris," he wrote to his old friend Geniès on June 25; "They are all for patching things up and having the King swallow these insults. We shall see in a little while what will happen. Meanwhile we must not sleep."[6] It was not Guise but the King whom Navarre now carefully watched. Guise had made his position clear; the fate of France depended on Henri de Valois' response. He could no longer brush aside the warnings that the League was involved in a traitorous plan, for the role of Spain in French affairs was daily more manifest. If he realized that the fate of France depended on his holding firm against the League, then he might, thought Navarre, be willing to ally himself with the Huguenot forces. Once again he exhorted the King to action, promising his soldiers, whatever revenue he had, even his own life for the preservation of the French kingdom. This was no time to haggle over the religion of his soldiers, Navarre argued, but to strengthen his army by every means he could. Queen Elizabeth, always prodigal with advice if not with assistance, affirmed this advice in her instructions to Sir Thomas Leighton who was to say that the Queen "cannot but marvel that a prince of his greatness and quality should take so weak and strange a course." She urged her fellow sovereign to rouse himself, to use the forces offered by those of the Religion, assuring him that no one who had the interests of France at heart would quibble because they were not Catholics. If he would but take courage, call Guise the traitor that he was, he would find his position immeasurably strengthened.[7]

Advice, however, to be of value, must be tempered to the capacity of the one who receives it, and the virility that shaped the policies of his cousin Navarre and of Elizabeth of England was totally beyond Henri de Valois. His mother's advice was more suited to his ability, for as Catherine worked in Paris against impossible odds, she saw but one course: conciliation. Seeing no way out but to capitulate to Guise's demands, she wrote to Bellièvre: "I should prefer to give away half of my kingdom and to give the lieutenant generalship to Guise, and to be recognized by him and by the whole kingdom, than still to tremble, as we do now, lest worse befall the King. I know that this is a hard medicine for him to swallow; but it is harder yet to lose all authority and all obedience. It would be much to his credit if he were to come to terms in whatever way he could for the present; for time often brings many things which one cannot foresee, and we admire those who know how to yield to time in order to preserve themselves. I am preaching a sermon; excuse me, for I have never been in such trouble before, nor with less light to see my way out of it. Unless God put His hand to it, I do not know what will happen."[8]

Ultimately her son followed her judgment and conceded to all of Guise's requests. On only one point did he stand firm: he would never return to Paris. Neither threats nor promises could move him, and Guise, who had demanded a meeting of the Estates in Paris, was forced to concede to an assembly at Blois instead.

In June the King left Chartres for Rouen, and it was there that Guise sent to him a document requiring his signature: the Second Edict of Union, as it was called. It was simply a confirmation of the Act of Union which had been signed just three years before. Its keystone was the "extirpation of heresy" and its most important practical achievement was the reaffirmation of the Cardinal de Bourbon as heir apparent to the throne. "Let us declare as rebellious and disobedient to our commands and guilty of *lèse-majesté* those who refuse to sign this oath or who sign it and then contradict the oath they have made," ran the document, thus ensuring full power to the League.[9] It was said that the King wept when he signed it and that torrential rains fell upon the city, for although the Act demanded nothing new, his signature upon it was for the King a visible symbol of his servitude.

On the second Sunday of October, the Estates formally opened. It had been twelve years since the last Estates which had also been held in the splendor of Blois. Now as then the King held to the tenuous hope that through the Estates he could regain something of his lost kingship. From the beginning his hopes were but illusions. When the delegates were seated in the vast banquet hall, it was not the King who drew their gaze but the Duc de Guise. Although the King was but thirty-six, he looked far older with his narrow shoulders and stooped walk. His dark eyes were lusterless and the hair beneath the crown gone entirely gray. Guise had the lean vitality of a man at the height of his power. As he led the King in solemn procession to his royal dais, an aura of majesty was about him. He had dressed in white satin, his scabbard and sword-belt flashed with pearls, and about his neck hung the jeweled orders of chivalry—the cross of Saint Michael and the silver dove of the Holy Spirit.

On October 16, Guise, in his position of Grand Master, took his place at the foot of the throne. Next to the King sat Queen Louise and the Queen Mother, an old lady with the quickness of mind and body dimmed by age. The first general session of the Estates was opened and the King rose to make his initial speech. The speech was intended to be a League triumph, for Guise had coerced the King into asking for a public reaffirmation of the Oath of Union. It had not been an easy measure to establish, for the King was solidly opposed to such an action, as was a large proportion of the First Estate; but Guise, "by money and presents" had won sufficient support to overrule the King. Now the King, as he had promised, read the oath and asked that "all swear to it with one voice." There was no room for dissent, and the small group of those who would protest were lost in the swell of upraised hands that attested their approval of the Act.

Worsted as he was, the King still had fire for one more speech, and his address to the Assembly lacked the conciliatory tone that the League had expected. In his contempt for the King's incompetence, Guise had forgotten Henri de Valois' power to win his audience and now he sat angry and a little frightened as he listened to the King's words. While the King could not afford to make overt accusations, he made it clear that he was ill-pleased with Guise and his followers, that he questioned their loyalty to France, and that if he had the power he would take his revenge. In a totally unexpected statement he condemned the Catholic League and those who had instigated it, declaring anyone belonging to such "leagues and associations" to be guilty of treason. It was a moment of courage and resolution such as Henri rarely showed, but ultimately it availed him nothing; for the Duc de Guise and his brother the Cardinal refused to have the speech published as the King had made it and he was forced to make whatever retractions Guise found expedient.

When news reached Navarre of the Estates formal action on the Oath of Union he was not surprised, for the composition of the assembly had made such a step inevitable. It did nothing to change the Huguenots' position since it merely reiterated the clauses of the Edict of Nemours. Yet to have it proclaimed not simply by Guise and his Leaguers, or by the King in private council, but by the representative body of the French nation, added a weight which made it harder to bear. Even before this action had been taken, Navarre had taken a step of his own. Perhaps to gain time, perhaps to indicate his good will and stave off a renewed war, he addressed a memorial to the Estates asking for a council, composed of a certain number of theologians from both sides, which would discuss the problem of his religion and "instruct" him in the truths of the Roman faith. The climate of the Estates made such a request ludicrous. Although the King asked mildly that it be considered and that his cousin be given another chance to

sign the Oath of Union, the clergy replied unhesitatingly that delay
was useless. When the King again suggested that Navarre should be
given an opportunity to defend himself before being condemned,
his petition was scarcely heard. Without further investigation a resolution was passed stripping Navarre of all his rights as First Prince of
the Blood and, consequently, of his claim to succeed to the throne.

The reply reached Navarre at an inopportune moment, for he was
presently presiding at a Huguenot assembly being held at La Rochelle.
When the more conservative among the Huguenots heard of his request
for a council to "instruct" him, they were outraged. Their zeal knew no
temporizing and for their avowed leader to make such overtures behind
their back seemed to them singularly disloyal. The consistorial party, as
the more rigid Huguenots were known, tended to be men who had
relied on Condé rather than Navarre, and they now looked askance
at this willingness to bargain with Catholics.

When Navarre rose to address the assembly, however, there was
little that was conciliatory in his speech: he argued for strong opposition to the enemy whose aim was directed not only against the
Protestants but against the King and the state. "As for myself," he
continued, "I have spared neither property nor life in this holy cause.
. . . If the difficulties continue to increase, I feel that God will redouble
my courage in the resolution we have taken: to expend, in the defense
of the Churches the last drop of my blood, and the last item of my
possessions. . . . I regret that there are some who have failed to recognize my labors and by whom my actions have been misrepresented.
I pray daily that God will grant me his Grace to lead his people through
so many horrors and frightful deserts to a place of safety and rest."[10]

There could be no quarrel with zeal such as this and even the
"grave ministers" responded favorably. Before the assembly was over,
they, too, had addressed a request to the Estates meeting at Blois.
"We very humbly beg Your Majesty," it read, "that it may please you
to restore to us the liberty of the first edict, made for our relief as
soon as it was discovered that we are altogether different in matters
of state and religion from what we have been calumniously called,
the edict that from the name of the month in which it was published, has been called the Edict of January."[11] It was a mild request,
signed deferentially "your humble and obedient subjects," but it received no more attention than Navarre's earlier petition. The Oath of

Union said nothing about "conciliating" heretics, only of "extirpating" them. There was to be no quarter now.

The Huguenot assembly continued into December; although it won no concessions from the crown, it had strengthened its own goals and affirmed Navarre's leadership. On December 17, Navarre wrote to Corisande indicating that the assembly had gone "well and very well," but adding, "if there were to be another assembly, I would go stark mad."[12] The interminable theological discussions, the high moralism, the republican tendencies—all ran counter to Navarre's instincts. When, in addition, he was lectured for the immorality of his conduct, the levity of his life, his favoritism to Catholics, he found it harder to sustain than a battle. In the past it had been the barbs directed at Corisande that had wounded him most, but for the past year he had not seen his mistress, although his letters continued as before. Each letter protested his love and his "wild desire" to see her, yet he never made his way to Bidache.

Those months following the "enterprise of Paris" had been hectic ones for Navarre. While he sought for money and men from the Protestant nations, at home he did all he could to increase the courage of his soldiers by taking a town, winning a skirmish, promising them victories over the enemy. Another man might have been more easily excused for not finding time to visit his mistress, but Navarre was made of different stuff and his mistress's expectations had grown extravagant. When the months passed without a visit from her lover, Corisande lost faith in his avowals. There is no record of her letters to him, but in Navarre's replies one catches that uneasiness that attempts to cope with doubt and misunderstanding. Toward the end of October, after describing the difficult but successful siege of Beauvoir-sur-mer, he continued: "I read your letter every night. If I love it, ought I not to love the sender? Never have I had such a desire to see you as I do now. If the enemy is not pushing us, I would like to steal away for a month after this assembly. . . . There are always a thousand things which cannot be written. . . . Ah, my love, you are mine. . . . Would it be possible that with a gentle knife I might cut the thread of your caprices? I would like to believe it. I am going to ask you a favor: forget all the hatred that you bear toward those who belong to me. This is the first change that I would like to see in you. Do not fear or believe that anything can shake my love. I love you more than ever. Good night, my heart."[13] It was a tender, loving letter but there was an undercurrent which had not been there earlier. The Corisande with whom

he had fallen in love had been a perfect being; there was nothing in
her he would alter, nothing he would wish her to relinquish. Now
there is talk of her "caprices," of her "hatred" for those in his service,
things he hopes she will "change." No avowal that his love is change-
less could balance for Corisande the knowledge that in her lover's
sight she was no longer peerless.

It is impossible to untangle the mystery of their romance begun so
idyllically. It had been not simply a meeting of hearts but of minds
as well. During those first years, the letters that came from Navarre
hardly seemed like love letters at all; they might have been intended
for a comrade in arms rather than for his mistress. But the news of his
skirmishes with the enemy, of the exploits of his loyal soldiers, of his
plans for new victories was like mountain air to Corisande; she grew
heady on all that he shared with her. At some point, however, their
relationship had shifted and the trust on which it had been built had
slipped. It is perhaps too simple an explanation to label Navarre
fickle, to assert that he could never sustain a love affair beyond a given
span. Nor can one cast Corisande in the role of the ambitious woman,
possessive and dominating, who—perhaps unconsciously—had thought
to draw Navarre entirely to herself. Somewhere between these extremes
must lie the answer: a woman made capricious by her insecurity; a
man made restive by her demands. In any case the flower had withered
despite Navarre's continued letters and avowals of enduring love.

In December he had still not taken the month of leisure he had
promised in October, and shortly before Christmas he wrote to Corisande: "I am well, thanks to His Grace, having nothing on my heart
but a wild desire to see you. I do not know when I will have that
happiness. . . . I beg you to love me. . . . There are two things of
which I have no doubt: you, your love and your fidelity. . . . Truly
I would pay dearly for a chance for three hours with you. Goodnight,
my love. I would like to be in the corner of your hearth to heat your
soup."[14]

Four days later, however, Navarre's world was turned upside down,
for on December 26 he received word that the Duc de Guise was
dead—murdered by the King's order. Etienne Pasquier caught the
mood of many Frenchmen when he wrote from Blois: "I will tell you
a story; the most tragic story that has ever occurred in France. Monsieur
de Guise has been killed in the King's chamber. . . . And now we are
like a bird on a branch waiting for news. Four days have passed since
this tragedy has been played." There had been signs aplenty of an

approaching storm, but the court had grown so used to the King's indolence that they had underestimated his capacity for revenge. Mendoza had been almost prophetic when he had written in early August: "The only real danger the Duc de Guise runs is to be attacked and killed in the King's chambers." Guise had been warned a dozen times from a dozen different sources and had himself written on December 10 to the Spanish agent Moreo, "You could not believe all the warnings I have received since your departure. I am well taken care of by the help of God and the assistance of my friends of which I have had and still have a good number with me, so that my enemies do not know how to attempt anything against me. . . ."[15]

Henri de Valois, having endured beyond his capacity, acted at last. The immediate cause of his action was the rumor that had been brought to him that Guise plotted to remove him from the throne altogether by forcing his abdication and shutting him up in a monastery. But Il Vescovo, as he had been contemptuously nicknamed, was not ready for a monastic existence, and he determined to fight for his kingdom in the only way he knew—by dispatching the man who threatened it.

On the morning of December 23 the Duke and his brother the Cardinal were summoned to the King's apartments. Shortly after seven o'clock Guise walked from his lodgings through the gates and up the steep way that led to the château. As Guise continued his way up the stairs, the gates of the palace swung shut and the royal guard closed in behind him. If he knew what was happening he gave no sign but made his way to the King's antechamber while the Cardinal went to attend a council meeting. While he waited for the royal summons, the Duke nibbled on a few dried prunes. The clock was striking eight when Revol, the newly appointed secretary of state, came to lead him to the royal presence. He stepped through the narrow door which led to the "old cabinet" of the King, raised his hand to push back the velvet arras, and was attacked without warning. He had not a moment's grace, only time to cry, "My God, I am killed," before his life poured out through a dozen wounds. In the council chamber the Cardinal de Guise, hearing the scuffle, rose to his feet, but was restrained by the naked swords of the King's men and the cry, "Let no man move unless he wants to die." He, in his turn, was arrested along with the Bishop of Lyons, and led to a solitary room of the château where the day following he was put to death.

Only when all was over did the King come from his chamber to look upon the man who was his rival no longer. For once he had acted without his mother's advice and now he made his way to the sick room with the elated cry, "Now I am King of France!" There was no answering elation in his mother for she understood far better than he what he had done. She had once commented cynically, "So many more dead, so many fewer enemies," but with the death of Guise this was not so. If the King thought that he would now reign more secure, he fooled himself for by this act he had but multiplied his enemies. Sick as she was, she tried to rally to advise her son for the last time, reminding him of what must be done and done with haste: orders given for the control of the cities, plans formulated for dealing with the chief Guisards, explanations made to the Papal Legate before his mind was poisoned by other sources. When the King left her, she lapsed into silence and depression, and one who served her heard her say, "I have been crushed in the ruins of the House."[16]

Word of the murders reached Paris as it chanted the matins of Christmas. The city, wild with grief and anger, spent Christmas Day destroying and looting and hurling invectives against the "tyrant" who called himself their King. In the pulpits the preachers of the League fulminated against the "odious Valois," and the royal arms were torn down from the portals of churches and public buildings and thrown into the river.

When news reached Blois of the uprisings in Paris the Queen Mother was again shaken with fear. Guise's death had been no answer, for with this death the King's position was further threatened. Her son needed her now, she reasoned, and she made a final effort to meet the crisis. Soon, however, even the strength to worry deserted her and she slipped into unconsciousness. On January 5, she died. L'Estoile wrote, brutally, of the event: "She died in the Château de Blois, Thursday, January 5. She was seventy-one years old and carried it well for a plain fat woman. She ate well, but did not understand matters of state although she had as great importance in them as any Queen in the world in the thirty years since her husband died. . . . She was mourned by some of her domestics and a little by the King, her son, who still had some dealings with her."[17] Perhaps it was Cavriana, the Florentine agent, who came closer to the truth when he wrote: "We all remain without light, or counsel, or consolation, and to tell the truth, with her died what kept us alive. From now on we must turn our thoughts elsewhere and find some other support. The kingdom will suffer more than is believed, and the King remains without the most faithful and necessary support that he had. God help him."[18]

Even in death the Queen Mother brought not peace but further contradiction. In Paris hundreds of students and clergy marched through the streets with lighted torches to Notre Dame and there extinguished the flames with the cry, "So perish the race of Valois!" The events in Paris must have indicated to the King how insecure his position was; yet he gave no sign, maintaining the palace as usual and insisting that the Estates continue their affairs. On January 4, the Edict of Union was solemnly confirmed and on January 11 the closing session of the Estates was held, as though, wrote De Thou, "the kingdom were in a state of profound peace."[19]

Word soon came from Rome of Henri III's excommunication, for despite all of the Legate's efforts to convince the Pope that Guise was a traitor who had to be killed before he should kill his King, the League had far more power at the Vatican than the French agents. The Pope was adamant: the King could not kill a cardinal of the Roman Church without grave consequences.

Meanwhile the Duc de Mayenne made his slow way from Lyons where he had received the news of his brothers' death. Always a prudent man, he now took time to strengthen his position as he rode north, augmenting his power in such cities as Dijon, Champaigne, Orléans. When he arrived in Paris the citizens were prepared to offer him the throne, but like his brother before him, he recognized the danger of such a step and satisfied himself with the title of "Lord General of the Estate and Crown of France." The King's seals had been broken and now new ones were made for Mayenne: on one side was engraved the arms of France and on the other an empty throne with the name and title of the Duc de Mayenne inscribed about it.

The King's unnatural calm had deserted him with the closing of the Estates. With no one to turn to now that his mother was dead, he took to his bed, weak with a series of hemorrhages and in a lethargy of despair. If he were to find help anywhere it would be in an alliance with Navarre and yet he hesitated lest by allying himself with heretics he lose even the meager remnant of royalists still loyal to him.

Navarre had kept a strange silence about the events at Blois, saying little beyond his first comment written to Corisande, "The King has triumphed." It was hardly a thoughtful appraisal of the situation and in the months that followed, it became obvious to Navarre how

misplaced his earlier enthusiasm had been. At the height of the troubles
at Blois, Navarre had been stricken by so severe a case of pleurisy
that those who nursed him despaired of his life. For days he lay racked
with fever and so weak that unaided he could not turn in bed. No
sooner did he regain a little strength than he wrote to Corisande,
"Yes, my love, I saw the heavens open but I was not good enough
to enter. God still wishes me to serve him here."[20] The first act of
that service was to place himself once more at the disposal of the King
his cousin. Each successive courier brought news of fresh uprisings
against the Valois. This, Navarre conjectured, might be the strategic
moment for converting the tragic events at Blois to his own advantage
and that of the monarchy. If he could convince the King to accept
the help he offered, together they might find deliverance from the
League.

While the King remained at Blois alone and shorn of power, Navarre
with his expert sense of timing continued to take advantage of the
confusion to seize a number of towns: Loudun, Mirebeau, Vivonne,
L'Isle-Bouchard. There was no longer a place for moderates and many
who had hedged before now swung closer to Navarre's side. With this
increased strength he tried once more to use his position to pull
France together and save the monarchy. On March 4 from Châtellerault he launched his famous manifesto, written in large part by his
adviser Duplessis-Mornay. Moved, as he said, "only by the miseries of
the country, the love of peace and the glory of the fatherland," he
pleaded with all true Frenchmen to come together in union and
concord. With his recent victories attesting to his power, he was in a
position to ask for peace not as an underling about to be vanquished but as a victorious leader. He can afford to boast of his
military strength, of his successful exploits even under adverse conditions. Yet, he reminds them, it is not a successful war that he wants,
but what he has always wanted, what he has always asked for: Peace.
He is aware, he points out, that many will say that if he were sincere
in his desire for peace he would have become a Catholic as they had
asked. "I have often been asked to change my religion," he admitted,
"but how? With a dagger at my throat! Even had I no respect for my
conscience, my respect for my honor would have kept me from making
such a change. . . . To have been nurtured, instructed, and raised in
one faith and then . . . suddenly to catapult myself on the other side!
No, gentlemen, the King of Navarre will never act in such a manner
even were there thirty crowns to be gained. . . . Instruct me; I am

not hopelessly opinionated. If you can show me a truth other than the one I now believe, I am ready to yield to it." It was not a new statement, but the times had changed, and many who would have scorned his leadership a year before, now began to look in his direction. They recognized the truth of his words when he said: "I am in great danger—so is the King . . . so are all of you. . . . We are in a house that is going to fall, in a boat which is sinking. There is no remedy but peace."

Navarre's answer to the establishment of peace was the reestablishment of a strong monarchical government, for he saw in the overthrow of the King the ruin of the country. Even those who had preferred to remain blind before were now forced to admit that the League was in alliance with Spain. The manifesto was deftly worded, appealing to the interests of each group to recognize that only in the reestablishment of the crown would they find their own security. "What will become of the face of this state if this evil continues? What will become of our nobility if our government is changed as it will undoubtedly be. . . . What will happen to those citizens who hold from the crown positions in finance or justice, police or soldiery? All this is lost if the monarchy is lost. Who will guarantee their possessions? Who will hold the authority for justice? Who will command the armies? In short, what order will there be? And you, the people, when the nobility and the cities are divided, what security will you have? . . . To whom will you have recourse? The King? He will command no one. The officers of justice? Where will they be? Wretchedness, confusion, disorder, misery everywhere. This is the fruit of war. . . . What is the only remedy for all this? There is no remedy but peace, peace which will restore order to the kingdom. . . . I call all those to me who have this holy desire for peace, of whatever quality and condition they may be, hoping that God will bless my plan. . . ."21

A few days later the manifesto bore its first fruit in a cease-fire established between Navarre and the King. The King's troops were now at Tours, and the remainder of March and April was spent in negotiations for a truce between the two leaders. It was not an easy matter to handle and might not have been so amicably settled were it not for the prudent Duplessis-Mornay gifted as he was with infinite patience in arranging details. Navarre, a born tactician, with reserves of energy and courage which often left his troops lagging far behind, felt an understandable impatience with his royal cousin's sporadic and ill-timed activity. Henri de Valois' failure to take advice had marred his rule from the first day. Now, however, he found he had to deal not with a deferential council but with a man who did not hesitate to command kings if such arrogance were necessary for kings' success. When Navarre learned that Henri, against all counsel, was planning a campaign into Brittany he was violent in his denunciation, warning, "If the King goes into Brittany, he is ruined." The King deferred to his advice. But Navarre grew weary of his cousin's insistence on getting the best of everything, of dallying to gain time and so win better terms. "These shilly-shallyings are out of season," wrote Navarre, well aware that the King was now largely dependent on Huguenot strength if he were not to be swallowed up by the League.[22] These were thorny weeks for both leaders, but finally toward the end of April a one-year truce was signed between the King and Navarre. At Navarre's demand, the Huguenots were given the town of Saumur so that they could safely cross the Loire and engage the army of Mayenne which was presently besieging Château-Renault.

On April 30 occurred the event which confirmed the treaty: the meeting of the kings at the château of Plessis-les-Tours. The Huguenots had from the start disapproved of this move. They feared it might be a Catholic trap in which their leader would be killed. Navarre, however, recognized that no truce would be lasting unless there was some evidence of mutual trust on the part of its leaders. On Sunday, April 30, shortly after dinner, Navarre with a troop of his soldiers crossed the Pont-de-la-Motte leading into Tours. With his doublet worn thin at the shoulders and on the side where his cuirass hung, he was dressed like a soldier rather than a king but his cloak was of scarlet and he wore the white plume for which he now was famous. The King's men were awaiting him at the bridge and led him through the park crowded with anxious onlookers, and into the garden of the château. It took them almost fifteen minutes to push their way through the excited crowd, however much the King's archers kept it in place. "Long live the Kings," came the spontaneous cry, which led Navarre to say, "I'll die happy with today whatever death I die."[23] The Kings talked for two hours, and at the end the truce was assured.

That night Navarre wrote to Mornay, who waited south of the Loire: "The ice has been broken, but not without numerous warnings that if I went I should die. As I passed over the water I commended myself to God who in His goodness has not only preserved me but has made the King's face radiant with joy. As for the people, there was unparalleled applause as they cried, 'Long live the Kings,' which made me very happy. . . . Please send me my baggage and have all the troops advance. The Duc de Mayenne has besieged Château-Renault, but hearing of my coming he has lifted the siege without warning and has gone on to Montoire and Laverdin. Tomorrow you shall have more news from the outskirts of Tours where our army is quartered."[24]

The truce with the Huguenots brought fresh wrath from the Vatican and on May 24 a *monitum* was issued from Rome ordering Henri III to free the Cardinal de Bourbon and the Archbishop of Lyons and to appear in Rome either in person or through his legate to explain why he should not be excommunicated for the murder of the Cardinal de Guise and why his subjects should not be delivered from their loyalty to him. All privileges granted to French kings were thereby revoked and he was henceforth to be known simply as Henri de Valois. This gave fresh fuel to the Leaguers of Paris; but, for the first time in years, Henri de Valois was in a position to ignore the insults and threats of the League, for he was drinking the cup of victory. Early in May Mayenne had planned a surprise attack on Tours, but Navarre with a quick and clever use of his cavalry had turned him back. From then on all had been success as the combined armies rode northward toward their goal: Paris. Gergeau, Pluviers, Etampes, Poissy, Pontoise all fell before the royal armies and by July they had secured those three important rivers, the Oise, the Seine, and the Marne. Startled by these unexpected victories, the people began to ascribe magic powers to Navarre, and the English agent wrote to Walsingham, "The King of Navarre is thought to do what he does by sorcery, for all places do yield to him."[25]

On July 31 the two kings established themselves at Meudon only a few miles from Paris. Mayenne had ridden ahead of them and was already in the city, preparing for its defense. The peasants, terrified at the approach of the royal army, gathered together as many of their possessions as they could, and pushing their wooden carts ahead of them, made for the safety of Paris. The city was soon filled far beyond its capacity and the leaders began to fear the consequences of a long siege. When Henri III had fled from Paris a year before, he had vowed that he would never return unless it was as a conqueror. At the time the threat seemed ludicrous, but now the chiefs of the League were forced to admit that the King's threat, which they had listened to so disdainfully, might come to pass. It was inconceivable that this shadow of a king, nerveless and dispirited, repudiated by his people, and excommunicated by the church, that this "Valois monster" whom they had baited and ridiculed should have roused himself at last. The League had anticipated nothing like this. The English agent watching the preparations at the camps at Meudon wrote exultingly to Walsingham that there was now "great hope of success," adding cautiously, "if Fortune play not her part."[26]

But Fortune was to play her part, and on August 1 she gave her wheel an unexpected turn. Early that morning a young Dominican, Brother Jacques Clément, walked up the hill of St. Cloud to the house of Cardinal Gondi where Henri III had set up his headquarters. He was a mild-mannered young friar of twenty-four, who explained to the guards that he had a private letter to deliver to the King. The King, always fearful of further antagonizing the clergy, ordered him to be brought in at once although he had not yet finished dressing. Deferentially the friar approached and gave the King the letter. Lost in thought as he perused it, the King did not see the quick gesture with which Brother Jacques slipped a knife from his long friar's sleeve. Within seconds the King had toppled over, the knife penetrating deep into his stomach. The guard, vainly set to guard the King, set upon the friar and killed him on the spot, while the King, his shirt covered with blood, was carried to his bed.

Here the doctors examined him and gave him great hope that the knife had missed his vital organs, although there was much whispering among themselves that there might be greater internal damage than they could immediately determine. After the first shock the King seemed to rally. Navarre was sent for at once and a little after nine o'clock he was with the King. As the day wore on, it seemed that Henri de Valois would live. He wrote to Queen Louise in his own hand and then dictated several other letters which he was able to sign. He assured his friends that his wound was not mortal and that his surgeon had promised that he would be back on horseback within ten days. To the English ambassador he was equally optimistic, saying, "I am sure the Queen your mistress will be sorry for this but I hope it will be quickly healed and so I pray write unto her from me."[27]

When the doctors assembled for a further conference that evening they were less hopeful. Massive internal bleeding had begun which they were powerless to control; and as night drew on the King's temperature rose and he grew considerably weaker. Navarre, who had returned to his own camp after being reassured that the King was in no danger, was recalled as the King sank rapidly. When he entered the King's chamber shortly before dawn, he came too late. Henri III was dead.

Death could not have struck at a more ironic moment nor in a more ironic mode. For the fifteen years of his reign, Henri de Valois had plunged from failure to failure; now he had seemed on the verge of success. A little of his youthful animation had returned, and the League for the first time was on the defensive. Had he been killed in battle, or even had the League poisoned him, as rumor had it they wished to do, his death would have seemed less ironic. Instead he had been killed by a strange, fanatic friar from the little town of Sens, who one night while he slept thought that an angel with a great light and a naked sword came to him saying, "Brother Jacques, I am a messenger of Almighty God and I have come to tell you that it is by your means that the tyrant of France is to be put to death."[28] Having lived so long among men who had hated him, having lived through sieges of war and pestilence, death had now come to him in its most macabre form and at a moment when he had least fear of it. Perhaps, as rumor said, Brother Jacques had been an instrument of the League; but this no one was ever to know for Brother Jacques had been killed before he could tell his story. Those who knew him put little credence in his playing the role of hired assassin; they saw him instead as a man convinced of his divine mission, a solitary man who needed neither accomplices nor masters, for to him his deed was no merely human act but a stroke of the divine vengeance. He was, if anything, an instrument of God, a man divinely chosen to free the world of a sinful and reprobate king.

It was a pathetic death for Henri III to die, but not inconsonant with the life that had preceded it—a life that had always just missed the mark, with its mortal mingling of ambition and indolence, generosity and gullibility. A little more virtue or a little more vice might have enabled him to side-step failure. But Henri de Valois had only half-read his Machiavelli at a time when a sovereign needed to know it thoroughly. "Never," commented a contemporary historian, "never had a prince offered so much hope; and never had a king responded so badly." L'Estoile's final judgment was more compassionate: "[he] would have been a very good prince, had he met with a good century."[29]

On one point, at least, the King had triumphed: he had not left the question of succession in the hands of the League; he had named his heir. In those first hours following the attack, he had called his nobles to him and in the presence of Navarre had proclaimed: "I beg you as my friends and order you as your king to recognize after my death my brother here and to have for him the same affection and fidelity that you have always had for me."[30] It was an ambiguous wish for in the last years of his kingship Henri de Valois had known little of devotion and loyalty even from those who were most his debtors. But the import of his words left no ambiguity: without hesitation or condition the throne of France was to pass to his Huguenot cousin Henri de Navarre. When, just before dawn on the morning of August 2, Navarre entered the King's chamber, it was to assume his role as Henri IV, King of France and of Navarre.

CHAPTER X

King of France and of Navarre: 1589–1591

A king without a kingdom, a husband without a wife, a general
without money.

Henri de Navarre

❦❦❦❦ There was silence in the Hôtel de Gondi in that hour before
dawn when one king lay dead and another stood at the foot of his bed
to take his place. Navarre, not knowing what the hasty message he
had received in the château of Meudon might omen, had come secretly
armed under his doublet; but there was, he found, no need of arms.
Death had brought, for a moment, peace and dignity to the presence
of the late king who for so long a time had lacked both. In that first
shock following the King's death, Navarre found no opposition to
his own position. He was undisputed master; he gave the orders
and they were obeyed without question, for there had been something
royal in that utterance in which Henri III had given over his kingdom
to his cousin.

The first silent reverence in the face of death was but short-lived,
however, and soon the "terrible confusion" which had been predicted by the Duc de Sully was in full sway. When the news of the
Valois' death reached Paris there was but a hesitant catch of the
breath before the storm broke loose. "The hand of God," shouted the
preachers, and the cry was taken up by the mob who rejoiced at their
divine deliverance from the "Valois dog," "the tyrant king," "the
perfidious ruler." The presses turned out endless reams of original
Te Deums to be sung and shouted and prayed. "What great spirit
guided thy hand," began one sonnet in praise of poor Clément who
had been killed before he could explain his mysterious design. But

to the Paris crowds there was no mystery for the hand of God was
obvious in this humble instrument. Was not Clément a martyr, meeting
his death in fulfilling the demands of his God? It was not long
before some of the more zealous suggested that a statue of "Saint
Clément" should be erected in Notre Dame. As for the former king:
Telle vie, telle fin concluded some verses applauding his death.

Not only in Paris but in many of the provinces the King's death
was a cause for rejoicing, and the English agent in Rouen wrote
to Walsingham of the "rejoicings" in the streets, the *"Ti dioms"* sung
in the churches, the proclamations in the squares affirming the Cardinal de Bourbon the rightful king of France: "They cried 'God save
Charles X, King of France, chosen by the princes and peers of France,
and for his lieutenant general of all provinces in France the Duke
Diman' [de Mayenne] and that all men must go and get their King
out of prison and in the meantime the Duke to be regent till the
coronation. . . . although that the King of Navarre is choosen in the
camp and hath made protestation to live Catholic, it is but to dissemble
as a heretic. . . . Two kings in France, the King of Navarre and the
Cardinal of Borbon!"[1]

Even in the Hôtel de Gondi the first shock of silence and regret
had given place to something less reassuring: a kind of embarrassment on the part of the nobles in the roles in which their King had
cast them. Loyal subjects of Henri de Navarre was the part he had
asked them to play. Their unthinking answer in the crisis of the
moment had been acquiescence. They had, in fact, been relieved that
the succession had been definitively established. But when the gray
clouds of early morning lifted, they began to see the twists and turns
in the course to which their obedience destined them. Put in its
simplest terms: France was to have a Huguenot king and they were
to sustain him in his position. Even the Huguenot leaders recognized
the difficulty of the situation, but the Catholics were appalled at the
trap in which they found themselves caught. Although Henri III's
last words had not demanded Navarre's conversion as a condition for
the throne, it was well-known that the late King had always maintained this as the only tenable position. Yet the new King showed but
little inclination to change his religious position. The Catholic nobles
could brook no delay, and after a short consultation sent a delegation
to Navarre, headed by Marshal d'O—a man known more for his
pleasures than for his integrity—indicating that his conversion to the
Roman communion was essential if he were to be recognized as King.

D'O pointed out that only by such a step could Henri retain the French nobility in his service. Although the Marshal did not speak for all the Catholic nobility, he spoke for a good part. There were few like the young Baron de Givri who would cry to Henri, "None but cowards would abandon you," or like the faithful Sancy who by some mysterious rhetoric cajoled the Swiss mercenaries to serve the new King for three months without pay. The lords of Auvergne and Picardy also announced their allegiance, but part of the nobility were represented by Epernon who, though too politic to refuse service, reminded Henri that the late King had some time before given him permission to retire to his lands around Angoulême to rest after the long campaign. Others, like Marshal Biron, used the opportunity to jockey for place in the great court game of self-aggrandizement. Biron, well aware of his reputation as one of France's most experienced men of war, offered his services in reward for the territory of Périgord when that land would be available.

By August 3, Henri, now the fourth of that name, was in a position to assess his situation. His army was tired and unpaid; many of its captains, following Epernon's leadership, were asking to retire into their own lands for a while—and from all sides came the battering arguments about religion. Navarre had been a leader of men too long not to know that leadership is a lonely thing, but he was to find that the loneliness of the crown was far deeper than he could have guessed. In a letter to his old friend, St. Geniès, now sénéschal of Béarn, he wrote. "Since God has called me to this estate, I have not had the opportunity or the time to write to you because of the endless work I have been involved in. I am living among strange people and far from the places where I have spent the last fifteen years of my life."[2] He now found himself with more sympathy than he had ever felt for his royal cousin who, gray-haired and friendless, had been tutored by experience in the knowledge that there are few men whom kings can trust.

On one side were ranged the Huguenots with their militant leader Mornay already suspicious that their old friend might now desert them; on the other, were the Catholic nobles who even while exhorting him to conversion were indicating in small overt ways that they were not sure that they could trust him even should he publicly retract his heresy. Navarre had hit the target well when in answer to Marshal d'O's importunities, he had replied "From whom can you expect such a change of faith except from a man who has none at all." This, indeed, seemed to Navarre the heart of the problem: who would trust him should he quickly make the move the Catholics were demanding. It would manifestly lead to the loss of the Huguenots, and this he could ill afford. It would, as well, have wider ramifications, for it would affect his relations with the Protestant states. He had spent too long building up alliances with the Swiss Cantons, the German Princes, with Elizabeth of England to risk forfeiting their friendship now. In the letters that went out to the leaders of the Protestant states on August 8, there was no word of future action, only a formal declaration of Henry III's death and of his own position and signed, "Henri by the grace of God King of France and of Navarre."

On August 4, from the camp at St. Cloud, the new King of France promulgated a document which he hoped would bring at least a temporary resolution of the problems that faced him:

> We, Henri, by the Grace of God, King of France and of Navarre, swear and promise by the faith and word of a King and by our present signature, to all our good and faithful subjects to maintain and conserve faithfully in our kingdom the Catholic, Apostolic, and Roman religion, without innovation or change both in its free exercise and in its ecclesiastical personnel, leaving them their lands, provisions, and governments in conformity with what has been done up to this time. We will be equally disposed, as has been stated in our letters published before our accession to the throne, to be instructed by a general or national council, promising to follow and observe what it would decide. And further to hold a convocation and assembly within a period of six months or sooner if that is possible.[3]

The main points of the document, then, were his promise to be instructed—he is careful not to say converted—in the Roman faith before the end of six months and to keep that faith intact in France. In addition, he purposed to call a meeting of the Estates General and to send an ambassador to Rome explaining the situation in France. It was all that the King could reasonably do, but for the Catholic lords it was not enough—and for the Huguenots it was too much. Although the King explained to the latter as well as he could that their salvation lay in a postponement of the issue, since immediate action would kill their hopes; yet they continued to look upon themselves as victimized and betrayed. They found the declaration to be "romish" in its wording and Mornay upbraided the King strongly on the use of the phrase "*la religion prétendue réformée*"; at least, chided the Huguenot minister, it could have been "*la religion dite réformée.*" Although it did not satisfy the malcontents of either side, yet for a considerable body (Biron, Aumont, Longueville, Luxembourg among the Catholics and La Noue, Guitry, La Force, Rosny among the Huguenots) it was a reciprocal agreement by which the new King promised to observe the rights of the French people while they, in their turn, acknowledged him as the rightful King of France.

Within twenty-four hours, the Declaration of St. Cloud was answered by the League in a document issued by Mayenne who at this time was exercising what he considered a sort of regency. Mayenne's statement was not only a call to arms against Navarre and the Huguenots, it was also a reiteration that the rightful King of France was now the Cardinal de Bourbon. "While awaiting the liberty and presence of our sovereign lord," the document read, "we ask all princes, prelates, officers of the crown, lords, and all by the obedience that they owe to God and to their natural and legitimate king to join us in bearing arms against the Huguenots."[4]

Whatever other results Mayenne's declaration had, one was to increase the rigor of the old Cardinal's imprisonment. He had for the last few months been kept in the fortified château of Chinon poised on a pile of massive rock with a sheer drop to the valley below. Although it was an awesome prison, it was also beautiful and it was not far from the Cardinal's ancestral lands of the Bourbonnais. Now, however, the old Cardinal was, by the King's order, moved south into Poitou, lands strongly guarded by those strange Huguenots, his enemies. Yet Mayenne, for all his solemn declaration that the Cardinal was now to be acknowledged as Charles X of France, took no action to rescue the so-called King from his imprisonment. Indeed the League's choice for the royal succession was a far more devious affair than the Cardinal in his imprisonment could have dreamed of.

The list of claimants for the French throne was long. There was Mayenne himself who though offered the crown by the enthusiastic Parisians had more far-reaching schemes; there was young Guise, son of the murdered Henri de Guise, now a prisoner in the Château of Tours; there were, if one could abrogate the Salic Law, the Duke of Savoy, the Duke of Lorraine, and, perhaps most important of all, the Infanta, Clara Eugenie, daughter of Philip of Spain by his marriage with Elizabeth de Valois.

Until the death of Henri III, Philip II had played a quiet if powerful game, but with the Valois dead and claimants to the throne in open competition, he dared to show his hand more openly. Six weeks after the murder of the King, Philip wrote to his agent Mendoza: "The offer you made to the Duke de Mayenne in my name, after the death of the king, for help in maintaining the Catholic religion in that kingdom, was very well done, and at the right time. No less opportune was your declaration to the same Duc de Mayenne in favor of the Cardinal of Bourbon at a time when they were confused and doubtful as to which way to turn. The Cardinal of Bourbon has such a good legal right to the throne, is as Catholic as can be desired, and has proven his integrity by many trials and sufferings for the cause of religion, that they should in no wise neglect to accept him as their king."[5]

While this dispatch seems on the surface a simple acceptance of the Bourbon as the rightful King of France, Philip's French policies were never simple. He recognized that even the League was not yet ready for direct Spanish intervention especially in the choice of a sovereign, but he knew, too, that there was no surer way to ingratiate himself with the League than by a disavowal of anything but the interests of the Catholic religion. So well did his pretensions work that there soon appeared in Paris a document counseling the people to place themselves under the protection of the King of Spain who, it said, has clearly indicated that he has but one motive: the integrity of the faith in France. "The salvation of the people is to be placed above all things," continued the document, and Philip alone with his great power is capable of protecting them from the enemy. But not all Parisians were so guileless and a short time later another document appeared in Paris entitled "Anti-Espagnol" indicating "the true goal King Philip tends to is meddling in the affairs of France."[6] His true goal was, it became increasingly apparent, the aggrandizement of Spain. Far from hoping for the conversion of Henri IV as the means of delivering France from civil strife, settling the question of succession, and maintaining the Roman faith intact, Philip began to make it clear that he intended to fight such a step from every side. In a letter to Mendoza written in September of 1589 he advised: "In the event that Béarn proclaims his intention and desire to be reconverted, there is little I can prescribe to persons as familiar as you are with his motives and the deceit in which he envelops himself. But endeavor to see to it that all the

Catholics are on the alert and advised to this truth so that such talk from him will not be listened to."[7]

It was especially in his relations with the Papacy that Philip's "true goal" became obvious. He had been elated at the decree of excommunication which Sixtus had leveled at Navarre in September 1585 and had every hope that this policy of severity would continue. The League, about which Sixtus had at first been chary, had won his sympathy when its leader, the Duc de Guise, and his brother the Cardinal had been murdered. Yet now the dispatches which the Spanish minister Olivares sent from Rome were distinctly disquieting. When Venice publicly acknowledged Navarre as King of France, the Pope angrily questioned the right of any Catholic state to acknowledge a heretic prince; but as the affair drew on, the Pope's anger calmed and no punishment was meted out to Venice. In actual fact, Sixtus was forced to sympathize with the courageous little state that recognized the necessity for keeping down the preponderance of Spanish power. It was a position which Sixtus saw more and more as his own, for he found the growing Spanish arrogance intolerable.

When in early January, the Duc de Luxembourg, sent from the Catholic nobles who were with Navarre, arrived in Rome, no amount of Spanish opposition could keep the Pope from welcoming him with far more tolerance than Luxembourg had been prepared for. Shortly before the Duke's arrival, weary of the fulminations of Olivares and the Spanish party, the Pope had said openly to Cardinal Montalto that he did not think that the war in France was entirely a question of religion and that he wanted to hear the explanation that Luxembourg would bring. The Duke, encouraged by this attitude, made bold to quote Navarre's final words to him: "Bear witness to the Holy See on my royal word that my actions will be proof that I wish to live and die as the eldest son of the Roman Catholic Church." But Sixtus, whom events had made something of a skeptic, said only in reply: "Tell him to free his uncle the Cardinal and then we will see about receiving him as a penitent son." Even the possibility of Navarre's conversion being accepted by the Holy See was more than Philip could endure, and he wrote in angry contempt of the wolf "who wants to clothe himself in a sheep's pelt in order to wreak greater carnage among the Catholics." Antoine de la Broderie, Henri's agent in Rome, seeing the increasing intolerance of the Pope for the Spanish faction, wrote earnestly to the King: "For the love of God, Your Majesty must not let this good opportunity slip."[8]

But while Rome and Madrid tried to force the fate of France through
the avenues of diplomacy, Henri IV had found his own way to maintain his power. From the moment of the former King's death, he had
realized that his position at St. Cloud was untenable. Although only
a month before he had written to a friend of how close they were
to the spires of Paris, that dream had now to be put aside. His forces
were far too small for either battle or siege, and before the end of
August the King had headed north toward Normandy. Even so small
an army was more than he had the finances to maintain, and soon
Robert Cecil, who had seen the King sell the few valuables he still
possessed, reiterated his pleas to Elizabeth to send money or troops
or both to help the French King. Meanwhile the King moved slowly
through the countryside where the grain which should have been ready
for the August harvest had been cut and trampled by war. It was a
strange procession which moved slowly along the banks of the Oise,
for Henri carried the body of the late King with him to give it what
burial he could in the abbey church of St. Corneille. Here beneath
the walls of Compiègne, where that other champion of royalty, Joan
of Arc, had met her doom, the last of the Valois found a temporary
burial place. Much of the ceremony of royal burial was omitted and
Henri, having done what he could in simple dignity, moved on toward
Dieppe. Along the way the towns of Meulan, Gisors, Clermont fell
into his hands and his easy successes caused it to be rumored that he
was on his way to besiege Rouen.

The rumors, instigated by Henri to draw Mayenne into battle, succeeded; for the burghers of Rouen, fearful of attack, begged the chief
of the League to come to their assistance. Toward the end of August,
Mayenne left Paris at the head of an army of more than 15,000 men;
victory seemed inevitable and as he said farewell to the Parisians he
assured them that he was going out to take the Béarnais and bring
him back through the streets bound hand and foot. But even in such an
emergency the Duke moved heavily—"his flatterers call this Gravity"
wrote a contemporary historian in contempt—and it was the third week
of September before he arrived at his goal. Henri, having no intention
of seizing Rouen, had already moved into the little town of Arques,
some two leagues southeast of Dieppe, and had spent the days of
waiting in constructing fortifications. Everything about Arques was
in his favor. Its marshlands, its little hills, the dense vineyards with
their opportunity for concealment, all made Arques a spot easy to
defend and difficult to besiege. By the time "the Fat Duke" arrived,

Henri had dug himself in with ditches seven to eight feet deep and had placed his cannon in strategic spots on the hill where rose the Château of the Dukes of Normandy. With his own city of Dieppe at his back, Henri felt secure; but his captains, measuring their small force against the massive army of Mayenne, found it hard to share their King's confidence. When one of them mentioned how outnumbered they were, the King was reputed to have said, "You are not counting everything; you have left out God and the cause of right which is on my side."[9] Yet Henri took no chances and on September 20 with Mayenne no more than "two volleys away" he spent the night in the trenches bearing the full responsibility of general and king. With the first light of dawn the battle broke, and in the initial charge of the cavalry it would seem that Mayenne's boast might prove true. But protected by their fortifications, the King's troops held firm against the waves of men that poured against them. Mayenne's mercenaries proved less than valiant, and when toward noon the morning fog lifted and the King's cannons from the hill began to find their target with stunning accuracy, the battle was all but over.

The battle of Arques was neither a great nor a decisive victory; years of warfare still lay ahead, but to its commanders—and to the people of France as well—it had a profound psychological value. The King had reaffirmed what he had always maintained: that it is leadership and strategy not numbers which win battles. Mayenne was forced to take a long look at his basic premise: that the League was invincible.

The King was gaining ground; many whose sympathies had been with him but who had felt his cause was hopeless now joined his army. At the same time the reinforcements promised him by Elizabeth arrived and money from Holland enabled him to make some payment to his troops. When in October he moved out of Arques in the direction of Paris, he was at the head of over 20,000 men. Even so his forces could not match those of the League and for the most part his men were tired and poorly equipped. The King realized, too, that not all of these would remain loyal to him; some of them were fair-weather soldiers fighting wherever Dame Fortune had established her court. It was, however, a beginning. It was enough to march on Paris—and Paris had always been his goal. To Frenchmen, taking Paris was a symbol of taking France itself. When after the death of Henri III the King had announced his withdrawal from the city, his old friend Givri had admonished him: "Who will believe that you are the King of France when they see your ordinances dated from Limoges?"[10]

In one of those sudden moves which Mayenne could never match, the King came out of the North and on November 1, day of All Saints, he was before the gates of Paris. It was 6:00 A.M. when his army, protected by the fog that rose in waves from the Seine, attacked the suburbs. Simultaneously his forces divided into three sections and forced their way into the five faubourgs on the right bank of the Seine. The King himself led the troops which besieged St. Jacques and in the first wave of the attack he was surprised to hear a few royalist voices crying, "Vive le Roi."

For the most part, however, the Parisians fought hard, and a bloody battle continued throughout the morning. The Huguenots were paying an old debt and some of them as they rode through the streets with drawn swords cried a word to make the Parisians cringe: "Bartholomew." They fought in a kind of fury, spilling blood recklessly to avenge the blood spilled seventeen years before. The excesses of those first hours did nothing to make Henri more popular nor did it win him a victory. Had the first charge been enough to force Paris, the people might have capitulated, for the number of malcontents was growing. The price of wine and corn had soared and even the necessities of wood and bread and hay were very dear. "The people are in misery and discouragement," wrote the Spanish agent,[11] and yet the fomenters of the League could still make Paris seethe with the memory of the murder of the Duc de Guise and the injustices to which they had been subjected during the reign of the Valois. Once again Mayenne was importuned, and on the morning of November 2 with more speed than he had ever shown before, the Duke arrived in the city which was close to ruin. The fact that he had been able to gain entrance at all was one of those ironies with which the King's military career was dogged. Despite the care with which the royalist attack had been mounted, one bridge, that of St. Maxient over the river Oise, had been left unguarded, and Mayenne, with no more than a skirmish to impede him, had made his way into the heart of Paris.

The King learned of Mayenne's arrival just as he was signing a letter to Mornay, describing his attack on Paris, and in a postscript added, "I have decided to remain here until tomorrow to see what Mayenne will do and then to withdraw in hope that he will intercept me—something he hasn't dared to do until now."[12] With Mayenne's arrival, Henri's chance to win Paris was at an end. On the morning of November 3 he attempted, as he had planned, to engage the Duke in battle; but although he had his troops drawn up in battle formation at Pré-aux-Clercs until almost noon, Mayenne was too cautious to attack. The Duke, unlike his more reckless elder brother, was a calculating soldier; he never courted honor at the risk of death and he saw no reason now to engage in combat with the Béarnais when Paris would obviously be his in any case. By the afternoon of November 3, the King had withdrawn his troops and left the city free. He knew he had neither the army nor the provisions for a siege and he saw no use in prolonging his stay. But the Huguenots who had thought to make Paris their own were but ill-pleased with the course of his action. The Protestant minister Gabriel d'Amours, who never feared to speak his mind, was particularly bitter as he railed at the King: "You would not take Paris when God gave it to you; one day you will wish to take it and God will not give it to you. The fine army of French gentlemen which you would not use will melt away." But Henri, knowing he had done the only prudent thing, would not argue, answering only: "I do what I can."[13]

The failure to take Paris had been a bitter blow to the King, made all the worse by the nearness of his victory. "Undoubtedly they were lost and would have given themselves up," he wrote to his captain, Bournazel, "if only the army had been just a little bit delayed, as indeed they would have been if the passages of the river had been more carefully secured." Yet disappointed as he was, he was not without hope and not long after he wrote in good humor of "the Duc de Mayenne who takes his ease in Paris where some day I, in my turn, hope to take my ease."[14]

Once again he left Paris behind him, this time traveling south through Orléanais and taking his ancestral city of Vendôme before reaching Tours where he hoped to spend the first part of the winter. There was a royal welcome waiting him in Tours and the light-hearted Tourangeaux led him through their city with the conventional procession of torchlight and pageantry. Despite their warmth it was a bleak winter for the King; the wind from the Loire was damp and depressing, the water itself locked in ice, and he longed for the clear air of the Pyrenees with their purple peaks glazed with snow in the winter light. "A king without a kingdom, a husband without a wife, a general without money," he sardonically characterized himself in these chill days. Even now, however, he was not without his humor, his warmth, his hope. There was nothing he feared so much as sad people and he would never join their ranks no matter how many misfortunes befell him. "I cannot have a melancholy man in my service," he told a friend, "for if a man is not good for himself, how will he satisfy others? Can one hope for satisfaction from a man who cannot satisfy himself?"[15]

Actually, the King had good reason for melancholy that winter. Unless his army increased he could hope to do very little and the foreign troops on whom he was counting had not yet arrived. Sancy had been successful in raising about 5,000 Swiss, but many of them, hearing that the King had no money, had turned back, some had died and now less than 2,000 were available. German troops, too, were slow in coming and although Elizabeth of England had promised to do her best to hurry things she had not been successful. Elizabeth alone had faithfully kept her promise of both men and money. He wrote to her in sincere gratitude, avowing, "You will never have to accuse me of ingratitude." Her answer had a warmth about it that was stronger than diplomacy. Now that the Valois were gone from France, the chess game was not quite so complex and Elizabeth could afford to write to her old friend Navarre: "There is nothing in the world that could make me happier than to hear that my troops have in some way assisted a prince whom I would like to see completely served." From time to time there slipped through the fog of distrust and anxiety which surrounded him a gleam of devotion and affection which warmed him even in his failure. One day at his camp at Lisieux a young religious was discovered, disguised as a soldier, for no other reason than to be near the King and to serve him. Henri was both amused and touched and while he would not keep the boy, he wrote to Claude Groulart in Caen: "I have just taken a little Cordelier, who was found in my army, dressed like a soldier, who says he left his monastery because he was beaten for being on my side. . . . I am sending him to you and if what he says is true, have him return to his monastery and give orders to the prior that he is not to be mistreated any more."[16]

With the new year, the King's fortunes improved. As his army made its way through Normandy, they took town after town with little difficulty: Argentan, Falaise, Lisieux, Verneuil, Honfleur all fell to the King. In exultation he wrote to Corisande toward the end of January: "My heart, God continues to bless me for I have taken Lisieux without even firing a cannon. . . . This is the strongest place I have conquered yet and the most useful." His hope soared, and that same month he wrote to the Duchesse de Montmorency, "I hope that in eight days Normandy will be free from the Leaguers and that Brittany will soon be in the same state."[17]

With these successes, his hope of taking Paris returned, for if he controlled Normandy he controlled many of the life lines on which the Parisians depended. He longed to confront Mayenne in a more decisive victory than that of Arques and he was jubilant when he learned in early March that the League army had crossed the Eure near Ivry. This time Mayenne could not evade his opponent and on March 14 he gave battle to the King's army. It was not a propitious spot for a conflict. The open plains stretched on all sides without bush or tree to break the skyline. The field was soft and muddy so that the cavalry could never achieve more than a slow gallop. In addition, the wind was against the royal army, blowing the smoke of their muskets into the faces of the King's men. Yet Henri made of it a battle for all time. He would bring the League to defeat and he would brook no obstacles. It was a battle not simply of military genius but an occasion when the full force of the King's personal magnetism was brought to its peak. His courage, his dynamism, his reckless confidence were not simply his own personal qualities but qualities which he communicated through sheer force of personality to his men. The noise, the confusion, the violence seemed only to steady his judgment and confirm his will. "He was everywhere," wrote a contemporary biographer, "as if he had a hundred eyes and as many arms." This was the battle of the white plume, that fabled feather that was to become symbolic of his greatest gifts. For, so the legend goes, Henri addressing his troops before the battle, cried: "If you lose your ensigns, cornets, or banners, rally round my white plume for you will always find it on the road to victory and honor." It was no empty boast, for by afternoon the field belonged to the King and Mayenne had retired to Nantes. Impatient for his victory to be known, he wrote that same evening to Elizabeth, to various members of the nobility, to Corisande to tell them that heaven had smiled on him once more. "God has blessed us," ran the letter to the faithful Huguenot La Noue. "This day, the fourteenth of the present month, we have given battle, a battle that was well fought. God has shown that he loves right more than might. Our victory was complete."[18]

For Mayenne the defeat was equally complete, for he recognized that Ivry was more than a single battle; it was a triumph which might well change the course of France. The Duke's initial popularity was waning; twice he had faced the King in open battle and twice he had been routed. His retreat from Ivry was described in contempt and even in Paris there were those who called him "the Fat Pig."

Mayenne was seriously frightened by the thought that his cause might be lost, for Spain alone could be counted on for money and men and he feared what this defeat would do to his Spanish prestige. Hardly had he taken off his boots when he wrote in near despair to the Spanish agent Moreo then at Paris: "It is with deep regreat that I tell you the sad news . . . death would be a thousand times more agreeable to me."[19] But Philip's displeasure at his failure was relatively mild, for it was to his own advantage to keep the League dependent. Victory might have gone to Mayenne's head and Philip preferred to keep his servants humble.

If on one side Mayenne had to use all his diplomacy to maintain Philip's assistance, on the other he had to be equally ingenious to justify his dependence on Spanish strength. Not only did many Frenchmen object, but the Pope, too, seemed increasingly mistrustful of the role Philip played in French affairs. Shortly after Ivry, Mayenne, fearful lest Sixtus withdraw his support from the League, wrote to the Pope:

> Your Holiness, as head of the Church, you less than anyone else should let yourself be impressed by the political reasoning of those who say that if we were too strong our prosperity would go to increase the grandeur of the Catholic king of whom everyone is jealous. Religion should come before every other consideration as indeed it does. But besides this, the king of Spain does not dream of conquering another crown and we have never seen in him any object other than to conserve religion in the kingdom. . . . But if there is reason to mistrust King Philip who more than Your Holiness would increase this danger in making us, through your hesitation, debtors to this Prince.[20]

"He has spoken very well, if he is telling the whole truth," wryly commented Sixtus on reading Mayenne's letter.

By the spring of 1590 Sixtus had too much evidence of the Spanish will to power to credit Mayenne's simplistic avowal. Sixtus had never been Philip's man and even before the death of Henri III he had begun to doubt that the preservation of the Roman faith was the only motive behind Philip's moves. His doubts were now increased by the Spanish ambassador's threats that if Henri de Navarre's Catholic supporters were not immediately excommunicated the Spanish King would withdraw himself from his obedience to the Holy See. Had Olivares been less arrogant he would have realized that every threat drove Sixtus more closely to the French position. Yet even Philip, usually more astute in diplomatic situations, failed to realize that Sixtus, like any man goaded too far, was soon to turn.

Although the Holy See was becoming increasingly sympathetic to Henri's position, yet in practical terms France had little to show for it. The Papal Legate, Errico Cardinal Caetani, had shown himself from the first day of his arrival to be a man of Spain and the League. His appointment had been due largely to Spanish influence and although he was a man whose birth and experience seemed to fit him for this delicate job, the Pope had misgivings from the first. From the moment of his arrival at Lyons in November he had shown himself a militarist rather than a conciliator. When Caetani reached Paris on January 21 his fame had spread before him and the volatile Parisians mobbed the streets shouting "Long live Sixtus V; long live the Holy See." Impressed by the flattery and luxury with which the Parisians surrounded him, his mission of conciliation was soon forgotten as he openly espoused the cause of the League. Meanwhile another mission, quite contrary to that of the Pope, was being worked out for him by Philip II through his ambassador, Mendoza. "The pretensions of the Prince of Béarn should be emphatically disavowed," wrote the Catholic King, "because he is an obstinate and confirmed heretic who was suckled on heresy along with his milk."[21] To almost every point that Mendoza suggested, Caetani agreed: he declared Navarre unable to assume the title of King of France; he demanded the release of and support for the Cardinal de Bourbon; he forbade prelates to attend the assembly of the Estates which Navarre had called at Tours.

This was the meeting which Navarre had promised in the Declaration of St. Cloud and at which the bishops would have had the opportunity of "instructing him" in view of his possible conversion. In February the legate, determined to block such a dangerous assembly, sent a circular letter to the bishops of France, thanking them for their invitation but assuring them that there was no need of such a convocation and reminding them that no heretic had the right to call a council. If, he continued, it was a question of theology, then let the *soi-disant* King of France discuss it with the Sorbonne; if he wanted to hear the true voice of the Church then let him listen to the Pope. If the King truly desired instruction, he remarked contemptuously, it would be quite enough to send one or two clergymen to him with the decrees of the Council of Trent and a copy of the Roman catechism. It was an incendiary message, and Henri when he heard it registered his own protest through the Parlement at Tours against the "*soi-disant* Legate of the Pope." It was, however, the Cardinal Legate not the King who held the ear of Catholic France, and the Sorbonne, taking its cue from Caetani, reiterated its unanimous decision that Catholics could not receive Henri as their King, that those who helped him in any way were "deserters from their religion and live in a perpetual state of sin." Following this decision, "in order to animate the people further," a procession took place in the streets of Paris led by such zealous Leaguers as the Bishop of Senlis and the Prior of Chartreux, "holding one hand on their crucifixes and the other on their halberds." All the religious orders, both old and new, took part—Capuchins, Feuillants, Jacobins, Carmelites. The historian De Thou sensing the irony of this commingling of religion and violence commented: "the old ones were grinding their teeth and walking with a warlike air; the young ones following armed. They sang as they went and called themselves the Church Militant."[22]

Whatever the Sorbonne might decree, whatever might be sworn on the great altar of Notre Dame was at best a matter of theory and Henri de Navarre had never been a theorist. The fact was that he had won Normandy, had routed Mayenne, and now in the beginning of May stood once again before the gates of Paris. Admirers of the King found it hard to explain where those two months had gone between his success at Ivry and his arrival at Paris. Philippe de Cheverny, who would later be Henri's chancellor, pointed out in some embarrassment that like a solicitous general he wished to give his troops time to rest and that, furthermore, he had had to wait for war supplies which were coming from England—but actually the supplies had arrived before the end of March.[23] His enemies found his conduct quite what they would expect: mercurial, reckless, irresponsible, lazy. Pierre Corneio, a Spanish monk who lived in Paris during the second siege, writes with the clarity of hindsight that had Henri come to Paris immediately following Ivry the city could not have withstood him. It was badly provisioned, the people were demoralized, the government incompetent. When the citizens heard of Mayenne's defeat at Ivry they were sure that the end had come. The Duke de Nemours, nominal commander of Paris, desperately levied a tax so that the walls of the city, but poorly mended since the days of Henri II, could be repaired. But the Parisians, weary of years of heavy taxation, responded half-heartedly, unwilling to believe that their walls could be so easily breached. Yet as peasants from the countryside, pushing their awkward wooden carts ahead of them, begged sanctuary within the protection of the capital, and as messengers, breathless and frightened, described the grain fields trampled and the mills in flames, the citizens began to wonder if they had counted too much on their security. By mid-May, chastened by news of the King's successes, they offered themselves to do whatever they could to strengthen their position. They carted dirt, dug trenches, dragged wooden beams to strengthen the pointed spikes of the palisade. Fear goaded them, for this time the King's army seemed invincible. Henri, too, had a sense of victory as he wrote to Corisande from the little town of Chelles: "I am now before Paris where God will help me. If I take it, I will at last begin to feel the effects of having the crown. I have taken the bridges at Charenton and St. Maur . . . tomorrow I will capture the suburbs of Paris by force. The enemy has lost much but we have lost very little. I have burned all their mills, as I have done all along the coast and within twelve days they will be forced to surrender. . . . May God give me peace, for I would like to be able to have a few years of rest. I am growing old."[24] Sometime during the bustle of those May days came the news that Charles, Cardinal de Bourbon, had died in the village of Fontenay-le-Comte in Poitou. His last words were as ambiguous as his life: "What I have done, I have done for the King, my nephew, and my other nephews. The late King and Queen knew my intentions very well."[25] It was a message that needed a ciphering hand; but no one cared enough to bother, not even in those great palaces where other rulers had acknowledged him as King. Neither in Paris, nor Rome, nor Madrid did his dying cause more than a momentary stir.

The twelve days which Henri had given the Parisians to surrender passed and still the city held out. It was obvious now both to the besiegers and the besieged that this was to be a long siege. Normandy was in the King's hands and so were all the river passages—Corbie, Melun, Lagny. Paris, it was apparent, was to be starved into submission. On May 26 an inventory of the grain supply was taken; the city had enough wheat for one month provided it was carefully rationed. When that gave out there was a small supply of barley to feed the 220,000 people then in Paris. Already famine was a substantial threat yet when in early June the officials examined homes to see that the rationing laws were being carried out, the Jesuits and Capuchins, reported L'Estoile with his usual cynicism, were found to have hoarded enough food for a year.

Henri had never wanted a siege; he was not a soldier of sieges but of quick battles and violent actions. To kill in the heat of conflict, to inflict pain and to endure it, this was a portion of life he knew and accepted. Wounds, mutilation, death these were part of a soldier's lot, part of any brave man's life, for in these days every man loyal to his country was in part a soldier. But the slow warfare of a siege needed a kind of sang-froid which Henri lacked. He had put towns under siege before and he knew the terror, the apathy, the despair that starvation inevitably brings. He had seen the dead in the streets and the dull-eyed listlessness of the survivors. To inflict this upon Paris, the queen of his kingdom, the symbol of his power, was intolerable. On June 15 he wrote to the people of Paris assuring them of his good will, of his paternal concern, indeed of his affection, and begging them to surrender before they should feel the full horror of the siege.

> We know, as you see, what you have and how long you can subsist; and we know even more than you because we know how you have been deceived. The help that has been promised you is imaginary . . . the journey we have just made has shown us even more clearly than before what you yourselves must also have seen: that the Duc de Mayenne is withdrawing from you rather than approaching, which is sufficient indication that his plans are only for his own advantage. Nevertheless, recognizing that your obstinacy can be of great service to him, this alone is responsible for his continued contact with you. Should he succeed better than there is any reason to think he will, he will just that much more easily deliver you into Spanish hands, since it is common knowledge that he treats with them and has made certain bargains with them.[26]

It was a letter of powerful logic based on the incontrovertible principle of self-preservation. Henri no longer spoke of loyalty to France, to the crown, to himself as King. It was no longer a matter of honor but of life. Yet strong as his rhetoric was, there was abroad in Paris a rhetoric still more authoritative because its argument was not to life in this world but to life after death. "What does it profit a man if he gain the whole world and suffer the loss of his immortal soul," the Paris preachers cried. Would the Parisians suffer the risk of eternal damnation by accepting a heretic king? Would they give up the crown of glory for a little bread, they demanded of the starving citizens. To exhort the people, the Leaguers organized on Ascension Day a religious procession which wound through the streets of Paris and reached its culmination in the Cathedral of Notre Dame. Here the great Catholic lords advanced to the main altar and there swore to use all their means and even life itself to maintain the Catholic religion in the city of Paris and throughout the kingdom. The crowds fired by the dedication of their leaders swore to die rather than to accept Henri the Huguenot. By mid-July the people were beginning to feel the sharp edge of their promises. The stores of grain were gone and the ration of bread was reduced to four ounces a day. "Although it is not Lent, they are fasting," wrote the Spanish ambassador Mendoza who used whatever money he had to help the Parisians and to exhort them to patient endurance.[27]

Corneio watching the slow destruction of the city he had so much admired wrote: "All is changed from the glory and triumph of this lovely city, for in place of the elegant and expensive tapestries, the silver plate, the precious jewels, in place of the great carriages with their horses which carried the lords and ladies about the city, now one sees only pots full of pulp and boiling herbs and kettles full of horse meat, donkey, and mule by which this poor people, so religious and so Christian, sustain themselves."[28] Soon, however, even horse meat was too expensive for anyone but the very rich and the people were forced to eat candle grease, grass, even rodents. Garbage was fished out of the river and men argued and fought over the bits of slimy refuse washed up from the Seine. Dead dogs, themselves having died of starvation, were carried from the streets and boiled in kettles which were too often empty.

Mendoza, whose instructions were to keep the Parisians from capitulating to the King at any cost, knew that Paris could not hold out much longer without help. When in the beginning of July, letters came to Paris from Mayenne promising them aid at the end of the month at the latest, Mendoza breathed more easily. Some, however, felt that the promise was simply a hoax to keep the people loyal to the League, and L'Estoile noted sardonically: "These beautiful words served the foolish people for bread . . . so anxious are they to attain that wonderful paradise which the preachers assure them will be gained by dying of hunger."[29] As the death toll mounted, the theoreticians at the Sorbonne continued their academic question: "Whether the people constrained by famine would incur excommunication by giving in to a heretic prince." But while Caetani and Cardinal Bellarmine, who had accompanied the legate to France, honed their wits on this delicate problem of salvation, the King wrote once more begging his people to cast the scales from their eyes and face the fact they were being duped by those who would subjugate France to their own interests. On July 16 he wrote: "If reason, natural duty, or the ancient laws and constitutions of this realm have not persuaded you of your lawful duty to this crown, abused by the wiles of those who, at the expense of your lives and substance, dare aspire to its usurpation, then the necessity to which you are now reduced and the frustration of waiting in vain for the help they have promised you ought to open your eyes." St. Denis was already in royal hands and even the leaders of the League realized that Paris was coming to the end of her rope. Desperately the people gathered at the Palais, willing now to settle for peace at any price, but instead of the hearing they had hoped for, soldiers charged into the crowd, arresting some, wounding others, and threatening with death any who would assemble under such traitorous standards. By mid-July Mayenne had not yet arrived, and Henri wrote to Corisande from St. Denis: "Paris is at bay so that this week there will have to be either a battle or a delegation. The Spanish will join the Fat Duke on Tuesday next; we shall see then if there will be blood about our ankles. The following week Henri wrote to Matignon that the enemy were no more than fifteen leagues distant and he was sure they will give battle within a few days, for "they cannot wait any longer or they will lose Paris before their very eyes since it cannot hold out any longer than that."[30] Once again Henri's optimism was unfounded, and even during the first hot week of August with the stench of the dead poisoning the streets, Paris still refused to capitulate.

Now, however, even the militant clergy recognized that steps must be taken to succor the starving city. With the permission of the Sixteen, Pierre Gondi, Bishop of Langres, and Pierre d'Epinac, Bishop of Lyons, able diplomats well-trained for their task, arranged for an interview with the King. A few days later, Henri recieved the bishops in the cloister of the Abbey of St. Antoine-des-Champs. He was gracious and reserved, listening readily while Gondi proposed that they should be given passports in order to act as intermediaries between Mayenne and the King. Henri, amused at their studied refusal to grant him the title of King of France, pointed out that since they spoke of the King of Navarre he was doubtful if the King of Navarre was in a position to give them what they asked. But there was little amusement in his tone as he continued, expressing his astonishment at the use of Spanish power, "Paris and the kingdom of France are a choice morsel for the mouth of Philip of Spain," he pointed out caustically and then continued to Cardinal Gondı: "You, Your Eminence, ought to have pity on them [the people of Paris]; they are your sheep . . . I am not much of a theologian but I know that God will not listen when you treat your people thus to please the King of Spain and Bernardino Mendoza. Your feet will be burned in another world. . . . I intend," he concluded, "to enter Paris and I will hang those who have caused the death of so many poor people." Still he continued to offer his mercy to Paris, his "eldest daughter," but only on condition that she acknowledge him as her rightful King. Otherwise, he threatened, he would use his full power as victor. The chastened bishops returned to the Sixteen with little to report beyond a reaffirmation of the King's position.

Despite their failure, within a week the prelates were asking for a second conference with the King. It is difficult to measure their motive for it seemed that there was little they could expect to gain. Perhaps they were, as they said, moved at the plight of the people, by the staggering mounds of corpses that were carried away each dawn, by the terrifying rumors that cannibalism was rife in the dark alleys where children unaccountably disappeared. The motive of the Sixteen in encouraging the bishops to treat with the King was easier to assess: they let them go, interpreted Palma Cayet, to stall for time, simply to keep the people peaceful until the sluggish Mayenne, joined by Spanish forces under the Duke of Parma, should come to relieve the siege. This second interview, however, had an unlooked for result: the King was so moved by the description of his starving people that he offered on August 20 safe-conduct to all women, children and scholars who wished to leave Paris, enjoining the surrounding towns to receive them well and take no vengeance upon them. Such kindness was an ambivalent blessing for, as L'Estoile commented, "Such humanity was one of the principal causes why the siege did not have the success it might have had.[31] He was not the only one who upbraided Henri for his mercy, for later that fall Elizabeth of England, annoyed at the outcome of the siege, asked the King querulously how he could have rendered his own siege ineffectual by giving permission for people to leave the destitute city.

By the end of August there were rumors that Mayenne and Parma had joined forces at Meaux and were on their way to Paris. Although Alexander Farnese, Duke of Parma, was a most able military leader, he was far from enthusiastic about his expedition into France. When he received his orders from Philip, he at first demurred, pleading that his work to establish peace in the Low Countries was far from finished. Philip, annoyed at his general's apparent lack of zeal for the Spanish cause, only reaffirmed his orders; and Parma, with misgivings which he could not articulate, joined Mayenne's forces on their march to Paris. The King, hearing of their advance, organized his men in an ideal battle situation outside the town of Chelles. This time he would force Mayenne's hand and so repeat his success at Ivry but on a grander scale. With Mayenne defeated, Paris would have no other course but surrender; and with Paris gained, all of France would capitulate. His confidence was full and his eagerness for battle unrestrained. But when September 1 dawned, no battle took place. For the next few days he harassed the enemy, forcing them in every way he knew to confront him. But Parma remained firm: his instructions had been simply to succor Paris not to engage himself in a full-scale conflict. Even Mayenne could not persuade him otherwise. For a week the game of cat and mouse continued while Henri became increasingly restless, sleeping but little, constantly reassessing his own position, reassuring himself that Parma was not planning a surprise attack.

For all his care he was unprepared for the simple scheme which cost him Paris. The Duke's combined forces successfully attacked the river town of Lagny which had neither sufficient ramparts nor garrison to defend it. With Lagny in their hands, Parma, with that brilliant strategy for which he was noted, and protected by darkness and fog, constructed a bridge of boats across the Marne and thus put his troops on a straight path to Paris. So quietly had the maneuver been accomplished that Henri knew nothing of it until it was over. Paris was freed almost without bloodshed, for the King in his determination to give open battle to the Dukes had pulled his troops into camp at Chelles, leaving Paris virtually unguarded. Within a few days the starving Parisians had been relieved by 1,500 wagons of provisions which Parma had sent into the city, and on September 18 the Fat Duke, ponderous but victorious, made his triumphal entry. Paris was wild with joy but among the applause for Mayenne was heard a cry that fell strangely on French ears: "Long live the King of Spain!" The people whose diet had been for three long months the unpalatable "bread of patience" would have cheered the devil had he brought them food. The League had once more justified itself and the preachers had material for a thousand sermons on the value of suffering nobly born, on God as the lord of hosts, on that holy Providence which will always give victory to the cause of right.

Meanwhile Henri sat amid the ruins of failure. Paris had but few happy memories for the King. Here his father had been bedizened with bright promises that a less vain man would have recognized as false. Here he himself had spent part of his childhood, the third of that triumvirate of the Three Henris of whom he alone remained. It was in Paris that his mother had died alone among those who had ridiculed and exploited her. And it was in Paris that he had watched the river run red with the blood of his friends during those terrible days of Saint Bartholomew. Paris was in a sense, if he relied on memory alone, his enemy. And yet whatever it had meant for Henri de Navarre, for Henri, King of France, it had its magic lure. From his camp he had seen the bell tower of St. Germain l'Auxerrois which had once rung the alarm for Saint Bartholomew; he had seen the high hill of Montmartre with its famous abbey; he had watched the spires of Notre Dame catch the light of the morning sun. Three times he had been before the gates of Paris; three times he had known the excitement of near possession. But three times he had failed, not in combat—that would have been more desirable—but by being out-thought, out-witted. It was a bitter failure because he had failed others as well as himself. He had failed his captains, some of whom had advised that he stay at Paris and await Parma's arrival; he had failed his soldiers who during the weary months of the siege had been bolstered by the thought of the ultimate conquest. Perhaps most of all he had failed Paris, for no one knew better than the King the numbers of the dead, and the extent of suffering through which the living had passed. Suffering often made men into beasts and he knew the murders, the looting, the savage brutality that starvation could awaken in a city. His failure lay like a great stone upon his shoulders. Henri had, from his youth, been brought up to responsibility; he had fought battles before and recognized, as any general must, the sorrow of knowing that one's orders must inevitably cost some men their lives. But his failure at Paris was a very different thing. Here he could not talk of "the enemy." Paris was no enemy; Paris was his own. He was its King and its citizens were his people, his people to cherish and protect, never to destroy. Not many years later, William Shakespeare, imagining the lonely burden that another king had felt would write:

> Upon the King! Let us our lives, our souls,
> Our debts, our careful wives,
> Our children and our sins, lay on the King!

"Upon the King," the phrase was heavy with meaning as Henri sat to write the letters which would attempt some justification of what he knew would look like a stupid ending to a long and expensive siege.

CHAPTER XI

The Struggle for a Kingdom: 1591–1592

It is difficult to determine *de futuris*, and this cloudy time threateneth a very great storm.

English Ambassador

Although the letters which the King wrote explaining the debacle at Paris lacked nothing of that fresh rhetoric by which he won men so easily to his side, they were not good enough to save him from rebuke. Elizabeth of England with reasons that ran closer to the bone than mere friendship was both angry and frightened by the turn things had taken at Paris. Henri had been so confident, the Parisians so disadvantaged, and Mayenne so halting in his efforts that she, like the King himself, had never thought of failure. Now, as token of her continued friendship, she sent him a scarf embroidered with her own hand; but although it was a precious gift, the King felt the prick of the needle as he read the accompanying letter: how could he have been tricked into two lengthy conferences with emissaries from the League who were obviously playing to gain the precious delay by which Mayenne had triumphed; how could he have rendered his siege ineffectual by his misplaced kindness to the inhabitants? "If God makes you victorious through His gracious mercy—yes, I dare to say it to you—it will be more than your carelessness deserves. . . . You like to gamble better than you like to bring things to a conclusion," she ended sharply.[1]

Whatever options Henri might once have had, no other course was left to him now but to withdraw his troops from Paris. Part of his forces he temporarily disbanded, sending them back to their homes for rest and food, for the devastated lands around Paris could not sustain an army. Yet even in defeat he could not resist the opportunity to follow upon Parma's heels as the Spaniard led his army back into the Low Countries. Although he was no match for the Spanish forces, he nipped and badgered, trying to turn Parma's triumphal withdrawal into the appearance of a defeat. The next few months he passed at Senlis, that little town from which he had escaped his royal imprisonment fourteen years before. The throne of France was something he had never thought of in those days when his single aim had been to rid himself of the tricks and chicanery of the Valois and return to his mountains of Béarn; now Béarn had been left far behind him and all his energies were directed to the heavy responsibility of winning the kingdom which was his only in theory.

He knew that Parma's withdrawal did not mean the end of Spanish force, and by November word reached him that Spain had taken the town of Hennebont and fortified the port of Blavet with both men and vessels. He wrote at once to Beauvais La Nocle, his ambassador in England, begging him to try to get together at least 2,000 foot soldiers and as much ammunition as possible. At the same time he wrote personally to Elizabeth with one of those cavalier gestures of flattery and dependence which Elizabeth, despite her shrewd bargaining, found hard to resist: "Madame," he wrote suppliantly, "it is one of your glories with which God has particularly wished to honor your reign that you be the recourse of the afflicted . . . and that you should have received, sustained and preserved from his enemies a king unjustly despoiled of his crown."[2] Elizabeth, moved less perhaps by the graciousness of the compliment than by her practical appraisal of the danger to England should the Spanish entrench themselves on the northwest coast of France, was quick to promise help.

While Henri waited to see what shape events would take on the coast, he made one last desperate surprise assault on Paris. Some three weeks earlier, the Leaguers, under the leadership of the Duc d'Aumale, nephew of Mayenne, had attempted to regain St. Denis. The weather had been bitter cold and the attackers had been able to cross the frozen moat and scale the walls. They were already at the Abbey before the night alarm was given, and Governor de Vic had been hard pressed to drive them back beyond the gates.

This enterprise, although unsuccessful, had stirred the King's daring, and on the night of January 20 he carried out his own dramatic

scheme for entering Paris. He had secretly maneuvered a large part
of his army beneath Montmartre where they waited in the faubourg
St. Honoré. Meanwhile ten wagons, filled with sacks of flour, and
assisted by fifty or sixty men disguised as peasants, sought entrance
through the Porte St. Honoré. The governor, Belin, however, having
heard rumors of a scheme to get through the gate, had had the
entrance filled with earthworks and requested the "millers" to take
their flour down river to another entrance. The "millers," realizing
that the ruse had been discovered, ran for their lives, surrounded
by the thousand armed men who had hoped to win entrance behind
them. Ultimately the *Journée des farines* did more harm than good,
for through it the League leaders convinced the citizens that they
needed additional protection against the usurping King; and on February 12, 4,000 Spanish troops were garrisoned in the city of Paris.

Although Henri had counted little on his latest scheme, yet the
weight of another failure dulled his spirits; he needed a success for
his own morale as well as that of his men, and toward the end
of January he sent Biron south across the plains of the Beauce
to surprise the city of Chartres into submission. Biron was often
his own man rather than the King's and now, despite Henri's orders
for haste, he did not arrive at the walls of Chartres until mid-February. By this time the city was alerted and when the King joined
Biron some days later, it was obvious that Chartres would not be
taken without a long and bloody siege. The city was of little military value and built in a way that almost defied siege with its
high eastern hill and sudden drop into the plains on its western
side. But Henri, made stubborn by failure, refused to listen to the
advice of his council, and for two long and costly months he laid
siege to Chartres. In a letter to Montmorency, then busy in Languedoc repulsing the aggressive Duke of Savoy, he was forced to
admit that the siege was of far longer duration than he had anticipated.

For the first few weeks the Catholics within the walls refused to
believe that a city consecrated to the Blessed Virgin could ever
fall before heretics, but as their food and ammunition grew low
and Mayenne's promises of help failed to materialize, their faith
grew dim. On April 11 the King wrote to the Duc de Nevers—
who after months of vacillation had finally cast his lot with Henri
—that the city had agreed to capitulate on April 19. "All the preachers
cried out against this," L'Estoile wrote from Paris, "and made the

ladies cry hot tears by the beautiful apostrophes they made to Our
Lady . . . reproaching her for deserting them in their hour of need."
The Catholics, nourished so long on sermons which told them that
God would never fail the League, were bewildered at the capitulation
of Chartres. What did it mean, they asked, that this city, the citadel
of the Virgin Mary herself, should have been brought to its knees
by a Huguenot prince? L'Estoile, never at a loss for a rejoinder,
retorted wryly: "What does the taking of Chartres prove? According
to the Paris preachers that Notre Dame de Chartres has not the
same power as Notre Dame de Lorette who guards the keys of
Paris."[3]

Whatever it meant at Paris, at Chartres it meant that the King
had his victory, and in a magnanimous gesture he bestowed the
keys of the city on the former governor, Sourdis, who some years
before had been driven out by the League. It was to all appear-
ances a routine political appointment, but those who had served
the King most closely in those last few months found a more devious
thread. The thread, if followed, led past the politic Monsieur de
Sourdis to his niece whom the King had met five months before.
It is not difficult to understand how this *amour passionel*, which was
to dominate the next ten years of Henri's life, began. Perhaps it
is true as a contemporary conjectured that the stars were in their
proper places; but it was more than that: the events of earth had
also conspired to that moment in the château at Coeuvres when the
King first looked at Gabrielle d'Estrées.

The affair with Corisande had faded. For three years they had
not met, and although his letters continued, they were increasingly
less frequent and more conventional. The protestations of love, of
fidelity, of desire were dry and withered. They had lost their bloom
and no passionate response on Corisande's part could revive them.
The King's wild rides through the countryside—fording rivers, evading enemy outposts, arriving breathless but joyous at the gates of
Hagetmau—were over. She had followed with her keen intelligence his
military strategies, the diplomatic tangles between himself and the
Valois, the political scheming of both Huguenots and Catholics. She
had shared his dreams and when they were shattered she had helped
him to shape new ones. She did not always agree with him, but
she understood him as no one else did. Her love had been far
from blind; she had had few illusions about her lover, and she had
sometimes denied his advances, refusing to go with him from town

7. Gabrielle d'Estrées (Photo Giraudon—Paris)

8. Henriette d'Entragues
   (The New York Public Library,
   Astor, Lenox and Tilden Foundations)

9. Corisande d'Andoins (Photo Giraudon—Paris)

10. Henri de Lorraine, Duc de Guise
    (Photo Giraudon—Paris)

11. François de France, Duc d'Alençon
    (Photo Giraudon—Paris)

to town like some camp follower; she would wait for him at Hagetmau —and he had respected her for her decision. She had been his star but sometime during those busy years the star had grown too remote and when in November of 1590 the King met Gabrielle d'Estrées he needed her nearness, her youth, her beauty, even her ignorance of royal affairs.

It was on November 7 that the King, made curious by the high praise of his Grand Master, Roger de Bellegarde, rode with him from his temporary camp at the border of Picardy to the estate of Antoine d'Estrées at Coeuvres. Even had there been no Gabrielle, the château of Coeuvres would have had its charm. The King, despite his natural resilience, was drained by failure and anxiety: the unabating search for arms, for men, for money; the constant scheming to win allies and outwit his enemies; the weeks on horseback broken only by the uneasy sleep of a camp pallet had taken their toll. He had been in arms for so long that the luxury of ordinary living was almost beyond his imagining. At Coeuvres, despite the war, that luxury was still maintained. The long garden paths bordered by arbors and flower beds, the pool with its careful landscaping, the long branches of the shade trees had, even now, in the gray November afternoon, something of tranquillity. This was the palace of a lord of some renown, and although the fortunes of the d'Estrées had dropped sharply during the period of the wars, their heritage was one of prestige. Jean d'Estrées had been honored by Henri II as a man of valor and faith, and his son Antoine had, until the League had overcome him, acted as governor of La Fère. The King was impressed as, with Bellegarde at his side, he rode along the avenue across the wide moat and into the lower court whose ornamentation of cannon and cannon balls gave tribute to the military interests of Captain Jean d'Estrées. The spiral stairs, the lord's mansion with its wide front and elaborately decorated dormer windows bespoke both grace and power.

But if Gabrielle's paternal heritage was for fidelity and valor, she had inherited something quite other from her mother. Françoise Babou de la Bourdaisière, while hardly more than a child, had fallen heir to the sins of her family and she, along with her six sisters, became known ironically as the Seven Capital Sins. By the time she had given birth to her first children, the number of her lovers was legion, and Antoine, her husband, a temporizer with no taste for duels, set himself to live in amity with the beautiful and self-willed

Françoise. "Astrée," the poet Ronsard had once called her, but the star had hung too low, and in 1584 with reckless braggadocio she had left her husband and children to follow the Marquis d'Alègre into Auvergne. For eight years she lived with him at Issoire until one day the years of her passion overtook her and she was brutally murdered in her bed along with her lover.

The title of the Seven Capital Sins she willed to her children, who, following either the prudence of their father or the folly of their mother, attempted to cut out their own careers. Although Gabrielle was probably no more than seventeen at that first meeting with the King, she had already appeared at the Paris court and was encircled by rumors—probably false—that she had been the mistress of the murdered Duc de Guise, of Henri de Valois, and of the Italian Zamet. True or false, many were amused by the irony that the d'Estrées house in Paris was on the rue des Bons-Enfants.

There was very little of romance in the royal figure that Roger de Bellegarde presented to the demoiselles d'Estrées, Diane and her younger sister Gabrielle. The King was thirty-seven but looked older with his graying hair and lined face. His doublet was worn and dusty, his boots were scuffed and cracked with long use; and Gabrielle had the opportunity to learn at firsthand that the rumor that His Majesty smelled more like a cowherd than a king was true. For Henri, however, there was not a moment's hesitation; in a second the world swung from its orbit and rested upon Gabrielle d'Estrées. His cares were swept from his back and all victories were caught up in this one siege in which he could not be defeated. She was all youth, and no care had yet violated her. The clear blue eyes, the flush of her skin, the golden sheen of her hair—these were the charms of some young goddess who had known nothing of conflict and hatred, of tricks and duplicity. She had never been ravaged by war, and he, who all his life had been dogged by battles and persecution, longed for her as saints long for heaven. His passion, as usual, was immediate and imperious and Bellegarde received his cue to meddle no more in the King's interests.

The King, however, was not able to pursue the prize as wholeheartedly as he wished. The siege at Chartres occupied his time and his visits to Coeuvres were necessarily infrequent. When he did come, it was Diane not Gabrielle who played the attentive hostess. When, according to legend, the King disguised himself as a peasant to get through the enemy lines, Gabrielle, far from being thrilled at the danger he had risked for an hour with her, seemed simply ill at ease in the presence of this ludicrous figure. The King, shuffling beside his goddess in his dusty smock and awkward sabots, knew that this was not the hour to make love. Despite Gabrielle's initial indifference, however, she could not long resist the King of France. The feints and counterfeints that ultimately installed her in the royal favor can never be more than conjectured, but by April Gabrielle d'Estrées was openly known as the King's mistress. Many of Henri's contemporaries were patently cynical about the power she wielded, commenting that it was not the King who conducted this siege but the whole tribe of D'Estrées who successfully besieged the King. Whether or not Gabrielle was fully aware of her role in the political maneuverings, it is true that within months the family fortunes had been restored. Monsieur de Sourdis, husband of her aunt Isabelle, was once more governor of Chartres, and soon her father was appointed governor of Noyon and her brother François-Annibal its bishop.

As the D'Estrée's family fortunes grew more secure, the King's became more precarious. In the year that had passed, his relations with Rome had grown steadily more vexing. Although he had never considered as his friend the Pope who had formally excommunicated him with that thundering bull, *Ab immensa*, yet with the death of Sixtus in August, 1590 the King had, in fact, suffered a loss. Although Sixtus had had no love for heresy, yet he had had too strong a political sense not to be aware that the troubles in France could not all be listed under the cause of religion. As Spain had shown its hand more and more, Sixtus' sympathies with the Huguenot King had increased.

Frightened by this shift in papal policy, Mayenne had written in annoyance: "It is shameful that the heretic faction should be sustained and the piety of Catholics calumniated." It was no surprise that Philip should give expression to a certain joy in learning of the Pope's death, and one of his nobles, following his master's cue, wrote: "the more one reflects on this death, the more one rejoices. Many think and some even say aloud that whoever his successor, he could not be more the enemy of this crown and of the French League.[4]

Joannes Baptista Cardinal Castagna, who succeeded Sixtus, had

no time to declare his allegiance, for he was dead fourteen days
after his election. When, however, in late December Nicholas Sfondrato
assumed the tiara, Spain and the most radical of the Leaguers were
loud in their acclaim. Sfondrato was a quiet, gentle man given more
to his books than to the court and who numbered among his friends
and advisers such holy men as Philip Neri and Charles Borromeo.
He was an unworldly man who lacked political expertise and was,
unfortunately, easily dazzled by Spanish rhetoric. The Duc de Luxembourg, still in Tuscany at the time of the conclave, astutely assessed the situation and wrote forcefully to the cardinals of what
might happen in France if the papacy should lean too heavily toward
Spain: "If by false zeal you repudiate your promises and condemn
the deeds of a nobility which awaits your help, be careful lest you
cause a schism in the Church; for without doubt the Gallican church
will separate from the Roman church."[5] Luxembourg's letter, however, did nothing but provide the Spanish with further evidence for
their position that the French clergy allied to the Béarnais were
a factious and rebellious group which must be forced into submission
to the Holy See.

Sfondrato, who had taken the name of Gregory XIV out of respect
for that other Gregory who had given such unqualified support to
the French Catholics, was no match for the Spanish diplomats who
used their influence to see that the post of secretary of state went
to the Pope's nephew, a monkish man, easily addled by his first
experience of power. Philip's initial satisfaction with Gregory's election
soon grew to enthusiasm, for on every score he corroborated Spanish
policy. Before the end of January, the new Pope had promised a
monthly subsidy to the League, taking 400,000 scudi from the papal
treasury at Sant' Angelo for that purpose. He agreed, as well, to
send military assistance; and a papal expeditionary force was formed
under another of the Pope's nephews, Ercole Sfondrato, Duke of
Montemarciano. Meanwhile letters went out from the Vatican to
France urging that religious innovations be halted, that a strong
Catholic king be elected with haste, and that the French hierarchy,
specifically the Cardinals de Bourbon, Lenoncourt, and Gondi separate
at once, under pain of suspension, from the heretic who called
himself king. To ensure that these orders be carried out, Marsilio
Landriano, another "Spaniardizer," was sent into France as papal
legate. He carried with him monitory letters which even the Catholic
historian Davila described as full of "high and threatening expressions,

sharp and rigorous commands, and in sum such as seemed not to suit much with the present time."[6]

The letters were but prologue to the drama, for he carried with him as well two papal bulls, one addressed to the clergy and the other to the nobility, reaffirming the excommunication of the Béarnais and declaring excommunicate as well all those who did not immediately retract their loyalty to the so-called king and join the Catholic party. They were given fifteen days in which to make their decisions. Mayenne, more and more disenchanted with Spain and the Vatican, and aware that such interference would only strengthen allegiance to the King, protested in vain against their publication. With the fanatical Parisians solidly behind them, they were read from the high pulpit of Notre Dame and affixed to the four principal gates of the city. But Paris was not France, and in early August, the parlements meetings at Tours and Châlons declared the bulls "void, seditious, damnable, full of impieties and lies" and directly contrary to the rights of the Gallican church.[7] They were ordered to be torn to bits by the public executioner and burned to ashes before the door of the city hall.

Once again Navarre found that his bitterest enemies were often those most responsible for his success. In response to this invasion of their national rights, Frenchmen rallied to their King. For a moment his fortunes soared, and with a conviction and assurance he had not felt for months, he wrote an official letter to his people protesting against this action on the part of the Holy See: "The Pope has become the laughing stock of the people and under the pretext of religion is trying to ruin the kingdom and the crown. For what has religion got to do with his opposition, since I have more than once solemnly promised that I will not in any way or for any purpose interfere with the status of the Catholic, Apostolic, and Roman Church and have so far kept this promise inviolate under all circumstances. But now these unscrupulous men are suggesting to the Pope that I am rejecting out of hand all instruction and all advice, and that I am every day trying to introduce into the Christian community greater and more dangerous innovations. They know that they are lying when they say this. I, therefore, once more assert in the sight of God that I desire nothing so much as the convocation of a free council, or some other assembly, which shall be empowered to remove the great schism in religion. I am ready to be instructed and enlightened; my greatest ambition is to learn to know the truth, and to see it unanimously observed by all my subjects."[8]

Even as the King stated his position with vigorous cogency, papal strength was increasing in France, for fifteen companies of papal troops had reached Savoy, marching under a standard bearing the legend: "This is the victory which overcomes the world, our faith." Despite its invincible banner, the army which arrived in Lorraine that September was weary and ragged and had sustained great losses through both defection and sickness. Once again everything depended upon Spain and the arrival of Farnese, but Farnese was no more anxious for this French campaign than he had been for the last one. Toward the end of October, Landriano, considerably chastened by the threats against his life and the accusations that he was guilty of treason, wrote anxiously from the fortress of Verdun where he had taken up residence with the Duc de Lorraine: "If he [Farnese] does not come and any disaster overtakes us, France will rise in revolt, for the cities are filled with politicians and the enemies of Spain. If it were certain that Philip is only acting in his own interests, then the followers of Mayenne would join the party opposed to him. The only chance of salvation lies in detaching the nobility from Navarre, but anyone who understands the French character realizes that that can only be brought about by peaceful means, and not by force."[9]

Landriano's anxiety was well-founded, for by the fall of 1591 the League was beset with dissension. It was largely Spanish policy which formed the wedge which split the League apart: there were those who were willing to ally themselves with Philip no matter what consequences such an alliance might have for France; others, although they wanted the victory of the Catholic party, would not tolerate a France tethered to the power of Spain. In mid-August the division was augumented by the sudden appearance of the young Duc de Joinville, son of the murdered Duc de Guise. He had, since the death of his father, been imprisoned at Tours and had at last succeeded in escaping in that manner dear to Renaissance daring: a window, a rope, a faithful servant, a reckless leap, a Spanish horse —and a few days later accompanied by his "good angel," Monsieur de La Châtre, and two hundred horsemen, he arrived at Orléans. The name of Guise still had its magic power for the Leaguers, and in all the cities where the news spread, bells pealed and crowds flocked to their churches for hymns of rejoicing. Verses in honor of the "miraculous events" were written over night and the people sang with glee:

> It was on Thursday, about noon,
> That the brave Duc de Guise
> Saved himself in a wonderful manner.[10]

He was young, he was daring and valiant, and, most of all, he had through his father, a certain claim to the throne. All of this made him a threat to his uncle Mayenne, who did all he could to win his nephew to him. Young Guise, however, was not eager to take Mayenne for either his tutor or protector. It was but a poor uncle who with thousands of soldiers at his command would let his nephew languish in prison for close to two years and not lift a hand to draw him hence. Although Guise presented himself to Mayenne in the town of Rethel not far from Reims, it was not as a suppliant nephew but with 600 gentlemen riding at his side, armed and equipped as though to serve a king. Nor was it to Mayenne but to Philip of Spain that he wrote with ardor if not with wisdom: "I come to offer you my life and all that I have for your service now that I am in a position to do something."[11] Happily he was spared the humiliation of knowing that shortly after his letter reached Madrid, Philip, always the opportunist, had written to his agent in France to make the most of the dissensions between Mayenne and his nephew.

The young duke arrived on the scene at a moment when his uncle's popularity was waning; in addition, he had much that appealed to the popular imagination for as Davila wrote: "[he is] full of high spirits, of a handsome presence, courteous and affable in his behavior, and which imported more than all, heir to his father's name and to that love which all the people of France profusely bore him."[12] Paris, weary of Mayenne's moderation, turned with new hope to young Joinville.

The Sixteen, who for all practical purposes ruled the city, did what they could to undermine Mayenne's position, suggesting to the gullible people a system of government which would suspend Parlement and the ordinary judges in favor of committees appointed by the Sixteen. On September 2 they wrote openly to Philip: "We can certainly assure Your Catholic Majesty that the vows and wishes of all Catholics are to see Your Catholic Majesty hold the scepter of this crown and rule over us. . . . thus, we cast ourselves freely into your arms, as into those of our Father. . . ."[13] When Mayenne heard of this document, he demanded a prompt retraction, but instead he was faced with rebellion. In November, the Sixteen, enraged at this questioning of their authority, planned a "purge" of those politiques who were suspected of disloyalty to the Paris Sixteen or of undue sympathy toward Mayenne. On the "red paper," as it came to be called, were listed their proposed victims and next to their names the enigmatic symbols, "P," "D," or "C"—indicating whether they were marked to be hanged, stabbed, or merely expelled from Paris. Madame de Nemours, Mayenne's mother, wrote in terror to her son, begging him to come to deliver them. Moved by his anger to uncommon haste, Mayenne arrived in Paris on November 28, but it was too late to save some of the members of the Parlement who had already been imprisoned and summarily executed. He brushed aside the lame explanation that this action had been necessary to keep order in the city, retaliated by several summary executions of his own, and on December 11 left a chastened Paris behind him.

The King was put in high spirits by the news which reached him at his camp near Rouen, for every mishap to the League fortified his own position. "This will not go well with the King of Spain," he wrote to Damville in assessing the tensions and divisions which were splitting the League.[14] When that same month, he intercepted a letter from the Paris Leaguers, proposing that the Infanta be placed on the French throne and subsequently married to the young Duc de Guise, he sent it on without delay to the man it would most disturb—the harassed Mayenne.

Although the Duke of Parma was once again marching on France, although the papal forces were waiting in Lorraine for orders to join the Spanish forces, still to the King who had never had the experience of easy victory, the situation looked considerably less bleak than it did to Sir Henry Unton, that melancholy ambassador who wrote to Elizabeth of the "miserable and lamentable" state of France. As the King counted his blessings, he found not the least of them to be good English forces to assist him under the leadership of no less a person than "My Lord Essex." The coming of the royal favorite had caused no little stir; and when he had arrived on the last day of August, the King himself had come to Pierrefonds to meet him and to conduct him with full panoply into Compiègne. In gratitude Henri wrote to Elizabeth, confiding to her that without the help she had sent, he could never survive the strength of his enemies who were so anxious to defeat him and wrest the crown from him, and then ending with that strange mixture of flattery and sincerity which so frequently marked his letters to England's Gloriana: ". . . if for the space of two hours I could be with you, so that at last I might have the happiness of seeing at least once in my life, her to whom I have consecrated my person and all that I have, and whom I love and respect more than anything in the world. . . ."[15] But Gloriana was proof against even such graceful flattery as this, especially when the flattery ran counter to British interests. In late September Unton had written to her that King Henri had left the main body of his forces to go off fighting on his own, that he had failed to make a proper use of English forces, and had often coerced the vainglorious Essex into foolish and dangerous excursions, concluding, "Now what is it for us to think to be thus abused by a king of many ways bound to us."[16] Although Henri and Essex worked well together, they did not see eye-to-eye on the tactics for taking Rouen. As the months dragged on with little chance for that military glory for which Essex yearned, he grew restive. Elizabeth, too, was tired of the dreary news that came out of France: the French King bereft of money, English soldiers dying of plague, Spanish forces already in France. In January, Essex, at the Queen's command, returned to England.

Elizabeth, angry as she was with what she considered the King's extravagance and incompetence, was too shrewd to endanger her own interests and she replaced Essex by Roger William, a competent English captain. She knew from other sources that Henri's need was acute, for her agents had reported that the Papal companies under Montemarciano were heading out from Lorraine, that the Spanish and Neopolitan troops had left Paris for Normandy, and that at La Fère, Mayenne, the Duc de Guise and Farnese had combined forces. All of these troops were converging on Rouen, which the month before the King had begun to besiege in earnest. Although Henri was assisted by troops from Germany and the Low Countries, he would be no match for this combined army. Elizabeth could not withdraw her support, yet she found it hard to forgive the French king for having dallied so long in laying siege to Rouen. It was almost a year since he had received reports that Rouen was his for the taking: its walls were not well-armed, its fortifications in poor repair, its store of ammunition low. He had

promised to attack at once, but his head was more filled with love
than war, and at a smile from "Sainte Gabrielle," he had ridden off
to Noyon "to please her."

Now with the walls of the city repaired and its storehouses provisioned
for a siege, Henri's incomparable optimism assured his followers that
the taking of this city, by which he could control all the traffic of the
Seine, would be no difficult task. He had heard, he wrote to Nevers in
mid-December, that the governor and the people bore no love for the
Duke of Parma and would prefer to treat with him rather than with
the Spanish. With this in mind, he had high hopes for a favorable
answer to his proposal that Rouen accept him as its lawful king; but
the herald who returned bore the arrogant answer that the Rouenais
would rather die than admit their allegiance to him. That night, in
dramatic affirmation of their Catholic faith, a procession took place in
the besieged city with hundreds of men walking barefoot and carrying
lighted candles, followed by children clothed in white, singing the
hymns which symbolized their religious conviction.

As early as December, Henri had written to one of the Catholic
lords of the approach of Parma, sure that within days there would be a
chance of open battle. Parma, however, was a general of strategy
rather than confrontation. He had been sent to France to relieve the
French Catholics and pave the way for a Spanish heir to the throne;
if this could be done obliquely, without the shock of battle, then this
was the course he would choose. It had worked at Paris; it might well
work at Rouen. With measured pace he led his troops through Picardy
into Normandy, while Mayenne seethed with impatience. This time
the Fat Duke wanted haste and a definitive victory over Navarre, for
he was beginning to despair over the fate of France. The conferences
which he had held with Farnese at La Fère earlier that month had
stripped away his last illusion and he, who for so many years had been
content to play the game of cat and mouse, now waited in mortal
terror for the trap to spring. Farnese had been explicit in his demands:
the Salic Law was to be abrogated and the Infanta was to be placed
on the French throne. Perhaps she might, to reinforce her claim, be
married to the young Duc de Guise. To this end Mayenne was
to see that the Estates General met at once. When Mayenne demurred, Farnese made it clear that Spanish money and Spanish troops
depended on his assent. Desperately the Duke hedged, and helped by
that experienced politician Pierre Jeannin won some small delay. He
was neatly pinned in his corner, as cleanly trapped as any of those

stags he had once hunted with such zest—and as afraid. Perhaps it is true, as some of his sympathizers said, that he never actually signed the treasonous paper which Farnese held out to him; but it is equally true that in some form he acquiesced, for his acquiescence was the bitter price of the Spanish army which now rode through the countryside east of Rouen.

Advised of the enemy's approach and unwilling to suffer a repetition of that strategy by which Farnese had delivered Paris, Henri, leaving the siege to Biron, rode off with a small part of his army to provoke the Spaniard to battle. The King's army, even with the newly acquired Dutch troops, numbered no more than 14,000—hardly a match for the ponderous force drawn up against them. Even so, Farnese was not tempted by the bait offered him, and despite the harassment of the French soldiers, he made his unequivocal way toward Rouen. The months of inconclusive manœuverings continued, until on August 5 Henri led a small band of light cavalry on one of their regular forays into the countryside near Aumale; as they cantered up a little rise of ground, they found themselves gazing into the full phalanx of the Spanish army. Even the King's reckless daring had not bargained for this! For once Farnese's caution worked to the King's good; naturally wary, and deducing that this was a bait which would lead his army into ambush, he refused to advance. In the skirmish which followed, the King was wounded before his cavalry could get out of range of the Spanish guns, but this was but a small difficulty compared to the tragedy which might have befallen.

The King's wound although painful was not dangerous, for the bullet had passed through the saddle and so was deadened when it reached his body. For the next fortnight, unable to walk or ride, he endured the humiliation of being carried on a stretcher from place to place. Henri's humiliation, however, was nothing compared to that of Farnese when he discovered that no army had been massed behind the Béarnais, that with a little more expedition he could have made the so-called King his prisoner, and so ended by a single blow the whole problem of the French succession. In angry contempt and in an effort to justify his own costly blunder, he remarked disdainfully that he had thought Henri was a general of an army and not a captain of light horse. Henri cared little what Farnese called him, for he was overwhelmed with gratitude that his folly had not had a more costly conclusion. He had escaped death by the slightest margin and he well knew that his death would have ramifications far beyond his own person. His native daring had become a luxury he could no longer afford. It was a chastened monarch who read the pompous admonition addressed to him by his Huguenot counselor Duplessis-Mornay: "It is our glory and duty to die for you; and yours, I make so bold to say, Sire, to live for France."[17]

That melancholy diplomat, Unton, now added a wounded king to his long list of misfortunes as he wrote in dejection to Elizabeth: "It is doubtful to determine *de futuris*, and this cloudy time threateneth a very great storm; and without Your Majesty's gracious aid this tragedy is almost at an end."[18] Unton's vision was not entirely unfounded for the siege of Rouen was going badly. In the King's absence, Biron, usually so ardent in his military enterprises, seemed to be paying his vows at some other shrine than Mars. Villars, Rouen's governor, found he had time to improve the fortifications of his city and even received through an unguarded gate 1,200 men from Parma's army. Many of the captains murmured that the King should never have left the siege, but Henri, still hoping to meet Parma in open conflict, dallied in the lands around Aumale. Had he but known it, Spanish morale was far lower than his own. During that early spring when the unseasonable, warm days turned the fields to mud, contagious diseases swept through the Spanish troops until Ibarra wrote to Philip: "Our army is at the end of its resources; we suffer from all kinds of privations; the enemy's cavalry is always very close to us; we have no more money. Colonna has managed a loan of 40,000 *écus* which has been distributed to Mayenne for the wages of January and February, but Your Majesty's soldiers have received no pay since that which they received at their entrance into France."[19]

As Spanish spirits fell, Henri's rose, for that "itch for battle," as one of his companions described it, was, he felt, about to be satisfied. On February 27 he wrote to Montmorency in high spirits: "Fortune has at last begun to turn in our favor. The wind has just changed after five weeks so that the 3,000 soldiers from the Low Countries can come to us. I have just received word that they are at Dieppe and I have also heard that the help which is being sent to me from England has already embarked and should be here in a day or two. With this I hope to number between 16- and 17,000 foot soldiers, more than that of the enemy; but my greatest advantage is the number and quality of my cavalry." A week later he wrote of the approach of the enemy; they were exhilaratingly close now, so close that the King concluded, "At moonrise I will mount and follow them."[20] But he was destined never to meet in combat those blurred forms that he followed stealthily by moonlight. During the weeks of waiting, many of the English troops had died of plague, and the King's army was once more reduced to less than 14,000 men. Parma, quick to take his advantage, moved with relentless speed south toward Rouen. The road was free before him and in less than three days he stood at the banks of the Seine before the walls of the besieged city. On April 20, after almost five months of siege, Rouen was delivered. The city was at once provisioned, the works raised by the King destroyed, leaving no trace of the long and painful enterprise.

"Fortune has at last begun to turn in our favor," the hopeful King had written five weeks earlier, as he boasted of the forty cannon he had ready to train on Rouen. But he had spoken too soon, counted too easily on Fortune's constancy, forgetting that Fortune was a woman who could turn her wheel in less time than it takes a man to utter false promises. Fickle Fortune had wooed him and abandoned him; had he remembered his history lessons he would not have been surprised. It was Paris all over again, but worse; for with each defeat the acid of failure bit more deeply into his pride. Once again he had subjected the citizens of a fine city to suffering and death, and inflicted irreparable losses upon his own army. What Elizabeth of England would write to him now, he preferred not to think. He had missed the roles of both Alexander and Augustus.

Henri, however, was far from defeated, and when the League forces arrived at Caudebec he was hard on their heels. Anxiously he waited for Montpensier and Longueville who were on their way with 800 horse, and on April 26 he wrote to his trusted friend Souvré with the zest of youth: "Old Woman, today we are taking up camp only two leagues from the enemy; they can't avoid battle any longer. This is why I am asking you to come as fast as you can to Pont-de-l'Arche where I am located. . . . Perhaps I will write to you on the eve of the battle."[21] His desperate appeals had drawn his nobles to him and in the days between April 28 and May 10 he had come off victor in all encounters. The Spanish troops had been badly hit by sickness and desertion and Parma himself had been wounded in one of the skirmishes. The bullet had lodged between the bones just below the elbow and Parma endured three terrible probings before the surgeons were able to extract the bullet. Sick with pain and fever he was forced to his bed, while his troops, lost without the iron leadership of their general, withdrew to the village of Yvetot.

The camp at Yvetot was a scene of despair. For fifteen days the Spanish troops, many of them sick with fever, sprawled on the open plain of Caux, while their provisions dwindled day by day. Blocked from recrossing the Seine by the buoyant Henri—once again confident of success—and with nothing to fall back on but the waters of the Channel, they were neatly trapped.

It was Parma, however, who sprang the trap. Still too weak to walk, he worked out the strategy of a retreat that was in its own right a victory. Despite the fact that here the Seine was at its widest, he ordered the construction of a bridge of boats, and under cover of the night his army made its escape. As at Paris, the whole maneuver was accomplished so deftly that the French army was unaware of what was happening until the morning sun rose over an empty camp. Legend has it that Parma, gleeful over his success, sent to Henri asking him what he thought of his withdrawal and that Henri, true to his Gascon heritage, had replied that he considered any withdrawal, no matter how well ordered, no more than a retreat.

Once again the road to Paris lay straight before the Duke of Parma, for the King, despite the pleas of many of his captains to follow the retreating Spaniards, remained at Yvetot. Perhaps Elizabeth of England had put her finger on a dangerous weakness when she had earlier observed, "I think you prefer to gamble rather than to bring things to a conclusion." By the middle of May, Parma was in Paris, having left Mayenne behind to lick his wounds and, as some contemporaries note, to treat a "shameful disease" which he had contracted. Parma's victorious entrance into Paris lacked the vitality of popular acclaim and L'Estoile who watched it all observed: ". . . the Duke of Parma having crossed the water at Caudebec arrived with his army outside the city of Paris. His son, the prince of Parma, and Monsieur de Guise . . . dined the next day with Madame de Nemours. Monday the eighteenth . . . the whole army in full battle regalia, looking tired and harassed, passed through Paris, which surprised the people more than it pleased them."[22] Soon Parma was on the road to Château-Thierry and the Lowlands which he had left so regretfully.

Henri who, upon his accession to the throne, had observed that he was a king without a kingdom could reiterate this with increasing truth in the summer of 1592. Whether or not one wished to call Parma's clever withdrawal from Yvetot a Spanish retreat, no one would call it a French victory. The King's minor success at Epernon could not change the image of his failure. Philip, encouraged by events at

Rouen, now sent more Spanish forces to help the Duc de Mercoeur in Brittany while Languedoc and Provence also received strong Spanish armies. The Paris preachers, exulting in the King's defeat, hurled invectives against both the Béarnais and his followers—prophesying hell for those Catholics who still fought in his ranks. Should he ever keep the promise he had made and be received into the Catholic church, they ranted, then let him crawl in as some penitent monk, but never as King of France.

It was not the open hatred of the League that nettled the King most, but the insistent demands of another group closer to him, a group led by the young Cardinal de Bourbon which called itself the *Tiers Parti*. Charles de Bourbon, fourth son of Louis, Prince de Condé, and younger brother of the truculent Henri de Condé who had died some years before, considered himself First Prince of the Blood. His claim was a dubious one since Henri de Condé's wife had borne a son after her husband's death and since the Prince de Conti, although somewhat defective in both mind and body, was his senior. Upon the young Cardinal's shoulders, however, had fallen the cloak of his father's ambition, and from his vantage point the throne looked appealingly close. The men who gathered about the Cardinal were variously motivated. Some were angry at what they considered Mayenne's treasonous behavior with Spain, at the ambition and arrogance of the Spanish themselves who schemed to reduce France to the state of a Spanish province. Others, among them Epernon, Bellegarde, Marshal D'O—the lords and advisers of the former king—wanted, as they had from the first, the satisfaction of their own interests, interests which would never be satisfied by either Philip or Henri. Some sincerely wanted peace and saw no possibility to attain it unless the King were willing to accept the Roman faith. Many of the *Tiers Parti*, among them the Cardinal himself, were playing a dangerous game, for while they were overtly arguing for the King's conversion, they were secretly relying on his refusal to take this step. In this case, Charles de Bourbon would assume the crown in the interests of national peace and unity.

After the fiasco of Rouen, the number of lords loyal to the King diminished, and there were, he admitted, but few whose advice he could count on. Among these was Duplessis-Mornay and it was to him that the King wrote toward the end of August: "I am tired of always writing the same thing to you. I want very much to see you. Come; I need you for reasons that I cannot write." But Duplessis-Mornay, usually so punctilious in obeying royal summonses, this time hesitated. He knew well why the King had sent for him and like all the zealous Huguenots he was torn at the thought that their King might defect from their party. Even though the summer before Henri had held an assembly which effectively increased religious liberty for the French Protestants, yet from the beginning he himself had made no open protestation of the Huguenot faith. His letters were often couched in terms which the Huguenots associated with Roman Catholicism and in a hundred small ways he had allied himself with the Catholic position. Although he could say to his minister, the Baron de Rosny, "I can never use them ill . . . for I shall always love them"; yet the rift was there, and no protestations of affection would heal it.[23] Even among the Huguenots, however, there were those who recognized that if France were to be kept from Spanish domination, it could only be through the conversion of the King.

The growing power of the *Tiers Parti* was forcing the King's hand. Thus in the fall of 1592, Henri sent to Rome Jean de Vivonne, Marquis de Pisani, and Cardinal de Gondi on the delicate mission of expressing his desire to return to the Church. They were both diplomats of skill and experience and the letter which Pisani carried had been prepared by expert hands: "As we make ready," the King had written, "to render forever the obedience which we owe to Your Holiness and to the Apostolic See, we wish also to resume in all things the same means which were maintained and used by the Most Christian Kings our predecessors, in observing the honor and filial respect which are your due . . ."[24] At first Henri's filial protestations seemed destined never to reach papal ears, for when Gondi and Pisani arrived in Florence, they were met by an emissary from Clement VIII who informed them that the Pope could not receive the representatives of an excommunicated man. Even when, through the devious channels of papal diplomacy, the King's letter reached the Pope, His Holiness' response gave little room for hope: "How can we put faith and confidence in Henri de Navarre, when even one of his adherents has told us that if Saint Peter himself looked upon the conversion of that prince as certain, we ought not to believe it. And that is our own conviction. . . . By his negotiations with us, he only wishes to force the League to submit to him."[25]

Estranged from the Huguenots, denounced by the League, deserted by many of the Catholic lords and now rejected out of hand by the Pope himself—there seemed no place to turn. In those dark winter days, the King's single hope was that when the last card was played, Frenchmen, with their ancient tradition of enmity for Spain, would prefer a French devil to a Spanish saint. He was not alone in his opinion, for at the same time the Spanish agent Diego Maldonado, in an effort to prepare Philip for possible failure, wrote to Madrid: "These are all Frenchmen. They may differ in religion but they are of one mind in their desire to keep the crown from foreigners. To believe at this time that one can get anything in France by love or persuasion is absolutely mistaken: nothing has any value but force; it is force and nothing else by which necessity will be made a virtue. They would prefer the Béarnais who is of their race rather than any foreigner even if he were an angel."[26]

Although the King's plight was far from enviable, no man in France was more entitled to bad dreams than the Duc de Mayenne. For six months he had evaded Philip's demand that the Estates be called, for he feared that with that assembly his own power would come to an end. He could delay no longer, however, and on January 5, 1593, the plans for the meeting of the Estates were concluded; and Mayenne wrote to the people encouraging and exhorting them to respond to the assembly which would open on January 25. He explained their duties, their allegiance, the need the Church had for a strong, Catholic France. It was one of his last official letters as Protector of the Kingdom and to it he affixed the seal which for three years had borne not a king's image but the image of an empty throne. For three years that empty throne had been the root of Mayenne's power, but now he was well aware that his power was waning. The Sixteen both resented his leadship and found him too moderate in his goals; the *Tiers Parti* ridiculed him as Philip's man; while the people who had once offered him the crown, now laughed at the "Fat Pig" who spent his time sleeping with his "Sow." He who had tried so hard to make friends at any cost, now found all factions leagued against him. When in November he had met with the Paris Assembly and promised them what they had demanded—free trade and a meeting of the Estates—he had asked contemptuously: "What more do the people want?" The answer was unequivocal: "They want a king."[27]

CHAPTER XII

The Perilous Leap: January–July 1593

They told him that of all cannon, the canon of the Mass was best
to reduce the cities of his kingdom.

Péréfixe

On January 26, 1593, the Estates General of France was
solemnly convoked in the great hall of the Louvre. On this point at
least Mayenne had had his way. Earlier in the negotiations, Parma had
held out stubbornly for Reims or Soissons as the place of the assembly,
but Mayenne, backed by those who wanted to keep Spanish power to a
minimum, was intransigent. When Parma died suddenly on December 2
as a result of the wound he had suffered at Caudebec, Mayenne was
able to designate Paris as the place of the Estates without great opposition.

It was, however, but a minor victory, almost lost in the swelling
tide of defeats, for Mayenne found opposition wherever he turned.
Even Paris had lost its ardor for the cause it had so long and so painfully espoused. Late in 1592 Tassis had written to Philip: "The city is
full of *politiques* and perhaps partisans of the Béarnais as well; with
good reason they are all weary of the life they have been leading these
three years." At the same time, Mayenne echoed Tassis' fears when
he wrote to the Spanish King begging him to increase his help without
which he had no chance of victory, "not because of the strength of our
enemies," he explained, "but because of the impatience and despair of
those who, brought to their knees by their needs and miseries, have for
a long time lost their first ardor for the cause of religion, and think now
of nothing but peace."[1] They were weary of war, weary of hardship,
weary most of all of false promises, of which the calling of the Estates

was simply the last and the greatest. Neither Mayenne nor the Sixteen, despite all their fine talk, had brought freedom to France. They had simply changed one form of tyranny for another.

The Parisians with their natural gift for barbed satire which for so long they had aimed at the hapless Valois now turned their gibes to the Estates and those who—even while they nominally opposed tyranny —did their best to arrogate power to themselves. There was a good *politique* of Paris, recounted L'Estoile with obvious relish, who when he had counted his chickens one day and found that there were sixteen, immediately killed one, vowing that "sixteen" would never be found in his house. There was big Jacques the soup carrier, who was heard to cajole his ass with the words, "Move along there, Big Jean; let's go the Estates." Or there was the variant version which ran in quatrain with its special gibe at Spanish power:

> Come on, my ass! through the gates
> To Monsieur de Mayenne's Estates;
> So you can turn without a wrench
> Into Spaniard instead of French!

Best of them all was the *Satyre Menippée* which appeared later in Tours as a burlesque of the Estates and a denunciation of Spanish influence in French affairs. The League, the Paris preachers, the Papal Legate, Parma, Mayenne, and Guise were all roundly denounced as traitors to France. The "Tableau of the Estates," which formed the frontispiece, pictured Mayenne presiding over the assembly with the Sixteen on one side and the nobility on the other, while dominating the scene was an enormous picture of the Infanta. In the background was a forge where with desperate effort the delegates worked to "make" a king, but with no success for since the alloy was base, the "king" kept breaking.[2]

In such a climate Mayenne formally opened the Estates. Despite the royal dais with its cloth of gold flanked by chairs covered in crimson velvet, despite all that Mayenne did to bring to this convocation the solemnity of former assemblies, the first meeting was far from impressive. There was neither king, nor princes, nor marshal of France. The stir and movement of the solemn procession was lacking, for the number of delegates was few and representatives of the nobility noticeably absent. Gossip was rife that this was a bribed assembly paid for in Spanish doubloons, and when by the middle of February the number of delegates had increased, it became obvious that they represented Spanish power.

Those who sat in the places of honor had already indicated where their allegiance lay. Mayenne for years had been the pensioner of Spain; Cardinal Pellevé had spent the last twenty years in Rome under Spanish protection until in 1592 he had come back to France as archbishop of the League city of Reims; the Legate, Filippo Sega, although of Italian birth, was Bishop of the Spanish See of Placentia. It had been only after many difficulties that Sega had been admitted to the Estates at all, for the French had made it clear that they saw no reason why a foreigner should be admitted to a national assembly; only on condition that he have no voice, either deliberative or conclusive, was Mayenne able to seat him. The man who was to cause the greatest difficulty of all was absent from the opening ceremonies. Lorenzo Suarez de Figueroa, Duke of Feria and a special ambassador of the Spanish king, was traveling south from Milan by slow stages with a cortege befitting his rank and dignity.

Mayenne was at once relieved and fearful at Feria's absence, for by it his own position became even more ambiguous. Knowing the temper of the French people and having waged a hard fight to have even the Apostolic Delegate seated in the assembly, he was well aware that popular feeling was not in Feria's favor. He feared the pressure that the Spanish ambassador would attempt to exert both by bribery and coercion. He would have feared even more could he have foreseen the insolent and patronizing manner in which Feria would conduct himself. He was then partially relieved that at least the opening ceremonies could be conducted without the oppressive weight of Spanish presence; yet he had to face the fact that whatever his overt position, he was in fact bound hand and foot as a pensioner of Spain. That experienced statesman Bellièvre had once noted wisely: "History teaches us that he who calls upon the strongest for aid, most often becomes the subject of the strongest."[3] Although as Lieutenant-General of the realm Mayenne had presumed to call the assembly in his own name, yet it was Spain who had ordered him to do so; although it was he who would assume the prime role in the Estates' affairs, he was Spain's puppet for all that. There were those who were saying that he had sold France to the Catholic King; he hoped that that was not entirely true, but he knew that he had sold himself.

What might have been done in the Estates in those two months before the arrival of Feria, it is idle to speculate. Mayenne was not inept nor was he unintelligent. He was a slow man not simply in his ponderous physical movements, but a man ruled by a kind of native caution, who played his chess game with wary skill, never risking his bishop or his king where a lesser piece might do. He studied his field well before he made his moves; if other men moved more quickly than he, this did not always mean that they were victorious in the end. His cousin the Béarnais had once remarked when he had outrun Mayenne, "My cousin Mayenne is a wonderful captain, but I get up earlier than he"; and yet, Mayenne was entitled to reflect that it was not Navarre who had twice relieved Paris and delivered Rouen.

While the Duc de Guise lived, Mayenne had had his role clearly marked for him: he was the second son in every sense. He could never match his brother's stride. He lacked his quick charm, his passion for danger and success, his mastery of men. At his brother's death he might have found his own stride, his own power of leadership; but even there it was, in many ways, too late. The decisions were already made, the ties with Spain already irrevocable, and Mayenne could do little but play the role in which his brother's scheming had cast him. It would have taken a brilliant diplomat and a soldier of unparalleled prowess to free France from the cords which bound her to Spain. Perhaps no man alive could have done it; certainly Mayenne could not.

Another man, even now, might have grasped at the power that remained to him and used those two months before the arrival of the Spanish ambassador to his own advantage. Such a step, however, needed a daring beyond Mayenne's capacity, for his native caution had expanded into a way of life. Had he been willing to hazard a move, the outcome of which he could not clearly predict, the course of events might have shifted to his favor; but Mayenne had decided upon the most ruinous course of all: the course of inaction.

He knew, however that whatever his own position, he could scarcely keep the delegates waiting until Feria's arrival, and on January 26, just one day later than he had originally planned, he opened the assembly with a clear statement of the purpose of the convocation: to elect a Catholic king in order that by this means the miseries of the kingdom will be brought to an end. This opening speech was well made; it might even have been a powerful speech had the man who made it been recognized as anything but the shadow of Spanish power.

While Mayenne was exhorting the Estates to the election of a Catholic king, the King himself from his headquarters at Chartres was using every means in his power to stop this body from taking steps that would exclude him permanently from the throne. Henri had no love for the House of Guise. While he had been only King of Navarre, he had listened to the rumors that ran riot in the south that from the very beginning it had been Spanish money and Spanish influence that had kept the Guises and their League in power. They had laughed then at the number of Spanish agents in France and speculated on the force of secretaries kept busy in Madrid decoding French messages to the King of Spain. In 1585 he had heard of the secret treaty concluded between Guise and Spain in the Guise town of Joinville which had been the prologue to that terrible Edict of Nemours which in a single hour had crushed his hopes of peace, stripped his Huguenot followers of their rights, and set Frenchmen at each other's throats again. When, later that year, Sixtus V had issued that fateful bull *Ab immensa*, he had no doubt of the source of the pressure which had caused his excommunication.

As the years passed, there was less and less effort at subterfuge, until now those who had been inside Paris reported that it was like a Spanish bastion, full of Spanish agents, Spanish gold, Spanish armies— and behind it all was the Fat Duke who for the last ten years had not been able to bend enough to take off his own boots. He had eaten well at the Spanish table, while the people of Paris had died of the poisoned bread proposed by Mendoza's recipe or been killed as they crawled into the fields to pull the unripe grain from the ground to assuage their hunger. Henri had little love for the Guise; his own reckless spontaneity was repelled by the Duke's cold caution. Most of all, he was angered by this interminable chess game with Spain in which France was no more than a pawn to be moved and shifted and bargained for according to the humor of those two inscrutable players who would sacrifice any loyalty in order to build their dynasties. If, as he had been told, Spain was now willing to pour money into the Estates to buy votes, and if the delegates heeded the righteous and stirring exhortations to elect a Catholic king at all costs, then he would stand to lose everything he had fought for since his cousin's death. And worse: France would be no more than a tributary to imperial Spain.

It was very clear to the King what he must do if he were to save France from such imperial aggression. It was three and a half years since he had, at the death of Henri III, issued the Declaration of St. Cloud in which he had agreed to be "instructed" in the Roman religion. The time had now come for him to fulfill that promise and on January 27 two acts were promulgated under the King's hand. The first, although it was the more conciliatory of the two, was a declaration which would change the course of French history since it suggested a course of action which would ultimately lead the way to the King's "conversion."

Since, it ran, the war was obviously causing the ruin of the state, then the only cure was the reconciliation of the disputing parties. Toward this end, the King suggested a series of conferences in which the warring factions would be brought together to discuss their differences and attempt to reach some amicable conclusion. The second of the acts was entitled: "Declaration against the convocation called by the Duc de Mayenne." This was a direct attack against Mayenne, who, accused the King, has an ambition so swollen "that it has rent the very veil behind which it has sought to hide." It was this ambition, continued Henri, which led the Duke to perform certain acts which were the privilege of the King alone: convoking a meeting of the Estates, issuing invitations to it in his own name, sealing these same letters with the Great Seal of the realm. Such actions, judged the King, must be condemned as acts of *lèse-majesté*. In addition, he warned the people that any effort to abrogate the Salic Law was to act contrary to a fundamental law of the realm, cautioning them that the Spanish had long been enemies of France and were even now concerned with nothing but their own interests. He reminded them that if the leaders of the Estates were sincere in wanting a Catholic king, they might do well to consult their memories and recall that he himself had publicly announced his own wish to receive instruction and be received back into the Roman communion. His concluding point neatly invalidated whatever acts the Estates might pass, for it declared the present assembly to be contrary to the laws of the realm and the good of its citizens.[4]

Accordingly, there arrived on the following Thursday at the gates of Paris, a messenger from the man whom Paris would not acknowledge as its king. The messenger, one Thomas Lhomme, indicated that he had letters from his master for the Duc de Mayenne. Although the Duke was sick in bed, the messenger was brought to him nonetheless; but the wary Mayenne, not wishing to be involved in private communication with the so-called King, insisted on reading the letters in the presence of Jeannin, Cardinal Pellevé, and the Papal Legate. The message was simple: an offer on Henri's part to set up a conference at which both parties would treat for peace. The Legate hardly heard the letter out before he "rose up in choler," proclaiming that they must have nothing to do with such a suggestion, since it was not permitted for faithful Catholics to deal with heretics. But Jeannin, a tough-minded politician not easily intimidated by the Church, thought otherwise. Always something of a constitutionalist in his views, he now maintained that no small group of men could decide such a question and that it should be presented to the whole assembly. Since Sega continued to oppose this advice, the question was referred to the doctors of the Sorbonne for mediation. When the Sorbonne reaffirmed the Legate's position—as he had been sure it would—the others stood firm; and Sega, deprived of a deliberative voice in the assembly, found himself helpless to impose his position. After a month of hesitation, the Estates reached the conclusion that Jeannin had hoped for, side-stepping Sega's objection by saying that they were treating not with a heretic but with other Catholic lords who also wanted peace.

On March 9, after weeks of controversy, the Estates formally accepted the King's proposal for a series of conferences. Henri's offer had caught Mayenne in his own trap. He could not afford to displease his Spanish masters, yet neither did he wish to alienate the French who manifestly felt that Henri's proposal might be the first step toward a lasting peace. He managed to evade the issue temporarily by leaving Paris for Soissons on February 8 to meet the new Spanish ambassador who had just arrived on French soil. Mayenne's reasons for leaving the Estates were various, but all of them diminished the Duke in the eyes of the delegates whom he left waiting. He wanted to evade the issue with which Henri had confronted him. He wanted also to ingratiate himself with Feria by a show of splendor and cordiality—not simply in order to prove himself a royal host, but also to dislodge young Guise from any position of influence which he might have gained with the Spaniards. He had heard in Paris that his young nephew had been warned against putting too much confidence in his uncle Mayenne and had been urged instead to entrust his glory solely to the King of Spain. Having lost so much in other quarters, Mayenne was fearful lest he should lose ground here too.

The meeting at Soissons, however, achieved none of the results which Mayenne had hoped for; it was a failure from the first. Hardly had the ambassador and the Duke completed their formal embrace than a mutual distrust grew up between them that made amicable relations impossible. Mayenne was glad that his presence was needed at Reims, thus acquitting himself of his obligation to make the trip to Paris in Feria's company. Before they parted, however, Mayenne had once more given his word to do all in his power to see that the Infanta was placed on the throne of France.

It was the end of March when the Duke of Feria was received at the Porte St. Antoine in Paris. That evening he made his solemn entrance into the city. His suit of dark, green velvet and his small black Spanish hat looked austere and foreign beneath the light of the torches; and although crowds of people gathered to see him pass, they seemed motivated, as one observer commented, more by curiosity than enthusiasm. "In the rue St. Antoine when he went by not a soul raised his hat," observed L'Estoile.[5] He had brought with him 30,000 *écus* which he had thought more than sufficient for overcoming whatever opposition he might encounter; he was bewildered to find that although Paris was still suffering want, there were few who were interested in Spanish gold.

On April 2 Feria was scheduled to take his place in a meeting of the assembly. It was, as he knew, an occasion of supreme importance and he described it in some detail in the dispatch he sent to Philip: "Friday at three o'clock the Abbé Orlaix came to inform me that I was awaited. I went to the palace which they call the Louvre and I was received at the foot of the stairs by Gilbert Genebrard, Archbishop of Aix. The second son of the Duc de Mayenne came to lead me up the stairs. At the top the Cardinal de Sens and the macebearers were waiting for me. They brought me into a large room hung with tapestries. On one side there was a little platform where the Duchesse de Nemours sat with her daughters; in the room were benches for the deputies of all three orders and in the center a table for the secretaries. On a platform there stood a dais with an empty throne, symbol of royalty. . . ." Feria was seated at the left of the throne below the dais with the Cardinal de Sens at his right. From here he rose to deliver his address to the Estates. From the beginning his words betrayed him. With his foreign fashions setting him off from the rest of the assembly, he began his speech in heavily accented Latin which made even the familiar words sound alien. "When heresy began to take root in France," he proclaimed patronizingly, "it was the Catholic King of Spain who turned his thoughts to your salvation."[6]

With his first sentence he turned the assembly against him. Who was this who did not speak their language and yet in his strange, lisping voice spoke of heresy growing unchecked in France, of a

Spanish king in whom they would find their salvation? They had seen Spanish swagger before, but they had never seen Spanish arrogance so blatantly displayed. But Feria, insensitive to the hostile climate, continued his carefully prepared oration. The Valois were condemned, the anarchy of the years that followed was deplored, the Spanish were eulogized as saviors. And should his own words lack sufficient weight, Feria ended by reading a letter from The Most Catholic King which stated with a kind of naïve arrogance that in return for all they owed him, the Estates now had no choice but to elect a zealous Catholic king without delay. In place of the ovation which Feria had anticipated, he met with a coldness for which he was totally unprepared. Everything about Feria entrenched the delegates in their national pride. All unwittingly he had helped, not hindered, the King's cause, for within days after Feria's opening speech, the Estates chose their delegates for the King's conference which was to be held at Suresnes.

Of all those who had pinned their hopes on Suresnes, it was the King who realized most deeply the far-reaching results of what would happen there. Although there were few to whom he would admit it, he knew that he stood on the edge of ruin. His embassy to Rome had so far failed. Gondi and Pisani still waited impatiently in Italy with nothing to show for their five months abroad but the Pope's continued refusal to treat with them. At home the problems were graver still. Week by week he lost good men to the cause of the *Tiers Parti* which, with the Spanish party losing face, grew more assured of their plan to put the Cardinal de Bourbon on the throne. Soissons, Conti, Montpensier—all princes of power—were veering to the *Tiers Parti*. They no longer took seriously the King's promise to be instructed in the Roman faith, and even his recent declaration seemed to them a hopeless impossibility in the light of the Pope's continued refusal to treat with the ministers already in Rome.

If the Catholic lords took the talk of Henri's conversion lightly, the Huguenots took it as seriously as death. For them it was the end: the end of their Brother the King and the end of their hopes for religious liberty. La Faye, who had so long worked and fought with Henri, begged him not to let this misfortune fall upon him. But Henri, now firmly convinced that his return to the Roman Church was the only means to save France and to ensure that religious toleration in which he so strongly believed, could only reply: "If I followed your advice there would be neither king nor kingdom in a little while in France. I want to give peace to all my subjects and rest to my own soul; decide among yourselves what you need for your security and I will always be ready to satisfy you." The Catholic royalists, hearing the fears of the Huguenots for their own safety should the King become Catholic, attempted to placate them by drawing up a document which promised that "nothing would be done which would be prejudicial to the religion known as the Reformed."[7] For many of the Huguenots, however, even this was not enough; it was not the assurance of a political promise that they wanted but the assurance of a friend. For years they had been outcasts with an outcast king. They had been harassed and scorned, hunted and persecuted. They had sacrificed their wealth, their lands, sometimes their lives. Their movement had often been political in tone; they had fought for public justice and for their basic rights as citizens of France. But primarily their movement was one of religious belief. They were a sect, not simply a political party, and the ties that bound them were ties of faith. Drawing them together, fighting their battles, sharing their vision had been Henri de Navarre. He had been an outcast like them, a poor man like them, a man who had risked his life a hundred times for the cause which they, too, espoused. No promises of religious freedom, no declaration of liberty could make up for the loss of a leader. Do what he would, say what he would, it was hard for them not to think of their King as a traitor. "I would rather be king of a little corner of France while serving God," cried the passionate D'Aubigné, when he heard of Henri's plan of abjuration.[8] But as Henri well knew, this was the cry of a private man who would answer to God for no more than his own conscience. The King could not afford the luxury of being a private man. His decision to return to Rome was no private matter. It was a matter far beyond the issue of private conscience for it extended into those mysterious regions of political responsibility. "They told him that of all cannon, the canon of the Mass was best to reduce the cities of his kingdom," explained Péréfixe with disarming simplicity.[9] In fact, there was no simplicity in the issue which faced the King; it was one of those cases of *haute politique* in which the issues were so intertwined that any effort to unravel them would only lead to a further distortion of the truth.

On the afternoon of April 29, the delegates of the League, led by Pierre d'Epinac, archbishop of Lyons and the delegates of the Royalists, led by Renaud de Beaune, archbishop of Bourges, met at Suresnes just north of Paris. "There were tears of joy and hope for the happy conclusion of this conference," wrote Palma Cayet of this opening meeting.[10] For the people at large it was not the major issues which brought the "tears of joy" but the possibility of the truce which they had heard rumored. They had fought long enough for causes, they had starved for causes, and died for them. Whatever hopes and fears the preachers had played on to keep them faithful, they could play on no longer. They had worn out their ardor and nothing could again fan the flames. Only one cause had any reality for them now: the cause of peace.

As the deputies to Suresnes were leaving through the Porte Neuve, a crowd gathered to watch them go, shouting at the top of their lungs, "Peace; blessed are they who seek it and procure it and cursed be all the others!" Feria and Tassis heard them and knew that such a spirit could spell their doom. Despondently Tassis wrote to Philip: "The situation is so sad that all the mercy of God is necessary to lead us to a happy conclusion." The Spaniards, however, were far from finished, for they still wielded a considerable influence with a major portion of the League. The King was now doubly the butt of their scorn; he was not only a heretic but a heretic who sought to hide his evil heart beneath a Roman cloak. The League inveighed against this man who would pretend conversion for the sake of a crown; and in the streets of Paris some learned clergy recalled the case of the pagan Pretextat who was rumored to have said to Pope Damascus, "Make me bishop of Rome and I will become a Christian at once."[11]

Once again Mayenne found himself caught, fearful lest Henri's open talk of conversion bring the people to him, and yet relieved that the talks at Suresnes delayed the question of an election which the Spaniards were now pushing more strongly than ever. It was hard to play such a complex game under cover of religion, and Henri caught all the nuances as she wrote early in May to the Prince de Conti; "this fear [that of Spanish domination], together with their necessities because of the length of the war, has inspired them with a desire to come with me provided that I am of their religion. Those who are of another mind—and that is their leaders—pretend to the same intention because they do not wish anyone to see that they are motivated by any other cause but religion." The King would have understood perfectly the delegate who murmured bitterly, "out of the mantle of religion, a Spanish cape is being cut."[12] By mid-May the conference had proceeded so successfully that Henri made a solemn pronouncement that he was ready to return to the fold of Peter, as so many devoted Frenchmen had advised him to do. The day following, official letters bearing these tidings were sent throughout France: "Having to this end decided to gather together a number of prelates and Catholic doctors by whose good teaching I might be able—to the tranquillity and satisfaction of my conscience—to clear up certain points which have kept me separated in the practice of my religion . . . I ask you to come to me in this city on the fifteenth of July . . . assuring you that you will find me well-disposed and docile to all that befits a Very Christian King who has nothing more deeply engraven in his heart than the zeal and service of God and the maintainance of the True Church."[13]

If for many Frenchmen this news was a sign of life, for the Huguenots it was the final betrayal which they had long feared. On May 9, the King attended, perhaps for the last time, the services of the Reformed Religion and listened to the fiery Gabriel d'Amours, who had often upbraided him for his licentious life, now condemn him to eternal damnation. D'Amours was not alone, for as the days for the convocation grew nearer, the Protestants redoubled their opposition. Out of Switzerland came a letter for the King from that patriarch of the Reformed Religion, Theodore Beza, whom Jeanne d'Albret had once welcomed in Nérac. It was a voice from another world where faith alone triumphed, where God's mighty hand reached out to reward the good and strike down the evil—a world in which kings need only say their prayers and obey the Commandments to be assured of victory.

"All these preparations, Sire," Beza wrote, "will be useless toil if you are not disposed to see in them all the hand of God. . . . Surely it is not necessary to teach you that God is God, that He alone can raise up or cast down. . . . 'If my God wishes me to reign, then I will reign; if He does not wish it, then I do not wish it either.' These are words worthy of a Christian king."[14] It was a vision, exalted, pure, transparent in its simplicity but which, it was obvious to the King, could hardly replace Machiavelli.

It was a letter from D'Amours which had touched him most, for although D'Amours was something of a fanatic, he had known what Henri had endured for the cause of peace and the throne of France. D'Amours was always a man of passion, and it was a plea of passionate entreaty which he now sent from the Huguenot town of St. Jean d'Angeli. He recalled the honor that Henri had done him by numbering him among his preachers, he recalled that joyful day when the King had joined his troops to those of Henri III and promised his minister that he would be the first to preach beyond the Loire. He recalled the victory at Coutras, the battle of Arques, the taking of Alençon, Falaise, Honfleur. With each victory Henri had ordered D'Amours to chant the psalms—psalms of petition, of trust, of thanksgiving. When, he continued, has there ever been a danger from which God in his power has not delivered his loyal subject? What of the sudden attack at Vendôme where the King, mounted on his horse with his brown velvet cloak singling him out as a perfect target for the enemy, escaped unharmed while the shot fell harmless at his horse's feet; what of Dreux "where for three long hours you galloped about on your great gray horse, with your gray hat with its plume flying, while the fusillades whirled about you and your nobles were driven half-crazy at seeing you in such danger?" What of Dieppe and Paris and Saumur? When was the King ever in danger and not rescued by God? Then why now did he seek to find refuge in an act so contrary to his conscience? "Can it be that the greatest captain in the world has become so cowardly as to go to Mass out of fear of men? Where is that great magnanimity, that rare faith which I so often beheld in you when, from a human point of view, you saw nothing ahead of you but desperate straits? What have you accomplished in your lifetime with a great majority? On the contrary, what have you not achieved with a small number of true Israelites? Do you wish me to predict your ruin. . . . That I cannot do. I will believe good until I shall have seen the evil."

This appeal to the deeds and friendships of the past was not the most painful part of D'Amours' letter; there was another subject on which the King was still more vulnerable: "Did you but listen," the preacher wrote, "to Gabriel D'Amours, your minister, as you listen to Gabrielle, your amour-euse, I would see a generous king victorious over his enemies."[15]

D'Amours was not the first to suggest that the influence of the lovely Gabrielle was of prime significance in the King's determination to change his religion. Egged on by her unscrupulous family, ran the rumors, Gabrielle had from the beginning used her favor with the King to restore her family's fortunes and win the first place in the kingdom for herself. It surprised no one who knew the King that within months after their first meeting, Gabrielle had won exclusive rights over his affections. What did surprise everyone however, was the marriage which took place in the summer of 1592 between Gabrielle and Nicolas d'Amerval, Seigneur de Liancourt. The groom was of a good family from Picardy, a man in his late thirties, small, rather ugly, and of somewhat limited intelligence. That the marriage had taken place under royal approval seemed obvious, but the motives behind the liaison were more difficult to construe. It was conjectured by some that Monsieur d'Estrées was being difficult, and that the King preferred to get Gabrielle away from parental domination; by others that Gabrielle herself had felt that the marriage would be a "convenience." In any case, it was a strange move on the King's part, since the stern moralists who already condemned his licentious affairs would be sure to find a married mistress more scandalous than an unmarried one. What the King thought to gain from the arrangement has never been made clear. In fact, it simply increased the rumors that Gabrielle was no better than the rest of her family—a clever schemer who would stoop to any means to get her way. It was clear, the gossips said, that she realized that the only way she could ever become queen was through an annulment of Henri's marriage to Margot. Since only the Pope could arrange such an annulment, then the Pope was to be courted— and what better way to do this than to use her influence to have her Protestant lover return to the bosom of Rome.

Leaguers and Huguenots waxed eloquent in denouncing both the King and his mistress, and Paris was full of placards ridiculing Madame de Liancourt.

> Neither the high learning of the old Sorbonne,
> The bravado of the Spanish nor the clamor of the Legate
> Have as much power to make a renegade
> As the inviting eyes of an angelic face.

ran one verse; while a wit quipped: Do you remember the old days when Gabriel an-nounced the message of salvation? Now it is another Gabrielle by whom the King re-nounces his salvation.[16] Indeed it was true that in those months preceding his conversion, there seemed nothing which the King valued above his love for his mistress. Passionate, reckless, unconstrained where love was concerned, Henri was, by the winter of 1593, totally bewitched, "I do not know what magic you use," he wrote to Gabrielle in February, "but it seems to me that I have already been away from you for a century. . . . Believe me, my dearest sovereign, love has never done this to me before." Within a week he had written her three letters, although he often complained that he could hardly find time to sleep so pressing were the affairs of state. "Oh, Jesus," he wrote that spring, "I will see you the day after tomorrow. What joy . . . Goodbye, my all. I kiss your beautiful eyes a million times."[17] Had those who declared that he had sold his soul to his mistress seen the letters which he poured out in the effortless rhetoric of his passion, they would have found even further evidence for alarm.

In the matter of the King's return to Rome, however, neither love nor magic played a part. That was a decision long in the making, hard in the resolution—and it was a decision which was entirely his own. He acted through neither fear nor coercion. He had made a promise at St. Cloud and that promise was at last to be fulfilled. Whatever barbs were directed against his mistress, whatever condemnation was directed at himself, the King knew that his decision was irrevocable. To the Huguenots whose coldness increased daily, he could only reiterate his promises of friendship and loyalty, assuring them: "When I do this, you will have no reason for fear. . . . On the contrary, I enter the house not to live in it but to clean it. I promise you this. As for yourselves, you will have no worse treatment from me than you have ever had. Pray to God for me and I will continue to love you as always."[18]

It was ironic that both sides should condemn him at once and for the same act, for while D'Amours condemned him at the Huguenot Preachings, in the squares of Paris the League hung placards renewing their attack. In one grim poster were luridly portrayed the tortures of the damned with the Royalists easily discernible, and the Béarnais himself pictured as a large black devil writhing under the feet of an angel labeled "Guise the King." It was the last desperate battle waged by those who saw their own inevitable ruin in the King's projected conversion.

Mayenne, for whom delay had become more than ever the most trusted of weapons, now sought to impede the King's plans by placing further conditions. On June 5, therefore, the League replied to the King's promise of conversion by stating that such a step depended exclusively on papal absolution. Only after this were granted, would they discuss the King's assurances that the Catholic faith would be upheld in the kingdom. Not until both these conditions had been met would they discuss the peace treaty which the King had suggested. Mayenne, however, had underestimated the people's hunger for peace. When they heard of this postponement, for which they held the Papal Legate responsible, they banded together in open protest while the frightened Sega walled himself up in the monastery of St. Martin-des-Champs as in a citadel.

Still Mayenne hedged, caught now in the triple fire of Spanish power, French pressure, and his own intransigent ambition. In mid-May Feria had proclaimed to a small, carefully selected council his plan for the French throne: the Salic Law was to be abrogated and the crown given to Isabella Clara Eugenia, daughter of Philip II through Elizabeth de Valois, and thus eldest granddaughter of Henri II of France. Although the group that heard Feria was composed of the most devout Leaguers, their response was not enthusiastic. The Bishop of Senlis, long considered one of the most fanatic of the League preachers, rose in bitter anger, crying that "the *politiques* were right when they said that private interest and ambition played more of a part than zeal for religion." It was not only Feria who was the object of their hatred but those whom they now recognized as subordinating French interests to their own. "How terrible," wrote one of the delegates in shame and despair, "that we should have seen sixteen monsters from Paris offer for sale the crown of France to the King of Spain."[19]

When, two weeks later, a solemn meeting of the Estates was convened to discuss the Spanish proposal, it was not the impolitic Feria who presented it, but the careful diplomat Juan Batista Tassis. Even Tassis' fluent French and placating manner could not conceal the fact that France was being wrenched from the hands of Frenchmen. Feeling ran high, and the Procurator General, Molé, expressed the reaction of many of his colleagues when he shouted that he was born a Frenchman and would die a Frenchman.

At last Feria was beginning to understand the loyalty of the French people and their deep devotion to the Salic Law; thus in an effort to "sweeten" the suggestion he had already made, he now suggested that since they found it unacceptable to have a woman on the French throne, the Infanta might be married to the Archduke Ernest, brother of the reigning emperor and recently appointed governor of the Low Countries. It is hard to understand what devious process of thought had led to this suggestion, but from the moment it was made it became obvious even to Feria that he had miscalculated. There was hardly a man in France, no matter what his political or religious persuasion, who could contemplate without anger the thought of a Spanish princess married to an Austrian duke sitting on the throne of France. The Estates acted with remarkable restraint when they countered the proposal by saying that it was beyond their power to consider, since they had no authority to elect a foreign king. They could, they concluded, take it under advisement. The people were less politic and when Feria left the assembly, he was surrounded by a hostile crowd with stones in their hands. "To receive the Archduke Ernest as king," wrote one of the delegates, "as we are being pressed to do, would be to subjugate our lives, our honors, and the dignity of this kingdom to foreigners."[20]

Only Mayenne, to whom everything had become subordinate to his own ambitions, refused to oppose Feria's suggestion unequivocally and tried instead to manipulate it to his own ends. On June 20 he wrote to Philip in a further effort to win the throne for himself or his son: "If it would be agreeable to your Catholic Majesty, a choice could be made of one of the princes for king, and, if you would do us the honor, the Infanta your daughter might be given to him in marriage . . . thus we would hope by this means to put an end to all our miseries and to conserve both religion and the state."[21]

The answer was almost immediate, and before the end of the month Feria again presented himself in the assembly, this time to suggest that within two months the King of Spain should name a French Catholic prince—it was implicit that he be of the House of Lorraine— to whom he would give the Infanta in marriage so that they should rule jointly over the French kingdom. It was a major victory for Mayenne and the Leaguers, and brought the King once again to the brink of ruin. With his plans carefully made, with the conference at Mantes less than a month away, Henri saw the crown receding from his grasp. Move by move over the months, Leaguers and Royalists had played out their game. They had had their kings and their bishops, their knights and their pawns and they had used them with the skill of adroit players. Move by move, check against check they had arrived within days of that final play which would decide the destiny of France. And now Time, that inexorable force which had made heroes and broken kings, won victories and ordained defeats, Time which the King had tried to use so adroitly and of which Mayenne was so often careless—Time had thrown her power against the King. Mayenne, that master of delay, would win at last and by the bitterest margin of all—a hair's breadth. The Royalist lords who had grown used to the exhilarating air of victory in the weeks since the King's proclamation, now desperately urged Henri not to wait for the assembly at Mantes but to abjure at once. Make himself a Catholic now,

they begged, before the days run out. But the King, usually so quick
to act, refused their pleas, maintaining that to act in haste would
be to act out of weakness, and no king could win an incontestable
victory by weakness. He would not advance the assembly he had
convoked; he would wait.

The decision might well have been suicidal had not the ordinary
course of events as men had conceived them been thrown awry by
a totally unexpected act of the Paris Parlement. On June 28 the
Parlement, having long considered itself to be the guardian of French
liberty and law, issued a decision which brought to an immediate
halt the Spanish plans for the throne of France. Under the leadership
of Du Vair and Lemaistre—for whom the decree was later named—
Parlement issued a decision which stated unequivocally that the election,
as it was currently conceived, could not take place without violating
the most fundamental laws of the realm: "The court and all the
assembled chambers having now and always no intention other
than to maintain the Catholic, Apostolic, and Roman religion, the
state and crown of France under the protection of a Christian,
Catholic, and French king, has ordained and does ordain that no
agreement can be made that will transfer the crown into the hands
of a foreign prince or princess; that the fundamental laws of this
kingdom must be kept, and the decisions given by this court for
the declaration of a king who is both Catholic and French be
executed. . . . This court had declared and does declare that all treaties
made or to be made hereafter for the establishment of a foreign
prince or princess are null and without effect, as acts prejudicial
to the Salic Law and to the other fundamental laws of this kingdom."[22]

Mayenne, exhilarated by his apparent victory over the King and busy
undermining the prestige of the Duc de Guise, was totally unprepared
for Parlement's action. Bewildered when the news was brought to him,
"he made a short reply, changed color, and dropped his hat several
times," reported L'Estoile.[23] Bewilderment soon gave way to rage
against this body which would take such a step without consulting
him. Inveighing against such an affront to his honor, he peremptorily
refused to recognize the decision, and by a display of angry threats
attempted to frighten Parlement into retracting its decision. But Parlement had not reached its decision hastily; its members had weighed
the cost of their action before they took it, and now to all Mayenne's
threats they replied with implacable firmness that they would rather
face death than be untrue to the laws of their country.

It was hard to believe that the years of scheming could be overthrown in a single day. Two years before Mayenne had written home in triumph that he had the Béarnais holed up in a little corner of France where he would have to surrender or jump into the sea; but the Béarnais had escaped. Now once again he thought he had cornered him, yet suddenly it was he who was cornered. There were crowds at the Hôtel de Ville clamoring for peace; there were placards at the Louvre condemning the Legate and the Sixteen; Feria, frightened by threats of violence, had reinforced his guard and retired behind locked doors; and that morning, shortly before dawn, that experienced statesman Villeroy had, in dramatic protest against Mayenne and his plans, left Paris. Among the ruins he could hardly find a piece to salvage. Philip liked success, and Mayenne had nothing to offer him now but failure.

Feria, knowing Philip's penchant for victory was determined that his mission would succeed despite this insuperable obstacle posed by Parlement. In early July Feria made his last bid for success. Admitting at last that he could not get the throne for the Infanta, he now suggested the election of the young Duc de Guise who was at once Catholic and French and who, if one delved deep enough, could establish an hereditary albeit shaky claim to the crown. To show their continuing friendship to the new King, Spain would be willing to give him the Infanta in marriage, along with a dowry of 1,000,000 gold pieces, an immediate force of 8,000 foot soldiers, 2,000 cavalry, and a subsidy of 400,000 crowns, with an additional sum within a month. Mayenne himself was secretly offered, in return for his support, the province of Normandy, a number of important French cities, and a substantial subsidy. In order to prove the sincerity of this offer, Feria offered to remain as a hostage in the Bastille until the terms were concluded. But Mayenne, who had more than his fill of Spanish intrigue, replied wryly that "the head of Feria was no sufficient guarantee for the crown of France."[24] Despite the loyalty his father's name commanded, Guise had incurred suspicion by his open devotion to the Catholic King, and this, along with Mayenne's bitter jealousy of his handsome young nephew, doomed Feria's last plan to failure. On July 20, Mayenne, unable to see any other way out, replied that in the light of present events in France, he was forced to suspend the election, and four days later he asked that the Estates be adjourned. It was split second timing, for it lacked but twenty-four hours until the King's conversion.

The prologue to this drama had already taken place at Mantes where the theologians of both faiths had met and where the inexhaustible scholarship and persuasive eloquence of the Abbé du Perron, Bishop of Evreux, had won the day. Under Henri's direction, the prelates convened again at St. Denis on July 21 where the drama would be played to its close. Desperately the Apostolic Delegate, already feeling upon his head the weight of the Pope's anger, tried to save his cause by publishing an exhortation to the Catholics, begging them to oppose this act, since by its very nature it was null and void and would only lead them into further misery. But the assembly had taken its decision; they would be neither swayed nor hindered. On July 22, they declared the bulls which Sixtus V had published against the King to be invalid and contrary not only to the rights of French kings but to canon law itself which maintained that no one could be excommunicated without previous warning. Therefore, they maintained, the Archbishop of Bourges, as patriarch of France, would absolve the King "since it was more expedient to proceed without delay in a work so pleasing to God and so salutary to France."[25]

On July 23 the King himself was called before the assembled clergy to ascertain if he were ready for the final step. Although the prospect of victory was very sweet, the price of that victory even at the end cost the King dear. The night before he was to appear in the assembly, he wrote to Gabrielle: "Tomorrow I begin my talk with the bishops. . . . My hope of seeing you keeps me from writing a long letter. Sunday I will take the perilous leap. As I write to you, I have a hundred troubles on my shoulders so that I hate St. Denis as you do Mantes. Goodbye, my heart; come early tomorrow for it seems like a year since I have seen you."[26]

The five-hour conference which was held the next day was a strange combination of Henri's unquenchable wit, his sincerity, and his perplexity in the face of certain Catholic dogmas. When they began to discuss prayers for the dead he was manifestly ill at ease. "Let us pass over the requiem," he suggested, "I'm not dead yet and I don't want to be." Purgatory, the Real Presence, confession, papal power—all were reviewed for his affirmation. He was no theologian, and the abstract concepts of religion often seemed to him mere quibbling. Now as the bishops pursued their points, he turned wearily, saying, "I pray you, call them off; tell them I've done enough and that if they press me further, worse may ensue." Even in those things which he did not understand, he was willing to submit; moved not by theological faith but "touched by compassion at the misery of his people" and willing to do whatever was necessary to alleviate it. At the end he said to the prelates, "Today I put my soul in your hands. Take good care of it, I beg you, for where you have me enter today, there I will stay until my death, I swear to you"; "and," commented L'Estoile, "there were tears in his eyes."[27]

On Sunday, July 25, Feast of Saint James the Apostle, the procession formed which would lead the King to the Basilica of St. Denis. Despite the prohibitions leveled by the Apostolic Delegate, it was a joyous and colorful spectacle: the streets rich with tapestries and fragrant with flowers, the roll of the drums and the bright clear call of the trumpets, the pageantry of the Swiss Guard in their glitter of orange and black, the sober kilts of the Scotch Guard swinging in the distinctive rhythm of the Highlands. And, finally, the King himself dressed in white satin with a cloak of black and a black plume in his hat—interpreted by the Catholics as a sign of penitence and by the Huguenots as a sign of mourning.

The day was stifling although it was not yet eight o'clock, redolent of another day of sweltering heat when the nineteen-year-old King of Navarre had made his way through the streets of Paris. He had gone then, swaggering a little in his youth and resplendent in yellow satin, to the Cathedral of Notre Dame where his bride, sparkling with jewels and the faint glitter of scandal, had come to him. Charles, his cousin and his king, had given the bride away; and Catherine de Medici had stood in frank delight at the success of her plan. Anjou had been there with something of a reputation for courage and military skill, and young Alençon, trying to stand tall on his spindly legs, with the fires of ambition and contention already eating him away. Among the lords, assured and debonair, had stood the Duc de Guise, reputed even then to be Margot's lover. Now, of them all, only he was still alive—except, of course, for Margot, walled up in the citadel of Usson—Margot who had betrayed him in a multitude of ways but who had betrayed him most by giving him no heirs. All the others had gone to their deaths, many of them violently, most of them prematurely: Condé, mysteriously and unexpectedly; Henri III by an assassin's knife; Guise by his King's own order; King Charles and Alençon betrayed by their Valois heritage.

Only Catherine, fat and wheezing, with her swollen legs and watery eyes, had lived out her span. It had not been possible for him to like Catherine, but he had always given her the respect due a formidable opponent. Those graceful hands had been made of pure steel; she had reigned no matter who had held the scepter. Had they done her bidding, France might have had peace long ago.

Now, however, Notre Dame was closed to him, and although he was King of France, he must come like any suppliant begging before the door of the basilica to be received into the fold of Peter. A few feet from the entrance, the Archbishop of Bourges awaited him, seated in a chair covered with white damask and embroidered with the arms of France and of Navarre. From the tympanum of the great door, Christ, surrounded by angels carrying the instruments of the Passion, sat in sculptured calm; on his right, Abraham, symbol of the elect, was received into Paradise, and on his left, the damned suffered those eternal pains to which their perfidy had condemned them.

"Who are you?" asked the Archbishop according to the formula, and received the answer, "I am the King."

"What do you ask?" he continued.

"I ask to be received into the Catholic, Apostolic, and Roman Church."

"Do you truly desire this?"

"Yes. I wish and desire it."

Then, kneeling, he made his profession of faith, the profession of faith which would give him the right to the crown of France: "I protest and I swear, in the presence of Almighty God, to live and die in the Catholic, Apostolic, and Roman religion; to protect and defend it against all its enemies at the risk of my blood and my life, renouncing all heresies contrary to this Catholic, Apostolic, and Roman Church."[28]

It was done. He kissed the episcopal ring and received the absolution of the archbishop, and rising from his knees, was brought through the vaulted archway into the basilica. Up the long nave, cool and dark, protected by its massive stone walls from the heat of the morning, the King was led. The procession moved slowly along the uneven stones dappled with the blues and reds and greens of the high windows. Looking down upon him with folded hands and blank eyes were those other men who had led France: Pepin, Charlemagne, Robert the Pious, Louis the Fat. Mayenne had refused passports to the people of Paris, but it had made no difference. Wild with joy, they could not be stopped, jamming the streets and pouring into the vast reaches of the basilica. Through the throngs that pressed about him, the King made his way to the high altar and there, kneeling once again, made his confession. The *Te Deum*, that traditional hymn of gratitude, cascaded from vault to vault while like some antiphonal choir the people shouted, "Long live the King!" Finally he was led to the prie-dieu prepared for him, draped in crimson velvet and embroidered with the fleur-de-lys of France. Here he heard Mass, omitting none of the devotional acts which he knew were expected of him—kissing the book of the Gospels, taking part in the offertory procession, receiving the kiss of peace.

What their value was to Henri is questionable, but to the people it meant they had a king—a king like themselves: not a Spaniard, not a Huguenot, but a Frenchman and a Catholic. Many in their simplicity felt that now that Henri had heard Mass, France would be at peace again, made one by a simple act of religion. For others, what the King had done was no more than a conjuring trick to win himself a kingdom. Only the King, for no one else could read his mind, knew exactly what had been accomplished. He knew that peace was not yet; he knew that even while Mayenne had signed a truce with him, he had also signed a fresh pact with Spain; he knew that at least a third of his kingdom was still in revolt against him. He had written to Gabrielle two days earlier, "I have a hundred troubles on my shoulders"; no single act of faith could remove that burden. But Henri was filled with limitless hope; he had listened in a kind of ecstasy to those cries, "Long live the King" and found it a sweeter music than even the *Te Deum*.

That night he sent out a circular letter to all the provinces of France, confirming what had been done that day in the basilica of the kings of France: ". . . recognizing the Catholic, Apostolic, and Roman Church to be the true church of God, full of truth, unable to err, we have embraced it and have resolved to live and die in it."[29]

CHAPTER XIII

"Long Live the King": 1593–1594

O Lord, the King rejoices in your power . . . You have granted him his heart's desire, nor denied him what his lips entreated.

Coronation ceremony

❧❧❧❧ The "perilous leap" had been taken, yet the France that awakened on the following day seemed no different from what it had been before. The crowds that had thronged St. Denis had returned to their Paris homes and the gates had been barred against the King. The square in front of the basilica of St. Denis was empty with only the littered streets to attest to the excitement of the day before. Within the church, the thrones and prie-dieus were removed and the tapestries and rich hangings taken from the walls. The task of abjuration had been accomplished, but the difficult work of reconciliation still lay ahead.

The King had few illusions about the future: the Spaniards still plotted to win the throne and Mayenne was with them; the League continued to stir up hatred among the people; the Huguenots sulked over what they considered their betrayal; the Protestant Princes waited to see what shifts in diplomacy might follow upon the King's conversion. Although it was true that popular feeling was in his favor, the enmity in some quarters was more stormy than ever. In a letter to Brèves, then his ambassador in the Levant, Henri explained the decision which had led to his final step, describing with obvious elation the actual ceremony and the enthusiasm of the people "who not only seemed very happy but who showed a marked affection and courage in my service."[1] Yet the letter ended on a sober note:

Spain, he fears, having failed to win the French throne by diplomacy may now turn to force.

Although the month before Henri had been able to borrow a large sum of money from the Duke of Tuscany, he was not in a position to face a strong Spanish assault. He continued to depend —as he had for years—on the resources that he hoped Elizabeth would make available to him. His conversion, however, had made relations with England ambiguous if not actually hostile. His Huguenot friends had used as one of their arguments against his abjuration that once he had acted against his conscience and so impugned his own integrity, he would lay himself open to contempt and scorn, and Henri was now experiencing the truth of that warning. The Earl of Huntington in a letter to Lord Burghley, having explained the circumstances of the King's conversion, concluded contemptuously, "I hope we shall hear of his hearty repentance for his late foul fall."[2]

Henri, fearful that Elizabeth might in retaliation sever friendly relations and withdraw English troops from the north of France, wrote at length to Beauvais, his ambassador in London, of the necessity of keeping English forces in the field and advising him to build his arguments upon Elizabeth's fear of Spanish domination. If Philip should be victorious in France, he warned, then all of Europe is lost, for it is "on this that he builds his dreams for the universal monarchy of the world."[3]

It was to England's self-interest to fight Spanish power in France, and the King could always be sure of Elizabeth's clear vision where matters of self-interest were at stake. It was the enemy at home, whose interest it was to invalidate the results of his conversion, that caused his darkest thoughts. The exuberance of the crowd that witnessed his abjuration had been short-lived. The rhetoric of the League preachers had never been more violent, one of them fulminating that now any dog that trotted to Mass on Sunday might expect to find a crown on his head, another begging the people to pray that God may raise up another Jacques Clément to rid them of this heretic as he had formerly rid them of the Valois tyrant.

In mid-August it seemed that God would answer their prayers, for there arrived one day in Melun, where the King was staying, a young man of twenty-seven, Pierre Barrière, a native of Orléans, who had come to Melun with the express determination to kill the King. It was much the same tale as that of Jacques Clément: he thought to do a service to both God and his country by ridding France of an unworthy king. He claimed that he had gone to seek advice and been told by a certain Jesuit, Varade, that if he carried out his plan he would receive the reward of paradise. In preparation for his deed, he had made his confession to a Dominican at Lyon, one Séraphin Bianchi. Unable to dissuade him, Bianchi had reported the plot to the officials, who arrested Barrière before he had the opportunity to attempt his plan. He denied nothing; repeating, during the long hours when he lay bound on the rack, that although he had been encouraged in his design, its execution was entirely his. Three days later, torn and bleeding on the scaffold that had been erected in the marketplace of Melun, with his offending hand chopped off at the wrist, his arms and legs broken, he still maintained that the plot was his own. The King when told that the parricide was dead, took no joy in the fact but brooded on the fate of kings and assassins, avowing that he would have pardoned the regicide had he asked grace before him.

The League was bitterly disappointed when they heard of Barrière's frustrated attempt, for in their fanaticism they approved any means to rid them of the Béarnais. Having fought so long against the possibility of the King's conversion, they now refused to accept the accomplished fact. "Even if he drank all the holy water in Notre Dame, they would not believe him," commented a contemporary. "The King of France is a Catholic now," wrote one of his officers, "yet they want to see him barefooted before the door of the Vatican, in the midst of the flock of penitents, on his knees before the priests, weeping for days and nights, and scorned by the buffoons and pedants of the Roman court."[4]

Although Henri was willing to do much to win Rome, he was not ready to replay the drama of Canossa. Word of Henri's step had reached Rome in mid-August. The Spaniards were wild with anger and the Pope was inclined to enjoy their discomfort, although he was alarmed at the position of the Holy See. He had no desire to augment Spanish power which he already found insufferable, yet neither could he afford to alienate Philip and the League. To absolve Henri meant to acknowledge him as King and the theologians of the Sorbonne had already pronounced against this. The two ecclesiastics most violently opposed to showing any clemency to the French King were the exiled Cardinal Allen of England and the Spanish canonist Francisco Peña, both of whom argued that since the bishops who supported Henri had been excommunicated by Gregory XIV, it was the sheerest nonsense to talk of their having power to absolve him from heresy.

In their excommunicate state, they could do nothing but heap further sins on their heads by arrogating powers to themselves to which they had no right. If, they warned Clement, he were to accept the King and should he then relapse—not an unlikely possibility in view of his past vacillation—the Pope would be responsible for the state of France. It was a powerful deterrent, but it was neatly countered by the argument of the Venetian ambassador who pointed out that by refusing to acknowledge Henri the Church might well lose France as it had once lost England. It was a dilemma in the full sense of the word with each horn sharpened to a fine point. In the end it was the quiet logic of Venice rather than the bombast of Spain which won Clement, and he privately acknowledged: "We intend to wait for a while the development of affairs in France; if God favors the course of Henri, then neither shall we oppose him but will bow to the inevitable."[5]

While fact and rumor poured into the Vatican concerning this latest outrage of the Béarnais, the Béarnais himself finished two letters addressed to the Pope which he planned to send by Brochard de la Clielle who had had the experience of several Roman missions. The first letter was a formal statement notifying the Pope of his conversion and assuring him of his filial happiness in returning to the flock of Peter. The second letter was more political in tone. He spoke openly of his enemies, of Spanish intrigue, of the means they were using in their effort to cast suspicion on his actions, of how they will attempt to discredit him with the Holy See, and concluded: "My enemies may surpass me in artifice and dissimulation but not in frankness and candor. I have my principal trust in God and in the goodness and justice of Your Holiness against the tricks and power which they have on their side."[6]

Clielle arrived in Rome on September 11 bearing not only the King's letters but also one from the Duc de Nevers, whom Henri had appointed as his ambassador to the Papal court, which expressed the new ambassador's confidence that now that his master had made his submission to Rome, his minister would be cordially welcomed in the Holy City. But Nevers' hopes soared too high, for Clielle found his reception far from cordial and would not have been granted even an initial audience were it not for the diplomatic finesse of Arnauld d'Ossat whose years in Rome had given him keys to many private doors. Even the audience which was obtained, however, was far from successful. Clement received Clielle's letters coldly and gave no sign of bending toward France. Within fifteen days after his arrival, Clielle was ready to take horse for home with no hope that his mission was other than a failure. But the night before his departure, d'Ossat, with his extraordinary gift for translating the ambiguities of papal diplomacy, sent for him to assure him that all was far from lost and advising him "that the King should go forward in showing himself truly converted, giving signs of being sincerely a Catholic, for the Pope had rejected the Duc de Nevers to satisfy his own conscience and to try the King's constancy; yet in time, he should at last obtain his desire."[7]

Fear of Spain was a major factor in Clement's reaction, for day after day the Spaniards harassed the Pope, threatening that a Spanish army in France would see to the election of a Catholic King, threatening to mobilize the Spanish forces in Naples, threatening violence even in Rome itself. "We find ourselves in a dark wood," sighed the bewildered Clement who could find no way to escape his dilemma.[8]

Toward the end of September, before Clielle could reach France, the Duc of Nevers began his journey to Rome. Nevers' mission had two elements: to request the Pope to confirm the absolution given by the French bishops insofar as this was necessary for its validity; to ask permission to make the *obedientia* in the name of His Majesty. When his magnificent entourage, which numbered three important ecclesiastics, arrived at Poschiano they were met by a Jesuit, Antonio Possevino, who explained that His Holiness refused to receive the ambassador of the King of France but would be happy to welcome to Rome Louis de Gonzague, Duc de Nevers, as a private citizen. On November 23, again through the ministry of D'Ossat, Nevers had his first papal interview. The Pope's attitude was inflexible: he waved aside Nevers' petitions, saying that even an angel of heaven could not convince him of the sincerity of Henri's conversion. The second audience, two days later, went no better, for Clement appeared incensed at the impudence of the French bishops who had taken on themselves the privilege which belonged to the Holy See alone. Although Nevers' visit had orginally been restricted to a period of ten days, he was forced to wait until December 4 before Clement would see him again. The Pope, meanwhile, called a consistory to discuss the case of the so-called King of France, asking what penance he had done in expiation for his sins, commenting contemptuously that anyone could hear Mass in order to usurp a kingdom, and then returning to that dominant issue: what would be the responsibility of the Holy

See should the Pope absolve Henri only to have him relapse into heresy?

The King, learning that his papal embassy had fallen on evil days, wrote to Nevers on November 20, begging him to "leave nothing undone which concerns the good of my affairs" and exhorting him to "undertake anything which can alter His Holiness," enclosing another letter to be given to the Pope. "Most Holy Father," it began, "after it has pleased God to call us to the knowledge and communion of this Holy, Catholic, Apostolic, and Roman Church and after the protestation that we have made to live and die in it, nothing can be dearer to us . . . than to see it approved and authorized by the blessing of Your Holiness."[9]

In France news of Nevers' rebuff had, quite contrary to the Pope's intention, simply massed more people about the King. Pomponne de Bellièvre, who had come out of his retirement to give his support to the King, wrote to Nevers: "The Holy Father is held to be a good and prudent prince, but from the news of this embassy to Rome, we judge our fear of the Spanish party to be just." Even more darkly came the fears of Nevers himself who wrote: "If the Pope does not receive me it will mean the ruin of France, the loss of millions of souls, and perhaps a schism."[10] Aware of the temper of the French people, Nevers made bold to tell the Pope in his final audience that if the Holy See continued to refuse Henri, then he would not be responsible for what might happen to the Church in France. It was a threat to schism; but still Clement did not capitulate. To Nevers' request for a written statement of the Pope's position, he replied that since papal writings had not been honored before by this king, he would not risk sending any more. To Nevers' desperate queries, asking what would convince the Pope of the King's good will, what course of action he should pursue, what acts of penance he should perform, the Pope either kept silence or evaded the issues. On January 15 Nevers left Rome, returning empty-handed to France, except for a small gold reliquary that Clement had given him as a present for his son.

Nevers' failure was a bitter shock to the King. Although he had been aware of Clement's anger at the initiative taken by the French bishops, he had felt that the Pope was too politically astute not to accept the fact of his conversion. He had deliberately picked Nevers, a fervent Catholic who had long struggled with his conscience in choosing his politics, and had deliberately provided him with a magnificent retinue as a sign of his royal power. He had done what he could to indicate the weakness of the League, his own popular acclaim, and the fraudulent ambitions of Spain. Beyond these worldly considerations was the possibility of schism which the Pope could hardly afford to disregard. Clement was no visionary monk who believed that men had but to await the manifest will of God; Clement was a Roman diplomat, a pragmatist, who knew how to assess and maneuver as well as any sovereign in Europe. Yet Clement, despite the facts which Henri had put at his disposal, had refused to accept him back into the fold of Peter. Everything he had done since that sweltering Sunday in July when he had knelt before the door of St. Denis had been done in the belief that Clement would accept him into the Roman communion. When the three months' truce which he had signed with Mayenne had expired, he willingly renewed it as he waited for Nevers' return—well aware that Mayenne's request proceeded from no desire for peace but for a delay which would enable him to build up his strength. He knew of the treaty signed by Mayenne and Feria just two days before his abjuration in which Mayenne promised that he and his followers would never recognize Henri and agreeing that the question of an election was not ended but simply deferred until the times were more propitious. He knew, too, that, in return, Spain had offered the League 12,000 foot soldiers and 10,000 cavalry with a monthly subsidy of 8,000 écus. He knew that before the delegates from the Estates were permitted to return to their homes the Duke had made them promise to be obdient to the decisions of the Holy See and to return to Paris in the fall to conclude the affairs of the realm.

During the first week of September, Mayenne, always nervous lest he fall out of favor with Philip, wrote to the Spanish King to explain to him that his only motive for signing the truce with Henri was to gain time, assuring him that he was still Philip's devoted servant. Yet even while he was writing deferentially to Madrid, he was continuing to meet Henri first at Andrésy and then at Milly to continue peace negotiations. Promises now came as easily to Mayenne as breathing and he had no difficulty assuring the French King that he would use his influence to obtain absolution from the Pope, that he would do all in his power to see that peace was permanently established. But just as too much caution had once undermined his power, now too many promises made him lose face everywhere. Neither Philip nor Henri paid much attention to his glib protestations of loyalty, and the people of Paris, still feeling the sting of suffering, while a permanent peace

lay just beyond their fingertips, were impatient with Mayenne's endless
exhortations to stand firm.

Through all of Mayenne's duplicity, Henri had remained silent
and acquiescent, determined to prove his good will to the Holy See.
Now with the Pope's refusal to acknowledge his conversion, Henri's
political maneuverings took another direction. The third renewal of
the truce which Mayenne asked for at the end of December was refused. "They have used it only to prepare for a new war," commented
the King as he received news of fresh Spanish forces assembling at the
frontiers. With the Pope's decision against him, his hopes of winning
his kingdom by peaceful means were shattered and he turned again
to the ways of war which he had longed to avoid.

There was, however, one more peaceful act which would strengthen
his royal position: his solemn coronation. No single act could affirm
his right to the throne more palpably than that religious ceremony in
which he would become not only the leader of his people but the
Lord's anointed as well. He had originally planned that his coronation
should take place in St. Denis immediately following his abjuration,
but then had decided to wait until he had received papal absolution,
thus indicating his filial obedience to the Holy See. Even late in
December he had written to Pisani that he still had great confidence
in the Pope's judgment and intended to postpone any plans for his
coronation until Nevers returned from Rome. Clement's action, however, had now made further delay futile and at the beginning of
January 1594, the King began serious preparations for his coronation.

The location for the ceremony was the first of the problems to be
met. Reims was the traditional scene for coronations, but Reims was
now securely in League hands. The problem was further complicated
by a decision taken by the Estates of Blois in 1588. The King of
France, the Estates had decreed, must be crowned at Reims and
anointed with the sacred oil there preserved, and this decision must
henceforth be regarded as one of the fundamental laws of the realm.
Even then many had considered this a ruse, since the power of the
League in Reims would effectively exclude anyone but a man favored
by the League from becoming the legitimate king. To bolster their
case, Henri's adherents dredged French history to find the names of
those who had been crowned elsewhere: Charlemagne, Louis the Pious,
the Ottos and Conrads and Henris all gave testimony that other cities
besides Reims could serve as the site for consecration. Since the
League refused him Reims, then, announced Henri, he would be

crowned at Chartres, a sanctuary dear to the Bourbon family since it lay within their ancestral lands. If the League refused him the sacred oil of Reims—held in veneration since it was reputedly used in the baptism of Clovis—then he would use the sacred oil preserved at Marmoutier, an oil made holy by that venerated French bishop, Martin of Tours.

On February 17 the King entered Chartres which he had once called "my beautiful city." This time he entered quietly, without a solemn procession, taking up residence at the archepiscopal palace. For a week the city concentrated its energies on preparing for the coronation which was to be held on Sunday, February 27. Beyond the normal preparations were those which years of war demanded. Many of the symbols of royal office had been stolen or defaced and everything had to be remade or newly fashioned. During that week, the holy oil was brought from the monastery of Marmoutier, outside Tours, and after solemn veneration by the people was deposited in the monastery of St. Pierre-en-Vallée. Bishops, peers, officers of the army, Princes of the Blood gathered in the city while the workmen at the catherdal grew dizzy as they hung tapestries high in the nave and carried chairs and thrones and canopies into the sanctuary.

Before dawn on Sunday morning those in charge of the ceremonies were checking last minute details in the catherdal while the Master of the Guards was already busy with the crowds jostling in the square for room to see this extraordinary coronation. Some had huddled in the streets all night or walked in the dark across the frozen, windy fields of the Beauce to assure themselves of a glimpse of this king who was already something of a legend. It was hardly light when the prologue of the drama opened before them: out of the darkness, stepping with care along the rough stones of the square, came a white palfrey, sheltered beneath a canopy of white damask embroidered with gold flowers, and on its back the sacristan of the abbey of Marmoutier carrying his precious burden, the Holy Oil of Marmoutier. Within the hour the cathedral began to fill with the dignitaries who would take part in the ceremony: the Princes of the Blood—Conti, Soissons, Montpensier—with their short tunics of silver cloth partially covered by the violet cloaks which fell free from their shoulders; the dukes of Burgundy, Normandy, Aquitaine; the counts of Toulouse, Champagne, Flanders—all of whom had declared for the King. Despite the poverty of France, they were dressed in splendor, their cloaks trimmed with ermine and fastened to their shoulders with metal clasps exquisitely wrought and ornamented with precious stones.

Shortly before eight o'clock, accompanied by the Bishops of Nantes and Maillezais, the King himself made his way from the episcopal residence to the main gate of the cathedral. Before him went the cross-bearer and the children of the cathedral choir, the trumpeters, the heralds, the knights of the Holy Spirit, the royal archers and, closest to His Majesty, his Scotch Guard. As they mounted the wide steps of the transept the crowd hushed, and the choir began its hypnotic chant *Domine in virtute laetabitur rex.* Preceding the King came Matignon, marshal of France, holding aloft a naked sword. Following him came Cheverny, the Chancellor, an ermine cloak trimmed with velvet covering his tunic of crimson velvet and on his head a black mortar, symbol of his office. Then came the King himself, dressed not in the full vesture of his royal office, but in the simple garments of his anointing: a shirt of fine Holland cloth, slit so that he could receive the sacred oils, a simple coat of velvet, and over all a cloak of silver cloth reaching below his knees. The portal beneath which he stood received the full light of the morning sun. High above him the kings of Judah stood erect, paying their homage to the King of Kings for whom they had prepared the way. Below them sat Christ Himself, surrounded by his Apostles. He was neither Judge nor Eternal Lawgiver, but Christ the Teacher, holding the Gospels in his left hand while with his right he blessed mankind. He was a Christ of infinite kindness, receiving from the kneeling figure of Charity the loaves which He will bless and give to the poor.

Almost dwarfed beneath the splendor of the tympanum, Henri made his way slowly into the nave of the cathedral. It was too early for flowers, but the air was heavy with the smell of musk and incense and alight with hundreds of huge candles, dimming the glory of the stained glass windows and casting strange, erratic shadows on the tapestries which lined the walls. At the entrance to the sanctuary the Archbishop, Nicolas de Thou, who would perform the ceremony, awaited the King. De Thou who had so often risked disfavor by his loyalty to kings, who had given sanctuary to Henri III when on the Day of Barricades he had come like a criminal in fear of his life before the gates of Chartres—De Thou was at last to receive his reward. To those of his court who had suggested a more prominent ecclesiastic, to Bourges who felt that as chaplain to the King the honor should be his, Henri had paid little attention. It was this old

man, who like Simeon had long awaited the coming of his lord, who
should anoint his body with the oil of kings. As the King entered the
cathedral, the choir ceased its plain-chant and in a glorious burst of
polyphony sang *Ecco mitto angelum meum*—"Behold I send my angel"
—the words with which God had announced the coming of His Messiah in whose name and by whose will Henri would now receive the
crown of France.

He ascended the wooden platform on which stood the royal chair,
draped in velvet and sewn with fleurs-de-lys. On either side of him,
along the steps of the platform, sat the chief men of the realm, while
the Archbishop took his place on the episcopal throne before the high
altar. Following the long introductory prayers, the sacred oil was
brought from its repository and the ceremony of the anointing began.
"I have found David my servant; with my holy oil I have anointed
him," chanted the choir. In reply, the King spoke for the first time,
taking the ancient oath of the kings of France: promising to the best
of his ability to build a kingdom of peace and tranquillity, to fight all
injustice and iniquity, to banish all heretics, and concluding, "I promise by my oath to keep all that I have said." He held aloft the
royal sword which was placed in his hand, its naked point reaching
toward the vaulted ceiling, while the Archbishop blessed it. He kissed
it and placed it on the main altar, and finally, on his knees, received
it at the hands of the Archbishop. Then in preparation for the anointing, he prostrated himself on the crimson carpet prepared for him while
the drone of the litany poured over him. At the end, he stood to
receive the holy oil. His clothing opened, he was touched on his back,
his chest, his shoulders, his arms, his hands; and before the other
symbols of his royal authority were placed in his hands, those hands
still wet with the sacred oil were gloved, lest the ointment should
touch some profane thing. The scepter, the staff, the royal ring by
which a king espouses his kingdom, all were entrusted to him. Finally,
the crown of France was taken from its pillow and held high over his
head while the peers stretched out their hands, symbolic gesture of
their affirmation, as the Archbishop set it at last upon his head:
"Receive this crown in the name of the Father and of the Son and of
the Holy Spirit." The "Amen" of the clergy was lost amid the tumult of
the crowd's "Long live the King!"

The triumph of St. Denis was thin compared to the full rich joy
that must have swept over Henri as he made his way to the royal
throne to receive the kiss of peace from the assembled peers. The

cries of St. Denis had been an omen, a presage of what the future might bring. Now the future was here; he had willed it and made it come true. With the weight of the crown upon his head and the ring of France upon his finger, the disapproval of the Pope died to a whisper. Let him accept or reject, let him hurl his anathemas and play his game with Mayenne and Spain. It was Henri who was king.[11] Now with his body anointed with holy chrism, there was renewed in him a dream which had twice before brought him to the edge of ruin: he would take Paris at last. He was more than a general now, more than a man seeking entrance into the Roman Church; he was the anointed King of France. He had held aloft the royal sword, grasped in his strong hand the royal scepter while the choir sang *Vivat Rex in aeternum*; and when the Archbishop had proclaimed those words, *Accipe Coronam Regni,* he had felt the full weight of the crown of France upon his head. He would take Paris, not by siege or by slow battle but with one of those lightning strokes which was part of his unique genius. From the beginning he was sure of his success and on March 17 he wrote to the Duc de Sully, "Come on the twentieth to Senlis, or to St. Denis on the twenty-first to help cry in the streets of Paris, 'Long live the King!' "[12] There was no Duke of Parma to stop him this time with clever feints and maneuvers, and if the reports he received were true, there were but few in the city who would risk their lives for Mayenne and his cause.

Mayenne, aware of his increasing unpopularity, tightened restrictions in Paris, while with a bravado he did not feel he commemorated the new year by the distribution of specially minted coins with his image, sword in hand, on one side and on the other, the arms of France and Lorraine, encircled by the words, "The throne being empty, the best captain rules me." By now, however, it was an ironic inscription and toward the end of the month a delegation of disgruntled citizens came to him to discuss their grievances. Even those who had worked loyally for the League from its inception had grown weary of Mayenne's empty promises. Actually, it was the recently appointed governor of Paris, the Comte de Brissac, long known as a zealous adherent of the League, who was instrumental in turning the city over to its lawful king.

Shortly after his coronation, the King had journeyed to Soissons and on March 10 had appeared at St. Denis much to the terror of the Sixteen; but in order to allay suspicion he had ridden away again, staying at Senlis until the night of March 21. Two weeks earlier the Duc de

Mayenne had left the city under questionable circumstances. Beset by angry citizens for his arbitrary banishment of six of the most articulate Parisians, and warned by his mother that even the Paris garrison was in league with the King, Mayenne took his leave early on the morning of March 6. Although he explained that he left in order to treat with other lords concerning the welfare of the kingdom, his departure had about it more the air of a flight than a mission. Mayenne's fortunes had reached their depth. People laughed openly in Paris at his pretensions of friendship with Philip, remarking that the Spanish were sick of the Fat Duke and that if they could get him to Madrid they would see that he was properly locked up where he could cause them no more trouble. The English ambassador reported that even with a Spanish subsidy behind him, Mayenne's finances were so reduced that he had to sell his silver plate to buy food. The Duke began to understand Villeroy's wisdom when he had pleaded with him the preceding December to make peace with Henri. "You think this is too dangerous and shameful, while I feel that no way could be more for both the general good and your own affairs," the minister had advised.[18] Mayenne knew now that no way was more shameful than the way of ambition scorned.

No sooner had Mayenne departed than Paris took on the aspect of a city under siege. The guards on the ramparts were redoubled, the gates closed and blocked with earthworks, and the keys brought to the Sixteen. Yet when the King came and left St. Denis without incident, the Sixteen, realizing that the citizens would not tolerate these precautions for long, relaxed their guard. Brissac had the signals well arranged and according to plan on the night of March 21 he left open the Porte-Neuve between the Louvre and the Tuileries. Shortly after dusk a Neopolitan soldier discovering this reported it to Feria. But Brissac, when questioned, assured the Spaniard that the gate was sufficiently guarded. Ibarra, unsatisfied, went to make the rounds himself, giving instructions to the Spanish officers on guard to use their daggers on Brissac should anything suspicious occur. When all was still quiet at three o'clock Ibarra, reassured, went to bed. Scarcely an hour later, St. Luc, his visor raised, appeared out of the driving rain, and Brissac, torch in hand, led him unnoticed through the gate with a hundred men behind him. Within another hour other gates were opened to the royal troops massed to enter. Between six and seven in the dull light of that rainy morning, the King himself, accompanied by an armed force of six hundred men, came through the Porte-Neuve—

that same gate through which Henri III had fled on the Day of Barricades. He had sworn that day that he would never reenter it unless he came as a conqueror and now his royal cousin was keeping his word for him.

There was little bloodshed as the King's troops entered the city, for many of the Spanish soldiers took refuge behind locked doors and the French soldiers were, for the most part, happy to put down their arms in favor of the King. Without hindrance Henri rode in triumph down the rue St. Honoré to the Louvre, with his white plume marking him even from a distance. About him the citizens thronged with white scarfs about their shoulders shouting their "Long live the King." As he continued on to Notre Dame, the church bells pealed, bringing people from their beds to hear the astonishing news that the heralds were crying in the streets. At the Pont Notre Dame the crowds were immense and his guards, fearful lest he be unseated, tried to push them back off the bridge; but the King would have none of it, ordering his men to let them be; ". . . they are famished for the sight of a king," he explained with evident joy.[14]

At the door of Notre Dame he was met by the dean, kissed the cross that was presented to him, and heard Mass. Overwhelmed with joy he returned to the Louvre for dinner with his chief officers, "as though he had always been there," commented Péréfixe. The Louvre —where as a child he had played and studied with those other Henris, Guise and Valois, to his father's delight and his mother's misliking; the Louvre—scene of his marriage night with Margot and of those bloody August days when he had been kept prisoner with his cousin Condé, while from the streets below he could hear the shouts and cries of the hunter and the hunted. The Louvre had had few happy memories for him, and when he had finally escaped he had thought that nothing would ever bring him back to those hostile walls. Now, however, the ghosts were gone; he had exorcised them by his victory. The wine he drank was not half so exhilarating as the triumph of those early morning hours when, without lifting his sword, he had won Paris. Intoxicated with his own success, he confided to those who sat with him: "I must confess that I am so happy to be here that I don't know what you are saying nor what I should say myself. . . . Should I believe that I am really here? . . . the more I think about it the more amazed I am, for surely there is nothing human in this; it is one of the most extraordinary works of God."[15]

While the King dined, his officers, accompanied by trumpeters and heralds, went through the streets of the city announcing grace and pardon to all. Simultaneously, handbills, previously printed, were disbursed among the crowds promising that the past would be forgotten for the King wanted all his subjects, especially those of Paris, to live in amity and concord.

At two o'clock that afternoon the King, dressed in gray, with a black hat and his great white plume, sat at a window overlooking the gate of St. Denis as the foreign soldiers filed out of the city: first the Neapolitans, then the Spanish under Feria and finally the Walloons under Ibarra. Their dream was over and Feria in despair over his failure had written, "We are going from fall to fall." Rumor had it that the King smiled as the troops filed by, lifting his hat in an ironic Spanish gesture and calling to them: "Adieu, gentlemen; commend me to your master. Go in peace but do not return this way again."[16]

Joy had given the King wings; he was everywhere, visiting churches, mingling with the citizens, taking the initiative of offering peace among those who might still be his enemies. He made it a point to see that Amazon of the League, as she was called, Mayenne's sister, Madame de Montpensier. Recognizing his victory, she was willing to forgive him everything, apologizing that her brother had not been there to lower the drawbridge for him. The King, amused that the woman who had done so much to ruin him should be so easily won, was rumored to have replied gallantly, "I only arrived very early this morning." But Brissac the Duchess could not forgive, commenting tartly, "I have long known that he was a coward, but I never knew until today that he was a traitor."[17]

The following day a circular letter went out to the provinces in which the King announced the taking of Paris, expressing special joy at the "cooperation" of Brissac which had permitted him to enter the city without bloodshed. At the same time he wrote to Pisani a letter both detailed and exuberant in which he rehearsed those triumphal hours when he had entered through the Porte-Neuve, passed before the Louvre, and entered as King into the Cathedral of Notre Dame. With an exultation typical of him, he noted that even this great church "was not big enough" to accommodate the vast crowd of people who flocked to him.

On March 29, just eight days after his victorious entrance, Parlement acknowledged him as their lawful king and issued decrees by which they hoped to reestablish order in France: Mayenne was removed from his position as Lieutenant General; all the acts and de-

liberations of the Estates of 1593 were revoked; all prelates and lords
were commanded to renounce their affiliation with the League under
pain of treason; all the "writs, statutes, and oaths given since December 1588 which were made without the authority of the King and
which were prejudicial to the laws of the realm" were declared null and
void.[18] It was not, however, until a month later that the reactionary
faculty of the Sorbonne signed a declaration acknowledging Henri to
be the lawful King of France and enjoining upon his people the
obligation to obey him.

CHAPTER XIV

The Wine of Victory: 1594–1597

By divine grace, by the prayers and good advice of my servants
. . . and by my own pains and labors, I have saved the kingdom
from loss.

Henri de Navarre

With the formal declaration of the Sorbonne, even those who had long fought the Béarnais were impelled to admit him as their lawful sovereign. Even so, however, Henri found that winning his kingdom was a slow and expensive business. For every Leaguer—mayor or governor or captain—had his price. When a member of the Paris Parlement remarked affably to the King that he was very happy to see him in Paris where he belonged and was glad that "what belongs to Caesar has been rendered unto Caesar," the King replied brusquely, "Ventre Saint Gris, I haven't been treated like Caesar; it was not given (*rendu*) to me but sold (*vendu*) to me."[1] Before the year was over, Henri was often to feel more like a merchant than a king; yet when Sully remonstrated at his buying what already belonged to him, he reminded him that it would cost ten times as much if he had to fight for it.

Four months before, at the expiration of the truce with Mayenne, a number of towns rather than engage in renewed fighting had capitulated to the King, among them Bourges, Meaux, Havre de Grâce. Shortly before his coronation, the important city of Lyons had acknowledged his rule. Now with both Parlement and the Sorbonne declaring in his favor, the threat of papal disapproval had but little power and soon a spate of towns in Picardy and Normandy swung to the King. Even Villars, who had fought so long to keep Rouen out of royal power, now capitulated to Henri. Devotion to the King was never sufficient motive for capitulation, however, and with each territory gained, the royal treasury dipped dangerously: for Toulouse, Joyeuse received 1,470,000 pounds; Cambrai cost over a 1,000,000 pounds while Amiens, Péronne, and Abbeville cost the King 1,261,000 pounds. Yet the King did not complain. To him France was worth a thousand treasuries.

That Easter he spent peacefully in Paris winning to him even those who still continued to doubt his sincerity, as he attended Holy Week services with obvious devotion. He knew what would please his people and he gave it to them in abundance: on Maundy Thursday he brought the poor to the Louvre and himself washed their feet according to the ancient custom; that evening he visited the sick in the Hôtel Dieu, distributing alms with a lavish hand. By torchlight he visited the prisons, pardoning those who merited it and freeing those who had been imprisoned by the League. "Gestures of piety which cost the King little but served him well in the opinion of the people," commented L'Estoile.[2]

He was still in the first flush of success when Gabrielle, who was noticeably pregnant at his coronation, gave birth to a son. On June 7, in the valley town of Chauny near the border of Picardy, was born the child who was grandiloquently named César. Gabrielle's reputation was far from untarnished and the attending physician was but repeating common gossip when he suggested diffidently to the King that there might be some question of the child's paternity. Henri was no blind lover; Gabrielle was young, she was beautiful and in her veins ran the questionable blood of Les Babous. It was a dangerous heritage. More than once the King had had to confront her with her "indiscretions," but Gabrielle, tearful and aghast, had protested against the gossip that her detractors had stirred up against her. In the summer of 1593, however, the King, with more than mere rumor to corroborate his suspicions, had written her a letter threatening the end of his love unless she could promise him fidelity: "There is nothing which continues my suspicions nor has the power to increase them more than the way you act toward me. . . . You know how I have been offended in your presence by the visit of my rival. The power your eyes have over me saved you half of my complaints. Yes, you made amends with your lips but not with your heart apparently. . . .

"All things considered, you must be the judge if you should not banish the cause of this trouble. This is what I hope for; can you swear to me that you have done so? Yet what faith can I put in your promises which you have already broken twice. I must see some results. . . . It is no longer enough to say, 'I am going to do it'; now one must say, 'I am doing it.' Take this resolution, then, my mistress, to have but one lover. . . . I have such a desire to see you that I would willingly sacrifice four years of my life for the power to do so. . . ."[3]

Now, however, so great was the King's desire to father a child in Gabrielle's womb that he was deaf to the rumors that questioned this child's paternity. What concerned him was not the question of César's paternity but of how to legitimate this doubly adulterous child. Thus were initiated proceedings to nullify the marriage of Gabrielle and Nicolas d'Amerval. The hearings were the stuff of comedy: the judge was selected with care and not long after the successful conclusion of the case came into a very profitable episcopal see. Gabrielle affirmed that despite her protests against this marriage, her father had stood firm and threatened her with the punishment of filial disobedience if she did not acquiesce. She assured the court that she had known nothing of D'Amerval's impotency before their marriage, and testified on oath that she had lived with him for almost two years —although it was common knowledge that they had not shared the same roof for more than a few months. D'Amerval's testimony was punctuated with even more discrepancies. It was true, he avowed, that their marriage had never been consummated; it was true that they had never lived together as man and wife. This was because of his impotency. Yes, it was true that he had had four children by his first wife, but since then he had suffered a serious accident. No, he had not told his wife this. No, there was no one who was inciting him to procure an annulment. The same questions elicited the same answers from Gabrielle: no, she did not wish to continue their marriage; no, there was no one who was influencing her to ask for this annulment.

Additional interrogations brought to light no further evidence; the case had obviously been settled before it ever came to court. On December 23 the official verdict was rendered: the marriage between Nicolas d'Amerval and Gabrielle d'Estrées was null and void. And young César was on his way to being the legitimate son of the man who had just been declared the lawful king of France.

Almost six months to the day after the capitulation of Paris, Henri made his formal entrance into the city. Just at dusk the King rode toward the Porte St. Jacques where the mayor and the officers of the

city, accompanied by troops from Mantes and St. Denis, awaited him.
His horse was dapple-gray and he himself was dressed in gray velvet
liberally embroidered with gold; on his head was the now legendary
hat with its white plume. Before him rode Gabrielle in a litter so
magnificent that only royalty would presume to use it. She was dressed
in black satin and so glittered with jewels that, as one Parisian commented, she dimmed the light of the torches. It was just eight
o'clock when the King crossed the Pont Notre Dame and joined the
members of Parlement awaiting him at the Cathedral. The King was
not an unimpressive figure on horseback; he was straight and lean and
rode like a master. His short, thin legs, which were always a source of
chagrin to him, did not matter here and even the great nose lost its
angular outline in the light of the torches. The King, however, had
little physical vanity and took his pride in the beauty of the woman
whom he loved. Gabrielle was thin and lithe again after the heavy
months of her pregnancy, and her blond beauty glowed against her
black satin gown. Although the King was generally impatient with
ceremony, he never grew weary of that spontaneous acclaim by which
the people acknowledged him as their King. "He was smiling," observed L'Estoile, "and very happy to hear the people shouting, 'Long
live the King.' His hat was in his hand most of the time, especially
since he saluted all the ladies in their windows."[4]

It was, however, to be one of the last experiences of unmarred joy
that the King was to experience for a long time, for his triumphant
entrance into Paris was the prologue to those years of kingship in
which all the burdens of his people weighed upon the head of the
sovereign himself. For years he had placed his happiness on some future event: a truce with his cousin Henri III, the overthrow of the
League, his conversion, his coronation, the capture of Paris. Once
Paris was his, he thought to reign secure. Paris was his now and in
his hand he carried the scepter of France. While it was true that this
brought its own kind of security, it also brought its own suffering. His
high hopes that the example of Paris would bring the rest of his
kingdom in its wake had diminished, and although the League's power
was weakened, Mayenne and Mercoeur obstinately retained the leadership of the party and continued their alliance with Spain. There were
those who averred that the leaders of the League would never recognize
him until the Pope did—and of that there seemed small hope. On the
other hand, his conversion had made his relations with England, the

Low Countries, the German Princes far less cordial; and yet it was upon them that he must count for help.

The loneliness and uncertainty of his position was augmented by the death of several men who had served him since the death of Henri III. Biron had been killed near Epernay the year before. The previous summer the young Cardinal de Bourbon, who had headed the *Tiers Parti*, had died. And that fall Henri had received word of the death of François d'O who had advised and assisted him during the uncertain days following the assassination of Henri de Valois. On December 14 the King celebrated his forty-first birthday with the melancholy awareness that none of his cousins had lived so long and that his own mother and father had both died at the age of forty-four.

Before the end of the year, death made its way to his side as well, for on the evening of December 27, as he held audience in Gabrielle's apartments, a young man—no more than a boy—slipped unnoticed toward the chair where Henri sat and thrust his needlesharp knife at the King's throat. The blow missed, for the King had just bent over as the assassin aimed his knife. The weapon spun from the criminal's hand and lay on the floor glittering in the light of the candles. In the confusion of assisting the King, whose mouth ran with blood, the Comte de Soissons noticed a small slight figure trying to make his way through the crowd. He was seized and after his first terrified denials he told his interrogators all they wanted to know. That same night, the King, who had sustained only a minor injury, wrote a circular letter describing in detail the attempted assassination. "This is the news of the tragic accident which was plotted against me and how it has pleased God in His mercy to miraculously preserve me from it. I had just arrived in this city about two hours before, returning from my trip into Picardy and I was still booted, surrounded by my cousins, the Prince de Conti, the Comte de Soissons, and the Comte de Saint-Paul, and about thirty or forty other men of the court. I had just received Ragny and Montigny who had not yet greeted me, when a young boy named Pierre Chastel [sic], a little fellow who could not be more than eighteen or nineteen, the son of a cloth merchant of this city, who had slipped unperceived into the room with the rest of the crowd, tried to thrust a knife into my body. Since I was bending over to raise up Montigny and Ragny, the blow only struck my upper lip, injuring a tooth. The poor wretch was seized at once and having at first tried to deny the deed, immediately confessed all without any force being used on him. There is very little to be gained from him except that he attended a Jesuit college for three years where, I presume, he received this excellent instruction. The first thing I thought of was to thank God for the singular grace to be protected from this assassin, and I immediately had the *Te Deum* chanted in all the churches of the city; in addition to which, the people had bonfires of gratitude in all the streets."[5]

In the interrogation that followed, Châtel made no effort to exculpate himself from the charges of regicide. He told his interrogators that for three years he had attended the Jesuit college of Clermont, particularly under the tutelage of Father Jean Guéret. Often a prey to despair and believing himself damned because of his sins and impure desires, it came to his mind that if he were to perform some great and extraordinary deed he might alleviate his sufferings. Thus, he thought to kill the King and so diminish the pain of his eternal torment. "Asked where he had learned this novel theology, he replied in the study of philosophy in the Jesuit college. When asked if he had ever been in the 'meditation room' where the Jesuits perpetrate their greatest crimes . . . he answered that he had often been in this room." He then added that he had been taught that "it was lawful to kill kings, even the reigning king, since he was not a member of the Church . . . because he had not yet been approved by the Pope."[6]

In addition to his own confession, there was found on his person several little religious charms and a note with the words: "Lord, give me strength to do to death Henri de Bourbon." There was no need for his judges to deliberate, and Jean Châtel, son of Pierre the cloth merchant, was condemned to the horrors of the death reserved to regicides. On December 29 he was carried in a tumbril to the Cathedral of Notre Dame and there in the pentrating cold, with a single coarse shirt clinging to his thin underdeveloped body, he knelt on the steps to ask pardon for his crime. His voice was strong and clear, undiminished by the tortures he had already undergone or the fear of those that awaited him. In the Place de Grève, before the throng that came to watch him die, his stoicism never deserted him, as though he truly believed that if he could escape something of those eternal pains which he so desperately feared, no other suffering would be too much to bear. By evening the crowd that had come to watch his pain was satisfied; his body had been destroyed, his ashes thrown to the winds, and the soul of Jean Châtel had gone to that unknown region where bewildered fanatics who destroy themselves and others in the name of God may find merciful judgment.

The death of Jean Châtel did not close the case, however; there still remained the evidence against the Jesuits. When the college of Clermont was searched, fresh evidence was produced, for there was discovered in the room of the rector, Jean Guignard, a collection of writings manifestly seditious. Guignard's judges found him guilty of *lèse-majesté* and condemned him to be publicly hanged. Jean Guéret was temporarily imprisoned, while the Society of Jesus (now commonly called the Society of Judas) was condemned to banishment from France as "corrupters of youth, disturbers of the public peace, enemies of the King and of the state."[7]

The King who had so often faced death at a gallop, had stumbled a little at this attempted assassination. There was a strong sense of paternalism in his concept of kingship and he was struck with horror before the crime of patricide. His spirit had been darkened by the sight of Jean Châtel, looking no more than a child, yet convinced that the King's death was the most pleasing act he could offer to God. As the *Te Deums* were chanted in the churches of Paris and the winter night blazed with fires of joy and gratitude, he could not throw off his unaccustomed melancholy. When, the following week, he attended a procession in Paris, L'Estoile observed: "He was dressed entirely in black, his face was sad and melancholy, with a small bandage over his wound. . . . One of the lords near the King, commenting on this, said: 'Sire, see how your people rejoice to see you!' But the King shook his head and said, 'These are a people, all right. If my worst enemy were now standing where I stand, they would shout even louder.'"[8]

It was not only the King who was frightened and depressed by this near escape from death, but his court officers as well, as they were brought face to face with the prospect of what would happen to France should the King die without issue. When Mornay received the news at Saumur, he wrote, "As I see it, we have been close to shipwreck"; and in a more explicit letter to the secretary of state, Villeroy, he wrote on January 1: "I maintain that if we wish to assure the life of His Majesty, it is necessary to urge his marriage. When one sees that the state will not die with his person, things will not have to be quite so vigilant. All other precautions are too weak against the devilish schemes of this world." With this as his goal, Mornay wrote to the King, encouraging him to marry and also to terminate his relationship with Gabrielle—a relationship which Mornay's strong moral sense could not tolerate. He grew thin-lipped with anger at the thought of this Circe with her golden hair, riding before the King on his solemn entrances, lying beside him in his bed when he received his ministers, as though she were truly queen. To Mornay a brush with death such as the King had experienced should be the means of drawing him back to his Christian duties, and in this tone he wrote to Henri: "God wishes to be heard when He speaks; he wishes us to feel it when He strikes us. . . . I am sure that Your Majesty will profit from this affliction . . . thus converting yourself entirely to Him in turning from all that provokes His wrath. Sire, it is not as a censor that I speak, for I would not be so presumptuous, but with the zeal of a servant."[9]

The King had indeed profited, as Mornay had suggested, from his brush with death; and he was also giving serious thought to his marriage. Perhaps he might also have agreed with his Huguenot minister that it was unseemly to treat his mistress as though she were his queen. For Henri, however, the simplest solution to the whole problem was to marry his mistress. Yet even Henri recognized that the time was not ripe for such a measure. The first step had been taken, however: Madame de Liancourt had been released from her marriage vows. The next step was to ensure the legitimacy of her child, César. The act which Henri sent to be registered in Parlement on February 3 read in part: ". . . since God has still not ordained that we should have children through our legitimate marriage, for the Queen our spouse has been separated from us for ten years, we have wished while awaiting children who can legitimately succeed to this crown, to have others who in their own place will be both worthy and honorable. . . . For this reason, recognizing those graces and perfections of both body and soul which we have found in the person of our well-beloved Gabrielle d'Estrées, since we have sought for some years for someone whom we judged worthy of our friendship, and since this woman after long pursuit on our part and in recognition of our authority has condescended to obey us and to please us by giving us a son who presently bears the name of César Monsieur . . . we have resolved in affirming and recognizing him as our natural son to accord these letters of legitimation."[10]

The implications of the document went far beyond the legitimation of César to the far more dangerous question of the King's marriage. It was obvious that the children whom he said he was "awaiting" would not come from Marguerite. There was then, without doubt, the question of another marriage; this, juxtaposed with his high praise of Gabrielle who "merits" his friendship, put his ministers in a state of grave uneasiness. The thought of Henri without an heir was unthinkable; but the thought of this demimonde sitting on the throne of France as Queen Consort was even more unthinkable. A worthy queen must be found. Thus began that long course of negotiations which eventually placed another Florentine at the right hand of the fleur-de-lys.

Even Mornay realized, however, that the King's marriage must wait upon the urgent state of France itself. A year earlier the King had written: "The King of Spain turns all his intention, strength, and plots to making war on me, thinking that if he succeeds in ruining me, he will be able to establish his rule over all of Christendom which is what he aspires to."[11] The year that followed had changed nothing. The Spanish troops that had been driven out of Paris had made their headquarters in the territory about Laon, and despite the mutual recriminations between Mayenne and Feria, the Fat Duke continued in the service of Spain.

For some months the possibility of open war with Spain had been in the air. Henri risked much should he make such an open declaration, and yet he knew also that he had much to gain. Such a decision would provide proof positive to the Protestant powers who had been watching him nervously since his conversion that he had no intention of capitulating to Catholic demands. Both Elizabeth and the Low Countries had their own reasons for wanting war with Spain and Henri felt assured of their help if he took the first step; otherwise, he feared that England's help might be drawing to a close. In October his ambassador to Elizabeth, Beauvais la Nocle, had reminded him of his great unpaid debts to the English queen; for reply Henri could only write: "I am so involved in business and so overwhelmed with difficulties and urgent needs that it is not possible for me to do any more at the moment. . . . Take courage, I beg of you, and live in the hope that I will not always be so short of means."[12]

Early in the winter of 1594 Henri called an assembly consisting of the Princes of the Blood, the officers of the crown, and the chief members of his council. On January 16, 1595, they issued a solemn declaration of war against Spain. Sully who, from the beginning, had tried to dissuade the King from this action could predict nothing but ruin for France, and the first months seemed to prove him right. Although Henri worked miracles in rallying the French leaders to his cause, in fortifying towns, in levying troops, yet from the start the advantage was on the side of Spain. Henri had not been unaware of the difficulties of open war, for even before the official declaration he had written to his ambassador in the Levant: "To speak freely to you . . . I cannot sustain alone the burden of this war, from which it seems that the Queen of England wishes to withdraw, so that if those of the provinces unite, I will find myself abandoned on all sides. . . . Yet there are ways of injuring the King of Spain even in his own country, which is what he fears most; for I know that the Moors and many other lords desire nothing so much as a change from the yoke of his tyranny—and this even in Spain itself."[13] But Henri's offensive war was doomed, for he had failed to take into consideration that if war can be the means of uniting all Frenchmen, then that same war will unite all Spaniards no matter what their personal dissatisfactions. The few victories gained in Beaune and Autun were small compared to the advances made by the Spaniards, especially in the north.

To the French troops that winter seemed endless. Days of blinding snow alternated with torrential rains until the French soldiers forgot what it was to have dry clothes on their backs or food in their stomachs. And through it all came the winds—strong, piercing, blowing across those vast fields which in summer were golden with wheat or yellow with rye. Now they were cracked and uneven with frozen mud, or even worse, flooded by the rivers that had overflown their banks. The huts of the peasants collapsed before the double assault of flood and wind, and in some places the plague broke out. Even the natural rhythm of the universe seemed disrupted for they spent Easter day trying to protect themselves from another snowfall.

Henri had gone to Paris for Easter, but it was rumored that he intended to spend it at Fontainebleau with his sister so that he could celebrate it *à la Huguenote*. He had made his public abjuration, he had asked Rome to affirm his act, he conducted himself as a Catholic, yet still the rabble bayed triumphantly at the smallest hint of his insincerity. To the man who had told him the gossip, he replied bitterly: "The people is a beast which allows itself to be led around by the nose, especially the people of Paris. . . . To show them how wrong they are, I shan't budge from this spot."[14]

It was not only religion that lessened the King's popularity, it was Gabrielle as well. The time he spent with her, the money and jewels which he lavished upon her made France wonder if the careless extravagance of the Valois were coming upon them again. Although the streets of Paris grew daily more crowded with beggars, Gabrielle rode abroad in a green riding dress lavishly embroidered with gold and which, it was rumored, had cost the King more than two hundred crowns. It was all very well for the King to say, "I pity my poor people," but words cost little and the people of Paris demanded a more tangible proof of his devotion. The King himself, the people knew, was a man of simple tastes; he had grown up on the mountain food of Béarn and had never acquired the tastes of his Valois cousins. A hard bed, a few hours' sleep, a little wine to chase his thirst— for he never became a hard drinker—was all he needed. Except for those occasions when he felt France demanded a pageant, his clothes, too, were those of the soldier rather than the king. Although he had had nothing but scorn for the childish irresponsibility of his royal cousin who had lavished his fortune on the schemers who surrounded him, now to those who watched he seemed blindly to follow the same pattern. He had once told Gabrielle that she bewitched him, and he had not exaggerated. Within months he had lavished upon her the abbeys of Longvaux, St. Corneille, Lessaydes, Fontenoy, La Ferté. The Florentine ambassador, amazed that this shrewd, hard-headed king should be so enthralled, observed that he treated her as though she were his legitimate wife.

In mid-May the King decided that the journey into the east of France which he had planned for so long could not be put off. By June he had reached Dijon where the Spanish forces were strong. Here the King sent Biron, the son of the old admiral, to reconnoiter in order to determine if the major body of the Spanish army under Velasco was in the neighborhood. On the way Biron met a French scout who assured him that all was clear, that only a small group of Spanish cavalry was in the vicinity. The message was relayed to Henri who began to advance with a small body of horsemen. But as Biron reached the top of a little hill, he saw massed in the valley below the full Spanish force. Retreat was impossible, and Biron's greatest fear was that he had unwittingly led the King into a trap. Henri in his turn was bewildered by the unexpected scope of the conflict; badly outnumbered and without even a breastplate to protect him, the King led the charge, thus saving Biron but badly jeopardizing his own life. Meanwhile Mayenne, excited at this unexpected opportunity to capture the King of France and thus bring the war to a speedy and victorious conclusion, urged Velasco to surround the French; but Velasco with Spanish caution hesitated, fearful lest this should be a clever ambush contrived by the Béarnais. The moment of his hesitation was all the French needed; reinforced by troops from the rear, they strengthened their position and after a hard skirmish, Velasco withdrew, fearful of risking a total conflict.

Later Henri was to write that while in other battles he had been fighting for victory, at Fontaine-Française he was fighting for his life. He was nonetheless exhilarated by the thrill of the battle and by a victory in which the odds had been so strongly against him, and a few days later he wrote with his old good humor to his compatriot Harambure: "Be hanged for not being with me in a battle I had with the enemy. . . . I will tell you all the particulars when I see you. . . . Hurry, for I need you." In his account to Mornay the cocky spirit of the Gascon came to the fore to replace the unnatural melancholy which had plagued the King. He made no mention of the small margin of his victory and wrote only of the ease with which he had vanquished the foe. The enemy, he wrote, "made an elephant out of a fly," continuing, "the whole army fled from the battlefield, leaving their camp and making for the banks of the river; thus crossing the Saône in great disorder . . . leaving it entirely free for me to transport my commodities."[15]

Fontaine-Française, however, was to be his last victory for many months. Reassured of his own powers, he moved eastward into Franche-Comté where for two months he tried in vain to draw the Spanish general into battle; they were wasted weeks which he could ill afford and toward the end of August, annoyed at his own poor judgment in planning his campaign and angry with both England and the Lowlands whose promises of help were growing cold, he journeyed south to Lyons where he made his solemn entrance on September 4. He was received with enthusiasm, for Lyons had grown weary of the demands of the League. Rather prematurely, a great Arc de triomphe had been erected and a high scaffolding built with ascending and descending stairs. Here on a dais richly draped in green velvet the King sat to receive the homage of the representatives of the Three Estates whom he promised to maintain in their rights and privileges.

Lyons was festive and at peace; Gabrielle was here waiting for him; and in the splendor and comfort of the archbishop's palace, Henri was lulled for a while into feeling that the war was almost at an end. It was to be but a short idyl, however, for word soon reached him that Cambrai was sorely besieged. The siege had begun in August under the redoubtable Spanish general the Comte de Fuentes, who despite his seventy years had never lost his military bearing nor his vigor in carrying out a campaign. Cambrai had been at war, however, before the Spanish had trained their cannon upon it. The governor Balagny was an opportunist who had left the League when he saw that its fortunes were on the wane. He had taken the money the King had given him but had done nothing to fortify the city for which he was responsible. At the same time that Balagny was sending for help to the King, the citizens of Cambrai were also sending delegates, begging to be delivered from their governor whom they accused of usurping power "at the expense of law." But as Henri had once written to Gabrielle, "There is no man so deaf as he who does not wish to hear," and in the soft September air of Lyons, the King was able to put aside the strident demands of the Paris bourgeoisie, the perduring vigilance of his mortal enemy in Madrid, the pleas for help from his beleaguered towns, and narrow his world to Gabrielle and the pleasures of love. Cambrai begged for help; messengers arrived at the archepiscopal palace with their reports of imminent disaster, but the King, though assuring them of his help, dallied. It was not until September 24 that he left Lyons for Paris.

It would have availed nothing to travel northwest to Cambrai, for Henri had neither men nor money to buy men; he must first go to Parlement and present his need for the funds with which to continue the war. On October 1, with the amorous days of Lyons far behind him, he presented himself in the hall of the Paris Parlement. He was again the leader, the man of decisive action, the man who could assess facts and face them squarely. He had little use for the ornate rhetoric of diplomacy, and his address to the members of Parlement was short and almost brusque: "I have come in haste on the advice of my counselors who tell me that my presence is needed here," he began, reminding them that so far he had done well in this war, that God had given him strength over his enemies, but that now there was grave danger in the north. Volunteer soldiers would never be enough; he must have mercenaries and for that he must have money. The Swiss were waiting at the Marne, he informed them, but they would not go beyond it unless they were paid. "Everything is going well. I came at a walk and will return at a gallop. The only thing lacking is money. I have lost my best horses and must get others for the journey." His need for money, he assures them—quick to read their thoughts—"is not for dances and ballets but to chase the enemy back into his own country. Help me and you will soon recognize that you could not have a better king."[16]

It was a stirring demand, but it came too late. Four days later he left Paris and on October 8 he was at Pontoise, but before he could reach Cambrai it had fallen. At the end, Balagny who "preferred to save his life rather than his honor" fled, leaving the citizens a prey to the mercy of the enemy. The fall of Cambrai deeply depressed the King. Once again the margin of time had turned against him, he complained, unwilling to face the fact that had he acted more quickly in Lyons, he might have turned the tide.

If many things had gone wrong in the months since his coronation, one, at least, had reached a happy conclusion. Shortly after Nevers had left Rome in the beginning of 1594, Clement had told D'Ossat that he had never meant to suggest that he was permanently excluding the King of France from communion with Rome; and a few months later, he confided to Cardinal de Gondi that he would consider receiving an envoy from Henri. This matter was kept highly confidential, however, and among the majority of Frenchmen there was open talk of schism. That summer a Catholic nobleman wrote to the King: "May I be allowed to remind Your Majesty that your predecessors often thought of ordering the establishment of an independent patriarch in Rome for much less reason than that now in question. A great part of your Catholic subjects and even many ecclesiastics would joyfully hail such a step. If the Roman Church will not open her doors to Your Majesty, then Your Majesty may rest content with a French Catholic Church in the bosom of which you can remain and make it independent."[17]

D'Ossat, well aware of the temper in France, did not hesitate to warn Clement during an audience on April 14 that if he overtly continued to take the part of Henri's enemies, he might well "lose the obedience of all France"; and that in addition "the Catholic religion would suffer a great setback and all of Christianity irreparable harm." Both Clement and his secretary of state, Aldobrandini, knew that this was no vain threat, and Aldobrandini wrote to Nevers assuring him that "if the King gave signs of repentance the Pope would acknowledge publicly that he had never actually closed the door nor excluded him absolutely; and that in all these matters he had been concerned not with human interests but solely with the service of God."[18] When Gondi returned to France in August, he brought a definitive answer from the Holy See: Rome was ready to receive an ambassador from the court of France. Two months later, Henri was further encouraged by a letter from François Cardinal de Joyeuse in Rome, who had been representing the League at the Vatican, begging to be received into the service of the King and promising his devoted service. On October 16 the King wrote to Joyeuse, assuring him of his gratitude and telling him that he could give no greater proof of his devotion nor render any more valuable service than to help in winning the Pope to believe in his sincerity and thus acknowledge his conversion.

At the very time, however, when Henri was protesting his sincerity to Joyeuse, he was engaged in drawing up a petition to Gondi asking for the dissolution of his marriage with Marguerite. Gondi was appalled, knowing that if word of this ever reached the Pope it might well end negotiations with the Vatican. The King's sudden and urgent interest in annulling his marriage could not have been more poorly timed and those who knew of it did not fail to make the parallel with another case of annulment and the fate of the kingdom across the Channel. The King was prevailed upon to postpone the question of his marriage till the primary issue with the Church was settled; and on the advice of Gondi he appointed Jacques Davy Du Perron, Bishop of Evreux, as French ambassador to the Vatican. Du Perron was in some ways a strange choice; a man of charm, influence, and immense learning, in his youth he had been a zealous Calvinist before converting to the Church of Rome. He had been an impressive figure in the negotiations preceding Henri's conversion and Gondi, who had had long practice in assessing the Pope's reactions, felt that no prelate in France was better equipped to undertake the present delicate negotiations.

When Du Perron's appointment was made public, Spanish tempers ran higher than ever, and D'Ossat wrote to France: "The Spanish continue their wicked schemes, calumniating the King and begging the Pope to send into France the troops that had been levied for Hungary."[19] Sessa, the Spanish ambassador to the Vatican, beside himself with anger, dared to recall to the Pope the day on which he had promised not to absolve Henri and suggested that Clement keep his word like a "gentleman." Insults, however, had never moved Clement, and D'Ossat felt certain that the Pope would not back down on his decision, for reconciliation with France was obviously to the interests of the Holy See. "By his refusal to admit you," D'Ossat wrote to the King shortly before Christmas, "he remains by that fact excluded himself from the first kingdom of Christianity and can enter it only by your grace and his absolution. . . . The Pope . . . has greater need for you to receive his absolution than you yourself. Thus, things being in this state, it is easy to judge who would lose more if this absolution is refused."[20]

Throughout the remainder of the winter the Vatican waited with increasing impatience for the French ambassador, and when by June Du Perron had still not come, D'Ossat wrote in some anxiety to Villeroy telling him that Du Perron's arrival was a major topic of conversation in Rome and that his continued delays were very displeasing to the Pope. At last on July 12 Du Perron arrived in the holy city, avoiding the crowds which gathered at the Del Popolo Gate with what the Pope felt was laudable humility. When, on July 16, he was received in official audience, the atmosphere could not have been more favorable. By the end of the month it was clear that Clement had made his decision. Although there were many difficult issues involved, both sides were willing to make whatever concessions were necessary for ultimate success. Clement, aware that the cardinals would demand some share in his final decision, yet fearful lest a consistory might swing the tide against the French King, spent the days from August 7 to August 23 seeing each member of the College of Cardinals individually to learn their views. It was a masterful stroke of diplomacy, and on August 30 at Monte Cavallo on the Quirinal, the Pope in consistory announced that two-thirds of the cardinals favored an absolution to the French King. Cardinal Colonna, who for months had devoted his energies to the cause of Spain, rose to speak to the Pope's decision, but Clement, with a gesture of pontifical finality, imposed silence and brought the consistory to a close.

The King upon learning the good news, wrote triumphantly from Lyons: "I have just had news from Italy informing me that the Pope will give me his absolution on the twenty-first of this month."[21] Du Perron had performed his task with consummate skill and the conditions imposed upon Henri were those he could easily accept: that the Catholic faith be reestablished in all places where it had been abolished (especially in Béarn); that the young Prince de Condé should be brought up in the Catholic faith; that the candidates for bishoprics and abbeys be submitted for approval to the Holy See; that the decrees of the Council of Trent at last be published in France—with the exception of those which would go against the peace of the realm; that the King promise to protect religion and to secure the clergy against violence. In addition, Henri was reminded of those devotional duties which had always been enjoined on the Most Christian King: to hear Mass every Sunday and feast day; to say the rosary on Sunday and the litanies on Wednesday, and to fast on Friday; to confess and communicate publicly at least four times a year.

On September 17 the ceremony of papal absolution took place in the basilica of Saint Peter. By early morning the square before the basilica was crowded with people, for it was not every day that they could watch a pageant on which the fate of Europe depended. In the hall of the consistories, thirty-four cardinals from the Sacred College gathered to escort Clement VIII to Saint Peter's. Surrounded by his cardinals, Clement, dressed in white vestments and gold slippers and with the full weight of the papal tiara on his head, took his place on the gold-draped dais outside the doors of the basilica. Here the representatives of the French King were brought and on their knees made the abjuration in the name of their sovereign. At the feet of His Holiness they recited the *Miserere*, David's psalm of repentance, while the Pope struck them lightly with a little scourge, as the ancient formula prescribed. When they had finished, the Pope, his voice raised to carry into the square, declared that Henri de Bourbon, King of France, was absolved from all ecclesiastical censures. It was the first time that Henri had received his full official title, "Most Christian King of France and of Navarre." With the words of the Pope's proclamation, the silence ended, the doors of Saint Peter's were thrown open, the bells from the tower pealed, the cannon from the Castel Sant' Angelo were fired, and in the heart of Christendom the *Te Deum* was sung to commemorate the end of a long and dangerous conflict. For most Frenchmen the event was one of spontaneous joy; only such an entrenched Huguenot as Agrippa d'Aubigné could write caustically that the Pope had "Cleaned his slippers on the fleur-de-lys."[22] But the King who guarded the fleur-de-lys never thought for a moment that the lilies of France had been humbled and read with exultation the papal bull which began: "When we consider the superabundance of the divine grace shown in your conversion and carefully ponder in our mind how you have been brought into the light of Catholic truth from the deepest obscurity of error and heresy, as though from an abyss of evil, by a mighty act of the hand of the Lord, we feel ourselves constrained in our wonder and admiration to exclaim with the Apostle: 'O the depth of the riches of the wisdom and of the knowledge of God!

How incomprehensible are His judgments and how unsearchable His ways!' "23

On November 12 Henri wrote to the Pope expressing his deep gratitude and assuring him of his filial devotion: "I am aware that no words can adequately thank Your Holiness . . . for bestowing your holy blessing and sovereign absolution. . . . I dare to assure Your Holiness that God will be glorified in this good work, His Church restored in France, the Holy See honored and respected as it should be, and the person of Your Holiness exalted, cherished, and obeyed uniquely and constantly by me and by all Frenchmen to the end of time. . . . I pray God, Most Holy Father, that He will preserve you long and happily in the government of our Holy Mother Church."24

D'Aubigné, however, was not alone in his cynical condemnation of the act which had taken place at Rome. For most of the Huguenots it was but one more measure that weighed the scales against them. Shortly after Henri's abjuration at St. Denis they were vocal not only in declaring their disapproval, but also in demanding a protector for the Huguenot churches—an implicit accusation that the King-turned-Catholic would no longer uphold them. When the King flatly refused, Mornay had written to him: "Do you wish to overcome the Huguenot desire for a protector? Then take away the need of one. Be yourself their protector." The King could hardly afford to turn his former coreligionists against him, and at his suggestion they assembled at Mantes in the fall of 1593. In December he addressed them, in another effort to convince them that his act of conversion was in no way a repudiation of his old friends: "I have sent for you," he began, "for three reasons. The first is that you hear from my own mouth that my conversion has brought no change in my affection for you."

But the Huguenot leaders had been embittered not only by the King's abjuration but by the clause of his coronation oath by which he promised to "drive out all heretics from the kingdom." Contemptuous too of his public libertinism, they listened with suspicious ears to his continued avowals of friendship. After Châtel's attempt on his life, D'Aubigné, with his usual moral righteousness, had presumed to say to Henri "God whom as yet you have abandoned only with your lips, has contented Himself with piercing your lips, but when the heart shall have renounced him, He will pierce the heart."25

While the King determined to give the Huguenots some measure of religious liberty, Gondi was cautioning him that acts favoring the Reformed Religion might easily disrupt the progress that D'Ossat was making in Rome toward recognition by the Holy See. In January 1595, however, the King presented to Parlement his desire to renew the Edict of 1577, the most liberal legislation ever enacted for the Huguenots, which permitted them not only a good measure of freedom of worship but also the right to hold public office. Yet even with the King's open approval, Parlement argued bitterly for almost two weeks; when it was finally put to a vote the measure was passed by the narrow margin of six votes. But the Huguenots, now become as captious as the League, would not be satisfied. The King, knowing that even this measure was being interpreted by the Spanish faction at Rome as a proof of his insincerity, realized that he could go no further. He had done all that prudence would permit; he could do no more. These were bitter days when, contrary to his own spontaneous spirit, he weighed and measured every act only to find that whatever decision he came to some faction would find a way of turning it against him.

Although the papal absolution was a further source of discontent for the Huguenots, it was, happily, a major factor in weakening the opposition of the League. When Dijon fell to the King in the summer of 1595, it left Mayenne neither a safe refuge, nor sufficient soldiers for battle. When news of the King's reconciliation with Rome reached France, Mayenne's hand was forced. Less than a week after the ceremony at the Vatican, Mayenne signed a preliminary peace treaty with the King.

In December the King went to the château of Folembray, one of the castles built by François I that had been abandoned during the years of war; and here, despite the bats and owls which had taken refuge in the chimneys and turrets, the King celebrated his forty-second birthday. It was a strange company that gathered to pay him homage, for along with the ever present Gabrielle and her child César, was his sister Catherine, and with her his former mistress Corisande. D'Aubigné, for whom any mistress was a scandal, leveled his shafts at Corisande as well as Gabrielle, accusing her of playing the part of Circe—an ironic barb when directed at the heavy, graying woman who sat watching Gabrielle wearing the King's favor with the same careless confidence with which she wore his jewels. For more than three weeks the strange menage continued. The King spent most of his days in the forest of Coucy hunting deer, while the women sat before the fireplace in the dark, barren hall of the château. For each of them her love for the King had been at some time the pivot of her life; yet now instead of drawing them together, their love was a two-edged sword that kept them apart—lonely, fearful and suspicious.

There was more than enough time for reflection in the weeks they spent at Folembray—more than enough for Corisande to appraise herself, her quondam lover, and the woman who had succeeded her. She had not been young when she had given herself to the King. She had been married and had borne two children; she had lived through war, fled from a besieged city, been widowed by the violent death of her husband. She had known suffering and had understood that love itself, if the jewel is properly cut, will have a facet of pain. Gabrielle had had none of this to offer to the King; but in its stead she had the self-assurance of youth, limitlessly hopeful in what life had to offer. Corisande could well be forgiven if she felt a flare of anger in Gabrielle's supreme self-confidence. What could this child share of the dreams of a king? What could she give him beyond the grace of her body? What did she know of passion who had known so little of danger or pain? It had come so easily to her; she was like some changeling from an old romance brought suddenly from the forest into the palace of the king to be clothed and fed, flattered and fondled. This was the stuff of fairy tales to be told in peasants' huts or nurseries. For Corisande, love was something quite different. She had thought once that it was eternal but Folembray with its broken windows and torn gables, its dust and barrenness proved to her that nothing is secure against the course of time.

Catherine, too, had little cause to look at Gabrielle with anything but jealousy. For Catherine, despite her narrow moral code, had escaped her mother's influence in many things: she loved masques and balls and elaborate pageants; and, strangely enough, for she was a plain, angular woman, she loved clothes. Having never lived in a world of fashion, she had constructed her own—strange bizarre fashions, wild colors in fantastic combinations, ill-chosen jewelry that flashed awkwardly about her thin neck or called attention to her plain, unflattering coiffure. Her speech, her dress, her halting gait all bespoke a woman who had come out of that strange southern province which had once provided such a rich source for her sister-in-law's caustic wit. It was, however, more than a matter of feminine jealousy which fostered her animosity toward Gabrielle for Catherine seemed largely unaware of how ludicrous her costumes often made her appear. As she watched the love that her brother lavished upon his mistress, it rankled deep that this brother of hers took his love wherever it pleased him, while he had moved her about like his pawn with no thought of her heart's affections. She must marry wherever her brother's interests dictated: the King of Scotland, the Duke of Savoy, the Duc de Lorraine—at various diplomatic crises they had all been mentioned. But Catherine, Jeanne d'Albret's child in more than appearance, had somehow worked her way free from the proposed alliances and in her own time—like her mother—she had fallen deeply in love.

Her cousin, the Comte de Soissons, loved her in return. It was, while it lasted, a true romance that glittered a little with the stuff of secrecy. They had first met as children during the days when their mothers had taken refuge at La Rochelle. They were as unlike as Antoine de Bourbon had been unlike Jeanne d'Albret. Charles de Bourbon had been brought up a Catholic but had not inherited the religious zeal that had made his father and his brother such staunch religious Huguenots. He was a Bourbon through and through, however, in his imperious temper, his reckless courage, his desire for glory. His household was not always moral but it was always intriguing. At first, Henri saw great advantages to having Soissons brought to his side by marriage; but the King, with his keen sense of men, could never quite trust Soissons. He was fractious, arrogant, an intriguer, and, rumor had it that for some time he had been in the pay of Spain. But by the time the King finally decided that this was no fitting match for his sister, his decision was too late.

Catherine, at the age of thirty-three, was passionately in love. Like her mother before her, she was oblivious to all the faults of her lover, to all the discrepancies that such a marriage would entail, to the anger of her brother should she run counter to his will. Helped by Corisande, the two lovers exchanged letters, sometimes met, and, at last, exchanged written promises of marriage. When during the siege of Chartres, the King learned of this he wrote in anger to Corisande whom he felt was largely responsible: "I would not have thought this of you, and I am only going to say one word: I will never forgive the people who are stirring up trouble between my sister and me." Undeterred by the King's anger, Corisande continued to play her role. A year later, Soissons, under pretext of going to see his sick mother, made his way to Pau where Catherine, in the company of Corisande, was waiting to pronounce her marriage vows. Henri, learning of Soissons' deceit, sent a messenger at once to Béarn, to the Seigneur de Ravignan, president of the council at Pau, with orders to thwart the marriage at any cost: "I have heard with great displeasure of the way in which the journey of my cousin Soissons has been arranged," the King wrote. "I will say nothing else about this except that if you consented or assisted against my will, your head will answer for it." Ravignan, who valued his head no less than the King's friendship, sent a company of soldiers into the courtyard of the palace, determined to take the aspiring bridegroom by force if need be. The lovers were parted, the written promises of marriage destroyed, and Catherine was forced to submit to her brother's will. The King, jubilant, wrote again to Ravignan, "I assure you that what you did at Pau was one of the greatest services you have ever rendered me."[26]

During those long days at Folembray, Catherine must have recalled bitterly that while she was expected to be faithful to her obligation to give herself in marriage only where it would most benefit the kingdom, her brother might love where he would. He, meanwhile, with that insouciance to domestic tension which made him a maddening husband and an exciting lover, seemed only to enjoy the winter weeks in the forest of Coucy. It was not all pleasure, however, for Henri was doing his best to conclude a truce with the Duc de Mayenne. The Duke, aware that he was not in a position to dictate terms, indicated that he was willing to make certain concessions, and on January 20, Gabrielle left Folembray for Montceaux to prepare the château for the King's conferences with Mayenne.

On the last day of January, the Duke, accompanied by six gentlemen, arrived at Montceaux where Gabrielle, now officially Duchesse de Montceaux, welcomed him and led him to the dais where the King awaited him. It was a moment which Henri had long prayed for, but its solemnity was tinged with humor for the King, as he bent over to help the ponderous Duke to his feet. "Well, my cousin, is it really you or am I having a dream?" he asked as Mayenne, who had not bent his knee for many a year, awkwardly regained his balance. Later, after a private conference in the King's study, they dined: Gabrielle seated beside the King, and at another table Mayenne in company with her sister Diane. The toast which the King proposed expressed his deepest desires: "To the lasting friendship of the King with my cousin Mayenne; and to the eternal peace of my kingdom."[27]

Mayenne could hardly believe that an enmity so long fostered could be so quickly healed; but that afternoon the King took his legendary revenge. He took his cousin along on his usual afternoon walk, striding along at his rapid pace, while the Duke, grossly overweight, and suffering from sciatica, strove desperately to keep abreast of him. The King talked gaily while his cousin, red-faced, panting, and gasping for breath, finally could continue no longer, but had to ask mercy of this wiry, indefatigable king. The King, amused and gratified, was quick to give his grace, saying: "There, let us shake on it; for by God that is the only suffering or trouble that you will ever receive from me."[28] On February 5 the King and Gabrielle returned to Folembray, and there the official treaty of peace between Henri and Mayenne was signed. By it Mayenne was given full and entire amnesty for himself and his followers, three towns of surety for a period of six years, and the enormous sum of 3,580,000 pounds.

France could ill-afford the price of Mayenne's alliance, but as the King pointed out to his outraged councillors, they could afford his enmity even less. The war was going badly. It was rumored that the King was in such straits that he had been forced to borrow 200,000 pounds from Venice on the royal jewels.

In early April, Calais, with its checkered history, again became a prize for contending forces. When the Spanish first began their siege, no one took them seriously for Calais was so strongly fortified by nature that it was almost impregnable. The citizens, however, had counted so heavily on its natural supports that they had let their fortifications fall into decay; and when on Easter Monday the Spanish bombardment began in earnest, the people sent in panic to the King. But Henri, already engaged in the siege of La Fère, feared that he could not transport sufficient troops to save the beleaguered city. Knowing, however, that Essex had a fleet in the Channel which could immediately be drawn up before Calais, he sent word to both Essex and Elizabeth of the plight of Calais. Essex, despite his friendship with the French King, was not free to move without the sanction of his sovereign, and while the walls of Calais were battered by Spanish cannon, Essex lay at anchor in the Channel waiting for the command that would send him to assist the French. The command never came, for Elizabeth, in answer to Henri's plea, answered that she would succor Calais only if it were given to England. When word reached him of the Queen's answer, he was appalled. He would, he said, rather lose Calais to his enemy than to his friend; and he wrote at once to Elizabeth: "Madame. I have received your letter through Sir Sidney and have heard the proposition which he was charged with making me on your behalf—a proposition which I have found so little resembling the sincerity of that perfect affection which I have always found in you, that I believe rather that it has come from those who do not know your heart. . . . Permit me to say, Madame, what I have already said to Sir Sidney, that I find it unbelievable that in a matter so important and so urgent you would measure your friendship by the advantage that you can derive from it."[29] On April 24, Calais, the invincible, fell before the onslaught of Spanish forces under the command of Archduke Albert, while the sails of the English ships bellowed white and clear in the Channel. If Elizabeth and Henri had sought to outbluff each other, their gamble had benefitted neither of them, —now the Spanish flag flew from the citadel of Calais.

In the summer of 1596 the King assessed his position. He recognized that although there had been some victories, they had been won at a great price. Mayenne had come over to his side, and following his example, Nemours and Joyeuse. But their reconciliation had been a costly business. Marseille had expelled the League and, under the leadership of the young Duc de Guise, had declared for the King. After a bloody siege of seven months La Fère had finally surrendered. These were his victories, but they were but one side of the coin. Picardy after months of fighting was ravaged; during March alone 6,000 impoverished people had come to Paris, crying of hunger in the streets, while the Parisians had hardly enough to sustain themselves. On the first day of March a woman had been condemned to death for having killed both her children because she had no food to give them and could not bear to see them slowly starve to death. The king's army had not been paid for months; they were overwhelmed with fatigue, weakened by sickness, depressed by the show of Spanish strength. Although through the influence of Jerome de Gondi he had been able to borrow 300,000 *écus* from the Grand Duke of Florence, he knew that he could not continue to count on foreign loans. Realizing that there were many matters of state that should be settled and encouraged by Sully, recently appointed a financial councillor, he called a meeting of the leading men of the realm to meet in Rouen in November.

A month before his Assembly of Notables was to open, the King arrived in Rouen accompanied by Gabrielle, who was already nine months pregnant. On October 16 Henri made his solemn entrance into the city which was enjoying a day of Indian summer after interminable days of rain. Six trumpeters announced the King's entrance as he took his place, dressed in pearl-gray satin with his white plume riding high, on the dais erected for him and decorated in green velvet embroidered with golden fleur-de-lys. Here he received the people come to pay him homage; his own speech was a single joyous expression of his delight to be in this city so long the chief city of Normandy and the scene of so many of France's joys and sorrows.

By the beginning of November, the delegates had begun to assemble, and on November 4 the Assembly, composed of nine members of the clergy, nineteen of the nobility, and fifty-two freely elected from the Third Estate, opened its sessions. The meetings were held in the chapter room of the Monastery of St. Ouen; here the King opened the meetings with an address which Sully later wrote was "uttered with dignity becoming a great prince, and a sincerity with which princes are unacquainted. . . ." The King's style, so different from the fulsome rhetoric of the Valois, left some of the delegates dissatisfied; they had expected the pompous oratory, the emotional flourishes which they identified with royal oratory. This King seemed to them brusque, unpolished, too much the soldier and too little the diplomat. It was a speech which L'Estoile characterized as a "fine speech, but brusque and short, in keeping with his humor which was very military at the moment."[80] "If I wished to acquire the title of orator," the King began, "I would have memorized some long, beautiful speech and delivered it solemnly to you; but Messieurs, my desire is for two titles far more glorious: those of liberator and restorer of this state. To this end I have assembled you. You know to your sorrow, as I do mine, that when God called me to this kingdom, I found France not only near to ruin but almost lost to Frenchmen themselves. By divine grace, by the prayers and good advice of my servants, by the swords of my courageous and generous nobility, by my own pains and labors, I have saved the kingdom from loss. . . . My very dear subjects, participate in the second glory with me as you did in the first. I have not called you as my predecessors did, simply in order that you might ratify their plans; I have assembled you to receive your counsels . . . and to follow them. In brief, I put myself into your hands as a student into the hands of his tutors."[81]

Much of what he said, however, was vitiated by his conduct, for it was a known fact that while he earnestly argued his need for money for the salvation of the state, he continued to surfeit Gabrielle with gifts. Even now her presence at the assembly displeased many and antagonized still more when they discovered that she had been hidden behind an arras while the King delivered his speech so that she might pass judgment on what he had said. On November 2 she gave birth to a girl and two weeks later Catherine-Henriette was carried with the pomp reserved for royalty to the baptismal font. There were pages carrying lighted torches; there were trumpets and tambourines and violins. The Swiss Guard led the procession and various dignitaries were pressed into service, with Nevers carrying the sacred oil, Matignon the candle, Epernon the silver basin, and the Prince de Conti the infant herself. The ceremony was performed by the Cardinal de Gondi, who was heard to murmur nervously that he could hardly refuse. The Apostolic Delegate, Alexander de Medici, who had arrived in Paris the previous July, was also in attendance. Although some maintained with embarrassment that it was unbecoming that a bastard be baptized in front of the Papal Legate, the Legate himself, a man of immense sophistication, seemed quite capable of absorbing the subtleties of his position. Catherine de Bourbon alone maintained her moral indignation, objecting that this was no Child of France and three times refusing to play the part assigned her—to lift the poor controversial child and place her in the arms of the Prince de Conti.

Meanwhile the assembly continued on into the new year. Their thorniest problem was—as the King knew it would be—that of finance. The question of taxes, of bribery, of embezzlement; the demand for a more foolproof plan to ensure the royal revenue; the need for a special council to deal with financial problems—all were discussed in endless sessions. Plans which seemed feasible on paper often failed when put to a practical test. These men lacked the experience of financiers and although they were aware of the grave abuses that would have to be corrected if France were to become solvent, they were incapable of drawing up a practical schema of reform. The English ambassador wrote home in disappointment that the assembly had "concluded none of the matter for which it was called"[82]; yet it had not been entirely a waste of time: an opportunity for free discussion had been provided; the problems of corruption in the ranks of all three Estates had been squarely faced; and many of the delegates were given their first opportunity to become acquainted with the King.

The King, however, continued to throw away half of his influence, for although he seemed to have deep concern not only for affairs of state but for the lives and happiness of his people, this concern was not translated into practical terms. Even as the assembly wrestled with the problem of an empty treasure, the King was ordering large quantities of young apricot trees to be transplanted from Pau to the gardens of Fontainebleau and St. Germain-en-Laye. When Gabrielle attended the baptism of Damville's son, the King complained that she did not have enough diamonds in her hair. "There were only twelve and there should have been fifteen." The Tuscan ambassador voiced a popular opinion when he wrote in his report: "It seems that it is not so good for the health of His Majesty to be always with Madame de Montceaux . . . The love of the King for this woman is still increasing and will become an incurable evil unless God stretches forth his holy hand."[83]

God, however, seemed content to stretch out his hand only in blessing, for everything that Gabrielle touched prospered: her father, her brothers, her sisters were living in luxury far greater than they had ever known; and she had already begun to dream of a marriage with the King of France. When on February 13 they returned to Paris, the round of parties and balls continued, and it was often daybreak when the King returned to the Louvre. When his counselors brought to him the pasquinades that were appearing daily in the Paris streets he had no time to listen; and when a scurrilous pamphlet entitled *The Life and Morals of Henri IV* was shown him, he was only amused by its tale of libertinism. Henri would never be reformed by insults; he had lived with them too long for them to do more than prick his skin. Failure alone could prick his conscience to repentance, and on March 13 such a failure was his. As he lay drugged with sleep following a ball, a messenger brought him the news of the fall of Amiens.

CHAPTER XV

The Years of Peace: 1597–1599

I have made peace abroad; now I want it at home. . . . I shall cut
at the root of all factions and all seditious teaching, putting an end
to those who excite it.

Henri de Navarre

❧❧❧❧ There was no dallying in the King's apartments when he
heard the news. He was on his feet in seconds, questioning the
messenger, summoning his council, sending for Sully, dressing even
while he talked. Sully recounts that he himself ran all the way to the
Louvre, not knowing what had happened, but interpreting the "consternation" on the face of the messenger as an omen of ill tidings.
"I saw him walking about very fast, his arms folded," he wrote of
the King, "his head reclined, and all the marks of deep uneasiness
impressed on his countenance. The courtiers stood in different corners of the room, leaning against the hangings, without uttering a
single word. . . . The King said, 'Amiens is taken.'"[1] The shock was
like that of an unexpected and violent death. Sully was silent, as the
King, torn by rage and regret, continued to pace the room, making
plans for ordering up more forces, for beginning a counter siege, for
leaving Paris for Amiens before the morning was over. It was an impressive display of energy, of courage, of decisive action—but it came
too late. Amiens was already lost.

Henri's popularity had waned in the past year and with the Spanish
victory at Calais it had dipped suddenly and frighteningly. Had he
been worsted in battle he would have been met with loyal compassion,
but Calais had not been lost in fair conflict; it had been lost, so it
was said, through negligence. Message after message had been sent to

Lyons, but the King had been like a man dreaming, who will not let harsh facts encroach upon his illusory happiness. When, at last, he had acted, it had been too late. The fact of Calais might have been forgiven, but such mistakes were too costly to bear repetition. With the news of Amiens, a pall fell upon the court, and the Venetian ambassador wrote to the Doge: "Amiens was lost yesterday. It fell to the Spaniards through secret intelligence and agreement which they had with the population. This loss is of such moment that all that has happened hitherto may be reckoned as naught when compared with it."[2]

The loss of Amiens was more than a military casualty; for the French people it became a symbol of failure, a symbol of disappointment in the man whose leadership they had trusted to restore France to her former glory. They had heard his voice above the rancor of conflicting parties, for it had cried "Peace," which was their own deepest aspiration. Yet what peace had he brought them? While he was still battling the intransigent elements of the League, he had declared war on Spain. They were weary of war, weary of hunger, of besieged cities, of fields burned and men killed. The King had promised them that his war with Philip would be an offensive war, but it was a rash promise made without a careful assessment of the enemy or of his own resources. It was not long before the war was back upon French soil—and even so, the defeats had outnumbered the victories. He had promised them that Elizabeth, in her hatred for Spain, would be generous in assisting them, but Elizabeth was playing for her own interests and it was hard to forgive what she had done to them at Calais. While the Archduke Ernest had kept the French engaged in the north, Philip's colleague, the Duke of Savoy, had turned his attention to winning Dauphiny and Provence for himself.

Meanwhile, as the need for men and munitions grew more imperative, taxes continued to increase; yet although his army had not been paid, there was always money for Madame la Marquise, that blond witch who kept him in thrall while fine cities like Amiens fell to the Spanish. Now the Somme was in Spanish hands and once again the road to Paris lay open. Neither strength nor courage had won Amiens, but trickery— and that was the most painful wound of all. The Spanish governor of Doullens, Portocarrero, had planned a ruse of classic simplicity. In league with some Spanish sympathizers in the city, he had led a fairly large force close to the walls. Then, a lumbering cart made its way through the carefully guarded gates; as it stopped, a sack of nuts rolled to the ground, broke, and spilled. While the guards helped the "peasants" reclaim their goods, another man immobilized the wagon by cutting its shafts. With the cart strategically placed so that the portcullis could not be lowered, it was the simplest thing in the world for Portocarrero to march his men into the unsuspecting city. There had been no battle, scarcely any bloodshed; the Spaniards had sacrificed nothing, but had gained all they wanted. They had, in fact, gained more than they could have hoped for, for with the loss of Amiens French morale plummeted to a depth it had not reached since Henri had ascended the throne.

When, several hours after he had received the news, the King left Paris accompanied by a sizable force, he was greeted by little popular acclaim. It was a silent Paris that watched him go, for they could not but think that had their King engaged in more battles and fewer balls this tragedy might have been averted. "I must leave these arms for other arms," Henri had reputedly said to Gabrielle, as he kissed her goodbye; but it would take deeds not words to win back the trust of his people.[3] The King, however, was determined that they would see those deeds. The anxiety which Sully had noted as he waited in the King's apartments was something Henri would not let his people see. It was courage and determination that they needed to witness now, and he would give them an impressive display. It was this which several foreign agents noted in their dispatches; but Villeroy, who knew that no display of courage, however dramatic, would be enough to win back Amiens, wrote to a friend: "The further we advance the more our loss is confirmed. The King has enough courage for everyone, but unless we are helped by men and money and munitions, things will go very badly."[4]

The day following his departure from Paris, the King reached Beauvais, and a week later he set up quarters at Picquigny between Amiens and Abbeville. Here he found conditions worse than he had anticipated; the garrisons were in a bad state; there was no food, no money, no help for the sick; and there was already talk of mass desertion. Frustrated and angry, he turned on those whom he had always considered his friends, accusing them of the hapless position in which he found himself. "Sancy, Sancy," the Venetian ambassador heard him say, "You and the Maréchal de Bouillon advised this war and your ill-starred advice is like to be the ruin of France." Even Biron, who had once saved the King's life, did not go unscathed, as Henri remarked caustically in front of his general that it was strange that whenever he was not present in person things went on "either with little fortune or much negligence." Late in March, in answer to a letter of complaint, he wrote with a kind of brutal realism, the bitter fruit of seeing evils and injustices which he was helpless to remedy: "I received your letters . . . and learned through them of the evils and miseries that afflict Poitou, but these public misfortunes are now so common in my kingdom that they have become the custom." "There is no one to help me," he wrote in his despair to Mornay when he learned that Elizabeth had sent a message indicating that she would help him at Amiens only if Calais were given over to her. Once again he refused, for, as the Venetian ambassador reported, "he would rather be skinned by his foes than scratched by his friends."[5]

On April 12, the King returned to Paris, for without further money at his command it was useless to attempt the recapture of Amiens. It was a strange King who returned to Paris, a King whom few had ever seen before: a silent, withdrawn man, a man who spoke prophetically of his own death, a man quick to anger, unjust in his judgments. His efforts to borrow money from Venice had failed, and he spoke frankly to the ambassador, Duodo, who quoted him in his dispatch: "I am in such a state that I am on the road to ruin and I cannot see the remedy (his very words), and if my dearest friends and confederates do not help me, who will . . . My people are so absolutely ruined that I can look for no help from them. Everything is in such decay that the whole world sees it only too well."[6]

Meanwhile he wrote to Parlement asking that they hold a general assembly in order to get money to help the state, "which is in a more weakened condition than it has ever been." But Parlement, never docile in matters of finance, was loth to give him what he asked. Four days later the president and several members came to the Louvre to confer with the King. Henri, usually so adroit in matters of diplomacy, was beside himself with rage. He would not be questioned, he would not be delayed, certainly he would not be crossed. Three weeks later, he wrote to the Constable: "I am sorry that the gentlemen of Parlement are still making fools of themselves. If it is necessary for me to go to them myself, I will do so; I would prefer to go a dozen times than to see France lost."

On May 21 he made good his threat and came to address Parlement in person: "It is for me a matter of extreme regret, Messieurs, that the first time I should come to my Parlement should be for such a cause as now brings me. I am impelled to come here because of your procrastination, your obstinacy, and your disobedience—and still more for the salvation of the state, of which I have tried to make you see the imminent peril; yet even this has not moved you. I am so driven by my desire to save this state that it has, perhaps, caused me to speak with more sharpness than I ought, and yet it seems that the corruption of this present time demands it."[7]

Five months later, Henri had proved his determination to save the state. Throughout the summer months he had carried on the siege of Amiens with a vigor and resolution which won him the loyalty of his soldiers and the hopes of his people. By the end of August it was apparent that the Spanish could not hold out much longer. On September 15 they acknowledged their defeat and on September 25 formally withdrew from Amiens. The elated King who watched the withdrawal bore little resemblance to the dark, taciturn figure who had ridden out of Paris in June. Mounted on his charger, elaborately bridled and with an embroidered saddle, he was again the master not only of men but of events. The royal baton was in his hand and about him were gathered the Princes of the Blood, the marshals of France, and a good portion of his nobility. From ten o'clock in the morning until well after noon, the Spanish forces filed before the King, doing him reverence as they passed. When the Spanish leader, Montenegro, dismounted before the King, and as a symbol of his defeat, kissed the royal boot, his victory was very sweet. It was sufficient to overshadow that terrible March morning when he was shaken to wakefulness with the news that Amiens was lost.

Success, as always, was the magic formula which drew people to their leader, and from all sides congratulations poured in. From Usson, Margot wrote praising God "for the happy victory it has pleased Him to give Your Majesty. I must express the great happiness with which I received the welcome news." From Rome, D'Ossat assured the King that "victory will help French affairs in Rome." "Let us sing in a thousand ways the praise of this courageous undertaking," ran the songs that were sung in the Paris streets."[8] The King's triumphal entrance into Paris was the capstone of his joy. Although it was not quite noon when he arrived at the Tuileries, the vast crowds made the streets almost impassable and it was close to five o'clock before the ceremonies in Notre Dame were completed and he was free to return to the Louvre.

When L'Estoile had written a few months earlier that "all Europe hangs on the outcome of this siege," he had not exaggerated; for

the question of peace depended in large measure on whether Henri
could make good his promise that he would rout the Spaniards from
Amiens. With the French victory, Philip's proud boast that "it did not
become his dignity to make peace with . . . a relapsed heretic" grew
faint. Spain needed peace and the King of France, finding himself
at last with the edge of victory, intended to push his advantage
hard. The Pope had long urged Spain to settle its difficulties with
France, and as early as September had written to France that the
Holy See would gladly act as mediator in drawing up a treaty. By the
beginning of 1598 Henri wrote jubilantly, "The ministers of the Spanish King are suing for peace more warmly than ever"; on February
3, Bellièvre and Sillery left Paris for Vervins, a town not far from
Cambrai, where peace negotiations were to be carried on.[9]

The negotiations so eagerly initiated were, however, not so easily
concluded. It was not, Henri found, the enemy who posed the
thorniest difficulties, but his major ally. He had foreseen Elizabeth's
objections and had tried to prepare for them by sending De Maisse
as his special ambassador to England to discuss the French position
and listen to Elizabeth's proposals. De Maisse's embassy, however,
had not had the success that the King had hoped for. His first interview
with Elizabeth was an uneasy affair with the Queen restless and
ill-at-ease. He was surprised at how old she looked; her face drawn
and wrinkled, her speech hard to understand because so many of her
teeth were missing. When De Maisse returned to France toward the
end of January, Elizabeth remained opposed to the peace, although she
had agreed to send commissioners to Vervins as Henri had suggested.
Even so she upbraided him roundly through her ambassador, saying
that she could not believe that he was contemplating such perfidy as
breaking a treaty with someone who had always helped him. In a
personal letter, she concluded caustically that "if there were a sin
against the Holy Ghost in temporal affairs, it was that of ingratitude."[10]

The criticism was hardly fair, for Henri had done his best to indicate that he would remain faithful to his promise never to make
a separate peace. Henri could ill afford to sacrifice England's friendship.
Not only did he need her as an ally, but should he ever bend toward
Catholic Spain at the sacrifice of Protestant England, he would lose, as
well, the precarious loyalty of the Huguenots within his kingdom.
The path to peace, he was discovering, was as filled with ambushes as the path to war. He was not unsympathetic with Elizabeth, for her fear of Spanish aggression was by no means unfounded.

The preceding fall Philip had again sent a fleet toward England; like the Armada, almost ten years earlier, it foundered before an adverse wind and was driven back to Spain at a loss of 50,000 ducats. It indicated plainly, however, that Philip's will to power was far from dead.

At the same time that negotiations continued at Vervins, Henri rode into Brittany to come to terms with the last of the League lords to make his submission. Philippe Emmanuel de Lorraine, Duc de Mercoeur, had been one of the most powerful of the League captains. As half-brother to Henri III's Queen Louise, he had been an influential figure, and in his own right an implacable soldier, courageous and resourceful. Even when Mayenne had been reunited to the King at Folembray, Mercoeur still held out, hoping perhaps to realize his aspirations to revert to the old feudal order. When negotiations with Spain began, his position grew increasingly untenable; many small towns had submitted to the King, and many of his own soldiers would prefer peace with the King rather than defeat at his hands, as now seemed inevitable. On March 6, the King met the Duchesse de Mercoeur at Pont-de-Cé and by the end of the month an edict of peace was concluded. Two days later the King and the Duke met in Angers where the peace was confirmed by the betrothal of their two children: Françoise de Lorraine, daughter of the Duke, aged six; and César, Duc de Vendôme, son of the King, aged four. It was a generous peace, for complete amnesty was given Mercoeur and his men; and in return for Brittany he received a large payment and a substantial pension. Sully, impatient with such undeserved generosity, avowed that he would not treat with Mercoeur with anything but a cannon; but the King knew that revenge could never produce a lasting peace and that Mercoeur was a man whose loyal friendship was more valuable than money.

With Mercoeur safely on his side, and with Elizabeth's ambassador, Robert Cecil, sending favorable reports of the proceedings at Vervins, peace with Spain moved forward more rapidly. On May 2, the plenipotentiaries signed the completed documents and on June 21 Paris celebrated the solemn proclamation of peace. It was a ceremony of elaborate proportions, for the fact it celebrated was almost more than Frenchmen could conceive: France was at peace. Neither civil strife nor foreign enemies was battering at the gates. Grandfathers had told stories to their grandchildren of far-off days when France had been at peace, when towns were not always guarded, when it was safe to work in the fields. They were golden stories, dimly remembered, of days that might never come again. But now the King, who for close to ten years had fought to bring peace to his kingdom, had won it at last. The last of the League lords had made his submission, Brittany was back in royal hands, Cambrai was under French rule again, and the Spanish were withdrawing from all the other towns on French soil that they had captured in the last three years. It was hard for the old to remember what peace had been like; it was harder still for the young to conceive what they had never known—yet for all of them the word was a magic incantation, and on June 21 Paris was wild with joy.

The preceding week Alexander de Medici had arrived in Paris. Papal legates had not always been popular in France, but this time an immense crowd followed his red satin litter through the streets, blessing and applauding him as one of the chief instruments of the peace. Five days later, on Sunday, June 21, the formal procession made its way from the Louvre. Scaffolds had been erected along all the streets where the dignitaries would pass, and long before dawn guards were on duty to keep the crowds in place. An hour before noon the King left the Louvre, accompanied by his chief nobles: Montpensier, Nevers, Nemours, Joinville, Mayenne, Epernon, Biron. The King glittered less than his nobles; he was dressed solemnly in black while they had spared no expense on their array: their sword belts flashed with jewels, their small velvet caps were embroidered with seed pearls and thread of gold, their horses were covered with saddle cloths of elaborate tapestry.

Following the Mass, the King rose and walked to the center of the main altar of Notre Dame; here Villeroy, his secretary of state, handed him the illuminated parchment which contained the formula of peace. With his hand on the Gospels, the King proclaimed the words that all France awaited: "We, Henri IV, king of France and of Navarre, promise on our faith and honor to observe and accomplish fully and in good faith all the articles of this peace concluded at Vervins on May 2. . . . I wish to the King my brother a long life that he may enjoy the fruits of this peace."[11] It was, however, too late for such a wish, for even as Henri proclaimed the peace in France, Philip lay dying in the Escorial. Covered with ulcers, unable to move, he was too weak to sign the document; that task was left to his ineffectual heir, Philip III.

The following Tuesday, Paris, which loved ceremonies, was given another one. That day the King came to the Place de Grève, so often the scene of brutal executions, to set fire "with his own hand" to the carts of pikes and halberds and spears which had been gathered there and to the effigy of war which was erected in the square. Nicolas-Edouard Olier, who watched the scene, wrote in his journal: "The Spaniards were at their windows admiring the joy of this great concourse of people which numbered more than five thousand, all bareheaded. . . . When the King arrived to start the fire, there was carried before him a torch of white wax weighing two pounds. Three times he circled the fire accompanied by all his nobility, by the Swiss and Scotch guards, along with the fifes and trumpets which sounded and made a great fanfare along with the people who in their joy cried at the top of their voices, 'Long live the King!' "[12]

If France was at last free from war, she was not yet free from dissension. No sooner had the Papal Legate taken leave of the King at Fontainebleau than the issue which had been stirring since the preceding winter came to the surface. While his emissaries had been coming to terms with the Spanish and Dutch and English at Vervins, Henri had brought together a group of men to discuss and resolve the growing problem of religious freedom in France. Since his conversion four years before, the Huguenots had become increasingly difficult. Even during the war with Spain, they had continued to hold synods, demanding the right to practice their religion throughout France and to resume the full dignity of public life. Whatever the King's personal response to such requests, he was, politically, in no position to grant them, as the Huguenots well knew. "I am offended and annoyed with them," the King had written in the summer of 1596, "as I truly have great reason to be." But the royal displeasure did not impede them, and a year later they published a memorial addressed to the King, entitled *Plainte des Eglises Réformées*. It was a stormy document, angry and resentful, for they feared the results of peace with Spain and objected to the influence the Papal Legate might have in France. As always, the document took its cue from those early days when the King was one of them, and played heavily upon the theme of his betrayal: "We are neither Spaniards nor Leaguers," it read, "nor have we served Your Majesty and the state so poorly that we deserve to be always wretched. We have had the happiness of seeing you born, and cradled, and raised among us; we have brought our goods and our lives themselves to impede the evil will of those who from your infancy sought your ruin."[13] The implications were clear: the enemies who had once sought his life were now in high favor, while the staunch friends of his childhood have been cast out.

Although Henri was often impatient of these appeals to his sentiment, he recognized that the Huguenots were a powerful force, a force sufficient to disrupt the state, which he was striving with all his power to bring to peace. Perhaps with the external pressures removed, he could afford to quiet the tension within by granting the Huguenots the measure of religious freedom they had been demanding for over thirty years. Those seasoned politicians, De Thou, Jeannin, Schomberg, and Calignon were appointed to draw up the terms of such an edict. The document which emerged in the spring of 1598 was not considerably different from some of the legislation that had preceded it. The element which marked it off was not so much its terms as its implementation. On April 13, in Nantes where he was then in residence, the King affixed his royal seal to the document. It provided in effect that Protestants were free to live in all parts of the kingdom of France without fear of being molested. They were free to worship in royal cities and in those places in which such worship was already established, as well as on the estates of Huguenot nobility. Protestant worship was still forbidden at court, in Paris itself, and within a radius of five miles of the capital as well as in episcopal cities. In addition, Protestants were able to hold any office except ecclesiastical ones, to maintain their own schools and printing presses, to inherit, to hold synods and consistories. The edict granted a great deal—and, as soon became apparent, more than the Catholics were willing to concede.

In Paris the storm was more violent than the King had anticipated. As in the days of the League, the preachers took the lead, arousing the people, making incendiary statements about the King, threatening another Saint Bartholomew Massacre. Henri, however, had listened to too much ranting rhetoric to be unduly moved by it; what did concern him was the reaction of Parlement, for sooner or later Parlement must be coerced into registering the edict before it could become effective legislation. Thus on February 7 he addressed himself to the whole body of Parlement. The tone was carefully chosen: it was paternal rather than royal, pleading rather than commanding, and yet it left little room for dissent:

> "I come to speak to you, not in royal dress or with my sword and cape as my predecessors did, nor as a prince comes to speak with foreign ambassadors, but dressed in my doublet as a father of a family comes to speak familiarly with his children.

What I have come to say is to beg you to verify the edict which I have accorded those of the Religion. What I have done is for the good of peace. I have made peace abroad; now I want it at home. . . . You have a duty to obey me . . . if obedience was due my predecessors, it is due as much or more to me, for I have reestablished the State, God having chosen to put me in this kingdom which is mine by inheritance and acquisition. The people of Parlement would not be in their seats were it not for me. I do not wish to boast, but I wish to say clearly that I have no precedent to invoke except myself. I know very well that there are intrigues in Parlement, that factious preachers have been incited; but I shall bring these to order. . . . This is the road to the Barricades and which led little by little to the assassination of the former king. I am going to be on my guard against all this. I shall cut at the root of all factions and all seditious teaching, putting an end to those who excite it. I have leaped over the walls of cities; I will easily jump over barricades. Don't allege the Catholic religion against me; I love it more than you; I am more Catholic than you. I am the eldest son of the Church, none of you can vie with me in this. You are mistaken if you think that you are on the right side of the Pope; I am even more so. . . . Those who do not wish my edict to be promulgated want war to come upon us. I would announce it to those of the Religion tomorrow, but I will not do this to them; for you would all go, with your robes, and assemble a procession of Capuchins who carry their muskets under their habits. . . . Concede to my pleas, what you would never have conceded to my threats. Do what I ask of you soon, I beg of you. Do not do it only for me, but for yourselves, also, and for the sake of peace."[14]

Had Navarre been aware of the full extent of the storm brewing at the Vatican, he might have been more hesitant in avowing that he rather than his conservative Parlement was at the "right side" of the Pope. Even before the edict was fully registered, Clement had said to D'Ossat: "As for me, when I hear tell of such things, they crucify me; please write and tell him so on my behalf." In early March word reached Rome that the edict had been formally registered on February 25. Although both Cardinal de Joyeuse and D'Ossat tried to assure His Holiness that this was simply a political move aimed at the ultimate conversion of the Huguenots, the Pope remained obdurate. Not even the affirmation of the Papal Legate, recently returned from the French court, could allay the Pope's misgivings. "I reaffirm," the Legate averred, "that if the King could wipe out heresy and still maintain peace he would do so. I know that this is contrary to general opinion, but it is true."[15] A month later, D'Ossat wrote at some length to the King, summing up the audience he had had on March 27. "The subject of this letter will be irritating both for us to write and Your Majesty to read," wrote D'Ossat, prefacing his letter with avowals of his own loyalty to the King and begging Henri to interpret the Pope's response as Clement's deep zeal and concern for the Catholic faith. "When we came into his presence," D'Ossat continued, "he said that he had asked us to come to tell us of the great suffering which he was enduring, that he was the most sorrowful and afflicted man alive because of the edict which Your Majesty has made in favor of the heretics and to the prejudice of the Catholic faith and which was finally passed and made public contrary to the hope he had been cherishing since he had first heard of this edict. His Holiness had hoped that Your Majesty had made it to keep the Huguenots happy, but that Your Majesty was sure that the clergy would oppose it and the court of Parlement would refuse to pass it, which would give you an excuse with the Huguenots. Now, however, he sees the opposite of what he had hoped. First, he sees an edict which is worse than any he could have imagined (these are his words . . .), for by this edict, liberty of conscience is granted to each individual which is the worst thing in the world." When D'Ossat tried to explain that this edict was not seriously different from previous legislation, the Pope interrupted, saying that other kings had been forced into such acts, but that this act was a free choice on the part of the King. He feels, concluded D'Ossat, "that the edict has wounded his own reputation, that he has been struck in the face."[16]

Had the edict been the King's only open act of independence of the Holy See, it would have stirred sufficient papal anger, but simultaneously Henri was engaged in preparations for marrying his Huguenot sister to a Catholic lord without either papal approval or dispensation. It would have been hard for the King to remember when the question of his sister's marriage had not been a thorn in his side. There had been suitors aplenty but always there had been what his mother-in-law had been accustomed to call a "tail"—some small point, some sticky detail that kept the union from fulfillment. Alençon, the King of Spain, the Duke of Savoy, the King of Scotland—all had made their suits but without success. For years Catherine herself had acted with marked indifference until she had fallen in love, much to her brother's annoyance, with the Comte de Soissons. For some years following his brusque termination of the Soissons affair, he had made no further plans for his sister's marriage; but in 1595 another suitor appeared: the Duc de Montpensier. Catherine was now close to forty; "well-painted, ill-dressed, and strangely jeweled," Robert Cecil wrote of her. Although a marriage with Montpensier would not be a brilliant union, it would, so it seemed to the King, be a satisfactory one. His sister would be married at last and his relationship with Montpensier would thereby be cemented. Catherine, however, saw things quite differently, and, reported the English ambassador, "said she would never marry him although she live a maid all her life."[17]

Henri, accustomed to winning people to his side by his charm, his power, the sheer force of his personality, could never accept his sister's obduracy in the face of his wishes. He, who could cow governors and win parlements, could never coerce Catherine de Bourbon. Had Henri not been so blinded by his own will to conquer, he would have recognized in his sister the qualities he had loved and admired in his mother: her loyalty to a cause she had espoused, her fearless devotion, her inflexible will. But in Jeanne d'Albret these were qualities he had watched from the distance of childhood; he had never pitted his will against his mother's, nor known the chagrin (which her contemporaries had sometimes suffered) of being worsted by a woman. Instead of acceding to her requests, he continued to investigate the possibilities of an advantageous marriage, and Catherine, close to exhaustion, wrote to a friend: "I do not know where I shall live nor where I am going. God wishes to lead me Himself and He gives me patience, of which I have more need than ever because of the way I am treated; if I told you about it, you would be filled with pity."[18]

Three years later, her brother wrote that he was still trying "to get her married as quickly as possible," and in August 1598 his efforts met with success. On August 5, at the château of Montceaux, in the presence of the King, his Chancellor, and the Constable of the realm, a marriage contract was drawn up between Catherine de Bourbon and Henri de Lorraine, Duc de Bar. The negotiations had been in progress for over a year, but at first there had been little hope of a successful issue, for the intended groom was a staunch Catholic and the King's sister gave little evidence that she would abandon her religion.

Under such circumstances, no dispensation could be obtained from Rome. Several bishops, feeling that the Edict of Nantes was a suf-

ficient cause of trouble, refused to perform the marriage, nor was it easy
to find a suitable place for the ceremony. The King, enraged by the
nervous groom, the obdurate bride, and the faint-hearted bishops, took
things into his own hands, coercing his natural brother, the Archbishop
of Rouen, to perform the ceremony and announcing that the marriage
would take place in his cabinet which was "as holy a place" as any
other. Early in the morning of January 30, with little pomp and less joy,
Catherine de Bourbon and Henri de Lorraine, pronounced their marriage vows. The King had had his way; what it gained him it is hard
to say, for after six more lonely years, his sister died, unwilling to believe that the tumor that filled her was not the child for which she had
hoped.

In the winter of 1599 it was not, however, the marriage of the
King's sister which absorbed the popular imagination, but the possibility
of the King's own marriage. The preceding fall Henri had been taken
dangerously ill. For days he lay at Montceaux close to death, and even
after the crisis had passed, Sully found him apathetic and depressed.
Although his physician assured him that despite the damage to his
urinary system, he could still have many years of healthy life ahead of
him if he took certain simple precautions, the King as well as his
statesmen were frightened by this dramatic proof of what slender
threads even royal lives hang by. The death of the King would be a
tragedy—but the death of the King without issue would be a cataclysm.
The old arguments that he must remarry for the sake of the kingdom
were articulated with increasing persuasion, for, as his friends pointed
out, the King was already in his forty-sixth year.

The first step toward remarriage was, of course, the annulment of
his union with Marguerite de Valois. For over ten years Margot had
lived her solitary life in the château of Usson; for the last five years
her solitude had been occasionally broken by messengers from her
royal husband testing her reaction to an annulment. As early as the
winter of 1593, on the advice of Mornay, the King had sent Erard,
his master of requests, to the Queen of Navarre, asking for her cooperation in the matter of an annulment. Three months later he received
a docile reply in which Margot assured her husband that she would
consent to whatever he wanted, but with certain "conditions." Even
while she was assuring Mornay that her actions would "never swerve"
from the service of her husband, she was patently indicating that a
large sum of money would help to cement the bargain. Henri, although impoverished himself, sent her the substantial sum of 250,000

écus. The letter of gratitude which he received the following fall was Margot at her most fulsome: she assured the King of her desire "rather to lose my life" than be false to her promise, avowing that "the respect and humble obedience I owe you" was the ruling principle of her life and signing the letter, "your very humble and obedient servant, wife, and subject."[19]

Despite Margot's acquiescence, the affair of the *démariage* was not to be easily settled. Since the Holy See had so far refused to acknowledge Henri's abjuration, it would certainly not concern itself with his annulment. On the other hand, the French bishops had no desire to endanger their position further by arrogating to themselves a right reserved for the Pope alone. Despite some sporadic correspondence between Henri and Margot, serious negotiations concerning the marriage question were dropped until papal absolution was granted to Henri in the fall of 1595. Despite the ingenuity of the King's ambassadors at the Vatican, it was difficult to find grounds for an annulment. Although it was true that Henri's marriage to Margot in 1572 had taken place without the necessary papal dispensation, it was equally true that following Henri's "conversion" after the Bartholomew Day Massacre, a dispensation had been granted. It was the Duc de Luxembourg's argument that such a dispensation had been granted to a Catholic, and that since Henri's "conversion" had been made under constraint, he was not in fact a Catholic and the dispensation was, therefore, invalid. Since an unconsummated marriage was easier to annul, Margot avowed that she was willing to swear that their marriage had never been consummated, although her spouse was rumored to have replied in answer to this that anyone who knew either of them would never believe it.

The attitude of the Holy See was at best ambivalent. Clement was as anxious as any Frenchman to see the King remarried, for unless he had an heir the throne would by rights pass to the Condés. In October and again in May 1598, Bonciani wrote to the Grand Duke that he had every reason to feel that the Pope looked favorably upon an annulment if only he could be sure that the King would not marry Madame de Montceaux. Of this no one could be sure, for, as the Papal Legate had written earlier, the King was entirely "in her toils." "No one speaks to him about this, because no one has the courage," concluded the Legate.[20] In this matter, the King sought no counsel and brooked no opposition. If one can trust Sully's account, Henri did discuss the question of his marriage with him in the spring of

1598; but when Sully warned him that marriage to Gabrielle might be sufficient to cause an uprising among his nobility the King seemed deaf to his advice. The Legate summed up the situation graphically when he wrote toward the end of June: "His Most Christian Majesty is more determined than ever to procure the dissolution of his marriage by the Holy See, and all his actions are directed toward this end. I have been warned that he will speak to me about this . . . no one dares speak or give him contrary advice. Monsieur de Sancy who has frequently and courageously expressed himself, for he wishes to reconcile the King with his present wife, the Queen, has lost much and is presently almost in disgrace."[21]

By the beginning of 1599 there was little doubt that, despite the talk of eligible European princesses, all the King's resolve was set upon a marriage with Gabrielle. Although both the Edict of Nantes and his sister's marriage had won him the severe disapproval of the Holy See, he now wrote personally to the Pope on January 20 begging for permission to marry his mistress. Although Margot—true to her promise and in return for another generous sum to pay her exorbitant debts— had already sent her signed statement agreeing to an annulment, the matter moved slowly, and that spring Henri wrote to Cardinal de Joyeuse in Rome, exhorting him to do everything in his power to hasten the decision.

Yet even while he wrote supplicatingly to the Holy See, he had begun at home the proximate preparations for his marriage with Madame de Montceaux. There was little that the French found to admire in Gabrielle. They saw none of the gentleness, the affection, the quiet devotion which kept the King faithful to her; instead, they condemned her for her parentage, her ambitious relatives, her love of luxury, her own talent for intrigue, her insufferable confidence that she could rule the King as she wished. As the King's mistress she was at best unfortunate, as the Queen of France she would be intolerable. On her head had fallen the blame for the loss of Calais, and far more seriously, for the capture of Amiens. "Mars exalted thee, but Venus hath laid thee low," wrote one poet, indicating how their warrior king had been undone by love. Had they seen some of the letters which the King wrote to his mistress, they would have been confirmed in their fears. "My beautiful love," he wrote in the fall of 1598, "two hours after the arrival of this messenger, you will see a knight who loves you dearly and who is called King of France and of Navarre. It is an honorable enough title, but a very painful one; that of your subject is much to be preferred."[22] This was precisely what his people feared: that something of the King had been lost in the lover, something of his valor softened, something of his vision obscured.

Simple and frugal himself, he let money flow like water about Gabrielle. He had bought a house for her which had originally belonged to his zealous councilor Schomberg, a house so discreetly situated that she could gain entrance to the royal apartments quite secretly. She had only to go through the gardens of the Tuileries, through a small wicket-gate which led to a staircase leading directly to the King's chamber. The house was more than convenient, it was elaborate as well. Turkish tapestries covered the walls. In the dining room a handsomely carved table, fifteen feet in length, was embellished with a silver service and handsome enamel dishes. The walls of her bedroom were covered with Flemish embroideries done in green silk and thread of gold; the chests and closets were piled with clothes, carefully styled to enhance her blond beauty. The King loved her most in green or in black satin, but there were also dresses of crimson velvet trimmed with grey, white satin embroidered with gold, yellow silk with full gray sleeves. After her death, one gown was valued at 1,200 *écus*. The King seemed to have no will against her magic, for while he upbraided Parlement for not according him the money he needed for his army, he bought the duchy of Beaufort for her and elevated her to the rank of duchess. Two years before, Margot had written to Gabrielle, proffering her friendship and her devotion: "Please accept my assurance—and be so good as to convey it to the King—that my desires are completely conformed to his will and to yours. . . . I hope you will accept what I have spoken so freely to one whom I hope to have as my sister and whom I honor and esteem second only to the King himself." It was not long, however, before Margot's generous offer of friendship cooled before her wounded vanity and she wrote to a friend: "I am loath to have in my place a woman of such inferior birth and infamous life about whom all kinds of rumors are flying."[23]

On Shrove Tuesday, the last day before the purple shadows of Lent would fall upon Christendom, Henri IV announced that his marriage to Gabrielle d'Estrées would take place the Sunday following Easter. As a sign of his troth, he placed upon her finger his coronation ring, that ancient symbol by which a king espouses his country. Lent fell like a pall upon France as the clerics pulled their cowls over their heads and the alleluias were stricken from the church ceremonies. It was a time of sorrow, of fasting, of supplication; but Easter would bring no surcease, for Easter would but see the climax of the tragedy. "We shall have a dynasty of bastards," murmured one courtier grimly. It seemed an ill-timed ceremony in every sense, for the bride was already six months pregnant. Only the King was jubilant—and Gabrielle, of course, who was heard to exclaim, "Only God or the death of the King can keep me from being Queen of France."

Part of March the King spent making final preparations for his marriage. The queen's apartments were redecorated; Gabrielle's wedding gown was cut and fitted. On March 21 Henri, always restless in the atmosphere of the Louvre, set out with his mistress for Fontainebleau. The King insisted that they make the journey slowly for he would take no chances with Gabrielle's pregnancy. The heavy mule-drawn wagons lurched and shuddered, for the spring thaw had set in and the roads were deep in mud, but no amount of mud could quell Henri's enthusiasm. Of all his castles, Fontainebleau was his home. Paris, for all his pride in her, was always alien to something in the King's blood. Cities made him nervous and constrained; the country was his atmosphere and Fontainebleau satisfied his country longings. For two weeks they enjoyed their idyl together. On April 5, however, the idyl came to an end and Gabrielle prepared to leave Fontainebleau to spend the solemn days of Holy Week alone in Paris. It was a decision that had been urged upon the King by his spiritual councilors, who advised him that this act of penance and sacrifice would place him in a more favorable light with those who felt that his marriage was at best a scandal and without a papal dispensation an act of the most flagrant disobedience to God and his vicar.

There seemed little chance that a dispensation would ever come from Rome. Clement VIII was beginning to agree with those who had warned him that he would rue the day he granted absolution to the heretic king. Within five months Henri had granted full liberty of conscience to the Protestants of his kingdom, married his Huguenot sister to a Catholic lord despite the specific prohibition of the Holy See, and now had publicly announced his marriage to his mistress although no pronouncement had yet annulled his first marriage. The Pope had every reason for anger against this fractious son who wrote letters of filial devotion while he conducted himself as he pleased. Clement might well have taken wrathful steps had not the memory of how England had been lost to the church over a simple annulment stayed his hand.

The King, however, was too preoccupied by his sorrow at parting from Gabrielle to be upset by papal disapproval. It is difficult to know the facts of that parting, for all the details were recast in the light of the tragic events which followed. If one follows the main lines of the legend, a legend enhanced now with all the paraphernalia of blighted romance, the sorrow of the parting lovers was immense— a sorrow out of all proportion to the event which caused it. In a matter of days they were to be together again, and in little more than a week the event on which both of them had set their hearts would take place. It is true that the atmosphere which surrounded them must have clouded their own exultation. Paris had, as always, made it more than manifest that it did not care for the marriage. Gabrielle had not been spared. Her relationship to the King had been expressed with the robust vulgarity of which sixteenth-century France was master; her mother, her sisters, even her aunt, Madame de Sourdis, had been fixed with epithets which were far from flattering. Gabrielle herself had found insulting verse pinned to a tree in the orange grove at Montceaux, and it was said that even the King's bedchamber had been violated by a sheaf of scurrilous verses. Yet none of this was enough to account for the pall which fell upon the lovers.

Again, if one follows the legend, it was not the shafts that were leveled against them—love provides its own armor against barbs such as these; it was something against which they had no protection, something that rose up within them, making them mistrustful of the happiness which was so close to their grasp, as though their own love carried within it the seeds of their destruction. Perhaps it was the shadow of Lady Fortune, who, in the employ of the gods, would turn her wheel at the moment of fulfillment lest mortals enjoy the bliss that should be reserved for the gods themselves. Later it was rumored that the night before they parted at Melun both the lovers wakened in terror, Gabrielle shaken by a dream that she had been caught in a terrible fire, and the King that he had watched his mistress die. Sully adds to the mysterious legend by affirming that Gabrielle, always a prey to superstition, had paid many diviners to tell her the future, and that always the prophecies had foretold her doom: that she would be married only once, that she was fated to die young, that she would be the victim of a great betrayal, that the fruit of her womb would be her destruction. Frightened and tearful, Gabrielle made the short journey to Paris, arriving in mid-afternoon under the shadow of the Bastille where her sister Diane and her husband Balagny awaited her.

She slept that night at her aunt's residence in the cloister of St. Germain l'Auxerrois and on Wednesday went by litter, accompanied by a portion of the King's guard, to the little chapel at Petit-St-Antoine which had been reserved for her. When she returned home, she complained of feeling sick, but the next morning she was well enough to attend the long services of Holy Thursday. By Thursday afternoon, however, she was seriously ill. She burned with fever, her throat seemed on fire, and pains, sharp as knives, shot through her stomach. During a moment of respite she wrote to the King, telling him of her sickness, and begging him to come to her. The doctors watched with her throughout the night, but they were powerless to help. On Friday she was worse and by early afternoon she was taken with severe hemorrhages. As Paris knelt, intoning the sorrowful office of the Lord's death, the doctors worked in their barbarous way to remove Gabrielle's child. The child, still-born and mutilated, was taken from her womb, and the mother, wracked by convulsions, passed into unconsciousness.

By nightfall there was little that was recognizable in the King's mistress. The beautiful body was torn beyond redemption and the face, contorted with pain, bore little resemblance to the beauty which, as the English ambassador had written shortly before, "possesses the King entirely." It was now only a question of time. Cheverny, then chancellor of France, wrote of those hours: "Her pain was so great that everyone stood helplessly by. Her servants were unable to do anything. Someone suggested the Last Sacraments but she was not capable of receiving them and so must be content with her Easter duty which she had made a little while before. Her face once so beautiful, now, in a moment, became hideous and frightful to look on."[24]

Even at the hour of her death, Gabrielle d'Estrées did not cease to be a subject of intrigue. La Varanne who attended her and who had sent a message to the King describing his mistress' perilous condition now sent another. Statesmanship triumphed over compassion, and, fearful lest the King marry his mistress on her deathbed and thus set his bastard sons upon the throne of France, his second message to the King informed him that there was no point in his hastening to Paris for Gabrielle was already dead and he had best save himself the grief of seeing his disfigured mistress. The King, who had been riding hard toward Paris, received the news at Ville-Juif. Bewildered by his grief, he returned to Fontainebleau to spend the dark hours of Good

Friday night in his own lonely vigil of death. Even while he wept for her, recalling her strange fears, her terror at their separation, Gabrielle lived on. She died at daybreak on Holy Saturday amid the muted alleluias of the Lord's resurrection. She had swayed a King and perhaps a kingdom; she had worn a King's ring upon her finger and borne a King three children. Proud, vain, foolish, clever, ambitious, devoted, exploited, besmirched. There is no lack of adjectives to choose from in describing Gabrielle d'Estrées. At some time or other they were all predicated of her. There was little that she was not accused of, little for which she was not blamed. One must walk warily among the gossip, the rumor, the legend, for while one can find evidence for almost every interpretation, none of the evidence is conclusive. Out of the welter of misshapen fact, there emerges but a single incontrovertible reality: for nine years Gabrielle had held the King faithful in his love for her. No one had ever done so much before—nor would anyone else again. That love had never diminished, and when she died, he wrote: "the root of my love is dead; it will not spring up again."[25]

CHAPTER XVI

Royal Husband: 1599–1601

Do everything I wish—that is the way to govern me.

Henri de Navarre

❧❧❧ Paris spent Easter week in mourning for the woman who had threatened the glory of France. Now that God had delivered them with frightening punctuality, they could well afford a token of sorrow. The God of hosts had saved them, that God, whom the scriptures avowed would protect the just and put sinners to rout, had heard their prayers. The sorceress was dead with her still-born child. They stood in the squares and listened to the heralds as they cried: "Pray to God for the soul of Madame d'Estrées, in her life time Duchesse de Beaufort and Marquise de Montceaux. . . . May God preserve her soul." They crossed themselves and murmured their *Requiescat in pace*. The sorceress was dead, the spell was broken, and their King was free.

In fact, the King was far from free; if once he was obsessed by love, now he was obsessed by grief. It was a man grown visibly older who rode from Fontainebleau to the rue Froidmanteau where funeral preparations for Gabrielle were underway. The Venetian ambassador noted that although he was but forty-six he looked closer to sixty. He was thin and bent, his hair and beard were entirely gray, and his face, always swarthy, was now yellow and dry as parchment with deep furrows about the mouth. The violet mourning customary for members of the royal family was not enough to symbolize his grief, and for several days the King dressed entirely in black.

In Gabrielle's apartments a bed of state had been erected over which a baldachino of cloth of gold was hung. Sitting erect on the bed was the funeral effigy, clothed in white satin covered with a golden cloak lined with ermine, and on its head a ducal crown. At the foot of the bed stood two heralds, holding vessels of holy water for the people who came to pay their respects. Although in life Gabrielle had been a subject of mockery and contempt, now Paris flocked for a glimpse of her effigy. She had become a legend during the nine years that she had been the King's mistress: a legend in her beauty, her influence, her elegance. She had taken her place among those fabled beauties who had been the *fol amour* of Kings. The sudden shock and violence of her death had added another dimension to the legend. This was the woman who had been struck down by the hand of God himself. At the climax of her greatness, Death, unbidden and unexpected, had made his way to her side. He had defaced her beauty and maimed her body and now on the very day chosen for her marriage her mortal remains lay hidden in a sealed coffin under the bed of state. Curiosity, self-righteousness, superstition drove people to line the streets as the funeral cortege left Paris that they might catch a glimpse of the royal litter which carried the body of the woman who had missed by a hair's breadth the crown of the Queen of France.

No sooner had Gabrielle's body been laid to rest than the King's counselors took up their old theme: the King must marry, not only for the good of France but for his own good as well. He had told one of them in the days following his mistress' death that he had lost half of himself. Now they argued that he must find himself again, must put aside his grief and take up the reigns of government. It frightened them that this man, now looking so much older than his years, should still not have provided an heir for the throne. He made few demurs to their suggestions, but neither did he show any enthusiasm for the list of suitable princesses they presented to him: the Infanta was old and ugly, the German princesses were hardly to his taste, the Princesse de Guise might not be trustworthy, the niece of the Grand Duke of Tuscany—perhaps. She was reputed virtuous, of stable character, and with a certain queenly bearing. Beyond that was the practical consideration that if the King were to engage in such a marriage her uncle might cancel the enormous debt that Henri owed to Florence. The counselors, seizing their advantage, pushed the benefits of such a union. It would be entirely acceptable to the Holy See, they argued, and would no doubt facilitate the problem of his marriage annulment which still hung fire. Marie de Medici was young and strong and there was every reason to hope that she would provide him with healthy offspring. Margot, too, who had shown a certain hesitancy in facilitating an annulment which would have placed a woman of questionable life on the throne, would have little reason to demur were Henri to marry a woman of such reputed virtue and background. Scarcely a month after Gabrielle's death, the Venetian ambassador wrote to the Doge: "He [the King] declares openly that he intends to marry again, and has shown some inclination toward the Princess Maria, niece of the Grand Duke of Tuscany."[1]

From the beginning of his reign, Henri's relations with Tuscany had been cordial. Following the death of Henri III, the Grand Duke had done his best to have the new King acknowledged as the legitimate sovereign; during the years of turmoil, he had been more than generous in lending Henri the money that he needed to keep his army in the field. In addition, he had used his influence at the Vatican to obtain the absolution about which the Pope had been so reluctant. Some time earlier, however, Henri had made overtures concerning a possible marriage with Marie de Medici; but then, beguiled by Gabrielle, he had turned aside and done nothing further about it. The Grand Duke had resented such treatment, and now when the subject of marriage was again broached, he was more cautious in his responses. He was made doubly hesitant by the gossip that Henri was proposing such a marriage only in order to win an annulment from the Holy See, and was in fact already deeply involved with a young Frenchwoman from Auvergne, Henriette d'Entragues, whose parentage seemed as unsavory as that of Gabrielle d'Estrées.

It was far more than gossip which linked the King with Henriette d'Entragues, for by the summer of 1599 he was plunged into what was to be the bitterest and most tumultuous affair of his life. It was in every sense a *fol amour*. Always impetuous in his love affairs, he was, also, imperious. He commanded, and there were very few who withstood his commands. He had often made mistakes but he had never paid a high price for them. If there were heartache involved, it had never been the King who suffered. Only twice had he fallen deeply in love and in both cases the women had proved worthy of his devotion. Now, however, he lost not only his heart but his head as well, for there is little that is rational in his passion for Henriette.

The D'Entragues were a family known as intriguers and oppor-
tunists. Marie Touchet, the mistress of Charles IX, had married in
1578 François de Balzac, Sieur d'Entragues, and had borne him a
son, the Duc d'Angoulême who was ultimately to prove himself a
worthy member of this conniving family. D'Entragues, at the time of
the Barricades, declared himself for the League and as governor of
Orléans had held this city against the Huguenots. When the League
leaders began to capitulate, however, he, too, changed his colors,
offering Orléans to the King for the exorbitant price of 20,000 *écus*.

The King had first met Henriette in the company of his friend
Bassompierre. Bassompierre, certain that the King would find solace
for his grief over Gabrielle only by putting someone equally entertaining in her place, had suggested that they visit Malesherbes, half-
way between Blois and Paris. D'Entragues, flattered to have the King
in his house, invited him to return often to enjoy the excellent
hunting. "Hunting," however, is an ambiguous term to describe the
King's activities of the next few months. Soon he was staying in
a château only a league from Malesherbes, and his attraction for
Henriette was a matter of common knowledge. He seemed to have
discovered for himself the truth of the proverb: one nail pushes out
the other. By mid-July Henry Neville was writing in his dispatches
to London: "The King rode post yesterday . . . upon no occasion
but to see Mademoiselle d'Entragues; . . . and for anything I see, he
minds nothing else, but that and hunting and hardly stays one whole
day with his council. We know not when to look for him here
again. . . . For his marriage with the Princess of Florence goeth
rather backward than forward."[2]

Even those who had had nothing but contempt for Gabrielle while
she lived, liked even less what happened following her death. Those
who had most violently opposed the King's marriage to his mistress,
now began to manifest a certain compassion for the woman who had
died so tragically while giving birth to a son for the King. Now,
in place of the barbed satires which had formerly been directed against
her were pathetic verses in her favor such as those entitled "The
Shade of the Duchesse de Beaufort to the King," in which Gabrielle
upbraided her royal lover for forsaking her memory as soon as her
body was laid in the tomb.[3]

Time frequently suffuses the harsh facts of history with a romantic
light, and in no place is this more true than in the affair of Gabrielle
and her royal lover. If she were ambitious and scheming, as many

of her contemporaries suggested, these qualities were blurred by the
tragedy of her death, when time, inexorable and prompt to the
second, robbed her of a royal marriage. Her vanity and extravagance
were lost in the anguish of those last terrible hours and in the
final pragmatic betrayal which kept the King from being present at
her death. If the events that followed were the work of fiction, then
fiction would have the King bereaved, persuaded perhaps to marriage,
but only a marriage of state which would never violate his heart's
affection. Fiction would never permit in its pages the facts which
history cannot deny; for history must record that within six months
after Gabrielle's death, the King was, quite literally, at the feet
of a girl less than half his age, a girl of whom contemporaries, to
a man, can say little that is not damaging.

Few of those who describe her are concerned with her beauty; it
was not her beauty alone that won Henri, but a kind of charm.
Henriette was small, lithe, graceful, almost feline in her movements.
She had an immense vitality of both body and mind. She was alert
and limitlessly alive. She missed no nuance, lost no possibility of
meaning. Her mind was not unlike her body, quick, sinuous, and
kept in excellent condition. Her conversation was rarely reflective,
but always penetrating. For all her charm, her wit, her gaiety, she
was seldom spontaneous. Ambition was the leitmotif of her life, and
ambition is best served by caution and self-possession. Her ambition
goaded her to be Queen of France, and toward that end she worked
with a skill and ingenuity far beyond her years. Sully wrote tersely
of her, "The Lady is no novice."

Yet neither was the King a novice. In his forty-six years there was
little he had not experienced of lust, romance, affection, love. Now,
however, he plummeted from folly to folly, careless not only of the
hurt to his own person but to his kindom as well. Shrewd almost to
a fault, with those quizzical eyes able to read men at a glance, he
now acted with less caution than a peasant with his first wench. It
is hard to believe that Gabrielle was so easily forgotten, so soon
replaced. Perhaps Henri's own words should be taken more literally
when he said, "I have lost half of myself." For following Gabrielle's
death something had gone, something of himself he seemed never
to regain. The man who offered himself to Henriette d'Entragues was
far from the aspiring prince who had shared his dreams with Corisande
at Hagetmau, far from the indefatigable King who had found comfort
in Gabrielle's young, responsive love. His affair with Henriette was

marked by neither happiness nor peace; it was from beginning to end violent, unsatisfying, tumultuous—and often bitter. It was, however— and perhaps this was its root force—compelling and totally absorbing. At a dozen points he stripped his mistress of her veneer, lashed her with his certain knowledge of what she was, and threatened to terminate his relations with her; and a dozen times he returned to her, vanquished by a compulsion he could not conquer, knowing himself exploited, yet powerless to withstand her spell. Gabrielle, it had been said, had bewitched him; Henriette's sorcery was of another kind. It did not blind him, but, even more invidiously, it impelled him, without illusion, to a course of action which he could not justify.

Henriette was indeed no novice. From her first conversation with the King she charted her course with meticulous foresight. She could afford no misstep and—at first—she made none. The role she assumed in the summer of 1599 was that of the virtuous daughter of virtuous parents. She was wide-eyed before the King's advances, she refused to see him unchaperoned, and when he sent her a pearl necklace, the compromising gift was returned to him. Impelled as always to shower gifts on those he loved, he sent her a basket of apricots instead, which she received with gracious thanks. By August, apricots had become an insufficient token of his love; when he gave her a house at Beaugency, near Blois where he was staying, she continued to play the role of a diffident demoiselle, entranced but still timid before such unwarranted largesse. Before his advances she demurred naïvely, saying that her mother had forbidden her to stay under the King's roof.

Henriette lacked for no parental advice. Her father was an opportunist to the core, whose loyalty extended no further than his own interests; her mother had had the experience of being a king's mistress at a court far more complex than than that of Henri IV. Under their direction, Henriette continued her role; flattered, enchanted, bewildered, fearful, she finally admitted in the face of the King's persistence that her parents would never permit her to do what His Majesty asked, unless—unless there was some promise that would ensure her own good name, a written promise that would ultimately lead to marriage. The proposition was outrageous and unthinkable. By comparison, the King's proposed union with Gabrielle had been a conservative and rational action. It was intrigue of the most obvious kind, too bold-faced even to be clever. Even more inconceivable than the proposition itself was the King's response. By October 1 he had drawn up a document agreeing in effect to the terms the D'Entragues had proposed, and reading: "We, Henri IV, by the grace of God King of France and of Navarre, promise and swear on our faith and word as a king to Monsieur François de Balzac, Sieur D'Entragues, knight of our orders, who gives us as our companion Henrietta-Catherine de Balzac, his daughter, that should the said Henriette-Catherine de Balzac within six months, beginning from this day, become pregnant and should she bear a son, then at that time we shall solemnize the marriage publicly in holy church according to the required customary ritual."[4]

Sully, always a dramatic if not a trustworthy reporter, recorded in his *Mémoires* the occasion several days earlier when the King had called him into the gallery at Fontainebleau and showed him the promise which he had just composed, asking him to tell him freely what he thought of it. Sully said nothing, but in a dramatic gesture tore the paper in pieces. Although he tried to reason with the King, it was useless; and Henri, taking the pieces from the minister's hand, withdrew to his own cabinet and rewrote the document which was to give him more grief than any battle he had ever fought.

The D'Entragues' first exultation in the piece of paper on which they intended to build their fortunes turned to bafflement as they watched the King quite openly pursue a totally contrary course of action. He had acceded to the demands of his council to marry a "virtuous princess" and thus give France an heir so that past calamities might be avoided. He agreed that negotiations with the Grand Duke of Tuscany should be pursued, he wrote to Cardinal de Joyeuse in Rome exhorting him to push the investigation of his annulment, and announced openly to Bellièvre, his newly appointed chancellor, his intention of marrying Marie de Medici, concluding: "Advance this affair as much as possible, so that I can be married shortly, which is what I want most in the world."[5]

On December 17 the Holy See decreed that since the union between Henri de Navarre and Marguerite de Valois had been the result of coercion the marriage was null and void, thus leaving both spouses free to contract new marriages. Later that month the King wrote to Margot a letter of gratitude and devotion in which he assured her that he still wished to love and cherish her as before, having more concern for her than ever before, hoping to be her true brother in act as well as title. It was a strange ending to a marriage begun in blood, complicated by romantic and political intrigue, and of which the dominant motif seems to have been mutual indifference.

With the question of the King's annulment satisfactorily settled, the marriage negotiations with the Grand Duke moved rapidly to a conclusion, and toward the end of April, in the Pitti Palace at Florence a solemn contract was signed between Marie de Medici and His Most Christian Majesty. Wild with anger, Henriette dropped the mask by which she had won the King, and there showed forth that sharp, unbridled ambition which had once led her to say that she would bear the King a son, and if the King himself did not suffice, then she would become pregnant by whatever means were necessary. Happily or unhappily, the King had sufficed, and by the time his marriage contract with Marie de Medici was signed, his mistress was in the seventh month of her pregnancy.

She could not complain that the King had not treated her generously; he had installed her luxuriously in the Hôtel de Larchant in Paris, justifying his extravagance by saying that such a bird demanded a beautiful cage. But it was not luxury that Henriette had set her heart on—nor was it faithful and abiding love. She was single-minded, with all the ruthlessness which single-mindedness demands. She wanted but one thing and she did not care what it cost: she would be Queen of France and nothing else would suffice. It was not jealousy that had unsheathed those claws; her lover could take as many mistresses as he wished, provided that she felt the weight of the crown upon her own sleek head. To appease her, Henri secured the territory of Verneuil in Picardy, raised it to the status of a marquisate, and named Henriette the Marquise de Verneuil. It was a foolish and expensive bribe, for neither Henriette nor her parents had any intention of releasing the King from his sworn promise for any paltry honor such as this. In the ensuing storm, it was Marie Touchet who acted as arbiter. When the King explained that although he could not marry Henriette, he would always keep her as his mistress, her mother in her quiet way seemed to acquiesce in his decision. She had had enough experience with kings to know that they cannot be pushed beyond their limit; but even more important, she knew that they had the King's signed promise—a document more deadly than any subtle poison—and more far-reaching.

On April 21, the King, brought face to face with the folly of his promise to this family of intrigants, wrote to Henriette from Fontainebleau: "Mademoiselle: Love, honor, as well as all the favors you have received from me would have sufficed for the most frivolous soul in the world, unless she were gifted with a naturally evil character such as yours. I will not wound you any more although I could and should do so—as you well know. I am asking you to return to me the promise in question and not to give me the trouble of recovering it by some other means. Please return also the ring which I gave you the other day. This is the subject of this letter to which I would like an immediate response." On the same day he wrote to Monsieur d'Entragues, again enjoining him to "return the promise which I gave to you at Malesherbes," affirming that the reasons for his decision were "personal reasons, not reasons of state," and concluding by reminding him that he remained his "good master."[6]

Neither letter received an answer. Henriette could hardly risk an overt refusal of the King's demand, nor had she any intention of acquiescing in it. Her child was due in less than two months, and on that fact her destiny depended. In the days when first pregnancies often ended in death for both mother and child, those last few weeks of waiting must have been a torment. To augment her anxiety was the clause of the promise which indicated that only a male child would satisfy the King's requirements. This was an element she could not control, and for a woman like Henriette, who left nothing to chance, whose efficient scheming covered every aspect of her life, her helplessness must have been intolerable. Throughout May and into the beginning of June she waited, taking every precaution to bear a healthy child, and using the time to placate the King's displeasure, to cloak something of her own ambition, and to resume her role as the King's loving and dependent mistress.

When her pregnancy had reached its term, the King had her brought to Fontainebleau and installed in the Queen's apartments. She begged him not to leave her, pleading that she needed him to be with her when her child would be delivered; but although she had won him back to her side, yet on this point he remained firm. He reminded her that matters of state, too important to be postponed, demanded his presence elsewhere. While it was true that he was needed elsewhere, it was equally true that he recognized Henriette's pleas as but another element of her scheming; for she hoped that if the King were present at her delivery, he would be moved to keep his promise to her even if the child she bore were not a son. But Henri, as quick to discover her wiles as Henriette was to employ them, remained unmoved by her tearful entreaties. By the end of June, he was off for Lyons, leaving his mistress to deliver her child alone.

Not all of Henriette's tearful pleas were simulated, however. She was genuinely frightened and overwrought. Fearful of the suffering and danger in bringing forth a child, her terrors were heightened as she recalled the fate the King's last mistress had met in childbirth. Ultimately, however, her anxiety had its root in the fact that she had placed all her happiness in the successful issue of her pregnancy. To bear the King a son: on this hung her fortune, her happiness, her life. Her keen and indomitable will had directed itself totally to this end. If resolution alone could have forced the issue, there is no doubt that the King would have had another son; but, ironically, the very force of her determination brought about her downfall. Restless and keyed to fever pitch, she could find peace nowhere. Accustomed to controlling not only every jot and tittle of her own life, but also those of others, she was unable to reconcile herself to the slow summer days, to the measured pace of her pregnancy, which she could neither hasten nor retard. Most of all, she could not reconcile herself to the absence of the King. When, after an oppressive day of sultry heat, a violent thunderstorm broke over the castle, Henriette became hysterical. Terrified by the crashes of thunder and the lightning which grew more lurid as night fell, she became irrational and uncontrollable. No one could quiet her, and before morning she had given birth prematurely to a stillborn male child.

Her attendants feared that she, too, might die, for when she was told that her child was dead, she fell into a despair from which nothing could rouse her. All the plotting and intriguing had come to naught; all the hours of family conferences in which mother and father and brother had helped her form her strategy, all the weary and heavy days of her pregnancy—all come to naught. The King's signed promise, so cleverly obtained, so resolutely guarded, now was worthless. She had known, from the beginning, that he might well try to escape from his part of the bargain; but she knew, too, that there were sudden ways by which she might trip him up and she would not have hesitated to use them. But it was not the King who had failed to keep his bargain, it was she. The limitless confidence that she could bear the King a male child had played her false. Her despair was made more bitter by the knowledge that she had, in fact, conceived a son and brought him to the rim of the world, and that only in those last hours had something inexplicable and uncontrollable entered unbidden into her designs. It had been her terror, she reflected, that had plunged her into labor— her terror at finding herself alone as the thunder crashed over the château hour after hour. Had the King been there he could have calmed her, and the child she had carried so carefully would have been brought alive into the world. In that case she could have held the King to his promise, and she would have reigned as Queen of France. Now she was but Madame la Marquise—and she had little hope of anything more.

For long weeks she lay in bed, beyond the reach of sympathy or hope. She frightened her servants, for the mistress they had served seemed dead. In her place lay a girl, still beautiful but subdued and withdrawn. The wit which had made her such charming company, the vitality, the quick shifts of mood had given way to the lusterless tone of depression. When the King came to console her, even he could not rouse her from her despair. She had staked everything on his promise of marriage and she had lost. It mattered little to her now that the King told her that he loved her unless he also promised to make her his wife—and this Henri did not do. Even his sympathy did not keep him with her long, for by the second week of July he had returned to Lyons and the problem of Saluces.

The marquisate of Saluces had long been disputed territory. François I had acquired it during his lifetime by right of reversion, since there were no male heirs in the direct succession. When, following the Day of Barricades in 1588, France seemed fair game, the Duke of Savoy, brother-in-law of Philip II, had seized the territory with no claim beyond that of force. Although the question had long been a source of irritation for Henri IV, he had not been in a position to attend to it while his own kingdom remained in a precarious state. The issue had been raised at Vervins, but Henri, eager for peace, did not wish to retard the treaty with Spain for a matter which he felt he could settle personally with the Duke of Savoy. Meanwhile Henri suggested that the Holy See act as arbiter in the case; but the Duke, fearful perhaps that the Holy See might rule against him and with limitless confidence in his own powers of persuasion, suggested instead that he come to France and settle in person the ownership of the disputed territory.

Charles-Emmanuel, Duke of Savoy, was a strange man, superstitious and eccentric, who several times postponed his visit to France on the grounds that the omens were unpropitious. At the end of 1599, however, the stars were in their proper places and he set out for France with an entourage of 1,200 horsemen. It was a somber if impressive procession that arrived at Fontainebleau in mid-December, for the Duke and his attendants were in elaborate mourning for his wife who had died shortly before. Although he was treated with the greatest pomp, the King remained suspicious, having written earlier to one of his ambassadors that although Savoy assured him that the point of his visit was to return Saluces, yet he would believe this only when it happened. If the Duke of Savoy did not charm the King, however, he won many others to his favor. Savoy had a great reputation for his largesse and soon the whole French court was profiting from it. On January 1, he celebrated the coming of the new year by giving gifts everywhere: two beautiful crystal vases and elaborate bowls to the King; a necklace of precious stones to Henriette; horses, jewels, pieces of crystal offered almost indiscriminately. Henri remained unimpressed by his largesse; he called it by another name: bribery.

Even while he flattered the King and offered him not only his friendship but his effective military assistance, Savoy wandered through the court employing his other gift: his supreme talent for sowing discord. Recognizing the D'Entragues for what they were, he did what he could to set them against the King, to suggest other schemes whereby their ambitions could be satisfied. Biron, too, was a man worth having on his side, and to that end he incited his jealousy, noting with surprise that the King had never treated him as he deserved, that a man who had saved not only the kindgom but the King's life as well should have been advanced to far higher positions. Biron, passionate, envious, superstitious, was supremely susceptible to Savoy's technique. In the two months the Duke spent at the French court, he sowed not only discord but treason—treason which would one day cost Biron his head.

The King was not unaware of what was happening, and yet the Duke, the diplomat to his fingertips, made open confrontation impossible. Yet if Henri could not stop his bribes and intrigues, he could at least wrest from him an acceptable treaty in the matter of Saluces. On February 27 a treaty was drawn up and signed. Its main terms indicated that by June 1, the marquisate of Saluces would be returned to France; that if the Duke refused to give up the marquisate, then he would give in exchange the Comté de Bresse. He agreed to advise the King by June 1 which he had chosen and abide by his decision. Soon after, Savoy left France, assuring the King and his court that he had enjoyed two months of unparalleled happiness. While he had made some friends, most of the court was glad to see him go; they put little faith in the signed treaty he left behind, remarking that they feared that his promises were as fragile as his gifts. Within weeks, as the King had predicted, Savoy had resumed relations with Spain; and when June came there was no effort to comply with the terms of the treaty. Early in July Henri wrote to him, warning him that affairs must be settled when he reached Lyons later that month, meanwhile giving directions to Sully to levy troops and set his artillery in order. By July 9 the King had arrived in Lyons and serious preparations for a war with Savoy had begun. Even this patent threat did not move the Duke, and Henri, convinced now that he was simply stalling for time in order to build up his defenses, made a public proclamation of war on August 11.

Meanwhile, Henriette continued to absorb the King's attention. He wrote to her almost daily, and by the end of August he acquiesced to her pleas to come to him as soon as her health permitted. Henri was inexpressibly relieved at Henriette's failure to bear him a son. The terms of his contract no longer obtained; he was free of his impulsive promise. Since he could no longer be constrained to be the husband, he could well afford to resume his role as lover, and his old fascination with Henriette returned. For his mistress, however, everything had changed. The bitterness of her disappointment had sharpened her dangerous claws and she awakened from her despair more ambitious and more *intrigante* than ever. If the paper promise she still held from the King was not enough to win her the Queen's crown, it might at least be the instrument for seriously discomfiting the King. This was not the prize toward which she had aspired; but in its own way it was something— and it would give her a certain pleasure to use it well.

About the third week of October, Madame la Marquise arrived in Lyons, "in an uncovered litter as though she were the queen," wrote young Cheverny in disapproval. He continued: "The Marquise followed him [the King] everywhere, playing more the role of a mistress or a trollop than of a woman who was to be a queen, as her ambitious imagination had made her hope."[7] From Lyons she moved south to La Cote-St.-André near Vienne. Henri was at Grenoble when he learned of her presence, and, taking Bassompierre with him, made the exhausting journey with scarcely a stop.

The welcome he received scarcely repaid him for his pains. In place of a loving mistress, he found an enraged fury, for Henriette had recently learned that Henri's marriage with Marie de Medici had been celebrated by proxy the week before. The King, usually gifted with a certain ironic detachment and rarely given to emotional scenes, became as uncontrolled as his mistress. Henriette had the power to evoke a certain violence in him. Another woman might have driven him from her by such irrational and unbridled fury, but, in a paradoxical way,

Henriette's rages drove him to her. He fought with the weapons she had chosen, determined to conquer her on her own terms. But Henri was no match for his mistress. Although in his fury he ordered his horses and shouted that he was leaving that same night, in the end he stayed, and the following morning Henriette, reconciled to her lover once more, rode with him back to Grenoble. The English agent, observing the King's relations with his mistress, wrote in his dispatch: "The King hath brought his mistress hither whom he doth embrace with more kindness than kings commonly do their wives, and doth honor with as much respect as if she were his queen. She doth dine ordinarily and publicly with him when he is attended on by the Princes of the Blood."[8]

For a few weeks they lived together in tranquillity, but the peaceful idyl was short-lived, for at the beginning of November the King received word of the coming of the Papal Legate, Aldobrandini, who was to act as mediator in the affair of Savoy. He could hardly have arrived at a more embarrassing moment. Since it was he who had officiated at the marriage which had been celebrated between Marie de Medici and Henri IV in Florence, Henri could scarcely afford to have his mistress at his side when he extended a welcome to the Cardinal. "This was when the greatest quarrels and fallings out between the King and his Marquise recommenced," wrote Cheverny, "for she did not wish to go but wanted the Legate and everyone else to hear the promises that he had made to her, for she felt that they were sufficient to nullify the marriage which had just been made at Florence and to oblige him to marry her."[9]

It took all his influence and a little of his royal prerogative to cajole Henriette into returning to Lyons. He arranged for her to travel sumptuously by boat on the Lac du Bourget, then down the Rhône to Lyons where she was given a royal reception, reminiscent, some said, of that which had once been given for that other royal favorite, Diane de Poitiers. She might have stayed at Lyons to await Henri's return, but hearing of the imminent arrival of Marie de Medici, she left for Paris. From here she wrote a letter to the King which, if taken at face value, would establish Henriette as the docile and loving mistress, humbled but loyal, exploited but faithful. It is perhaps closer to the truth to interpret it as another element of intrigue. Threatened by the presence of Marie de Medici, and fearful lest her continued recriminations drive the King into the arms of his wife, she recognized the precariousness of her position. She knew enough of kings to know that they were often duped by flattery and flattered by submission. Thus, she wrote to the King sometime in November: ". . . in truth I am forced to confess my sorrow, not because you have any obligation to fulfill the vows of your subjects, but because your nuptials will be the funeral of my life. . . . In my wretched exile, I have nothing left but the single glory of having been loved by the greatest monarch in the world, by a king who has so wished to humble himself as to give the title of mistress to his servant and subject. . . . Remember, Sire, a young lady who once was yours with all that she sincerely owes you, with all that she can accomplish only in your trust which has as much power over her honor as Your Majesty has over the life of your very humble and obedient servant and subject."[10]

Henriette's letter bore no immediate fruit, for Henri was preoccupied with concluding the affair of Saluces and even more concerned with the arrival of Marie de Medici. His passion for Henriette was far from over, but for the moment he could feel only relief to have her safe in Paris. He dreaded what she might do, for by now he recognized that she was constrained by neither integrity nor ordinary feminine reserve. Although the promise he had made to her was no longer valid, still it could be a source of considerable embarrassment. While Henriette's assertion that it was enough to invalidate his present marriage was but part of her bluff, still he was willing to do what he could to keep the promise from the knowledge of the Papacy or the Grand Duke of Tuscany—who would hardly be impressed by a son-in-law who, while concluding marriage negotiations with his niece, was promising conditional marriage to his mistress. A docile Henriette was probably more dangerous than an infuriated one, but Henri, who rarely speculated on the future, rejoiced in the sudden calm and turned his eyes to the fleet that had sailed from Leghorn on October 17.

It had been originally planned that Marie de Medici would come to France during the summer of 1600, but the Savoy campaign made such a plan untenable and the King continued to postpone the arrival of his wife. In the interim, he wrote to her frequently; they were letters not only of a king but of a lover, for Henri was a supreme master of rhetoric, especially when the rhetoric was that of love. On May 24, a month after their solemn betrothal, he wrote one of his first letters: "The virtues and perfections which shine forth in you and make you universally admired, have for a long time now incited in me a desire to honor and serve you as you deserve. What Hailincourt has reported to me about you has increased my desire. Since it is not possible for me to express my affection in person, I have decided that while waiting for this happiness (which shall soon be mine if heaven listens to my prayers) to send my faithful servant Frontenac to perform this office in my name. . . . He will uncover my heart to you and you will find there an impassioned desire to cherish and love you all my life as the mistress of my affections, and henceforth to assume the yoke of your commands. I hope one day to be able to witness to this in person and to confirm the pledge of my fidelity."[11]

On October 7 in the cathedral at Florence, the event took place which Henriette had hoped so resolutely to avert and which the King's counselors were equally resolved to bring about. Henri IV, King of France and of Navarre, was espoused in marriage to Marie de Medici, niece of the Grand Duke of Tuscany. The ceremony was performed by the Pope's nephew, Cardinal Aldobrandini, with Roger de Bellegarde as the King's proxy. It was a ceremony of great splendor and magnificence, and was followed by a marriage supper in which even those masters of spectacle, the Italians, outdid themselves. The food itself had been shaped into the forms of birds and animals and rare plants, and following the dessert a cloud opened, revealing the person of Diana accompanied by a eunuch who sang alternately the glory of the King of France and of his queen. Through it all the affianced bride sat with a kind of ponderous majesty.

Marie de Medici was at the time of her marriage twenty-six years old. She was a woman of limited intelligence and equally limited passions. If she had her enthusiasms she rarely showed them. Like many people of limited gifts, she had identified the role into which she was cast and never let herself play beyond it. Queens were, as she understood it, women of dignity, of virtue, of high patronage. Their personal qualities were submerged beneath their royal destinies. It was to be her tragedy that she soon found herself in a part utterly unexpected and for which she had not the least ability to improvise. The man she married had no preconceptions of the role of kings. He played the man he was and let his own natural strengths define his kingship. He expected his queen to do the same, but Marie de Medici was in every way unequal to the task. She lacked humor, spontaneity, perspicacity. Her personality was in many ways defined by her appearance. Inclined to heaviness, she was not an unattractive woman. Her nose and mouth were well-formed, her eyes dark, her neck and arms (of which she was very proud) were beautifully shaped. Yet the mouth lacked expression and the eyes were a bit protuberant. The high forehead, usually interpreted as a sign of high intelligence, was at war with the thin, ill-defined eyebrows, which gave to her face a quizzical and unfinished look. Shortly after her arrival in France, the Duchesse de Bouillon wrote of her: "Marie de Medici: has large eyes, a full round face, like many women of her race; she resembles a rich bourgeoise rather than a queen. . . . Her skin is dark but clear, her mouth a trifle heavy, her eyes black, her forehead high; she is inclined to be a little heavy. There is a great kindness in her face, but there is nothing that even approaches Gabrielle d'Estrées."[12]

Just a week after her marriage, the bride, flattered and excited by the luxury with which she was surrounded and with high expectations of what awaited her, left Florence for Leghorn from where she would embark for France.

In spite of the luxury of the fleet which bore her, it was a hard voyage, for the winds were often contrary, and it was November 3 before they arrived in Marseille. Although it was already dusk, the wharves were filled with people eager to see their new Queen. For the most part they approved of what they saw. She was dressed in cloth of gold and about her neck was a string of large pearls. Her hair was piled high in the Italian manner and was unpowdered —even more surprising her face was unpainted. More important, however, she had a royal mien, and there was a certain kindness in the manner which acknowledged their cheers. The Chancellor of France, the Constable, four cardinals, and a number of noble lords and ladies were present to greet her, but her royal husband had sent his regrets, protesting his sorrow at not being on hand to welcome her.

It was a disappointment she had not bargained on, and even when the following day she was presented with the carriage which her husband had sent to her, she looked with indifference on the brown velvet, the damask curtains, and silver trimmings. The Marseillais did what they could to appease her disappointment: receptions, balls, processions took up her days until on November 16 the Italian women who had accompanied her (chief among them her aunt and her sister) returned to Italy. Two days later, she traveled north to Aix and then on to Avignon. It was two weeks since she had disembarked at Marseille and still her royal husband had not come. Although he had written to her several times, indicating that nothing

but the business of Savoy would keep him away, avowing his sorrow
and embarrassment at not being on hand to greet her at her arrival—none of this was sufficient to make up for those lonely, be-
wildering days in a strange country. On every side she was bom-
barded by a language she did not understand. She had studied her
French diligently, but the quick, voluble manner, the slurred speech,
made it impossible to disentangle the sounds into meaningful sen-
tences. She was not quick in either movement or speech, and although
this gave a kind of regal grace to her movements, it now put her
at a distinct disadvantage.

Even worse than the inevitable loneliness of those first few weeks
was the difficulty of the trip itself. Winter had already set in when
she left Marseille, and the trip to Lyons was a nightmare of hardship and confusion. The cold was penetrating and the wind swept
down from the Alpilles in great buffeting gusts. The stony ground
was frozen fast, and it was easy for both men and animals to lose
their footing on the dark shale. There was little to break the cold,
gray landscape except the small twisted bushes that grew rooted
in the stone. Huddled in her litter, she could never get warm, and
sometimes she feared for her life as the wind swept down from the
mountains, almost overturning both wagons and litters. When they
reached the Durance, the current was running dangerously swift, but
Marie, unwilling to delay, ordered the crossing. They began at noon,
but by nightfall only half of the baggage had been successfully
transferred to the other side. One page was drowned and another
of her Italian attendants came close to losing his life. Already the
company was exhausted, and they had only reached Avignon, less
than a third of the way to their destination. Yet even now Marie
refused to rest but insisted that they press on to Lyons, for it was
at Lyons that the King had promised that he would meet her.

It was not until December 2 that they reached the outskirts of
the city. Once again her husband disappointed her, and it was almost
the end of the week before she received a short note telling her
that his affairs with the Duke of Savoy were settled at last, that
he was leaving his army in the care of Biron, and that he hoped
to be with her by Saturday at the latest, concluding, "I have had
two bouts of fever; I am still not entirely well, but the sight of
you will cure me."[18] Many interpretations have been given of Henri's
long delay in coming to receive his wife, when he had urged her
so strongly not to delay her journey to France. The evidence is

clearly on the side of those who feel that despite the letters of devotion and affection the marriage to Marie de Medici was essentially distasteful to him—an affair which if he could not avoid he would postpone as long as possible. It was clear to many that the affair with Henriette was far from over, and Aerssens in his dispatch to the Netherlands wrote, "The clearest fact is that the King takes this one only for a pretext, for his thoughts are entirely on Mademoiselle d'Entragues."[14]

Whatever his motivation, the fact is that it was December 9 before Henri reached Lyons. Marie had spent Saturday in anxious waiting —wondering whether, since she had been disappointed so often, the King now, despite his specific avowal, might fail her again. At eight o'clock he still had not come, and Marie went to her supper alone. Hardly had she begun it, however, than La Varenne came to announce that the King would soon be in the city. Henri, despite his procrastination, had a strong masculine curiosity about the woman he had married, and feeling that he could assess her more objectively if he could observe her unseen, he did his best to gain entrance into the adjoining room without the Queen being aware of it. The inevitable flurry that his arrival caused spoiled his plan, however, and Marie, catching sight of the curtsies and bows of her attendants, refused the rest of her supper and retired to her room. Here she remained, awaiting the King's entrance in what the Florentine ambassador described as "respect and a joy mingled with fear."[15] A contemporary account gives a dramatic and detailed account of that first meeting: "After the table was removed, she returned immediately to her chamber. The King, who waited only for this, came to her chamber door, and ordering Monsieur Le Grand to go before, he knocked so hard that the Queen thought it must be the King; upon this she stepped forward at the very instant that Monsieur Le Grand entered the room, followed by His Majesty, at whose feet she immediately threw herself. The King raised her up, embraced her with great tenderness, and all that was polite, passionate, and respectful passed on both sides. After the first compliments were over, the King took her hand and led her to the fireplace, where he continued talking with her above half an hour; he afterwards went to supper and ate very sparingly. In the meantime, he bid Madame de Nemours tell the Queen that he had not provided himself with a bed, expecting she would give him part of hers, which from that time was to be common between them. Madame de Nemours, carrying this message to the

Queen, she returned for answer, that she had come thither only to obey His Majesty as the humblest of his servants."[16]

The following days were spent in mutual happiness; the courtiers who watched carefully could note in the King only "great satisfaction," "happiness and delight" and an expansive desire to tell everyone about the "rare and wonderful beauties of his new spouse." Thus, wrote Cheverny, "this marriage was happily accomplished after so many obstacles." The Queen, too, seemed supremely happy, writing to her uncle the following week: "The King my lord arrived about eight days ago. . . . I hardly know how to tell you of the many marks of honor with which he has surrounded me and with what kindness he has constantly treated me."[17]

On Sunday, December 17, Cardinal Aldobrandini was again at hand to solemnize the marriage which he had celebrated by proxy three months before in Florence. Henri, with small appetite for pomp, knew when the occasion merited it, and the ceremony at Lyons was gauged to impress not only his own people and his wife but especially her Italian entourage. The splendor of the King of France was spread out before them, and the Florentine ambassador, Vinta, wrote in awe, "I would not have wanted to miss this spectacle for all the money in the world."[18] Preceded by his trumpeters, the knights of the Holy Spirit and the Princes of the Blood, the King walked in doublet and hose of white. His richly embroidered collar was held by a golden clasp studded with diamonds, and about his shoulders was a cloak of black velvet. He did not wear his royal crown but had instead a small hat trimmed with heron plumes and heavily ornamented with precious stones. It was not upon himself but upon his Queen that he had lavished his jewels. Her dress was of Tuscan style with the bodice heavily ornamented with lace and trimmed with violet fleur-de-lys. Her violet cloak was covered with gold embroidery and lined with ermine and her long train was carried by four ladies of the nobility. Everywhere she sparkled with jewels—her cloak, her bodice, her neck—and on her head she wore for the first time the heavy gold crown of the Queen of France. Marie was always at her best when she could play the role of Queen to the full. She was regal, ceremonious, grandiose. On occasions such as this, her heavy style was impressive, and the people cheered enthusiastically as she left the cathedral.

For a month the King continued to enjoy "the first delights of his marriage," while the Queen's "virginal anticipation" turned to something more robust. Toward the end of January, Marie confided to her husband that she thought she was pregnant, and the King, happy in the thought that he had provided an heir to the throne, assured the Queen of his joy—but then pleaded urgent business and set out for Paris. Although Marie must have been surprised and disappointed by his sudden departure, those who knew the King were astonished that he had stayed so long at Lyons. In fact, the "urgent business" had been somewhat exaggerated, for a treaty had already been signed with the Duke of Savoy on January 17 in which Bresse and Bugey (in place of Saluces) had been ceded to France. Despite the perils of the winter roads, Henri made the trip to Paris in two-and-a-half days, but, remarked Cheverny who was one of the attendant company, he did not stay there but continued on to Verneuil. What blandishments he used to calm his mistress' wrath are not recorded, but before his departure, their quarrels were over and Henriette had once more "forgiven" her royal lover. By the time the King left Verneuil, his mistress was again pregnant.

The Queen, meanwhile, journeyed by slow stages toward Paris, arriving at Nemours in time to celebrate Candlemas Day. France had not felt such cold for thirty years and the travelers were literally frozen in their robes. Marie's face, although heavily masked by her veil, was chapped and cracked by the winds that had torn the entourage mercilessly, in some places even turning over the carriages on the roads. At Nemours the King joined them to take them to Fontainebleau. During his absence Marie had been heartened by the letters that came to her every few days—short letters, but letters avowing his love, protesting his sorrow at their separation. "Do everything I wish—that is the way to govern me," he had written, "for I want to be ruled only by you."[19] It was the most conventional of sentiments, but Marie, still in the first guileless flush of surrender, saw nothing but the literal meaning of the words.

On February 9, two months to the day since the King had come to her at Lyons Marie de Medici entered Paris. Although the cannon were fired in a triple salvo at her arrival, there was little pomp about her entrance. She rode alone in her litter with César, eldest son of the King and Gabrielle d'Estrées. Marie, used to the splendor and elegance of Florentine pageants, must have been surprised at the modesty of her entrance. She was further surprised when the procession did not take the route to the Louvre, but went to the Hôtel de Gondi where she stayed for the next three nights. Not

until February 15 was the Louvre ready to house its Queen. Having
been delayed so often, Marie could not but have found it strange
that even on the day of her arrival her apartments were still not
prepared. When she was finally established in the Louvre, she was
further bewildered, wondering if this were some strange French joke.
Walking through the cold, dark, badly furnished palace, she could
not believe that this was the home of the King whom she had
called "the greatest monarch in the world." Henri, with a distaste
for the Louvre, had never kept it in royal state. He avoided it
whenever possible, staying in other people's houses, spending as much
time as he could outside Paris. Having lived so long in camps and
journeys, he was accustomed to find his comfort where he could
and had but little sense of fitness about the splendor in which a
king should live. He had settled his mistresses in lovely houses,
but he had given but small thought to a worthy palace for his
Queen.

Scarcely had they been settled in the Louvre than that event
took place which was to color the remainder of Henri's married life.
At the command of the King, Madame de Nemours, dreading the
task yet unable to avoid it, presented Henriette d'Entragues to the
Queen. Although Marie's French was still halting, she had understood
enough of the gossip with which she was surrounded to be humiliated
and angered. What might have happened had the introduction ended
there, it is hard to say; but the King, hoping perhaps that candor
might clear the air, added, "This is my mistress who now wishes
to be your servant." No one records what was said on either side,
although some observers noted that the Marquise did not bow low
enough and that the King, angered by her arrogance, pushed her
to the ground. But no heavy hand upon her head could ever abase
Henriette. She knew it and so did the King; it was at once her
brightest charm and her most lethal weapon. "The Marquise, believing herself to have all kinds of power over the King, and availing
herself as usual of her vivacity and the sharp barbs of her words,
so pricked and offended the Queen time after time that at first
coldness, then indignation and anger formed between them, and
the King was constrained to separate them in order to maintain
peace on both sides."[20]

The meeting between Henriette and the Queen had been a public confrontation and it was not long before all of Paris knew of
it. In his dispatch to the Grand Duke, Giovannini reported it in

great detail, recording the King's words, Henriette's arrogant behavior, and Marie's equanimity. "The Queen received her in the usual manner and treated her thus throughout the evening without showing any displeasure," Giovannini wrote, describing in addition the "disgust and displeasure" which Paris felt at this humiliation to its Queen.[21] Marie's equanimity, however, was but the thinnest veneer. She was stricken and aggrieved that the King should have subjected her to such an ordeal. She was well aware that Henriette's curtsy had been an insufficient token of homage and that the gesture by which she had kissed the Queen's robe had in it something of disdain. Marie had had unlimited confidence that her royal prerogatives would put her beyond the reach of insults, but she was soon to learn that it was not so. The weapons of her queenship would never vanquish Henriette. Henriette had at her command weapons far more deadly, and she used them with the grace and skill of an accomplished swordsman. Alongside them Marie's pompous manner, and majestic style were clumsy and unwieldy. She had been in her husband's company little over two months and already seeds of distrust were beginning to root in her heart. She had heard rumors of his profligacy, but his loving letters had put her fears to rest. The days at Lyons had been both tender and joyous and in those first weeks she had proved her worth by conceiving the child he desired. Yet even while this child now quickened in her womb, the King her husband sat with his mistress at his side, laughing at her wit, and looking at her with something he had never shown to his wife. Bewildered and lonely, she turned for solace to those whom she knew best, the Italians of her retinue, chief among them Concino Concini and Leonora Dori, commonly called "Galigai."

Leonora Dori, a woman of "lowly birth," had been the daughter of Marie's nurse, and Marie had for her the affection of a sister. Thin, nervous, with pronounced features, and "great feverish eyes," Galigai had an insatiable ambition and a driving will. Impervious to insults, she took no notice of those who said she was no more than a carpenter's daughter; she kept close to the Queen, sympathizing with her in her misfortunes, making sure that she would soon be indispensable. Her "lowly birth" was not the only thing, however, that won the disdain of the French women of the court; even more notorious was her flagrant affair with her compatriot, Concino Concini, a handsome Italian of questionable reputation, whose conduct had compromised Galigai even before Marie's entourage had left

Lyons. Marie, eager for any solace, and with none of her husband's ability to read character, failed to recognize that her faithful Italians were exploiting her to their own advantage. Her favoritism soon won her the enmity of the French ladies who were put to serve her and her apparent approval of the Concini-Galigai romance did little to enhance her own reputation. She was soon accused of lack of circumspection, of neglecting the vigilance which it was her duty to exercise, of permitting licentiousness in those who served her.

When, at Galigai's request, she asked her husband to raise her Italian lady to a higher post, he categorically refused, telling Leonora that she must be satisfied with fixing the Queen's hair—and if she did not know how to do it in the French fashion, then she should learn. When, a little later, Marie approached him on the subject of a marriage between Concini and Galigai, he was even more vehement. If they wished to marry, he stated, then they could return to Italy and do so; but as long as they remained in France, he would never grant such a permission.

The Italians, however, were more than the King's equals in intrigue. Aware that his mistress could twist the King as she would, they now sought to exploit her to their own advantage. Leonora suggested to Henriette, with the subtlety of which she was master, that she might win the Queen to accept Henriette with better grace, might even induce her to grant Henriette a coveted part in the extravagant ballet which the Queen was planning, if, in return, Henriette were willing to use her influence to win the King's permission for her to marry her lover. Within a few weeks this amazing team had won its way: Henriette was "graciously" received by the Queen, Leonora was granted her coveted post—and on July 12 at the château of St. Germain-en-Laye she and Concini pronounced their marriage vows. It was the first in that remarkable series of intrigues by which they cemented their influence at court to the undying hatred of the French people—a series of intrigues which lasted beyond the death of the King and which ended ultimately in their downfall and violent deaths.

During the summer of 1601, however, the intrigues of Concini and Galigai became subordinate to that eagerly anticipated event: the Queen's delivery. Although the Queen bore her pregnancy with a minimum of difficulty, still the King was restive and anxious, recalling Gabrielle's death in childbirth and Henriette's stillborn child. His anxiety was not sufficient to keep him at court, however, and August and September were filled with short notes to the Queen, giving her the news of his affairs, affirming his sorrow in being separated from her, and encouraging her to be brave and patient as the time of her delivery approached. When Marie's labor pains began on September 26, the King was by her side, tenderly holding her during each spasm. Some time before, Marie was reputed to have said that if her child was not a boy, then she hoped that her bed would become her tomb. Marie had no cause to worry, however, for after twenty-two hours of labor, a son was placed in the King's arms at midnight of September 27. France had an heir at last. The King, beside himself with joy, flung open the doors of the waiting room, and into the Queen's chamber poured dozens of people. In answer to the midwife's reprimand, the King had only a simple answer: "This child belongs to everyone." Overcome with emotion, he touched the small hand to his own sword, saying: "Use it, my son, for the glory of God and for the defense of the crown and of your people."[22] The room was finally cleared, and the Queen, exhausted but triumphant, was put back to bed. For once she had pleased her husband; she had done what no other woman could do for him —she had borne him a son worthy to sit on the throne of France.

The following day a circular letter announcing the birth of the Dauphin went out to all the provinces of France: "Among the many miraculous signs of divine assistance that one has been able to notice in our favor since our accession to the throne, there is none that has made us feel more strongly the effects of His goodness than the happy delivery of our dear Queen, our beloved spouse and companion, who has just brought into the world a son which has given us a joy impossible to express."[23]

It was Giovannini, however, in his letter to the Grand Duke who best caught the note of messianic triumph in the birth of the Dauphin when he wrote succinctly: *Puer natus est nobis.*

CHAPTER XVII

The Bitter Cup: 1601–1604

France is like an apothecary's shop full of sweet things and pleasant
odors but also full of poisons and foul smells.

Henri de Navarre

❧❧❧❧ With the birth of the Dauphin an elation swept through the
French court. Mornay, Sully, Bellièvre, those influential statesmen who
had argued long and pleaded hard that the King enter into a marriage which would provide worthy heirs for the French throne, had
won at last. France had an heir. Within the week Henri had written
to the Grand Duke of Tuscany and his Duchess announcing the
birth of a son and thanking them warmly for having given him
his wife who had brought such great happiness to his kingdom. The
Duchess of Mantua, Marie's sister, was asked to be the godmother
and the Grand Duke to be the second godfather. The role of the
first godfather was to be filled by the Pope himself. For years all
Europe had watched nervously this aging King who had peopled
France with children from the wrong side of the blanket, but who
had failed to provide a legitimate heir to the throne. Now congratulations poured in on all sides.

To the Queen, however, congratulations meant little when compared
with her husband's smiles and approbation. He had told her that
she had "done well" and for Marie that sufficed. For a few weeks
she lived in sunshine as the King praised her for her health, her
courageous endurance during the long hours of labor, her fine powers
of recovery. The idyl was short-lived, however, for the following
month Henriette was brought to bed and this time gave birth to
a healthy boy. It came too late to fulfill the King's requirements of

her but Henriette, constitutionally incapable of admitting defeat, clung grimly to the King's promise, saying, "The Florentine has her son, but I have the Dauphin. . . . The King is my husband, for I have his promise."[1]

Marie's brief dreams of holding the King through her successful maternity faded. She had been in France less than a year and already the full weight of humiliation had fallen upon her. Less than a year before she had been deluged by letters from her husband, avowing his devotion, his love, his abiding fidelity; and she, who had known nothing of love before, had responded ardently. She had wanted no delays in her journey to France, for she had almost a child's eagerness in the marriage that awaited her. Even when Henri had not met her at Marseille, when she had made the long, cold journey to Lyons without him, still she had not doubted. She had believed without question in the notes that protested his sorrow at being kept from her, his determination to bring the affairs of state to a speedy conclusion, his joyful expectation in their meeting. The truth was obvious to her now, and anger, vengeful and bitter, shook her to her roots. With her anger, her goals shifted. She no longer set her sights solely on winning the King; now, she sought another object: to destroy her rival.

Before the year was out, opportunity played into the Queen's hands. She who could never match Henriette's cunning now found herself a party to a plot which would destroy the King's mistress at a single blow. It was Juliette-Hippolyte d'Estrées, Duchesse de Villars and sister of Gabrielle, who set the scheme in motion. At Gabrielle's death she had seen a chance of winning the King's affection, and she had never been able to forgive Henriette her success. Juliette's current lover was the young Duc de Joinville, youngest son of the murdered Duc de Guise. Like several young men, he had been seduced by Henriette and then dismissed. Joinville, determined to avenge himself, had at hand the perfect instrument: a packet of letters which Henriette had written to him during the month of the King's marriage negotiations with Tuscany. They were more than love letters—although as such they would be damaging—they were treasonous letters full of contemptuous remarks about the King and his "Fat Banker." Together, he suggested to Madame de Villars, they could bring Henriette to her ruin. The story was brought to the attention of the Queen, who acted precisely as they knew she would: triumphant, she revealed all to the King, producing the incriminating letters themselves as positive proof of her accusations. Henri had no illusions about Henriette's fidelity, but he was shaken with rage as he read the disdainful comments about himself with which the letters were filled. Sully later wrote that he had never seen the King in such a fury. A messenger was sent to Henriette to charge her with treason and to revoke all her privileges. But Sully, who was given charge of this delicate matter, walked cautiously, well aware that Henriette's wiles might be too subtle for the King's anger. Sully was, as usual, right; for Henriette, composed and innocent, soon had convinced the King that the letters were forgeries concocted by Joinville's secretary who had a reputation for such double-dealing. It was the thinnest of explanations, but Henri, who found it far less painful than the truth, appeared to accept it. It was not the King who forgave his mistress, but an aggrieved Henriette who forgave the King for his unjust accusations, even demanding an indemnity for libel of 6,000 pounds. Marie had not only failed to destroy Henriette, she had in fact destroyed something of herself. She had brought down upon her own head the contempt of the court, the anger of her husband, and, most painful of all, the laughter of his mistress. Henriette, more arrogant than ever, made arrangements for a great ball to be given on the Feast of the Holy Innocents, a ball to celebrate her rehabilitation.

When that spring the King and Queen went to Blois, Henriette went with them and was lodged with them in the royal château. Marie, knowing herself powerless, took refuge in her room, seemingly unaware that every burst of anger, every fit of sulking simply made the King's mistress more secure. Sophisticated and controlled, Henriette had the advantage in everything while the court was torn between pity and irritation for the Queen whose tears could never win back her husband. Sir Ralph Winwood observing the domestic squalls wrote to England of the Queen's conduct ". . . she kept herself retired in her chamber, either spending the whole day in bed, in tears and lamentations, or if she did rise, yet would not be persuaded to put on other clothes but those of her bed chamber. She refused to open the door to the King when he knocked, who returned with this answer, that she was *impedita*."[2]

In the spring of 1602, however, the King's domestic troubles were overshadowed by an affair that made the kingdom totter. Charles de Gontaut, Duc de Biron, peer and marshal of France, and close friend of the King, was accused and condemned of high treason. If Biron's treason rocked the kingdom, it rocked the King even more. For Henri it was a double tragedy: the King had been betrayed by his general; the friend had been betrayed by a friend. Henri, whose concept of kingship was colored by a large element of paternalism, had always been deeply disturbed by attacks on his life. When Pierre de Barrière had plotted to kill him the month after his abjuration, he had brooded for days, more disturbed by the assassin's attitude than by the danger to his own life; when Jean Châtel had attacked him after the recapitulation of Paris, he was depressed for weeks. Yet both of these attempts—and many others—had been plotted by men with strange fanatic aberrations for whom the King was not a man but a symbol of a cause they felt divinely called to oppose. But with Biron, the case was far different. Biron had led his armies and helped him conquer his kingdom; Biron had not only saved France but saved his king's life as well. And he had rewarded him: with money, with high positions, most of all with his trust. There had been times when the two men had clashed, when there had flashed through Henri's mind the thought that Biron sometimes played the game of war to his own advantage. He had not been pleased with the conduct of the seige of Rouen and later, in his anger over the loss of Amiens, he had indicated that Biron had not bestirred himself sufficiently. These, however, had been but passing episodes which the King had soon forgotten. They had never dictated his relations with Biron; if anything, he had treated him with more largesse. Biron, however, proud, ambitious, susceptible to slights, had forgotten nothing. He had that capacious memory with which petty men are sometimes endowed. It is difficult to know when the seeds of treason were sown, but many placed the date as January 1600, when the Duke of Savoy had walked through the French court lavishly bestowing presents with his right hand and flattery with his left—both with an eye to his own advantage. In Biron, Savoy found all he could have hoped for. When Savoy told him that he was a man of infinite capabilities, he had no difficulty in believing it. When he suggested further that these capabilities had never been properly employed, the marshal was equally credulous. Whether Biron and Savoy had already come to terms when Savoy left to return to his lands, it is impossible to say, but by 1601 Biron was already actively engaged in plans for marrying Savoy's third daughter and in doing what he could to assist the Duke and the King of Spain in their plans against France. This time, however,

Biron did not go through with the plot; perhaps, through fear, perhaps through remorse, he came to tell the King "all"—that he had been upset by the King's refusal to give him Bourges when he had been largely responsible for its capitulation, that he had entertained treasonous thought against His Majesty. Henri, who was incapable of resisting repentance, forgave him on the spot, assuring him that the past was already forgotten.

Although there had been those who had cautioned the King against continuing his trust in Biron, Henri had waved them aside, assuring Sully that Biron was basically loyal and brave—that his fault was impetuosity which sometimes made him say in anger things which he soon regretted. By the spring of 1602, however, Henri was forced to heed the various reports sent to him about his marshal. The man who finally provided conclusive evidence was one Jacques Beauvais de la Nocle, Seigneur de la Fin, a thoroughgoing villain himself, who doubtless betrayed Biron less out of loyalty to the King than for his own advantage. La Fin was known as a shiftless gentleman and small-time adventurer whose loyalties were always for sale. At first the King refused to listen to him, for it seemed like a case of a petulant lackey betraying his master. But the evidence which La Fin provided was incontrovertible. In his position as a kind of secretary to Biron, he had cleverly kept the originals of several treasonous letters while sending only copies to their destination. It was these he now presented to the King to substantiate his evidence. Whatever the personal character of La Fin, the King could not ignore the testimony of the letters.

The plot was in effect aimed at dismembering France. It had been hatched by that eternal schemer the Duke of Savoy, the Spanish ambassador Fuentes, and Maréchal de Biron. Toward the end of 1601, Biron urged on by Spain and Savoy had already begun to recruit an army from the off-scourings to be found in the city streets. Spain had agreed to take over Languedoc, Guyenne and Brittany; Savoy would invade Dauphiny, Lyonnais and Provence; while Franche-Comté and Burgundy would be left to Biron. The rest of France might, then, be divided among the other restless lords. It was the plan of a man who had never looked favorably upon a strong central government. Like Mercoeur, he harkened back to the days of feudalism, when a man could be truly lord in his own lands, with his own army, his own vassals, his own wars and revenges. Although Biron later affirmed that it was his dissatisfaction with the King's religious attitudes which had led him to an alliance with Spain, his own religious attitudes were both shadowy and unformed. Although he spoke of revitalizing the League with Spanish help, it was far less its religious goals than its opportunity for power which drove him on. It was later rumored that Biron had once been heard to say that he would not die happy until he had seen his image on a coin.

On one point Spain was adamant: it had no desire to invade a country where the King still ruled. Henri, his queen, and the Dauphin must be disposed of. It was suggested that the King be taken care of by a "hunting accident" or even by a simple assassination. Marie and the Dauphin would, then, cause little difficulty. They could easily be taken out of the country or imprisoned in some safe fortress. Regicide, however, was a serious business and some of those who were in the plot suggested instead seizing the person of the King and bringing him into Spain where he would be safe. In the *Procés Criminel* which followed Biron's arrest, it was reported that when Fuentes asked one of Biron's men what they planned to do with the King, he answered lightly, "Oh bring him into Spain; we'll give him a good time; he can play tennis and pass his time with the ladies."[3] The callous remark was, to the King who heard it, its own kind of assassination.

By the end of April, the King realized that he had to act on the evidence that continued to pour in. Several times he sent for Biron, in an effort to have him leave his territory of Bourgogne and force him to court to confront the King. Biron, however, stayed where he was. Even while the King wrote to La Force, Biron's brother-in-law, "I have discovered the greatest evils, treacheries, ingratitudes, and enterprises against me that you could possibly believe," he was also writing to Biron, assuring him of his affection and of his unshakable belief in Biron's fidelity.[4] Biron, however, despite the King's avowal of friendship, remained wary; he had no intention of stepping into a trap. It was not until the King sent Jeannin to deal personally with Biron, assuring him that whatever he had heard of the King's displeasure was entirely false, that he wanted nothing so much as the opportunity to clear up these misunderstandings that Biron agreed to a meeting.

It was the second week of June when Biron arrived at Fontainebleau, and the next twenty-four hours were hours of obvious anguish for the King. It had been no ruse when he had begged Biron to come to him, no ambush when he assured him of his continued affection. The King's role would have been far easier had his friendship for Biron turned to anger when La Fin had spread the treasonous letters before him. It was the King's strength to attract men to him and to respond to them by friendship; it was his weakness that his friendship was often misplaced, that it continued long after the object of it had proved himself unworthy. When he had begged Biron to come that they might clear up the false rumors that had been circulating, this was what he had really hoped for. He could not believe Biron innocent—the evidence was too conclusive for that—but he continued to hope that there might be some explanation, some small set of circumstances that could remove the ugly sound of treason in favor of a less bitter word. In effect, Henri's supreme desire was the desire to pardon. "If only he had asked my grace," he had sighed when he had been told that Pierre de la Barrière had gone to his death. It was this which he now wanted of Biron: a frank avowal of his fault, a plea for mercy, and a determination to face the future in fidelity. "He fights like a devil and pardons like a god," one of his contemporaries had said of the King; while another, less kind, interpreted the King's compulsion to pardon as a kind of pride, a desire to play the role of God with his subjects—bestowing his grace far beyond their deserts, that by that means the bonds which tied them to him might be strengthened. Like God, however, the King found his hands tied when his subjects refused to sue for grace.

Now, he turned the full strength of his desire into his interview with Biron. Had Biron recognized all the evidence that the King had against him, he might have made an open confession; but La Fin, the insatiable schemer, had whispered to him upon his arrival "take courage and stand firm, for they know nothing."[6] It was enough to give Biron that false confidence in which he played the next twenty-four hours. The morning of Biron's arrival, he had his first interview with the King. "You did well to come; otherwise I would have had to search you out," the King was reputed to have said to him. To all the accusations that Henri brought against him, the Marshal "haughtily denied all." When the interview was terminated, it was noted by those who had observed it that "the King's countenance had notably altered." After dinner, they talked again, but with the same result. The following day there was another long talk, but nothing was gained. That afternoon the King spent several hours walking in his gallery; he looked old and worn, helpless in the face of Biron's obstinacy. "I don't want to lose this man, but it seems to be his own desire to be lost," His Majesty observed. He had done his best, but he had lost. Biron had made his irrevocable error; it was not his treason which doomed him but his obduracy.

That evening they played cards together; a strange harassed game in which the King vainly tried to lose himself. Shortly after midnight the game broke up, but as Biron started toward his room, Vitry, the captain of the guards, and a good friend of the Marshal, put his hand on Biron's shoulder, and with his left hand on his sword, told him that he was under arrest. "The King has asked me to take charge of your person," he answered in reply to Biron's surprise. "Please give me your sword." With a show of anger and hauteur, Biron asked to speak to the King; but Vitry was firm, "The King has retired." That same night Charles d'Auvergne, Comte d'Angoulême, bastard son of Charles IX, and half-brother to Henriette, was also arrested on the charge of treason.

On June 14 the King wrote a circular letter advising the provinces of France of the discovery of the plot against his person and his state. It was a formal letter, doing no more than indicating the basic facts of the case and warning the people to take precautions to guard their cities. The following morning both men were brought under guard to the Bastille to await their trial. Ultimately, however, it was only Biron who stood trial, for the evidence against D'Auvergne was purported to be insufficient, although many murmured that it was his sister's influence that had won his freedom. Biron, meanwhile, had lost everything: his sword, his marshal's staff, the collar of his order, his ducal crown—and most of all, his dignity. For Biron, alone in the Bastille, facing death, was a far different man from the general who had captained armies in the field, a different man from the intrigant who had arranged to sell France to Spain. Biron, for all his pride, had few inner resources. He was a man of action, not a man of thought. Although he had always worn his religion proudly, it was in fact, a strange blend of superstition and bigotry—far from enough to sustain a man in the face of a humiliating death. He raged against the King and fulminated against the injustice that had brought him to such a downfall. But there was no one to listen, no one who could help. Brought up to give orders to others, he found himself strangely lost where there was no one to control but himself. Soon he grew quiet, and his guards discovered him painfully picking out the words in an almanac (for he was almost illiterate) in a desperate effort to see what the future held for him.

Some weeks later, Biron was brought to trial and condemned by his peers after several hours of deliberation. The judgment was inevitable, but it fell heavily upon the King for all that. On July 12, Henri wrote to De Fresnes his ambassador in Venice: "His treason is completely proved by his own confession. The Duke of Savoy and the Comte de Fuentes have been the main conspirators with Biron. . . . They have spared neither money nor any other kind of artifice. . . . Thus he was carried away by presumption and vanity and those to whom he sold his honor and his faith were of little trust and easy agreement."[6]

Despite his faults, however, Biron had been a popular soldier, and shortly after he was taken to the Bastille, Henri was confronted with a group of gentlemen led by La Force who came to plead in his belief. "Do all you can in defense of his innocence," he replied; "I will not oppose you in anything and I will even help you as far as I can."[7] But all their efforts could not negate the evidence, and the King refused to grant pardon where no pardon was asked. For all his courage, Biron did not die like a brave man. He could not believe that his life was over, could not believe that at the last moment, the King would not lift his hand to save him. But Henri did nothing, telling a friend that while he might have pardoned the injury to him, he could not presume to pardon the plot against the Dauphin and the state. On July 31, Biron, dressed in gray satin, wild with rage and still fulminating against the King who despite his hopes had not stepped in to save him, was beheaded in the courtyard of the Bastille. For Biron, at least, it was over; for the King it was but the beginning. With Biron's treason a weariness settled upon him; it was more than the weariness of age, more than the weariness of conflict. Treachery from his enemies was something that Henri had long lived with, as had his mother before him. Treachery by his friends was the bitter wine that had been saved for his last years. "The King was deeply touched by this treason," wrote L'Estoile. "Sometimes in affirming an incredible truth, he would say, 'This is also true, because it is true that Biron was a traitor.'"[8] "Avarice and ingratitude," wrote Giovannini to the Grand Duke some time later, in attempting to assess the motive for the conspiracy. For Henri, they were unnatural faults, and as such he could not understand them; it was to be his tragedy to be surrounded by them more and more in the years to come.

There were few joys in the months that followed. Biron had not been alone in his conspiracy. D'Auvergne had also been implicated and in his testimony had named as his accomplices Montpensier, Damville,

and Bouillon. How weighty the evidence against them or how trustworthy D'Auvergne's testimony, it is difficult to say, but by September
all charges had been lifted. For once the King's mercy did not meet
with popular approval, for it was, in D'Auvergne's case at least, so
palpably a matter of the King's infatuation with Henriette. Giovannini
wrote in surprise to the Grand Duke during the first week of October,
"The Comte D'Auvergne has avowed all. But through the influence of
the Marquise, his sister, he has been put at liberty." The verses which
made their round through Paris were more blunt in their judgment:

> Great God, what injustice:
> Two prisoners have merited
> The pain of the same punishment.
> The one who has always fought well
> Has died respected for his virtue
> The other lives for the love of vice.[9]

Marie was further humiliated by this public scandal which led people
to comment that the greatest betrayal of all was the King's own
betrayal of justice. When Henriette gave birth to a child just two weeks
after the Queen gave birth to a daughter, Marie's rages became frightening. Her majestic reserve had long since been cast aside and her
ladies-in-waiting, who had once criticized her pompous dignity, now
realized that it had been far easier to cope with than the scenes and
tantrums which now shook the royal apartments. The King confided
to Sully that they could not go for eight days without a quarrel, and
Sully himself recalled an incident in which the Queen scratched the
King's face in her anger, and would have struck him had Sully not
stayed her arm. Marie could not have chosen a more infallible way to
drive her husband into the arms of his mistress. Of this domestic
discord, Henri wrote to Sully: "I receive from my wife neither com-
panionship nor gaiety nor consolation, she either cannot or will not
show me any kindness or pleasant conversation, neither will she accommodate herself to my moods and disposition. Instead, she shows
such a cold and disdainful expression when I come in and go to kiss
and embrace her and laugh a little with her, that I am forced to leave
her in vexation and go look for my relaxation elsewhere."[10]

That spring however, just when things were at their worst, the King
and Queen were brought to a reconciliation when Henri fell dangerously ill. Like many people with strong constitutions, Henri paid

little attention to the advice his physicians gave him. He had been warned against the spicy foods he liked so well, warned against gorging himself on his favorite melons and oysters, but except when he was ill, he refused to heed his doctor's cautions. In mid-May, however, he was stricken more severely than he had ever been before. Later that month Cavalli wrote to the Doge, "The King has had a brief but very severe attack; they called it colic, but it was actually pain in the kidneys . . . so intense was the pain that he fainted twice."[11] This time Henri's natural optimism deserted him, and as he lay in bed he faced the possibility of death. Death had been on his mind in the weeks preceding his illness, for on April 3, Elizabeth of England had died at Richmond in the seventieth year of her age and the forty-fourth of her reign. It was hard for Henri to imagine England without Elizabeth. He had been but five years old when Elizabeth ascended the throne. During all the hazardous years of his own reign, Elizabeth had ruled England and had profoundly influenced the affairs of France as well. Although she had not always shown largesse in helping him, yet ultimately, doubtless for her own good as much as for his, she had stood by him with money and troops. Although frankly curious about each other, they had never met. It would have been an historic meeting, to see that interplay of subtlety and wit which marked them both. Now Elizabeth, twenty years his senior, had died, leaving the crown to her cousin James of Scotland, son of Mary Stuart, a woman whom she had always feared and for whose death she was responsible.

Even while he mourned England's sovereign, Henri himself had his brush with death. Although at first his physicians had assured him he was in no serious danger, his condition deteriorated and the bouts of pain became increasingly intense. On May 17 he sent for Villeroy and Sully, writing to the latter: "I feel so sick that there is a good chance that God wishes to dispose of me. Since, after the care of my soul, I have an obligation to take care of the usual measures for assuring the succession of my children, to reign securely to the advantage of my wife, of my state, my servants and my poor people whom I love as my own children, I desire to confer with you concerning all these things before coming to any conclusion."[12] "If only the Dauphin were a little older," the King was reputed to have murmured as he held a portrait of his twenty-month-old son.

During the days he lay in bed, the Queen was faithfully at his side. Moved by compassion for his suffering and made secure by that fact that it was she, not Henriette, who sat at his bedside, Marie was for a few days the woman she had always hoped to be: tender, gentle, understanding. So used to anger and recriminations, Henri basked in this display of unquestioning devotion. He discussed with her some of the affairs of state, told her that if he should die she must assume the role of regent, and encouraged her to learn as much as she could of the duties she might soon have to carry out. This mark of his confidence was the dearest thing he could have given her and she responded to it wholeheartedly. As it turned out, however, Marie was not to exercise her role as regent for another seven years; the King recovered rapidly and by the first week of June was able to travel to Paris although with the heavy burden of the doctors' advice: Let him abstain from every woman, even the Queen.

Even as his own health improved, however, his sister's grew more precarious. Whatever the King had hoped to achieve by her marriage had never come to fruition, for Catherine de Bourbon, after five lonely, tortured years of marriage died at the château at Nancy on February 12, 1604. As always, Henri, profoundly moved in the face of death, grieved over the death of this sister, six years his junior. He wrote to Beaumont, his ambassador in England, that he had just been informed of the "death of my sister . . . which has grieved and troubled me for I have loved her dearly; I could suffer no greater nor more painful loss (after that of the Queen, my wife, and her children—may God preserve them) than the separation of this only sister who has been my companion in all my adventures both good and bad."[18] So often calumniated in life, the calumnies continued after her death: Some said her death was a sign from God who had struck her down for her heresy as He had struck her mother before her: others that she was "helped" on her way because she had been an unendurable source of dissension at the court of Lorraine. Even her brother's grief was besmirched by those who said that he wept for a soul whose salvation seemed so uncertain. In fact, weakened by a hereditary pulmonary weakness, she had died of tumor, which she and even some of her physicians had misinterpreted as pregnancy.

For Catherine de Bourbon, however, with her perduring and visionary faith, death may not have been the final anguish, but a release from the loneliness and misunderstanding of her married life. For a while she had apparently been happy at the court of Lorraine, but soon her husband began nagging her insistently to renounce her heresy. In the summer of 1600 he journeyed to Rome, ostensibly to gain the indulgences of the jubilee year, hoping to influence the Holy

See to grant a dispensation, but privately seeking a sanction that would encourage him to "put Madame away publicly and never to return to her without a dispensation" since she was endangering his soul's salvation. It was a ticklish business, for should Bar repudiate his wife there would undoubtedly be a serious conflict between the King and the House of Lorraine; yet Clement, caught once again in a dilemma, would not permit himself to be badgered into granting a dispensation when there were clearly no grounds for it. "This affair of the Duc de Bar is a bad business,"[14] wrote D'Ossat to Villeroy in May of that same year.

Meanwhile, Catherine, unaware that her husband was secretly bargaining to repudiate her, wrote to her brother, "Here I am, wretched, far from my husband whom I love more than my life, to whom they preach every day that I am the cause of his damnation." The following year Catherine was invited to court to be present at the birth of the Dauphin, but also to be coerced into abjuring her religion. She listened to the preachers her brother provided, but she simply shook her head; she was not convinced. Henri, weary of her constancy, accused her of compromising the peace and destiny of France by her obduracy. Too weary to argue, she pleaded for permission to retire to Béarn which is all that she had ever wanted. Henri remained firm, until the day when Catherine, goaded beyond endurance, turned upon him saying, "Sire, they want me to believe that our mother is damned." Those who witnessed the scene said that the King, profoundly moved, turned away, saying to the Duc de Bar: "That's all I can do, brother; I am vanquished; now it is your turn to try."[15]

By the end of 1602, Catherine, already sick, was at the end of her resources; "God grant her His grace," wrote the sympathetic Duchesse de Bouillon. As a final resort she wrote to her brother begging him to use his authority with the Pope. "I am forced to implore you often on this subject which is now in such a state that I watch my husband in despair, seeing himself further from a dispensation than ever . . . have pity on us because as it is we live in every kind of suffering . . . the pain I feel is that of watching someone suffer who is dearer to me than anything in the world." Henri, perhaps more for his own sake than for hers, had already written to D'Ossat, assuring him that he had "employed every means to instruct and convert her to our holy religion" and begging the Cardinal to do all that he could to influence the Pope. "You are not unaware of the difficulties that could result in His Holiness' refusal to grant this dispensation," he concluded.[16] In

December 1602, the dispensation was granted at last—a conditional dispensation which laid upon Catherine the responsibility of taking instruction and of promising that her children be brought up in the Catholic religion. A year later, Catherine, without ever fulfilling the conditions of the dispensation, died in the château at Nancy at the age of forty-five. Although at the news Henri retired into mourning, his grief may well have been tempered with relief, that at least one unmanageable situation had reached a conclusion.

The King's anguish over the death of his sister was soon subordinated to a far more dangerous affair: another conspiracy against his person and the state. Ten years earlier the King had expressed a wish for peace, a wish that his old age might be spent in tranquillity, but it seemed to be a wish that would never be fulfilled, for he had no sooner come to terms with the enemies of his kingdom, than his friends set to work to undermine it. Once in a sardonic moment Henri had commented, "France is like an apothecary's shop, full of sweet things and pleasant odors but also full of poisons and foul smells."[17] In these last years of his reign it was the "foul odors" that came to the fore; the fetid smell of treason filled the court. This time it was not simply a warrior-friend who led the conspiracy, but the woman, who, it was said, having led the King to betray his honor now betrayed the King himself.

Henriette had long been playing a tortuous course. There had been lovers aplenty, barbs against the King, and insults directed at his Queen. During the winter of 1604 she had played a role that drove the King almost to distraction. It was a singularly inappropriate part in which Henriette had cast herself, for it was the role of remorseful penitent. She withdrew from the King, repulsing his advances, avowing that he had led her into sin, and that she wanted nothing but to do penance for her soul's salvation, declaring that she could no longer think of her past except with tears of repentance. She even spoke in vague terms of retiring to a convent to end her life in penitential discipline. Yet even as she wept for her sins, she entered into a conspiracy which, she hoped, would put her son on the throne of France and gain for her the ultimate power for which she had long yearned.

By the spring of 1604, rumors were pouring in from many sides of this second major conspiracy against the King; yet still the King hesitated, his need for Henriette eclipsing his responsibility to the state. The Tuscan agent wrote home in anger and bewilderment, "She has undertaken a thousand things deserving death and the King knows them all—absolutely all—and yet he puts up with them . . . in spite of all he loves her, tolerates everything from her, and cannot live without being near this woman." The King was not blind to Henriette's plots; his duty was clear to him, and yet he could not bring himself to exercise his authority. "It upsets me to have to use force against her," he wrote to Sully, "for she is very good company when she wants to be . . . and always has a joke to make me laugh, which I never find at home." On April 14, he again wrote to Sully, asking him to visit Henriette to advise her of his position, which, he said could be summed up in these words: *Caesar aut nihil.* Henriette, however, was far too confident of her power over the King to believe Sully's ultimatum and soon after Henri wrote to her himself: "If your acts followed your words, I would not be as dissatisfied with you as I am. Your letters speak only of affection, while your actions toward me indicate only ingratitude. For five years and more you have continued to live like this. . . . If you wish to treat me as I deserve, then I shall be yours more than ever; if not, however, then keep this letter, for it is the last you shall ever receive from me."[18] It was a brave boast, but one which the King was incapable of keeping.

By June, however, the King could delay no longer. An Englishman, Thomas Morgan, a former servant of Mary Queen of Scots, had been arrested and on being questioned had provided overwhelming evidence against Monsieur d'Entragues, his daughter Henriette, and the Comte d'Auvergne. On June 23, the Venetian ambassador wrote to the Senate: "The King has found from the English Catholic, whose arrest I reported, that Monsieur d'Entragues, father of the Marquise de Verneuil, has been plotting with the Spanish ambassador, in order to induce the King of Spain to support the claims of the Marquise's son to the title of Dauphin."[19] D'Entragues was arrested and many damaging papers, including one signed "Yo el Rey," were found in his possession. It was enough to imprison him, and Henri, momentarily finding himself with the upper hand, threatened him with death if he did not return the promise of marriage which he had made to Henriette four years earlier. On July 2, the foolish promise which had caused the King so much embarrassment was returned to him and in turn given to Marie de Medici who treasured it as a victor might treasure the standards of a vanquished enemy.

There still remained, however, the problem of the conspiracy. Henriette had for some time been under suspicion. She had spoken openly of being afraid of the vengeance of the Queen and of the possibility of seeking refuge outside France. She had insisted on taking lessons in Spanish, and had been reported as having entered into secret correspondence with Spain. Despite Morgan's incriminating testimony and the discovery of treasonous letters in the possession of D'Entragues, the King still dallied. When Henriette was faced with the details of the plot, she denied it all and her denial was reinforced by her father who assured the King that he was exaggerating the whole episode. He was willing to acknowledge a little "indiscretion," but nothing more. As for his daughter, she was innocent of it all. When the King sent Sully to his mistress to attempt to get a confession from her, assuring her that if she asked the King's pardon, he would forgive her everything, Henriette was her most arrogant self. Sully, for whom Henriette was the cause of every evil that befell the King, wrote of the interview: "I found a woman whom disgrace could not humble, whose insolence detection could not abate, and who endeavoring not to excuse herself or to implore a pardon, talked in the style of one who had suffered wrongs, not given them; . . . she complained, she raved against the King, she made new demands."[20]

Meanwhile, the King was doing all he could to get the elusive D'Auvergne back to court where he could be interrogated for his part in the conspiracy. But D'Auvergne, who had barely escaped unpunished in the Biron conspiracy, had no intention of placing himself in jeopardy again. His contemporaries could find little to say in favor of D'Auvergne. "Corrupt, fickle, cunning, inconstant," he had originally been destined for the service of the Church, but soon "threw off his cowl" to marry the oldest daughter of Montmorency-Damville. The Church lost but little, for D'Auvergne, even in the eyes of Frenchmen who were not above compromise, was a man rotten at the core. Finally it took force to bring D'Auvergne out of his own lands and to the court where he could be tried. He continued to deny his complicity, yet, wrote Sully, "fears, alarms, the wildness of his look and air, and the disorder of his whole person would have been sufficient testimony against him."[21] By December, both D'Auvergne and D'Entragues had been committed to the Bastille and Henriette was placed under guard in her own lodgings in the Faubourg St. Germain. Even this did not dispel Henriette's arrogance. She continued to speak "freely and proudly," saying she had no fear of death, and prophesying that should the King order her execution it would be his wife whom he murdered, for it was she and not Marie who had been validly married to the King. As for the rest, all she wanted was "a pardon for her father, a rope for her brother, and justice for herself."[22]

At the beginning of the new year their trial began. There were few who trusted their testimony for their perfidy was too well known; there were equally few who expected justice from the King. Sully, in despair over the King's weakness, wrote angrily, "Yes, perjury and lies; Henri, that man on every other occasion so upright, so open, so sincere, became acquainted with all these vices when he abandoned himself to love."[23] The trial was a network of evasions, contradictions, and counteraccusations. D'Auvergne was the most hopeless of witnesses; he shifted his ground from question to question; arrogant one minute, servile the next. He accused his half-sister of turning the King against him, exculpated himself from the implications of his deeds, refused to take seriously the evidence that was presented against him. Henriette was at least consistent, maintaining that she had nothing to fear and nothing to hide, indicating that D'Auvergne's damaging testimony against her was as false as all the rest of his statements.

It was Monsieur d'Entragues who played the most impressive role. He was quiet, deferential, logical. He made no accusations; he stood on his own "integrity," an innocent man caught suddenly in incriminating circumstances. He reminded the court of the many ways in which he had served the King and the kingdom and for which he had received little in return. His government of Orléanais had been taken from him and given to someone else; yet he had not complained—he had remained silent. Then his daughter, "the joy of his life," had been badly treated by the King and publicly insulted by the Queen. In addition, the promise which he had kept in good faith concerning the King's desire to marry his daughter had been forcibly taken from him. The atmosphere of France had become intolerable to him and he had thought of accepting the invitation of his cousin, the Duke of Lennox, to take his daughter for a visit to England. Henriette, fearing for her life in a court where the Queen's unreasoning anger was constantly directed against her, had agreed. However, before their plans for retiring to England had been completed, D'Entragues had been brought into the company of the notorious Spanish agent Tassis who had sown doubt in his mind about the validity of the King's conversion and recalled to him those glorious days when the League had risked everything for a truly Catholic France. It was not too late for such a dream to come true, Tassis had suggested, inferring that D'Auvergne might soon be carrying the red cross at the head of Spanish troops.

To all of this he had done no more than listen silently, adjured D'Entragues, never consenting, never allying himself with the conspirators. Yet his very presence at their meetings had incriminated him, and this fact Tassis had used as a kind of blackmail to implicate him further. Tassis finally arrived at the core of the matter: the right of Henriette's son to succeed to the crown, a right that could be implemented by marrying him to the daughter of the Most Catholic King, who could then take him—and the French throne—under his protection. D'Entragues denied emphatically that he had ever become partner to such a plot, that he had ever intended to give the King's promise into Spanish hands—although conclusive evidence of this had been found among his papers—denied everything in fact except that he had been exploited by a group of subtle intriguers. His conclusion was a master stroke: he could not reveal all, he said, without offending and injuring the King, and so out of his respect for His Majesty he was constrained to keep silent.

The accused had done their best, but it was not enough: on February 1 the court convened and convicted them of the crime of *lèse majesté*. D'Auvergne and D'Entragues were sentenced to beheading and the Marquise de Verneuil to spend the rest of her natural life in the cloister of Beaumont-les-Tours where she was to have no converse except with the religious.

The sentence of death had fallen, but it had fallen not only upon the conspirators but upon the King as well. He had been sorely wounded by Biron's treachery, but with this conspiracy the knife had reached his heart. "I have worked hard for France," he had once said to Sully. He had fought for her and suffered for her; despite his innate love of peace he had spent half his life in battle that the enemies of France might be vanquished and the kingdom restored to its former glory. That any of his subjects, whom he so often referred to as his "children," should wish to take his life, grieved and bewildered him; that Henriette should be willing to do so was beyond his conception. Had there been a single visible sign of remorse, a single plea for mercy he could have forgiven her. Even in her condemnation she held the whip hand, for he could not pardon her while she continued to deny her guilt. The paradox was that the more successful he became as King, the less personal happiness he experienced. He had done wonders for his kingdom, it was true, but now all his success seemed very dry and bitter as he listened to the verdict which pronounced those closest to him guilty of *lèse majesté*.

CHAPTER XVIII

The Last of Everything: 1605–1610

Kings are the living images of God . . .

Duchesne

❧❧❧ There were few who felt that the sentence passed by the
court on February 1 was final. The King would find a way to save his
Marquise, of that they were sure. That same day Anzolo Badoer wrote
in his report to Venice that the Duke of Lennox, cousin to the
D'Entragues and "ambassador of 'Great Britain' as he is styled by his
master" had had an audience with the King in which he pleaded in
behalf of the conspirators. "The King replied," continued Badoer, "that
he did not wish to interrupt the course of justice but that he would
remember the Duke's intercession when justice had run its course."
It was an ambiguous answer, leaving room for the King's subsequent
explanation that his mercy to the D'Entragues had been dictated by
the necessity for keeping relations cordial with the English ambassador.
Six weeks later, Badoer again wrote to Venice, this time presenting a
fait accompli: "The King to please the Duke promised to grant them
their life, their liberty, and their honor."[1] Whatever Lennox' diplomatic influence, it was, of course, Henriette who had turned the tide.
The prospect of a life spent within the cloister of Beaumont-les-Tours
had diminished her arrogance sufficiently to have her write at some
length to the King. While her letter could hardly be called either a
confession, an apology, or a plea for mercy, at least it provided the
King with a minimal excuse for shifting the course of justice. It was
a clever letter in which Henriette used to the full those ploys which
had never failed in the past to win the King: "I do not ask to be
able to justify myself by mere words, since my past actions provide

sufficient witness of my plans. . . . I ask only that in my sorrow I be permitted to have you hear my laments; and after all it is only right that since it is Your Majesty who wishes that I suffer like this that at least you should endure that I speak about it. . . . There was a time when Your Majesty received me with loving kisses, in place of the bitter remarks which come to me now, and with sighs of love instead of tears of distress. I was always pressed to your mouth and even better to your soul . . . now all that former happiness has been changed into distaste . . . unhappily the heavens have permitted my condition to be changed, but my affection has not changed. I love as before, I burn with as much ardor as before, but not with the same happiness . . . for he who once loved me more than his own life now looks forward to the hour of my death, which although he may not desire it, he is in some way the cause of.

"You have never really loved me, or if you did your love was not intense enough. . . . If you do not wish me to owe my liberty to my innocence, at least let me owe it to your goodness, in the same way that I am indebted to your past love more than to my own merit. Freed thus, I will be more than ever the slave of Your Majesty and much more your prisoner when I shall be least imprisoned."[2]

This was the chance that Henri had longed for, and with it the machinery of pardon was set in motion. Not long after, Monsieur d'Entragues' sentence of death was commuted, and within months he was permitted to retire to his home at Malesherbes, while Henriette was given her entire liberty. Only the unfortunate D'Auvergne was left indefinitely in the Bastille.

During the months of the Marquise's disgrace, the Queen had had her golden opportunity—an opportunity which a more intelligent and perceptive woman might have turned to her permanent advantage. Marie, however, resentful of the past and suspicious of the future, did nothing in those months to draw her husband to her. With the King's promise of marriage to Henriette in her hands and with Henriette herself in confinement, she had everything she had dreamed of. She was, for the moment at least, the victor; but her conquest brought her neither security nor happiness. She could not put down her arms, but continued to fight the shadow of her adversary long after Henriette had vanished from the scene.

In the first few months after he had granted Henriette her liberty, the King was prudent enough to keep her out of Paris, but in the summer

of 1606 she was again in the capital, more shameless and more auda-
cious in the awareness of having vanquished not only the King but the
interests of justice itself. Her ostensible reason for coming to Paris was
to congratulate Henri on his near escape from death when the royal
carriage, carrying both the King and the Queen, had plunged off the
ferry at Neuilly. Marie, hearing that Henriette upon learning of the
accident had laughed that had she been there she would have cried,
"The Queen is drinking," was beside herself with rage. "She and the
King went for fifteen days without speaking and it took the King's
most powerful and influential people to appease her," wrote the Princesse de Conti.[3] No one could calm the Queen and she swore that she
would never leave her apartments while Henriette remained in Paris.
Henri, unable to cope with the tempest, was forced to capitulate and
send Henriette back to Verneuil.

Her departure, as anyone but Marie could have foreseen, simply enslaved the King further, and the letters he wrote in the fall of that
year were more passionate, more unrestrained than ever before. Letters
followed fast upon each other that October—letters with a single
theme: without his mistress he could find no joy. "It is beautiful here,"
he wrote, "but no matter where I am unless I am with you I am so
bored that I can scarcely endure it." Find some means so that I can see
you in private before the leaves fall," he wrote with a certain autum-
nal melancholy. And a few days later: "Be assured, my heart, that I
love you with everything I am and with greater passion than I have
ever felt." For a while, Henriette seemed to respond, writing often to
him, and telling him the one thing that he wanted to hear. "I have
received three letters from you and hope to receive more . . . ," he
wrote on October 23. "Believe me when I say that this is the only time
I am truly happy. For outside of your presence or of news from you,
I find no more joy than I would find salvation outside the Church."[4]

Henriette's reciprocal devotion during these months may have been
caused less by her gratitude at being given back her liberty than by her
awareness that she was not the only object of the King's affection.
According to court gossip, royal favorites tumbled in and out of the
King's apartments with embarrassing frequency, but two of them remained long enough to pose a serious threat to Henriette. During the
period of the D'Entragues conspiracy, Henri had become interested in
Jacqueline de Beuil, a sixteen-year-old orphan in the service of the Princesse de Condé. Although she was not among the beauties of the
day, she had those qualities of gaiety and wit which always attracted

the King. Although the affair never took on the proportions of his affair with Henriette, it did, nevertheless, give him another son, Antoine de Bourbon, who joined the mélange of children in the nursery of St.-Germain and won for Jacqueline the title of Comtesse de Moret. Even before this affair terminated, however, the King had turned his attention to Charlotte des Essarts, who soon proved by her flagrant infidelities that she was far from the ingénue that the King had mistaken her for. She, too, gave the King a child, but even before its birth Henri had grown weary of her, and shortly after she was sent at the King's command to live a life of seclusion among the nuns of Beaumont-les-Tours—a monastery which by this time had about it the air of a seraglio.

The King's affairs could not have been more public or more debasing. "Has anyone ever seen anything more like a Bordello than this court!" wrote the Tuscan ambassador in exasperation.[5] Although the Queen had never been a popular figure at court, there were few who did not sympathize with her in the intolerable position in which she was now cast. There was even gossip that the marriage could not last, and that the Queen was already making secret plans to return to Italy in company with her favorite, Concini. But although the women who came and went in the King's affection were affronts to her majesty and her womanhood, it was still Henriette d'Entragues against whom her anger was directed. Here she would make no compromise, threatening violent action should Henri permit the Marquise to return to court. In her own ill-advised way Marie was dauntless, and in the beginning of March 1607, the King wrote in annoyance to Sully, whom he so often used as an intermediary with his wife, "I have just received a letter from my wife—the most insolent letter possible." The letter, examined dispassionately was far from insolent, for it did no more than plead with the King to undertake an action which would obviously be to everyone's advantage: "I am forced by my honor, my conscience, and my duty to your service to plead with you constantly to relinquish this friendship which is so distasteful to your most faithful subjects and so prejudicial to your health, your life, and to my own well-being and tranquillity."[6]

With no reply save the King's anger, she turned in her despair beyond the French court to her uncle, the Grand Duke of Tuscany. Even this communication required some ingenuity, for if Marie is to be believed, Henri had forbidden her to write openly to Florence. Yet Marie, at the end of her resources, braved the King's anger and wrote openly to her uncle: "Suffice it to say that I have no other suffering or anxiety except that which comes to me from the Marquise; whoever declares himself in her favor, declares himself my enemy. If I could have it my own way, I would avenge myself on her in the harshest way possible. May Your Highness come to my help in whatever way you can, for you must realize that there is no other recourse available to me and that my sole hope is in you. I commend myself to you in this distress with tears in my eyes, and if in my suffering I can find some assistance from Your Highness, then for the love of God and in the name of his holy pity, do not refuse me, for I assure you that I will compensate you for this in whatever way I can. This letter has been written at three different times and in secret because on one occasion the King has forbidden me to write."[7]

Despite her pleas, Marie was to receive little help from Tuscany. On the contrary, another uncle, Don Giovanni de Medici, who was currently at the French court, only did her further disservice by flattering the King and making light of the Queen's distress. Only the King could relieve Marie's suffering and this he showed no inclination to do, although in the fall of 1607 his relations with Henriette were once more discordant. His letters were a curious alternation of affection and recrimination. "I have received your letter," he wrote in mid-October. "It is true that on Sunday we decided to spend an hour figuring out some way of living which would bring us more happiness than your ingratitude and capriciousness has brought us in the last four years." Yet within days he was willing to assume the guilt of their tumultuous relationship: "I did not mean to offend you when I said that only you could turn my sadness into joy. . . . You say that my sadness is not your fault; I have never said it was. Since it does not seem to be caused by anything in this world, possibly it proceeds from the spleen. . . . I kiss your hands in all humility."[8]

The complexity of court relationships was further increased that summer with the arrival of Marguerite de Valois who had grown lonely in her mountain fastness of Usson and who had received the King's permission to return to Paris. The Marguerite who arrived in the capital that July was far from the beautiful creature who had been exiled by her royal brother just twenty-three years before. She was no longer "the glass of fashion and the mould of form." She had grown heavy and clumsy in the years she had spent at Usson. Isolated so long from the world of fashion, she had lost touch with it and still dressed and painted in the outmoded fashion of the Valois court. Her heavy cheeks were extravagantly rouged and she wore an elaborate blond wig to hide her premature baldness. She had lost nothing of her sense of romance, however, and her house, the Château de Madrid, was soon peopled with the poets and artists and philosophers whose conversation she found so stimulating. There was always in attendance at least one young man—sometimes more—and the people of Paris soon found that although Margot had changed in many ways, one characteristic still persisted: the faint aura of scandal was always about her. Of all the women who moved in the orbit of the King, however, his former wife caused him the least embarrassment. She had promised that she would be one of his most faithful subjects and she kept the promise well. Instead of her anticipated rivalry with Marie de Medici, there was instead a deference and respect which soon wore away the Queen's cold defenses. Far from being envious of the children who peopled the nursery, Margot, who had never had a child of her own, took the Dauphin as her special charge, showering him with both presents and affection and naming him her heir.

Margot's loyalty, however, was but small comfort to the King in the broils which continued to disturb France long after the D'Entragues conspiracy had been laid to rest. Chief among these was that stirred up by a faction of the Huguenots under the leadership of the Duc de Bouillon. Despite the King's efforts to satisfy their demands, the Huguenots had continued to be a factious group, and in August 1605, Henri wrote in annoyance to Mornay who was attending a Huguenot assembly: "I desire the well-being of those of my subjects who are of the Reformed Religion . . . but I cannot tolerate that under pretext of religion, they would wish to establish in my kingdom a faction contrary to my sovereign authority."[9] At the time of the Biron conspiracy, many accusations had been leveled against Bouillon, and after Biron's death, the charges against him had persisted.

By the beginning of 1605 Bouillon was again stirring up trouble, and Henri's agents brought him news not only of troops being levied in Germany but of plans for uprisings in Quercy, Limousin, Périgord as well. Throughout the summer and into the fall, the affair continued without resolution, with the King unwilling to take the initiative in the conflict and with Bouillon resolved not to back down, insolently boasting, according to Sully, that he had but to stamp his foot in order to bring 4,000 armed men to assist him in his own territory of Sedan. By mid-March, the King, recognizing that he had no alternative, set out from Paris to besiege Sedan.

The conflict that France feared, however, was destined never to take place, for Bouillon's bluster died in the face of the King's forces and by April 1 Henri was able to write, "The treaty is going to be completed and I hope it will be signed today or tomorrow."[10] When on April 28 the King entered Paris with Bouillon at his side, not simply fully reinstated in his lands but in the King's friendship as well, some who had served the King loyally at great personal expense, wondered cynically if perhaps treason rather than fidelity might not be the gate to royal favor. Bassompierre, Henri's friend and confidant, having described the scene in which the erring Duke had thrown himself at the King's feet, avowing his undying loyalty, concluded with some bitterness, "From that time on Monsieur de Bouillon lived as he had before."[11]

The more discord Henri found in his domestic and political life, the more he cherished the public image of himself as the *Rex pacificus*. When in 1606 the continuing hostility between Venice and the Papacy reached a point of open conflict, Henri offered himself as arbiter, a position which, as he explained, was based upon his "devotion and gratitude" to both parties. The role which Henri assumed with the mutual consent of Venice and the Papacy was a complex one. Venice was already under interdict—an interdict which failed to cow the dissenting leaders—and Paul V, who had succeeded Clement VIII the previous year, although assuring everyone of his desire to end the conflict, maintained that he could hardly initiate reconciliation without some token of good will on the part of the Venetians. It took months of skillful and devious French diplomacy before a compromise was reached in the summer of 1607. Although this was far from a glorious or permanent conclusion, it reaffirmed Henri's position as a Christian prince of power and influence, won the gratitude of the Vatican, and underscored his image of himself as the king of peace.

Although it had been as a military leader that Henri had first won the respect and admiration of his people, his aim had never been sheer conquest. He had fought without respite to win his kingdom because he saw no other way to peace; and peace, he well knew, was the fundamental requisite for restoring France to her former glory. In the years following Bouillon's submission, Henri found himself at last the king of a peaceful kingdom. The question which had plagued him so long had been amply settled: France had its heir, and not only a single heir—for Marie de Medici had proved as fecund as her kinswoman Catherine before her. By 1609 she had given the King three sons and three daughters. The nursery at St. Germain teemed with children, for the King paid scant attention to the Queen's outraged protests that her children should not be raised with the royal bastards. To Henri it was all one. He loved his children no matter whence they came and had no patience with the convention which would keep them separate. His children were often his greatest pleasure. He played with them, talked with them, listened to them. He was amused by their conversation, rejuvenated by their affection. When they were sick he waited anxiously for news of them, filling his letters with details of their colds, their measles, their fluctuating temperatures.

St. Germain-en-Laye became his favorite home, and now that he had more time and money at his disposal he set about beautifying it. Years before, even when he was straitened for funds, he had ordered apricot trees to be brought from Pau and planted in the gardens of St. Germain. Now he set about an elaborate plan of building and decorating. The Tuileries, St. Germain, Fontainebleau, Montceaux were all redecorated and in some cases enlarged. He was fascinated by the business of construction and was often out at dawn to watch the laborers as they worked. It was his gardens, however, that received most of his attention. Wherever he could he built parks rich with shrubs and shade trees, planted orange groves, and designed elaborate gardens. It was not only his own homes which benefited from his desire for beauty. Throughout the last years of his reign, France found herself in a fever of reconstruction: churches and convents were rebuilt, cornerstones laid for new hospitals, streets were paved, bridges repaired. Throughout the kingdom existing highways were improved and other roads cut through forests to improve communication. New wharves were built in Paris and the Pont-Neuf, begun long before under Henri III and hailed as a miracle of original construction, was completed. Whoever would have thought ten years ago, mused Sully with a certain complacence in his successful fiscal policies, that the King would ever be rich enough to do all this.

This, however, was the crux of the matter, for France as a whole was far from rich; and while the King extended his parks and lawns, the poor continued to murmur in their poverty. L'Estoile writing of conditions in 1608 characterized it as a year in which living was much more expensive than heretofore for the poor. "There is little fruit; bread, wine, and meat are dear and all other commodities and merchandise are equally so." That same year, an anonymous chronicler describing the exorbitant increase in taxes indicated the increasing unpopularity of the King's efforts to raise money: "Everybody is murmuring about it, especially the poor merchants who have been sheared so often that they are shivering of cold."[12] In 1609 the King sent several new edicts to Parlement for registration, but Parlement knowing that the people were already taxed beyond endurance, balked at the measures.

Had the cause seemed to warrant it, the people might have accepted the increased taxation with better grace. But everywhere they found the swell of luxury with its attendant licentiousness and they wondered if the days of the Valois were coming upon them again. Bribery and graft were infections that had spread throughout the realm. Dueling was at its height; financiers gave banquets which would have cost a lesser man his whole fortune; young gallants were bedecked in finery with jewels twinkling even on their shoes. When in September 1606, the Dauphin was brought to his solemn baptism, the court was resplendent. Few could remember more extravagant dress. The men were as bejeweled as the women. D'Epernon's sword was covered with hundreds of diamonds and Bassompierre's cloak was so heavy with seed pearls that he could hardly move. There were some who called it a display of unrivaled magnificence, but many among the poor uttered a harsher phrase.

Years earlier, in describing the court of Nérac, the Vicomte de Turenne had warned that luxury breeds vice as heat breeds serpents. Paris in these years might have drawn the same conclusion. At the end of 1608, L'Estoile summed up the spirit of the court in frightening terms: "At court one talks only about duels, whoring, and pimping; gaming and blasphemy are in vogue; sodomy (which is the abomination of abominations) reigns. . . . God has given us a prince totally unlike Nero, for he is good, just, virtuous, and God-fearing and naturally abhors this abomination. But there is no one to be found in all the court, neither cardinal nor bishop, nor chaplain, nor confessor, neither priest, nor Jesuit who will open his mouth . . . to remonstrate with His Majesty about this for fear of incurring the anger and dislike of some of the great who are called the gods of the court; preferring to go along with these handsome gods (who are actually only devils) than with the living God."

"The year of the hard winter" was L'Estoile's description of 1608, for in addition to the man-made privations under which the poor suffered, nature, too, had conspired against them. "No one ever remembered it so cold," L'Estoile commented as he described the vines

frozen and the trees killed; cattle dying in the fields and men freezing
to death in the streets of Paris as packs of wolves howled at the very
gates of the city. Then, in the fall, almost without warning, the Loire
had overflown its banks. "This whole passage was one continued sea,"
Sully wrote, "in which the boats swam over the tops of the trees and
houses that the water had yet left standing. . . . The desolation was extreme and the damage infinite."[13]

In the midst of the disaster, Henri wrote with compassion, "God has
given my subjects to me in order that I may protect them as my
children,"[14] but the words rang empty to many who watched him
squander his money at the gaming tables and his heart's affection on
the irresistible Henriette. Spring and summer of 1608 were filled with
letters to her, letters protesting his undying love, his need for her, his
single desire to be in her company. "I only wish that you were in my
arms," he wrote on April 10; and two days later, "I do not know how
to pass a single day without reminding you of me, loving you perhaps
more than I ought; but I have no regrets—on the contrary, I want to
love you more than I have ever done." When Holy Week had passed
without his writing to her, he hastened to explain, "My dearest heart,
it is not my devotions that have kept me from writing to you, for I do
not think it is wrong to love you more than anything in the world;
rather it is because I have been sick." But there had crept into even
these impassioned letters a note which had never been there before: a
nostalgia, a sense of something lost that could not be recaptured. It
was a new experience for the man of action who had always lived so
much for the future to find himself slowed to inaction by a melancholy
reminder of "days gone by." It was in such a vein that he wrote to
Henriette toward the end of May: "A hare led me up to the crags in
front of Malesherbes, where I experienced the truth of the saying that
'surpassing sweet is the remembrance of past pleasures.' I wished that
you were in my arms as I used to see you. While reading my letter, remember that this memory of what used to be will make you scorn all
that the present holds for you. . . . My dearest love, if I sleep my
dreams are of you; if I am awake my thoughts are just the same."[15]

Soon, however, even the nostalgic joys of past happiness were embittered by the increasing awareness not simply of Henriette's callous-
ness—that he had long acknowledged—but of his own waning attraction. In place of his old tendency to find excuses for her ill-temper and
infidelities he became increasingly angry at her treatment of him. "I
have never kept anything from you, but you have deprived me of every-

thing you could," he wrote angrily, adding, "Do not imagine that you can nourish me with stones, after having once given me bread." When he discovered Henriette's little son reading his prayers in Spanish, his anger was unbounded that his mistress, whom he had once so generously pardoned for her treasonous relations with Spain, should not only inculpate herself again but should try to influence their son in that direction. The letter in which he expressed his displeasure had a new note of finality about it: "The reason I wanted to see you was to put an end to our affair; but since you have other considerations, do as you please." "Your ingratitude has at last conquered my passion," he explained in one of his last letters to the woman who had bewitched him for more than eight years—always to his torment and often to his ruin.[10]

No man in France was happier at this turn of events than the Duc de Sully who had been the Marquise's avowed enemy since that day in October 1599 when the King had shown him his reckless promise of marriage to Henriette. Now that the King's mind was free from the distractions of love, he could be moved, so Sully hoped, to further implement that "Grand Design" which was to be the successful instrument for diminishing the power of the Hapsburg in both its Austrian and Spanish branches and shifting the balance of European power in favor of France. It was not a new goal. He was, in a sense, simply carrying on that ancient quarrel which had formerly been incarnated between François I and Charles V. The means by which Henri hoped to achieve his goal, however, was less a matter of direct confrontation than of careful and patient diplomacy.

Well aware that his alliances with Protestant princes were always interpreted by Spain as proof that his Catholicism was no more than a cloak to hide his true religious feeling, he now worked toward winning certain Catholic powers to his side. He hoped that his mediatorship in the Venice affair had won him the lasting confidence and good will of both Venice and the Vatican. He further encouraged the Pope by pointing out the immeasurable advantage should Milan and Naples be freed from Spanish rule and brought under the aegis of the Papacy. Savoy, whose lands were strategically located, he won, after years of enmity, by marrying his daughter to the Duke's son. Perhaps most important of all, he succeeded in January 1608, after years of encouragement and negotiation, in signing a treaty with Holland, a treaty which not only promised him practical help but had the added blessing of humiliating the King of Spain, who had fought persistently against such an alliance.

The stage was no sooner set than the curtain was raised on the act which would propel Henri's carefully wrought design into operation. On March 25, 1609, a petty German sovereign—known by the unprepossessing epithet William the Simple—died in his duchy of Cleves. No sooner had he breathed his last, than William, who had made but small stir during his lifetime, became the center of an international crisis. Shortly after receiving news of the Duke's death, the Emperor Rudolph II, claiming imperial prerogative and feudal rights, stepped in and appointed a temporary governor. It was not an unanticipated move, for William had left no children, and as always in such cases, there were a large number of claimants for the succession. Henri had anticipated such a difficulty several years before and had urged the German princes to forearm themselves against possible Hapsburg aggression by reaching some mutual agreement about the future heir. He had already written to the Landgrave of Hesse: "I have told you myself when I have seen you and I have often written to you . . . the reasons and considerations which have led me to exhort, counsel, admonish, and help you in forming a strong nation in Germany among those princes who are not allied with the House of Austria for the preservation of your liberties which are threatened on all sides."[17] The initial hesitation of the princes was dispelled during the intervening years when they were witness to many such acts of aggression; and in the spring of 1608 a small confederation of German states was formed which promised mutual help with a common army and a common treasury. They were, then, somewhat prepared when the Emperor deputed the Austrian Archduke Leopold as temporary ruler of Cleves. It was the tactical moment Henri had long awaited, and he announced without hesitation his resolution to assist his allies against their unjust aggressor.

His announcement was greeted with bitter accusation from many quarters. In mid-August he wrote to Sully informing him that the Emperor had already sent one of his servants to him "with the express purpose of advising me of his coming into the estate of Cleves and the reason for this. He has begged me not to involve myself against his imperial authority." It was clearly a threat, and Henri responded to it by reaffirming his decision. In answer to the remonstrance sent by Paul V, he simply reiterated his duty to see justice done, pointing out to his ambassador at the Vatican that the Pope, of all people, could not capitulate to the pressure exerted by the Hapsburgs since he has "a certain obligation in virtue of his duty as a common father." To those who accused him of deliberately propelling Europe into war for his own interests, Henri countered: ". . . it seems that you have been informed of my intentions on the affairs of Cleves and Juliers counter to the truth and sincerity of which my actions bear witness. I have never favored an invasion of this country, nor thought to prejudice the right of others, especially that of the House of Saxony with whom the kings my predecessors have always lived in friendship and confederation. This reproach would be better addressed to those who have no scruple about appropriating to themselves . . . goods to which they have no right except that of their own pleasure, than to me who have favored and preferred the advancement of peace for my neighbors over all other considerations." But, he continued, should the countries to which he is allied be threatened, then he had every intention of protecting them. If, under such circumstances, "fire and war" be rekindled in Christendom then "those shall be responsible who have favored the injustice of this cause."[18]

Throughout the fall and into the winter of 1609, anxious letters continued to pour into the French court: angry letters accusing him of warmongering, pleading letters begging him not to plunge Europe into a full-scale conflict; temperate letters arguing that even he would have more to gain from peace than from war. Through it all, however, there was no sign of capitulation on the part of the Emperor, and in response Henri gave commands that would put into action the machinery of war.

At best it was a complex and dangerous situation, for many of those whom Henri had hoped to entice by promises of Hapsburg lands remained unwilling to commit themselves until they had seen how the tide was running. Holland, despite her alliance with France, feared to violate her truce with Spain should she overtly throw in her lot with France; the Pope whose presence would be of infinite moral support, although tempted by the thought of the increase of papal territory, remained sufficiently intimidated by Hapsburg power and Hapsburg righteousness to cast his vote for peace at any price. Even to many in France who agreed with the King in principle, his plan seemed ill-advised. Victory was not self-assured, and no Frenchman wanted a part in such a failure. For many more, however, it was a scheme made murky not only by self-interest but by the ambiguous religious coloring which seemed to place the Most Christian King at the head of a Protestant alliance. Henri had once commented bitterly that one of the things that no one would believe was that the King of France was a good Catholic. It was even harder to believe it now when he set himself in opposition to the most formidable of Catholic rulers, and deliberately encouraged and championed a union of Protestant princes.

If the religious issues muddied the waters through which France had to pass, they were made murkier still by the last and most debasing of the King's *fols amours*. Henri who, it was said, had once sacrificed a military victory for the sake of seeing Corisande, who had brooked no opposition in his plans to marry Gabrielle, who had all but thrown away the queenship in his promise to Henriette—Henri was in love once again. "Romance" had often been the word which had been used to characterize his liaison with Corisande, "magic" of his relation with Gabrielle, "sorcery" of his affair with Henriette. This time his love was characterized by a baser word: "besotted" was the term which some used to describe this new passion for Charlotte de Montmorency, daughter of the Constable Montmorency-Damville. The King was fifty-four; Charlotte was barely sixteen. According to contemporary accounts, the King first noticed her as she rehearsed for a ballet, "Des Nymphes de Diane," at the Louvre in January 1609. Dressed as a huntress, she catapulted into Henri who was watching the rehearsal from a doorway. She raised her bow as if to shoot—and future events proved that the shot found its mark.

The fact that the lovely Charlotte was already promised by her father to the King's handsome young friend, Bassompierre, did nothing to allay his passion. Little more than a month after his first encounter, he sent for Bassompierre to explain to him that he was "overcome and beside himself" in his passion for Mademoiselle de Montmorency, suggesting that it would be better for all concerned for Bassompierre to relinquish his claim to her hand. Instead, the King would marry her to the Prince de Condé, a young man "who prefers hunting to women." The value of such a union was clear: Condé would receive a lavish fortune for his compliance; Bassompierre would retain his friendship with the King; Henri would be able to keep Charlotte at court where she would be the "consolation and care" of his old age. Bassompierre, angry and humiliated, yet recognizing that he was no match for the King, concluded his recital, "As he was speaking, I was thinking what I ought to say. . . . I decided that I should give in to him gracefully and I said,

'Yes, Sire, I shall desist forever and I hope that this new love will bring you as much joy as the loss of it will cause me sorrow.' "[19]

On May 17 of the same year, Charlotte de Montmorency was married to the Prince de Condé who was described as "little and thin," with the marked characteristics common to those of the House of Bourbon. Henri had decided that it was "wiser" for him not to attend the ceremony at Chantilly; yet his very absence, along with the extravagant gifts which he made to the bride, simply increased the gossip that this marriage was arranged simply in order to keep the bride available to the King. The Queen, always credulous to court gossip, now had more than her fill, and when she was told that the King had not only bestowed elaborate jewelry on the bride but had paid for her very wedding clothes, she was so openly enraged that "soon [she] put the whole court into an uproar." Her anger was increased through her sympathy with Condé, who, perhaps out of love, certainly out of shame for being so publicly cuckolded, "did not restrain from showing his discontent publicly [and] meditated from that moment the imprudent step he took some time later."[20]

Less than a month after the wedding, Condé, lacking Bassompierre's compliancy and feeling that the only way of avoiding trouble with his sovereign was to put distance between them, asked permission to leave court with his wife. The answer was an implacable No; but Condé, always impetuous, now threw caution to the winds and braved the King to his face, calling him among other niceties a "blackguard" and a "tyrant." The latter was a word that Henri, with his image of himself as a benign father to his people, found intolerable. "My friend the Prince was here, who raised the very devil," he wrote to Sully. "You would be angry and ashamed at the things he has said to me; finally my patience was worn out and I determined to speak frankly to him." This frank talk apparently included a declaration that the young Prince was a bastard, for L'Estoile reported that the King had replied to Condé's accusation of tyranny by saying that "he had never committed an act of tyranny in his life except to have him acknowledged for something he was not and that if he liked he would show him his father in Paris."[21]

A few days later, despite the King's threat to stop his pension, Condé left the court with his wife. Although they returned to Fontainebleau early in July to attend the wedding of the King's son, the Duc de Vendôme, to Mademoiselle de Mercoeur, it was only a short visit of courtesy. By August they had taken up residence at Muret near

Soissons. They might have stayed there permanently—and thus considerably altered the course of French history—had not the King undertaken one of those escapades which while amusing in his youth now won him nothing but scorn from his enemies and pain from his loyal friends who were embarrassed by his actions. Henri, disguised as a hunter—and made more rakish by a patch over one eye—came with a group of his nobles to the forest near Muret hoping for a sight (and perhaps something more) of his "beautiful angel." His angel, however, did not respond as he had anticipated. At first she failed to recognize him, and when she did, in place of the secrecy he had counted on, she screamed "as though she were beside herself, [crying] that she would never pardon this trick."[22]

For Condé, this was the end, and he resolved to make good the threats he had made to Sully earlier that summer—to leave France and take his wife with him. Shortly before midnight on November 28, Sully was summoned to the Louvre by a messenger of the King who greeted him with the words: "The man you know of is fled, as, the King said, you foretold; and what is worse he has taken the lady along with him." "When I came to the Louvre," Sully continued, "I found the King in the Queen's chamber, walking back and forth, with his head reclined and his hands folded behind his back. . . . 'Well,' said Henri, 'our man is gone and has carried all with him.'" This time Sully had no need to embellish the dramatic colors of the scene: Henri's grief was humiliatingly real. "I am lost," he said simply to Bassompierre; and the Marquis de Fontenay-Mareuil, who was no more than fifteen at the time, recalled later, "He was so deeply touched that for some days he remained in seclusion, wishing to speak to no one."[23]

Since there was every indication that the pair was heading for the Netherlands where Condé's sister was married to the Prince of Orange, men were sent posthaste to try to apprehend them before they reached the border. At the suggestion of Villeroy, other messengers were sent to advise the foreign ambassadors of the affair so that they might use their influence to get the couple back into France. Condé was too quick to be overtaken, however, and on November 30 he had passed the border and wrote from Landrecies, a fortified village of the Low Countries, to Archduke Albert, begging him for hospitality and security in his lands, concluding: "If you do not accord me this favor, my honor and my life will be forfeited."[24] Perhaps before he was fully aware of the implications of his action, Albert granted Condé a safe-conduct, and when the following day De Praslin arrived from the King asking that Condé be returned immediately to France, Albert found himself in a highly ambiguous situation. Henri's ministers had been right when they had assured the King that Albert had far too many obligations to France to wish to risk French hostility, yet Albert also had other responsibilities. Married as he was to the Infanta, he could ill afford to ignore the wishes of Philip III. His position was further complicated by his Austrian parentage and his relation to the Emperor Rudolph. Under the most peaceful circumstances his position would have been difficult, but now it was intolerably complicated by the Cleves affair. With French troops already levied and the French King intransigent in his determination to protect Cleves (and ultimately to diminish Hapsburg power in both its Austrian and Spanish branches) any friction was sufficient to light the tinder. The Archduke who had no desire that his should be the hand that would start the conflagration did his best to assume a conciliating position, explaining to Henri that since he had granted Condé a safe-conduct he could hardly revoke it without impugning his honor, yet averring that such a permission involved simply the right to travel through his kingdom and not the right to take up permanent residence.

Spain, meanwhile, was far more cordial to Condé whom they recognized as a possible instrument for stirring up further trouble in France. No matter what his personal qualities, Condé, as First Prince of the Blood, might be manipulated as a focus of opposition to the French King. Should Condé be led to question the integrity of Henri's abjuration—a problem increasingly to the fore with Henri's open espousal of his German allies against the Catholic Hapsburgs—should he be led to distrust the validity of the King's marriage to Marie de Medici, and, further, should his personal ambitions be incited, Spain might once more achieve a dominant influence in French domestic affairs. With this in mind, Philip assured Condé of his friendship, offering him either a permanent home in Spain, or if he preferred, the necessary assistance to take up residence in Italy. Meanwhile he directed the French ambassador at Madrid to explain to his master that his action was motivated only out of respect for a Prince of the Blood and his sincere desire to act as mediator in this difficult matter.

"Difficult" was far too mild a word with which to describe the interplay of foreign and domestic problems, the tension of interests, the congeries of motives which filled the first months of 1610. Spain continued to play her devious hand, the Archduke attempted to avoid giving offense to either side, the Vatican endeavored to assuage the

French King's anger without capitulating to Spanish pressure—and Henri himself became increasingly implacable. He remained implacable throughout the Vatican's renewed efforts to bring about peace through a series of marriage alliances of his children with those of the Spanish King. He grew increasingly impatient with the temporizing position of the Archduke. When his carefully chosen emissary, the Marquis de Coeuvres, returned from Brussels with nothing to report but Condé's intransigence and his arrogant role as upholder of liberty against a tyrannical King, Henri's determination to recover Charlotte de Montmorency became a mania.

Having lost his faith in both negotiations and threats, he set upon a more romantic (and more questionable) course of action. Under the direction of De Coeuvres, a plot was designed to "abduct" Charlotte (with her full consent!) and thus bring her back to France. According to the plot, the heroine was to slip quietly from her apartments in the darkness of the night, her face hidden beneath a black mantilla, make her way through a small breach that had been made in the wall, and then, accompanied by twenty-five knights waiting with fresh horses, gain the border before her absence was discovered. The plot was straight out of the medieval romances which Henri had always loved. It was, however, a plot doomed to failure. Too much unaccustomed activity, too many small hints and restless excitement gave the scheme away and Charlotte was subjected to closer supervision.

When word of the failure was brought to Henri, rage gave way to despair as he faced the possibility of defeat. Toward the end of February he wrote to his agent in Brussels, "I am so tortured by my anguish that I am only skin and bone. Everything bothers me; I avoid company, and if, in order to do justice to other people, I do let myself be drawn into some gathering, instead of cheering me, it only succeeds in deadening me." The King's description of himself was no exaggeration, for Don Inigo de Cardenas, Philip's ambassador to France, who had kept a close Spanish eye on the French King, wrote at some length in mid-March: "I have been told that the King of France would give the Dauphin and all his other sons for the Princesse de Condé which leads me to believe that he will risk everything for his love. His health is altered; he has lost sleep and some people are beginning to believe that he is starting to go mad. He who has so much loved society now remains alone for hours at a time, walking up and down in his melancholy."[25]

Shortly after the abortive plan to abduct Charlotte, Condé, further enraged by this treacherous act of "the tyrant," made plans to leave Brussels for Milan, having obtained a promise that his wife would be carefully guarded against the wiles of her royal seducer by changing her residence to the archducal palace. Since Charlotte had agreed to this proposal, the Archduke had no alternative but to agree. Condé's action shifted the ground of negotiation and in March, Charlotte's father, directed undoubtedly by his friend the King, began to sue for a divorce for his daughter. Once again, Charlotte—with what can only be described as an infinite capacity for compliance —agreed. No one could be sure of Condé's reaction to this proposal, although it was fairly clear by this time that whatever his initial passion, his love for his wife had cooled. Whatever role Charlotte played in the King's political designs, in Condé's view it was obvious that she had become a tool for self-aggrandizement.

It was precisely the effort to discover the King's true motivation that absorbed the foreign ambassadors and their masters that spring, for only if they could arrive at the "reason behind the reasons" would they be able to make counterproposals that might lead to a peaceful settlement. The truth doubtless lies someplace between the contemptuous appraisal of De Cardenas who interpreted the entire war effort as the irresponsible action of senile passion and Henri's own angry statements disavowing all motives but loyal assistance to his injured allies. On one hand Villeroy was reported to have said, "Whoever will find an expedient for returning the Princess will do the greatest favor Christianity has ever known," on the other he was reported to have declared to Pecquius, the ambassador from Brussels, "It is not the Princess who will be the cause of war but the Prince; the King will take up arms because they want to make his nephew an instrument for overthrowing the kingdom."[26]

The King's remarks were often equally ambivalent, for although he raged at the Papal Nuncio, who informed him that the common rumor was that the war had no motive but his illicit passion, yet when it was reported to him that Pecquius had compared Charlotte to Helen of Troy, it was said that he replied grimly: "I know the story but he ought to remember that Troy was destroyed because Helen was not returned." When, in addition, the pope accused him of sponsoring the German princes at the expense of devoted Roman Catholics, he wrote to his ambassador in Rome: "I have no wish to favor and sustain the Protestant princes of Germany in order to strengthen them for the destruction of the Catholic religion; but they are my friends and the ancient allies of this kingdom."[27]

By the end of April, all Henri's motives for war had converged, and on April 28 he wrote to his ambassador in England: "As for mine [his troops] they will soon be ready to be put to use, and I intend to march with them in person the twentieth of next month; and they will be of such quality that I am sure that my friends will be reassured while my enemies will be intimidated and held back."[28] Meanwhile Pecquius had kept the Archduke informed of war preparations in France. Albert had done all that he could to avoid offending Henri, but by the end of March he feared that nothing could avert an invasion of the Netherlands. Consequently, the borders were doubly guarded and the Estates convoked to vote the necessary funds for raising troops. Henri, however, continued to aver that his intentions toward the Netherlands were entirely peaceful and that the Archduke had nothing to fear at his hands.

On May 8 Albert received a formal request from the King of France asking permission for his army to pass through the Lowlands. "As I have always loved and by true and signal effects favored the public peace," the letter read, "I have still the same desire. This is also the true and proper role of a very Christian king which is the title I bear, thanks to the piety of the kings my ancestors, and I intend to preserve their honor by the same means which they have used." Avowing his intention to be faithful to the promises of help he has given to his friends "and true inheritors" in the Duchy of Cleves, he concluded: "having in order to do this to pass through some places and villages under your jurisdiction, I wish to know if I can do this as a friend who does not wish to commit any act of hostility and who has no other design in this journey than to bring to my allies the assistance which my faith toward them and the justice of their cause obliges me."[29]

To refuse permission would have been the sheerest folly, and Albert could do nothing but accept the King's word. A few days later a formal letter was sent out under the Archduke's seal granting the French King the permission he had requested.

Even as Henri waited for the answer, he made his final preparations to join his forces on May 20. He had made his plans carefully for the campaign which lay ahead. Three armies were already in the field, two of them led by competent and experienced captains and the third he intended to lead himself. At home his

plans were equally complete. Marie de Medici assisted by a council, had been appointed regent in his absence and to that end was
to be solemnly crowned at St. Denis. Some of those who observed
the King during his last weeks in Paris noted with satisfaction that
the thin worn figure who in February had fled from his friends
to walk in lonely melancholy in the galleries of St. Germain had
been replaced by the dynamic leader who knew how to order his
state and galvanize his army. It was with his usual energy that he
had written reviewing his plans for the coming week: "I shall lie
at St. Denis on Wednesday; I will return from thence on Thursday; I will put my affairs in order on Friday; on Saturday I will
run at the ring; on Sunday my wife shall make her entry; on Monday my daughter Vendôme shall be married; on Tuesday we will
keep the marriage feast; and on Wednesday to horse and away."[30]

Yet those who knew him best noted in him an underlying uneasiness, a sense of impending doom. Henri, who had always had
such limitless faith in his star, now could not shake off the feeling
that even the King's star might fall. He took little joy in the splendor
of the Queen's coronation at St. Denis or in the prospect of his
daughter's nuptials. Bassompierre, who was often his confidant in
those days, later recorded that Henri had confided to him his fear
of his approaching death, saying, "I don't know how it is, Bassompierre, but I can't convince myself that I shall ever go into
Germany." Sully, with his penchant for hindsight and his Renaissance
reliance on omens, later recalled that the King's uneasiness was so
profound that he had tried to persuade him to cancel the Queen's
coronation ceremony; the King, however, would change none of his
plans, although he confessed to Sully, "I shall die in this city; they
will murder me here; I see plainly that they have made my death
their only recourse."[31]

Friday, May 14, had been the day that the King had set aside
to put his affairs in order. Even this routine business seemed to him
fraught with danger, some of his court later observed, and the King
spent the morning uneasy and irresolute. About midafternoon he
ordered his carriage to take him to the arsenal for a conference
with Sully. Assuring the captain of the guard that he had no need
of him, he set out in an open carriage with the Duc d'Epernon
at his right and Montbazon and Laverdin facing him. It was a
warm bright day and the carriage was open on both sides. As it
entered the rue de la Ferronnerie, it was forced to stop because of

two carts that blocked the narrow street. Those inside the carriage
scarcely noticed the delay because their attention was absorbed by
a letter which the King had asked D'Epernon to read. Lost in
thought, they did not even see the man who leaped to the wheel
and plunged his dagger into the King's unprotected body. Henri
had time only to murmur, "I am wounded," before the assassin
struck the second time. They were his last words, for with the second
blow blood gushed from his mouth.

Lady Fortune who, against all odds, had raised Henri de Navarre
to the throne of France, who had steadied her restless wheel while
he had received the sacred chrism at Chartres and had entered victorious into his cheering capital, Lady Fortune who had so often
saved him from the fruit of his folly, had, in the blink of an
eye, played him false. He had not even a moment to steady himself
against her treachery, not even that precious moment in which to
prepare for the sudden fact of death. Henri, who had so often
ridden recklessly into danger that he was sometimes accused of courting
death, now received the scythe's stroke without warning.

Fortune's minion was François de Ravaillac, a native of Angoulême. He was no different from those others who had attempted
the King's life. Lonely, impoverished, a prey to nervous terrors and
morbid imaginings, he had believed, like Pierre de la Barrière, Jean
Châtel, The Dominican friar Ridicauwe, that he would do a service
to God and the Roman Church by ridding them of a King whom
he believed to be a heretic and a tyrant. Ravaillac differed from the
others in only one thing: his knife had gone unerringly to its mark.

At once D'Epernon took charge, assuring the gathering crowd that
the King was only slightly wounded and ordering the carriage to
return to the Louvre at once; but it was inevitably a slow, confused
journey and by the time they arrived the King was dead. He was
carried up the vast marble stairs to his own room and laid upon
the bed. He lay there completely dressed, his doublet open, his shirt
covered with blood. Someone had placed a crucifix on his mouth,
but it was too late for piety. His surgeons, who had been called
to dress his wounds, stood helplessly by, knowing they could no
longer serve him. For a moment they were stirred to hope, for it
seemed that the King had sighed—but it was nothing. Henri, King
of France and of Navarre was dead, in the fifty-seventh year of
his age and the twenty-first of his reign.

Within hours the tragic news swept through the streets of Paris.

It was not simply grief which moved the people but terror at what France might now have to endure. The Dauphin who would now assume the burden of kingship was but nine years old, and many Frenchmen could remember all too keenly what can happen to a kingdom when there is no strong hand to guide it. Although the last years of Henri's reign had been a disappointment to many, they were forced to acknowledge that during the twenty-one years of his reign he had attained a stature which placed him among the greatest of French monarchs.

In those dark confused hours following his death, the legend of Henri's kingship was already taking shape: the King who had put an end to civil war, the King who had won a successful peace with Spain, the King who had satisfied the Huguenots with the Edict of Nantes and brought back the Jesuits for the advancement of learning; the King of largesse, of wit, of humanity. This was the King who was true to his promises: he had promised his people peace and he had given it to them; he had determined to improve France's precarious economy and he had done it; he had promised justice to his people, equity to all men of good conscience, and rigorous justice to those who had "sold" justice for their own advancement. It would not be long before his people would recognize that this Henri merited to be called "the Great."

NOTES

CHAPTER I

1. Bernard Nabonne, *Jeanne d'Albret* (Paris, 1945), p. 44. Hereafter cited as Nabonne.

2. Nancy Layman Roelker, *Queen of Navarre: Jeanne d'Albret* (Cambridge, Mass., 1968), p. 112. Hereafter cited as Roelker, *Queen of Navarre*.

3. Marquis de Rochambeau, *Lettres de Antoine de Bourbon et Jeanne d'Albret*, Société de l'Histoire de France (Paris, 1877), p. 173. Hereafter cited as Rochambeau.

4. Roelker, *Queen of Navarre*, p. 127.

5. Théodore de Bèze, *Histoire ecclésiastique des eglises réformées au royaume de France* (3 vols., Paris, 1833), I, 121.

6. Lucien Romier, *Catholiques et Huguenots à la cour de Charles IX* (Paris, 1924), p. 35.

7. Roelker, *Queen of Navarre*, p. 162.

8. *Calendar of State Papers, Foreign Series, Elizabeth, 1561–1562*, nos. 461, 682. Hereafter cited as *CSP, For. Eliz.* with specific volume and dispatch number.

9. *Ibid.*, nos. 931, 945.

10. *Mémoires et poésies de Jeanne d'Albret*, ed. A. de Ruble (Paris, 1893), p. 31. Hereafter cited as Jeanne d'Albret, *Mémoires*.

11. Roelker, *Queen of Navarre*, p. 183.

12. Jeanne d'Albret, *Mémoires*, p. 25.

13. Nicolas de Bordenave, *Histoire de Béarn et Navarre*, ed. P. Raymond, Société de l'Histoire de France (Pau, 1873), p. 115. Hereafter cited as Bordenave.

14. Jeanne d'Albret, *Mémoires*, p. 4.

15. Bordenave, p. 116.

16. *CSP, For. Eliz.*, 1561–1562, no. 987.

17. *Commentaires et lettres de Blaise de Monluc*, ed. A. de Ruble, Société de l'Histoire de France (5 vols., Paris, 1864–1867), II, 443. Hereafter cited as Monluc.

18. *Lettres missives de Henri IV*, ed. B. de Xivrey (9 vols., Paris, 1843–1876), I, 3. Hereafter cited as *Lettres missives*.

19. Roelker, *Queen of Navarre*, p. 207.

20. *CSP, For. Eliz.,* 1563, no. 354.

21. *Relations des ambassadeurs Venétiens,* ed. N. Tommaseo (2 vols., Paris, 1838), II, 67. Hereafter cited as Tommaseo.

22. P. Champion, *Catherine de Médicis presente à Charles IX son royaume, 1564–1566* (Paris, 1937), p. 106.

23. Pierre de L'Estoile, *Mémoires-Journaux,* ed. G. Brunet et al. (12 vols., Paris, 1888–1896), V, 246. Hereafter cited as L'Estoile.

24. *Memoirs of the Duke of Sully* (5 vols., Edinburgh, 1819), I, 13. Hereafter cited as Sully.

25. Roelker, *Queen of Navarre,* pp. 402–403.

26. Sully, I, 12.

27. Bordenave, pp. 146–149. Translation from Roelker, *Queen of Navarre,* p. 404.

28. Jeanne d'Albret, *Mémoires,* p. 55.

29. Rochambeau, pp. 62–63.

30. Tommaseo, II, 105.

31. *Ibid.,* II, 106.

32. Michel de Castelnau, *Memoirs of the Reigns of Francis II and Charles IX* (London, 1724), p. 425.

33. Ludwig von Pastor, *The History of the Popes,* ed. Francis Kerr (40 vols., St. Louis, Mo., 1932), XVIII, 129. Hereafter cited as Pastor.

34. Roelker, *Queen of Navarre,* p. 347.

35. Monluc, III, 355. Translation from Roelker, *Queen of Navarre,* p. 343.

36. *CSP, For. Eliz.,* 1569–1571, no. 27.

37. Roelker, *Queen of Navarre,* pp. 368–369.

38. *Ibid.,* pp. 366, 371, 372.

39. Rochambeau, pp. 345, 352.

40. M. W. Freer, *The Life of Jeanne d'Albret, Queen of Navarre* (London, 1862), p. 376.

41. *Ibid.,* p. 382.

42. Rochambeau, p. 343.

43. *Lettres de Catherine de Médicis,* ed. H. de La Ferrière et B. de Puchesse (10 vols., Paris, 1880–1909), IV, xlvi. Hereafter cited as *Lettres de Catherine de Médicis.*

44. *Mémoires et lettres de Marguerite de Valois,* ed. M. F. Guessard, Société de l'Histoire de France (Paris, 1842), p. 25. Hereafter cited as *Mémoires de Marguerite de Valois.*

45. Roelker, *Queen of Navarre,* pp. 392–393.

46. *Bulletin de la société de l'histoire du protestantisme français,* LVI (1912), 142, 141. Hereafter cited as *BHPF.*

47. Roelker, *Queen of Navarre,* p. 409.

CHAPTER II

1. Tommaseo, II, 155.

2. *Mémoires de Marguerite de Valois,* p. 26.

3. *Lettres de Catherine de Médicis*, IV, 110.

4. *CSP, For. Eliz.*, 1569–1571, no. 581.

5. Conyers Read, *Mr. Secretary Walsingham* (3 vols., Cambridge, Mass.), I, 203. Hereafter cited as Read.

6. Dudley Digges, *The Compleat Ambassador* (London, 1642), p. 234.

7. Eugenio Alberi, *Relazioni degli ambasciatori Veneti al Senato* (15 vols., Florence, 1839–1863), IV, 285. Hereafter cited as Alberi.

8. Jacques-Auguste de Thou, *Histoire universelle* (11 vols., Basle, 1742), IV, 565. Hereafter cited as De Thou, *Histoire universelle*.

9. *Archives Curieuses*, ed. Cimber et Danjou (27 vols., Paris, 1834–1840), VII, 81. Hereafter cited as *Archives Curieuses*.

10. Jules Delaborde, *Gaspard de Coligny* (3 vols., Paris, 1879), III, 439.

11. Maurice Andrieux, *Henri IV* (Paris, 1955), p. 97.

12. Alberi, IV, 289.

13. *Mémoires de Marguerite de Valois*, p. 33.

14. *Archives Curieuses*, IX, 3–113.

15. All of the quoted conversation given here belongs to the legend and appears again and again in substantially the same form; it cannot, however, be substantiated as fact.

16. *Archives Curieuses*, VII, 217.

17. *Mémoires de Marguerite de Valois*, p. 34.

18. H. Forneron, *Histoire de Philippe II* (4 vols., Paris, 1882), II, 328. Hereafter cited as Forneron.

19. *Ibid.*, II, 326–327.

20. Felix Rocquain, *La France et Rome pendant les guerres de religion* (Paris, 1924), p. 126. Hereafter cited as Rocquain.

21. *Correspondance diplomatique de Bertrand de Salignac, Seigneur de La Mothe-Fénelon* (7 vols., Paris, 1838–1840), V, 122.

22. *Lettres le Catherine de Médicis*, IV, cxvii.

23. *Archives Curieuses*, VII, 65.

CHAPTER III

1. *Negotiations diplomatiques de la France avec la Toscane*, ed. A. Desjardins (5 vols., Paris, 1861–1865), III, 824. Hereafter cited as Desjardins.

2. *Lettres missives*, I, 36–38.

3. Rocquain, p. 151.

4. *Lettres missives*, I, 135.

5. *Archives historiques de Gascogne*, VI, 154–155. Hereafter cited as Archs. hists. Gascogne.

6. Rocquain, p. 165.

7. *Calendar of State Papers and Manuscripts relating to English Affairs in the Archives and collections of Venice*, 1559–1580, no. 573. Hereafter cited as *CSP, Ven. Eliz.*, with specific volume and dispatch number.

8. *CSP, For. Eliz.*, 1572–1574, no. 1372.
9. *CSP, Ven. Eliz.*, 1559–1580, no. 581.
10. *Ibid.*, no. 582.
11. *Lettres missives*, I, 60–70.
12. *Mémoires de Marguerite de Valois*, p. 40.
13. *CSP, For. Eliz.*, 1572–1574, no. 1403.
14. *Lettres de Catherine de Médicis*, IV, xxviii–xxx.
15. *Ibid.*, IV, ccvii.
16. *Lettres missives*, I, 70–71.
17. *CSP, Ven. Eliz.*, 1559–1580, no. 601.
18. *CSP, For. Eliz.*, 1572–1574, no. 1462.
19. *Lettres de Catherine de Médicis*, IV, 311. It is at this point that the portrait of Henri III given by his contemporaries moves from characterization to caricature. Since most of those who recorded their impressions were his enemies, the figure that emerges is that of a stylized tyrant, but a tyrant who lacks the stature of a villain. Perhaps when P. Champion completes his work on the last of the Valois, something more realistic may emerge. *CSP, For. Eliz.*, 1572–1574, no. 1509.
20. *Lettres de Catherine de Médicis*, V, 74–75.
21. *CSP, For. Eliz.*, 1572–1574, no. 1509.
22. Rocquain, p. 185.
23. *Mémoires de Marguerite de Valois*, p. 44.
24. *Ibid.*, p. 53.
25. *Letters of Ogier Ghislain de Busbecq to the Holy Roman Emperor, Maximilian II*, tr. and ed. Robert E. Jones and Bernard C. Weber (New York, 1961), p. 125. Hereafter cited as *Letters of Busbecq*.
26. *Ibid.*, *CSP, For. Eliz.*, 1575–1577, no. 106.
27. *Letters of Busbecq*, p. 113.
28. *CSP, For. Eliz.*, 1575–1577, nos., 176, 58.
29. *CSP, Ven. Eliz.*, 1559–1580, no. 636.
30. *Mémoires de Marguerite de Valois*, p. 64.
31. *Letters of Busbecq*, p. 139.
32. *Lettres de Catherine de Médicis*, V, 142, 139.
33. *Mémoires de Marguerite de Valois*, p. 66.
34. *Lettres missives*, I, 81–82.
35. *CSP, For. Eliz.*, 1575–1577, no. 605.
36. *Mémoires de Théodore Agrippa d'Aubigné*, ed. M. Lalanne (Paris, 1854), p. 192. Hereafter cited as *Mémoires D'Aubigné*.
37. L'Estoile, I, 114.

CHAPTER IV

1. *CSP, For. Eliz.*, 1575–1577, no. 605.
2. *Lettres de Catherine de Médicis*, V, 185.
3. *CSP, For. Eliz.*, 1575–1577, no. 614.
4. *Lettres missives*, I, 84, 86–87.

5. *Lettres de Catherine de Médicis*, V, 192.
6. L'Estoile, I, 142–143, 153.
7. *Lettres missives*, I, 115–117.
8. Jean Louchitsky, *Documents inédits pour servir à l'histoire de la réforme et de la Ligue* (1875), pp. 19–25.
9. *Mémoires de la Ligue* (6 vols., Amsterdam, 1758), I, 2–7. Hereafter cited as *Mémoires de la Ligue*.
10. *Les Mémoires de Monsieur de Duc de Nevers* (2 vols., Paris, 1665), I, 470.
11. *Lettres missives*, I, 113–116.
12. *Lettres de Catherine de Médicis*, V, lxxvi; Desjardins, IV, 110.
13. *Lettres de Catherine de Médicis*, V, 233–234.
14. CSP, For. Eliz., 1575–1577, no. 1368.
15. L'Estoile, II, 219–220.
16. CSP, For. Eliz., 1577–1578, no. 225.
17. L'Estoile, II, 235–236.

CHAPTER V

1. *Lettres missives*, I, 182, 185–186, 196.
2. CSP, For. Eliz., 1578–1579, nos. 607, 132.
3. *Lettres de Catherine de Médicis*, VI, 38.
4. *Ibid.*, VI, 46.
5. *Ibid.*, VI, 64.
6. *Mémoires de Marguerite de Valois*, p. 203.
7. CSP, For. Eliz., 1578–1579, no. 579.
8. *Lettres de Catherine de Médicis*, VI, 110, 117, 118, 120.
9. *Ibid.*, VI, 140, 100, 107.
10. Pierre de Vaissière, *Henri IV* (Paris, 1928), p. 181. Hereafter cited as Vaissière.
11. *Lettres de Catherine de Médicis*, VI, 181.
12. *Ibid.*, VI, 284.
13. *Ibid.*, VI, 358.
14. *Mémoires de Marguerite de Valois*, p. 159.
15. Jean-H. Mariéjol, *La Vie de Marguerite de Valois* (Paris, 1928), p. 154. Hereafter cited as Mariéjol.
16. Agrippa d'Aubigné, *Histoire universelle*, ed. A. de Ruble, Société de l'Histoire de France (10 vols., Paris, 1886–1909), V, 382. Hereafter cited as D'Aubigné, *Histoire universelle*.
17. *Mémoires de Marguerite de Valois*, p. 163.
18. *Lettres missives*, I, 239.
19. *Ibid.*, I, 294.
20. *Lettres de Catherine de Médicis*, VII, 253.
21. *Lettres missives*, I, 297.
22. *Ibid.*, I, 275–276.
23. *Ibid.*, I, 285.

24. *Mémoires de Marguerite de Valois*, p. 166.

25. *Lettres missives*, I, 304, 302–303.

26. *Ibid.*, I, 332–333.

27. *Ibid.*, I, 353, 354.

28. *Ibid.*, I, 365.

29. Claude Haton, *Mémoires*, ed. F. Bourquelot (2 vols., Paris, 1857), II, 1047.

30. *Mémoires de Marguerite de Valois*, pp. 162, 177–181. The whole episode of Fosseuse is taken from Marguerite's account.

CHAPTER VI

1. *Archs. hists. Gascogne*, XI, 27.

2. Charles Merki, *La Reine Margot* (Paris, 1905), p. 247. Hereafter cited as Merki, *La Reine Margot; Archs. hists. Gascogne*, XI, 23.

3. *Lettres missives*, I, 443, 446–447.

4. *Mémoires de Marguerite de Valois*, pp. 284–285.

5. Desjardins, IV, 421.

6. Raymond Ritter, *Cette Grande Corisande* (Paris, 1936), p. 89. Hereafter cited as Ritter, *Corisande*.

7. *Mémoires de Marguerite de Valois*, p. 292.

8. CSP, *Ven. Eliz.*, 1559–1580, no. 795.

9. CSP, *For. Eliz.*, May–December 1582, no. 69.

10. *Lettres missives*, I, 571–574.

11. L'Estoile, II, 132.

12. *Lettres de Catherine de Médicis*, VIII, 428–429.

13. *Mémoires de Marguerite de Valois*, p. 296.

14. *Lettres de Catherine de Médicis*, VIII, 170, n. 1.

15. *Ibid.*, VIII, 172.

16. *Lettres missives*, I, 632.

17. CSP, *For. Eliz.*, May–December 1582, no. 491.

18. Philippe Lauzun, *Itinéraire de Marguerite de Valois en Gascogne, d'après ses livres de comptes, 1578–1586* (Paris, 1902), p. 256. Hereafter cited as Lauzun.

19. *Lettres missives*, I, 624.

20. *Ibid.*, I, 645.

21. Lauzun, p. 281.

22. *Mémoires inédits de Michel de la Huguerye*, ed. A. de Ruble, Société pour l'Histoire de France (3 vols., Paris, 1877–1880), II, 294, 316. Hereafter cited as La Huguerye.

23. *Lettres de Catherine de Médicis*, VIII, 180–181.

24. Desjardins, IV, 463.

25. William Murdin, compiler, *A Collection of state papers relating to the affairs in the reign of Queen Elizabeth, 1571–1596.* (2 vols., London, 1759), II, 383. Hereafter cited as Murdin.

26. John Bennett Black, *The Reign of Elizabeth,* The Oxford History of England (Oxford, 1959), p. 357. Hereafter cited as Black.

27. CSP, *For. Eliz.,* May–December 1582, no. 138.

28. L'Estoile, II, 154.

29. CSP, *For. Eliz.,* May–December 1582, nos. 539, 587, 611.

30. *Lettres de Catherine de Médicis,* VIII, 188.

CHAPTER VII

1. Murdin, II, 411.

2. G. B. Harrison, *Letters of Elizabeth* (London, 1935), p. 162. Hereafter cited as Harrison.

3. Murdin, II, 411.

4. *Lettres missives,* I, 666.

5. De Thou, *Histoire universelle,* VI, 392.

6. CSP, *For. Eliz.,* July 1583–July 1584, no. 672.

7. Merki, *La Reine Margot,* pp. 307–308.

8. CSP, *For. Eliz.,* July 1583–July 1584, no. 710.

9. Rocquain, p. 265.

10. *Ibid.,* p. 266, n. 1.

11. CSP, *For. Eliz.,* August 1584–August 1585, p. 126. From August 1584 dispatch numbers are no longer used in this series; post-July 1584 references will be made to page numbers.

12. *Ibid.,* July 1583–July 1584, no. 752.

13. *Lettres missives,* I, 615.

14. Forneron, III, 223.

15. Hardouin de Péréfixe, *The History of Henri IV* (London, 1663), p. 52. Hereafter cited as Péréfixe.

16. Rocquain, p. 263; Murdin, II, 414

17. CSP, *For. Eliz.,* August 1584–August 1585, p. 275.

18. Henry Baird, *The Huguenots and Henri of Navarre* (2 vols., New York, 1886), I, 294. Hereafter cited as Baird.

19. *Archives Curieuses,* XI, 7–21.

20. *Lettres missives,* II, 38.

21. Henri de L'Epinois, *La Ligue et les Papes* (Paris, 1886), p. 20. Hereafter cited as L'Epinois.

22. CSP, *For. Eliz.,* August 1584–August 1585, pp. 343, 354.

23. Pastor, XXI, 277.

24. *Archives Curieuses,* X, 130–131.

25. *Lettres missives,* II, 25, 39–40, 46, 36, 211.

26. *Ibid.,* II, 63–64, 213.

27. *Ibid.,* II, 17–19, 54–55.

28. *Ibid.,* II, 79.

29. Black, pp. 364–365.

30. Bremond d'Ars, *Jean de Vivonne: Sa vie et ses ambassades* (Paris, 1884), p. 174, n. 1.

31. *Lettres de Catherine de Médicis,* VIII, 339.

32. L'Estoile, II, 199.
33. *Lettres missives*, II, 87–88.
34. Desjardins, IV, 620.
35. *Lettres missives*, II, 71–72, 87–88.
36. *Ibid.*, II, 98, 120.
37. Duplessis-Mornay, *Mémoires et correspondence* (12 vols., Paris, 1824), III, 159–182.
38. *Lettres missives*, II, 129–130.

CHAPTER VIII

1. *Archives Curieuses*, XI, 49–58.
2. Baird, I, 366.
3. *Lettres de Catherine de Médicis*, VIII, 350.
4. *Lettres missives*, II, 136–137, 172–174.
5. *Ibid.*, II, 147–150, 150, 152, 138–142, 149.
6. Lauzun, p. 310.
7. Merki, *La Reine Margot*, p. 317.
8. CSP, For. Eliz., August 1584–August 1585, p. 462.
9. *Lettres de Catherine de Médicis*, VIII, 318–319.
10. Merki, *La Reine Margot*, p. 348.
11. *Mémoires D'Aubigné*, pp. 68–69.
12. *Mémoires du Vicomte de Turenne*, ed. Comte Baguenault de Puchesse, Société de l'Histoire de France (Paris, 1901), p. 183. Hereafter cited as *Mémoires de Turenne*.
13. *Lettres missives*, II, 224–225.
14. *Ibid.*, II, 163, 166.
15. Baron de Hübner, *Sixte-Quint* (3 vols., Paris, 1870), II, 173–175.
16. *Ibid.*, II, 199.
17. L'Estoile, II, 337.
18. *Lettres missives*, II, 227.
19. Vaissière, p. 278.
20. *Lettres missives*, II, 251–252.
21. *Calendar of the Manuscripts of the Marquis of Salisbury at Hatfield House*, Historical Manuscripts Commission (19 vols., London, 1883) III, 219. Hereafter cited as Salisbury.
22. *Lettres missives*, II, 298.
23. Read, III, 207.
24. CSP, For. Eliz., June 1586–June 1588, p. 252.
25. *Ibid.*, p. 272.
26. Thomas Wright, ed., *Queen Elizabeth and her Times* (2 vols., London, 1838), II, 347.
27. *Lettres missives*, II, 309.
28. *Ibid.*, II, 308.
29. Vaissière, pp. 302–303; Baird, I, 440.

30. Péréfixe, p. 71.

31. *Calendar of Letters and State Papers relating to English affairs, preserved in the Archives of Simancas, 1587–1603*, no. 25. Hereafter cited as *CSP, Span. Eliz.*, with specific volume and dispatch number.

32. Forneron, III, 241.

33. De Thou, *Histoire universelle*, VI, 438.

34. *CSP, For. Eliz.*, June 1586–June 1588, p. 510.

35. *Lettres missives*, II, 341.

36. Ritter, *Corisande*, p. 212.

37. Joseph de Croze, *Les Guises, les Valois, et Philippe II* (2 vols., Paris, 1866), II, 28.

38. *Lettres missives*, II, 343.

39. *CSP, For. Eliz.*, June 1586–June 1588, p. 542.

40. Étienne Pasquier, *Lettres Historiques* (Geneva, 1966), p. 287. Hereafter cited as Pasquier.

41. Enrico Davila, *Historia delle guerre civili di Francia* (2 vols., London, 1752), I, 588. Hereafter cited as Davila.

42. *Ibid.*, I, 590.

CHAPTER IX

1. *Mémoires d'estat par M. de Villeroy. XLIV. Collection complète des mémoires relatifs à l'histoire de France*, ed. M. Petitot (130 vols., Paris, 1818–1829.) Hereafter cited as *Mémoires d'estat*.

2. *Archives Curieuses*, XI, 443–448; L'Estoile, III, 153.

3. L'Epinois, p. 125.

4. L'Estoile, III, 205.

5. *Lettres missives*, II, 379–380.

6. *Ibid.*, II, 378, 382.

7. *CSP, For. Eliz.*, January 1500–June 1500, p. 636.

8. *Lettres de Catherine de Médicis*, IX, 368.

9. *Mémoires de la Ligue*, II, 402–407.

10. *Ibid.*, II, 577–578.

11. *Ibid.*, III, 149.

12. *Lettres missives*, II, 411.

13. *Ibid.*, II, 395–396.

14. *Ibid.*, II, 412.

15. Pasquier, pp. 351, 356; L'Epinois, p. 199; Charles Valois, *Histoire de la Ligue* (Paris, 1914), p. 287, Appendix II.

16. *Archives Curieuses*, XII, 89.

17. L'Estoile, III, 231.

18. Desjardins, IV, 853.

19. De Thou, *Histoire universelle*, VII, 368.

20. *Lettres missives*, II, 427.

21. *Ibid.*, II, 443–458.

22. *Ibid.*, II, 466, 468.

23. L'Estoile, III, 277–278.
24. *Lettres missives*, II, 480–481.
25. *CSP, For. Eliz.*, January–July 1589, p. 351.
26. *Ibid.*, p. 351.
27. *Ibid.*, p. 394.
28. *Archives Curieuses*, XII, 385.
29. De Thou, *Histoire universelle*, VII, 493; L'Estoile, III, 306.
30. Palma Cayet, *Chronologie Novenaire*, Petitot XXXIX, 199–202. Hereafter cited as Palma Cayet.

CHAPTER X

1. *CSP, For. Eliz.*, January–July 1589, pp. 405–406.
2. *Mémoires de la Ligue*, IV, 13.
3. Duplessis-Mornay, IV, 381.
4. *Mémoires de la Ligue*, IV, 34.
5. De Lamar Jensen, *Diplomacy and Dogmatism* (Cambridge Mass., 1964), p. 193. Hereafter cited as Jensen.
6. *Mémoires de la Ligue*, IV, 36.
7. Jensen, p. 196.
8. E. A. Ségretain, *Sixte-Quint et Henri IV* (Paris, 1861), p. 177. Hereafter cited as Ségretain.
Edouard Frémy, *Essai sur les diplomates du temps de la Ligue* (Paris, 1873), p. 273. Hereafter cited as Frémy.
9. Vaissière, p. 339.
10. *Ibid.*, p. 334.
11. Forneron, II, 73.
12. *Lettres missives*, III, 64.
13. *BHPF*, I, 283.
14. *Lettres missives*, III, 166, 105.
15. Vaissière, p. 377.
16. *Lettres missives*, III, 134, 132, 117.
17. *Ibid.*, III, 136, 115.
18. Péréfixe, p. 114; Vaissière, p. 356; *Lettres missives*, III, 171.
19. Forneron, IV, 25.
20. Ségretain, p. 191.
21. Jensen, p. 200.
22. L'Estoile, V, 266, 271; De Thou, *Histoire universelle*, IX, 160.
23. *Mémoires de Philippe Hurault, comte de Cheverny*, Petitot, XXXVI, 155. Hereafter cited as *Mémoires de Cheverny*.
24. *Lettres missives*, III, 194.
25. L'Estoile, VI, 25.
26. *Ibid.*, V, 278.
27. Forneron, IV, 102.
28. Frémy, p. 310.

29. L'Estoile, I, 30.
30. *Lettres missives*, III, 217, 216, 225.
31. Palma Cayet, Petitot, XL, 106–107; L'Estoile, V, 50.

CHAPTER XI

1. *Lettres missives*, III, 285.
2. *Ibid.*, III, 320.
3. L'Estoile, V, 89.
4. René de Bouillé, *Histoire des ducs de Guise* (4 vols., Paris, 1849), IV, 18. Hereafter cited as Bouillé. Rocquain, p. 429.
5. *Ibid.*, p. 432.
6. Davila, II, 220.
7. *Lettres missives*, III, 414, n. 1.
8. *Mémoires de la Ligue*, IV, 267.
9. Pastor, XXII, 378.
10. Bouillé, IV, Appendix 1.
11. Forneron, IV, 103.
12. Davila, II, 236.
13. Palma Cayet, Petitot, XL, 360.
14. *Lettres missives*, III, 522.
15. *Ibid.*, III, 462.
16. *Correspondence of Sir Henry Unton*, ed. Joseph Stevenson, Roxburghe Club, LXIV (London, 1847), p. 92. Hereafter cited as Unton.
17. Sully, I, 284.
18. Unton, p. 336.
19. Forneron, IV, 122.
20. *Lettres missives*, III, 574, 577.
21. *Ibid.*, III, 621–622.
22. L'Estoile, V, 169.
23. *Lettres missives*, III, 613; Sully, I, 341.
24. *Lettres missives*, III, 674–675.
25. Pastor, XXIII, 68.
26. Forneron, IV, 191–192.
27. L'Estoile, V, 190.

CHAPTER XII

1. Forneron, IV, 188; Bouillé, IV, 121
2. L'Estoile, IV, 131; V, 212. *Satyre Menippée de la vertu du catholicon d'Espagne* (Tours, 1594).
3. Raymond Kierstead, *Pomponne de Bellièvre* (Northwestern University Press, 1968), p. 65. Hereafter cited as Kierstead.
4. Palma Cayet, Petitot, XLI, 231–248.
5. L'Estoile, V, 223.

6. Forneron, IV, 197–198; Bouillé, IV, 162.

7. Palma Cayet, Petitot, XLI, 368, 369.

8. D'Aubigné, *Histoire universelle*, VIII, 338.

9. Péréfixe, p. 165.

10. Palma Cayet, Petitot, XLI, 304.

11. L'Estoile, V, 239; Forneron, IV, 191; De Thou, *Histoire universelle*, XI, 761.

12. *Lettres missives*, III, 769; L'Estoile, VI, 35.

13. Palma Cayet, Petitot, XLI, 366–367.

14. *BHPF*, I, 44–45.

15. *Ibid.*, I, 280–285.

16. Vaissière, p. 426.

17. *Lettres missives*, III, 725, 736.

18. L'Estoile, VI, 19–20.

19. L'Estoile, VI, 291; Forneron, IV, 204.

20. Rocquain, p. 582.

21. M. A. Poirson, *Histoire du règne de Henri IV* (4 vols., Paris, 1862–1867), I, 421.

22. *Ibid.*, I, 440.

23. L'Estoile, VI, 43.

24. *Ibid.*, VI, 50.

25. Poirson, I, 477.

26. *Lettres missives*, III, 821.

27. L'Estoile, VI, 61–62.

28. *Archives Curieuses*, XIII, 343–358.

29. *Lettres missives*, III, 822–823.

CHAPTER XIII

1. *Lettres missives*, IV, 7.

2. Wright, II, 431.

3. *Lettres missives*, IV, 37.

4. Poirson, I, 490; Forneron, IV, 211

5. Pastor, XXIII, 78.

6. *Lettres missives*, IV, 12.

7. Davila, II, 428.

8. Pastor, XXIII, 86.

9. *Lettres missives*, IV, 56, 53

10. Kierstead, p. 74; Pastor, XXIII, 85.

11. A detailed account of the ceremonies is given in Palma Cayet, Petitot, XLII, 158–184; *Archives Curieuses*, XIII, 402–442; Théodore Godefroy, *Le Ceremonial François* (2 vols., Paris, 1649), I, 346–397.

12. *Lettres missives*, IV, 114.

13. *Mémoires d'estat*, XLIV, 482.

14. L'Estoile, VI, 186.

15. *Ibid.*, VI, 189.
16. Forneron, IV, 225; Péréfixe, p. 173.
17. Vaissière, p. 452; Forneron, IV, 224.
18. *Recueil des choses memorables* (Paris, 1603), p. 776.

CHAPTER XIV

1. L'Estoile, VI, 189.
2. *Ibid.*, VI, 205.
3. *Lettres missives*, IV, 288–291.
4. L'Estoile, VI, 226–227.
5. *Lettres missives*, IV, 286.
6. Palma Cayet, Petitot, XLII, 380–381.
7. *Ibid.*, p. 383.
8. L'Estoile, VII, 2.
9. Duplessis-Mornay, VI, 145, 142–143.
10. Raymond Ritter, *Charmante Gabrielle*, (Paris, 1947), pp. 262–263.
11. *Lettres missives*, IV, 89.
12. *Ibid.*, IV, 234.
13. *Ibid.*, IV, 475.
14. L'Estoile, VII, 22.
15. *Lettres missives*, IV, 375, 372–373.
16. *Ibid.*, IV, 414–416.
17. Pastor, XXIII, 104–105.
18. *Lettres du Cardinal d'Ossat*, ed. Amelot de la Houssaie (5 vols., Amsterdam, 1632), I, 418. Hereafter cited as D'Ossat; Rocquain, p. 514.
19. D'Ossat, I, 447.
20. *Ibid.*, I, 310–312.
21. *Lettres missives*, IV, 396.
22. D'Aubigné, *Histoire universelle*, IX, 231.
23. Pastor, XXIII, 139.
24. *Lettres missives*, IV, 447.
25. Duplessis-Mornay, V, 544; L'Estoile, VI, 106; D'Aubigné, *Histoire universelle*, IX, 104.
26. *Lettres missives*, III, 362, 588, 622.
27. L'Estoile, VII, 47–48.
28. Sully, II, 127.
29. *Lettres missives*, IV, 573–574.
30. L'Estoile, VII, 75.
31. *Lettres missives*, IV, 657–658.
32. Thomas Birch, ed., *An Historical View of the Negotiations between the courts of England, France, and Brussels, 1592–1617* (London, 1749), p. 47. Hereafter cited as Birch.
33. L'Estoile, VI, 83; Ritter, *Charmante Gabrielle*, p. 343.

CHAPTER XV

1. Sully, II, 164.
2. CSP, Ven. Eliz., 1592–1603, no. 553.
3. L'Estoile, VII, 84.
4. Lettres missives, IV, 698.
5. CSP, Ven. Eliz., nos. 571, 590; Lettres missives, IV, 727, 734.
6. CSP, Ven. Eliz., 1592–1603, no. 586.
7. Lettres missives, IV, 744, 764.
8. Mémoires de Marguerite de Valois, p. 329; D'Ossat, II, 488; Palma Cayet, Petitot, XLIII, 371.
9. L'Estoile, VII, 101; CSP, Ven. Eliz., 1592–1603, no. 537; Lettres missives, IV, 892.
10. Birch, p. 167.
11. L'Estoile, VII, 337.
12. Journal de Nicolas-Edouard Olier (Paris, 1876), p. 39.
13. Rocquain, p. 531; Mémoires de la Ligue, VI, 429.
14. Lettres missives, V, 89–93.
15. Desjardins, V, 366; L'Epinois, p. 649.
16. D'Ossat, III, 317–321.
17. Birch, p. 113, 48.
18. Lettres et poésies de Catherine de Bourbon, ed. Raymond Ritter (Paris, 1927), p. 129. Hereafter cited as Lettres de Catherine de Bourbon.
19. Mémoires de Marguerite de Valois, pp. 301, 304.
20. Lettres du cardinal de Florence sur Henri IV et sur la France, ed. Raymond Ritter (Paris, 1955), p. 111.
21. Ibid., p. 227.
22. Lettres missives, V, 28.
23. Mémoires de Marguerite de Valois, p. 330.
24. Mémoires de Cheverny, Petitot, XXXVI, 387.
25. Lettres missives, IV, 111.

CHAPTER XVI

1. CSP, Ven. Eliz., 1592–1603, no. 791.
2. Ralph Winwood, Memorials of affairs of state in the reigns of Queen Elizabeth and King James I (3 vols., London, 1725), I, 81. Hereafter cited as Winwood.
3. Vaissière, p. 521.
4. Lettres missives, V, 190.
5. Ibid., V, 224.
6. Ibid., V, 225–227.
7. Mémoires de Cheverny, Petitot, XXXVI, 466, 467.

8. Winwood, I, 225.

9. *Mémoires de Cheverny*, XXXVI, 467.

10. Charles Merki, *La duchesse de Verneuil et la mort d'Henri IV* (Paris, 1912), p. 77. Hereafter cited as Merki, *La duchesse de Verneuil*.

11. *Lettres missives*, V, 234.

12. Merki, *La duchesse de Verneuil*, p. 87.

13. *Lettres missives*, V, 362.

14. *Lettres inédites de François d'Aerssen* (Paris, 1908), 79.

15. Vaissière, p. 532.

16. Sully, II, 404.

17. *Mémoires de Cheverny*, Petitot, XXXVI, 484; Berthold Zeller, *Henri IV et Marie de Médicis* (Paris, 1877), p. 65. Hereafter cited as Zeller.

18. *Ibid.*, p. 69.

19. *Lettres missives*, V, 273.

20. *Mémoires de Cheverny*, Petitot, XXXVI, 494.

21. Desjardins, V, 459.

22. *Archives Curieuses*, XIV, 479–480.

23. *Lettres missives*, V, 479–480.

CHAPTER XVII

1. Merki, *La duchesse de Verneuil*, p. 98.

2. Winwood, I, 406.

3. Zeller, p. 130, n. 1.

4. *Lettres missives*, V, 594.

5. Zeller, p. 145. The details of Biron's arrest, imprisonment and death are from *Archives Curieuses*, XIII; Sully, III; the "Procés criminel" quoted in Zeller; "La Conspiration, prisons, jugement et mort du duc de Biron," quoted in Merki, *La duchesse de Verneuil*.

6. *Lettres missives*, V, 620.

7. L'Estoile, VIII, 29–30.

8. *Ibid.*, VIII, 40.

9. Desjardins, V, 505. Maurice Andrieux, *Henri IV dans ses années pacifiques*, (Paris, 1954), p. 208. Hereafter cited as Andrieux.

10. *Ibid.*, p. 209.

11. CSP, Ven. Eliz., 1603–1607, no. 64.

12. *Lettres missives*, VI, 87.

13. *Ibid.*, VI, 200.

14. *Lettres de Catherine de Bourbon*, p. 176; D'Ossat, IV, 14.

15. *Lettres de Catherine de Bourbon*, p. 176; La comtesse Armaillé, *Catherine de Bourbon* (Paris, 1872), p. 309.

16. *Lettres de Catherine de Bourbon*, p. 189; *Lettres missives*, V, 560.

17. Vaissière, p. 648.

18. Andrieux, p. 255; *Lettres missives*, VI, 227, 229–230.

19. CSP, Ven. Eliz., 1603–1607, no. 235.

20. Sully, III, 373.

21. *Ibid.*, III, 367.

22. L'Estoile, VIII, 169.

23. Sully, III, 378.

CHAPTER XVIII

1. *CSP, Ven. Eliz.*, 1603–1607, nos. 335, 351.

2. Merki, *La duchesse de Verneuil*, pp. 183–184.

3. Princesse de Conti, "Histoire des Amours de Henri IV," *Archives Curieuses*, XIV, 343. Louise Marguerite de Lorraine, Princesse de Conti, was the daughter of the Duc de Guise and originally published her narrative under the title "Les Amours du Grand Alcandre."

4. *Lettres missives*, VII, 12, 21.

5. Andrieux, p. 323.

6. *Lettres missives*, VII, 119.

7. Andrieux, pp. 324–325.

8. *Lettres missives*, VII, 376.

9. *Ibid.*, VI, 503.

10. *Ibid.*, VI, 596.

11. F. de Bassompierre, *Journal de ma vie* (Paris, 1870) p. 175. Hereafter cited as Bassompierre.

12. L'Estoile, IX, 190; Merki, *La duchesse de Verneuil*, p. 214.

13. L'Estoile, IX, 187, 142; Sully, IV, 341.

14. *Lettres missives*, VII, 635.

15. *Ibid.*, VII, 517, 518, 510, 557.

16. *Ibid.*, VII, 665.

17. *Lettres missives*, VII, 672.

18. *Ibid.*, VII, 789, 784–785.

19. Bassompierre, p. 217.

20. Sully, IV, 436.

21. *Lettres missives*, VII, 732; L'Estoile, IX, 280.

22. *Memoires de Messire François Duval, Marquis de Fontenay-Mareuil*, ed. J. J. F. Poujoulat et J. Michaud, *Nouvelle collection des mémoires pour servir à l'histoire de France* (32 vols., Paris, 1836–1839) V, 7. Hereafter cited as Fontenay-Mareuil.

23. Sully, IV, 446–447; Bassompierre, p. 256; Fontenay-Mareuil, V, 8.

24. Le duc d'Aumâle, *Histoire des princes de Condé* (2 vols., Paris, 1864), II, 445.

25. *Lettres missives*, VII, 838; D'Aumâle, II, 561.

26. Merki, *La duchesse de Verneuil*, p. 268.

27. Paul Henrard, *Henri IV et la princesse de Condé* (Paris, 1885), p. 247; *Lettres missives*, VII, 860.

28. *Ibid.*, VII, 890.

29. *Ibid.*, VII, 895–896.

30. Sully, IV, 530.

31. Bassompierre, p. 270; Sully, IV, 533.

INDEX